THE COMPLETE TEXTS OF

AMERICAN HISTORY & SCIENCE

A.S.A.P.*

*As Soon As Possible,
As Simple As Possible

Alan Axelrod, Ph.D.

Prentice Hall Press
Published by The Berkley Publishing Group
A division of Penguin Group (USA) Inc.
375 Hudson Street
New York, New York 10014

Previously published as *American History A.S.A.P.*,
Copyright © 2003 by Alan Axelrod and *Science A.S.A.P.*,
Copyright © 2003 by Alan Axelrod

Cover photo by Ryoichi Utsumi/Photonica

Library of Congress Cataloging-in-Publication Data available

Special markets ISBN 0-7352-0417-9

Printed in the United States of America

1   3   5   7   9   10   8   6   4   2

American History Contents

Science Contents

MEDIEVAL SCIENCE

RENAISSANCE SCIENCE

ENLIGHTENMENT SCIENCE

PRELUDE TO MODERN SCIENCE

THE ATOM AND THE AIRPLANE

OUTER SPACE, INNER SPACE, AND CYBERSPACE

MODERN SCIENCE

AMERICAN
HISTORY

A.S.A.P.*

*As Soon As Possible,
As Simple As Possible

What This Is and What This Isn't

The best way to explain the purpose of this book is to examine the tail end of its title: *A.S.A.P.*—"As Soon as Possible," and "As Simple as Possible." The "soon" and the "simple" parts are key, of course, but so is the "as possible." For the goal is to deliver, in an informal, enjoyable, and highly efficient one-stop source, all the American history the general reader needs to stake a legitimate claim to cultural literacy. This much and no more, but no less, either—which is what is meant by "as simple as possible."

American History A.S.A.P. is not a compact narrative history of the United States, nor is it a brief encyclopedia. Instead, it selects 200 events that everyone needs to know about American history and uses them as sturdy springboards to related events and, even more important, to the ideas, concepts, and themes that underlie and inform American history. There are just 200 events here, but they are leveraged into a full-scale appreciation of American history from the Ice Age to September 11, 2001, and beyond.

40,000 B.C.
(approximately)

The First Immigrants

A glance at a map of Alaska shows that North America and Asia are separated by a mere fifty-five miles of the Bering Sea. Now, fifty-five miles in some of the coldest water on the planet is a long swim, but it's not much of an ocean voyage, and if the geologists and paleontologists are right, there was a time when you didn't even need a boat. During the Quaternary Period (that is, the last two million years), a "land bridge" emerged in the Bering and Chukchi Seas as the sea level dropped because of the expansion of the ice cap surrounding the North Pole. It is believed that anywhere from 45,000 to 10,000 years ago, people used the Bering land bridge to enter the New World, emigrating from what is now northeast Asia to northwestern North America. Beringia, as the land bridge is sometimes called, disappeared when the major continental ice sheets and other glaciers melted, causing the sea level to rise again and thereby separate Asia from North America.

It is not that, 45,000 years ago or so, a group of Asians decided to take an evening's stroll. The trek across Beringia must have spanned thousands of years of settlement and re-

What was the population of "Native America" some 10,000 years ago? In the area that is the present-day United States, it is generally estimated that the Native American population reached 11 million—although estimates vary from about 8.4 million to 112 million. For comparison, in 1990, 1,959,234 Indians, including Eskimos and Aleuts, lived in the United States, and the Native American population is growing at a rate of 3.8 percent per year.

settlement. Presumably, the land mass supported such Arctic vegetation as dry grasslands and boreal forests, which supplied adequate food for grazing animals, including the horse and the reindeer, as well as such Ice Age species as the mastodon and the woolly rhinoceros. As the animal herds ate their way southward, the hunting-and-gathering migrants followed, across Beringia, then fanned out onto what we now call North America. By approximately 9000 B.C., it is likely that some of these former Asians reached Patagonia, at the southern tip of South America. The human population of the New World was complete.

5500 B.C.

The Anasazi ("Ancient Ones")

No written records exist of the vast American history that preceded October 12, 1492, the day Christopher Columbus landed in the Caribbean. Assuming a prehistoric population of about 11 million, it is most likely that early Native Americans were very thinly distributed over a vast area in bands of a hundred or even fewer individuals living on the ragged edge of subsistence. About 9,000 years ago, perhaps, some bands began to domesticate plants, and by the end of the fifteenth century—when the Europeans first arrived—Indians were cultivating maize, beans, squash, manioc, potatoes, and grains. Farming created a more stable and settled lifestyle than subsistence hunting and gathering. With stability came the time and resources to create *things*.

In the American Southwest, the Anasazi (from a Navajo word meaning "the ancient ones") appeared as early as 5500 B.C. Today, they are sometimes called the Basket Makers, because of the many beautifully woven baskets that have been discovered in sites associated with their culture. The Anasazi built communal dwellings, some of them of wood and thatch, and some no more than shallow caves closed off with rocks. By A.D. 400 to 700, the Anasazi settlements were becoming genuine communities, collections of pit houses, built over shallow excavations. From about 700 to 1100, the Anasazi started building what the Spanish invaders would later call pueblos (Spanish for "town" or "village" and also "people"). The Hopi and the Navajo today revere the Anasazi as the ancestors of the native people of the West.

Works of the Mound Builders

From the Appalachian Mountains to the eastern edge of the midwestern prairies, and from the Great Lakes to the Gulf of Mexico, from roughly 1000 B.C. until sometime after A.D. 1500, various Indian societies constructed great earthworks. These ranged from relatively simple burial mounds to elaborate temple mounds (which served as the foundations for important public and private buildings), as well as circular and geometric ceremonial earthworks.

What archaeologists call the Woodland Mounds were built in eastern North America from about 1000 B.C. to the beginning of the eighteenth century. The most impressive surviving examples are the mounds of the Hopewell people, so-called because the structures they raised were discovered at Hopewell, Ohio. Another type of mound was built by people of the "Mississippian" culture. These structures were actually villages consisting of palisades and flat-topped, rectangular mounds that served not for burial but as the foundations of temples and other important structures. The Cahokia Mounds in Illinois, just across the Mississippi River from present-day St. Louis, must have once contained as many as fifty platform mounds and probably supported a population numbering in the thousands.

986–1015

The Norse Landings

I n 986, a Norse navigator, Bjarni Herjulfsson—blown off course on his way to Greenland—sighted the North American continent. He made note of it, which may or may not have influenced another Norseman, Leif Ericson, who landed on the continent in the year 1000. Ericson established a settlement he called Vinland on Newfoundland, probably at the place now known as L'Anse aux Meadows.

During 1004–1008, Leif's brothers, Thorvald and Thorstein, explored more of the continent, and they may even have reached modern New England. Then, between 1010 and 1013, an Icelandic trader named Thorfinn Karlsefni visited the North American coast, and it is quite possible that Freydis, Leif Ericson's sister, sailed with Thorfinn to the New World in 1014–1015.

And then . . . ?

Well, apparently not very much. North America made so little impression on the people of Europe that no one thought of bothering with it for another 500 years, making the Norse explorations of the New World perhaps the most important *non*events in American history.

1492

Columbus Sails to America

Christopher Columbus, though born to a Genoa weaver in 1451, had no interest in his father's trade and, early in life, took to the sea. Unlike most seafarers of his day, he learned to read, and he devoured all he could find concerning westward sea voyages. His reading persuaded him that the world was round—something most well-educated people believed in the fifteenth century, but, then again, the vast majority of fifteenth-century Europeans were not well educated. Although Columbus neither "discovered" nor "proved" the roundness of the Earth, he came up with the boldly original idea of using that roundness to go east by sailing west. The East—Asia—presented many trading opportunities, but, most important, it was the land of spice, which, in an era before refrigeration, was the sovereign element of food preservation and palatability. As such, spice was more precious than gold. Fifteenth-century trade routes from Europe to Asia lay mostly overland and were slow, dangerous, and costly. The nation that could find a sea route to the lands of spice would become a mighty nation indeed.

Yet Columbus had a monumentally hard time selling his idea to those who could authorize and finance a voyage. King John II of Portugal turned him down, in part because he thought Columbus had underestimated the circumference of the Earth—which, in fact, he had. Columbus misused data from Marco Polo's travels in China, fudged them with the gross miscalculations of the Greek astronomer Ptolemy (ca. 100–170), then bolstered all of this with the bad guesswork of the Florentine cosmographer Paolo dal

Pozzo Toscanelli. He concluded that Japan—his proposed destination—was just 5,000 miles *west* of Portugal.

Booted by the Portuguese monarch, Columbus moved on to Don Enrique de Guzmán, duke of Medina Sidonia, who likewise turned him down. He next approached Don Luis de la Cerda, Count of Medina Celi, who was sufficiently impressed to arrange an audience, on or about May 1, 1486, with Queen Isabella I of Castile. But it was not until 1492, and only thanks to the influence of a courtier named Luis de Santangel, that Isabella and her royal consort Ferdinand finally agreed to sponsor the voyage.

On August 3, 1492, Columbus sailed from Palos on ships that were small even by the standards of the day, the *Niña* (Vincente Yáñez Pinzón, captain), the *Pinta* (skippered by Vincente's brother, Martin Alonso Pinzón), and his own flagship, the *Santa Maria*. For about a month and a half, it was smooth sailing, driven by highly favorable winds. Then, between September 20 and September 30, the winds died, progress all but halted, crews grumbled. Columbus began to keep two logbooks. One, intended for the crew, brimmed with fictitious computations of distances; the other, kept secret, consisted of accurate figures. This trip was taking *much* longer than Columbus had expected, and, to the crew, each day without sight of land seemed to prove their captain was very, very wrong. The men spoke of sailing off the edge of a flat Earth and of being swallowed up by demons. Even those who believed no such thing rightly feared endless drift and eventual starvation.

By the time land was sighted on October 12, 1492, it is doubtful Columbus could have held his crew off a day longer. Landfall came at a place the natives called Guanahani and Columbus named San Salvador.

Most modern historians believe Columbus touched land at present-day Watling Island, although, in 1986, a group of scholars suggested that the true landfall was another Bahamian island, Samana Cay, 65 miles south of Watling.

Columbus and his crew were greeted by Arawak tribespeople, who welcomed them in a most friendly fashion. Now, Columbus had sailed about 3,900 miles, and he believed Japan was 5,000 miles from Spain. Yet he persuaded himself that he had reached Asia, known as the "Indies," so he called the people he met *Indians,* and, from San Salvador, he sailed to Cuba, believing that he would find there the court of the Mongol emperor of China (for he at least understood that he had not reached Japan) and, with the emperor, he intended to negotiate an agreement for trade in spices and gold.

In Cuba, of course, he found no emperor, so he set off for Hispaniola (modern Santo Domingo, Dominican Republic), where, in a Christmas Day storm, the *Santa Maria* was wrecked near Cap Haitien. Columbus deposited his crew onto the shore, determined that here, too, the "Indians" were friendly, and, leaving a garrison of thirty-nine at the place he decided to call La Navidad in honor of the holiday, set off on his return to Spain on January 16, 1493, sailing on the *Niña.*

1493

The Letter of Columbus

Returning from what would be the first of four voyages to the New World, Columbus paused on February 15, 1493, at the Spanish-controlled Canary Islands to replenish supplies and to send a letter to Luis de Santangel announcing nothing less than the discovery of a New World.

When the precious letter reached him, Santangel instantly recognized its importance and wasted no time publishing it to the world, and it is this letter as much as the deed itself that made Columbus's voyage of 1492 so important in American history. After all, he wasn't the first European to visit the New World. What about those Norsemen 500 years earlier? But none of them had written home about it, and nobody much cared about what they had found. It was Columbus's letter of February 15, 1493, that brought the New World to the Old, and set into motion American history as we know it.

1493

The First Euro–Indian War

In countless poems, plays, histories, textbooks, and movies, Columbus is portrayed as the "discoverer" of America. Discounting the Norse voyages of half a millennium earlier, this is true enough—from the point of view of Euro-America. But from the perspective of the *Americans*—that is, the people Columbus misnamed "Indians"—Columbus was not a discoverer, but an invader, in whose wake violence and oppression were quick to follow.

When he departed La Navidad to return to Spain, Columbus left on the island a Spanish garrison of thirty-nine men. No sooner had he departed than the members of the garrison began stealing the natives' things and molesting the local women. The Indians, whose friendliness Columbus had misjudged as timidity, retaliated by night, murdering ten Spaniards as they slept. Then they hunted down the rest of the garrison. When Columbus returned in November 1493, on his second voyage to the New World, no Spaniard was left alive. It was the beginning of 400 years of almost continuous warfare between Europeans (and, later, Americans) and Native Americans. For while Columbus had "discovered" a *new* world, he also set into motion a very *old* process, the ancient engine of history itself, a hard-grinding machine that turns contact into conquest.

Coronado's Quest for
the Seven Cities of Gold

The conquistador Hernan Cortés conquered the Aztec empire of Mexico in 1521 and became a man of unimaginable wealth and power. His exploits ignited the hope that somewhere else in the New World another golden Aztec empire would be found. This hope was fostered by something the Indians had told Columbus years earlier: tales of villages that held vast treasuries of gold. Alvar Nuñez Cabeza de Vaca, a member of an ill-fated expedition led by Cortés's rival, Panfilo de Narvaez, wandered throughout the American Southwest for eight years beginning in 1520 and brought back to Spain accounts of fabulously rich pueblos, the "Seven Cities of Cibola," although he himself had not seen them. One survivor of the Narvaez expedition, a black slave named Estevan, joined an expedition led by Marcos de Niza in 1539 to locate the Seven Cities. Zuni Indians killed the unfortunate Estevan in a battle outside the Hawikuh pueblo, but Marcos returned to Mexico City and there rendered a vivid account of the pueblo and its treasures. It was true that Marcos had not himself entered Hawikuh, but Estevan had. Of course, he was dead.

Driven by these rumors, Francisco Vasquez de Coronado traveled throughout the Southwest, as far as present-day Kansas, during 1540–1542. In July 1540, he and his troops rode into Hawikuh and, in conquistador fashion, demanded the surrender of the pueblo. In response, the traditionally peaceful Zuni showered Coronado with stones, one of which knocked him unconscious. Within an hour, however, Hawikuh fell to the Spaniards, who, with great anticipation, rode into the village, and there they found—very little indeed. Hawikuh had no gold.

So Coronado continued his quest for the Seven Cities of Cibola. He traveled through the pueblo region along the Rio Grande, capturing one town after another, forcing the inhabitants into slavery and taking from them whatever food and shelter he required. His experience in the Southwest was typical of the early Spanish period of exploration, driven by dreams of wealth, guided by a ruthless disregard for the natives of the country. But with Coronado's disappointment, the legend of the Seven Cities of Cibola dimmed, as did Spain's interest in the American Southwest. More than a half century passed before the ambitious newly appointed governor of New Spain, Don Juan de Oñate, led an expedition in 1598 from Mexico City into the American Southwest. He reached the site of present-day El Paso, Texas, and claimed for Spain—as well as for his own governance and (he hoped) enrichment—all of "New Mexico," a region extending from Texas to California. Spain's North American empire was born.

1590

The "Lost Colony" of Roanoke

With the blessing of Queen Elizabeth I, Sir Humphrey Gilbert became the first Englishman to set sail for America in 1579. Forced to return when his fleet broke up in a storm, he embarked again in June 1583 and reached St. John's Bay, Newfoundland, in August, claiming that territory for the queen. On the return voyage, Gilbert's overloaded ship sank, and his royal charter passed to his half brother, Sir Walter Raleigh, age 31, and already a favorite of the queen.

In 1584, Raleigh sent a small reconnaissance fleet to America, which probed a place that would later be called Croatan Sound in the Outer Banks of North Carolina. The expedition returned with enthusiastic reports of a land inhabited by "most gentle, loving and faithful" Indians, who lived "after the manner of the Golden Age." Raleigh asked his queen's permission to name the new land for her. She suggested calling it "Virginia," to memorialize her status as the "Virgin Queen."

In 1585–1586, Raleigh dispatched Sir Richard Grenville with a small group of settlers to colonize Virginia. The great British sailor-adventurer Sir Francis Drake encountered this group a year later, starving and wanting nothing so much as passage back to England. Not one to be discouraged, Raleigh launched a larger expedition of three ships carrying 117 men, women, and children. They landed at what is now Roanoke Island, off the coast of North Carolina, in 1587. Their leader, John White, chose a particularly dismal spot on this swampy island to establish his colonists, then, after a time, decided to return to England to fetch the tardy supplies Raleigh had promised to send. (Unknown to White, the supply ships were stalled because of the attack of the Spanish Armada against England.) When White returned to the colony in 1590, he found no settlers and only the barest trace of there ever having been a settlement—a few rusted implements and what he took to be the name of a neighboring island carved into the trunk of a tree: CROATOAN.

What had happened? Did the colonists all sicken and die on this pestilential island? Did they starve? Or did not so "gentle, loving and faithful" Indians kill them or take them captive to a place called "Croatoan"? White didn't know, and he never found out. No one has. And thus, with a disaster as miserable as it was mysterious, began the most important phase of the European colonization of what would become the United States.

1607

Founding of Jamestown

T he first English attempts to settle in America were not part of some titanic government effort to colonize the New World. They were business ventures, and fairly modest ones at that. In 1605, two groups of merchants—the Virginia Company of London (also called the London Company) and the Plymouth Company—petitioned King James I for a charter to establish a colony in Virginia. Such matters were handled pretty loosely back then, and, as far as anyone knew, Raleigh's Virginia patent took in whatever parts of North America Spain had not already claimed. The Virginia Company was granted a charter to colonize southern Virginia, while the Plymouth Company was given rights to northern Virginia.

The Virginia Company quickly recruited 144 settlers, among them the families of moneyed gentlemen as well as poor people. Since passage to America wasn't free, the poor folk purchased their places on the ship and in the colony by binding themselves to serve the Virginia Company as indentured servants for a period of seven years, working the land and creating a settlement.

In December 1606, this small band of men, women, and children boarded the *Susan Constant,* the *Discovery,* and the *Goodspeed.* Travel in the tiny, filthy ships of the day was a terrible ordeal, and that 39 of the colonists died en route was hardly remarkable. The 105 survivors arrived at the mouth of a river—they called it the James, to honor their king—on May 24, 1607. No sooner had they landed than they began to scratch out Jamestown.

As history would see it, Jamestown was "the first permanent English colony" in the New World. "Permanent," however, may be too strong a word. For Jamestown was staked out in a malaria-infested swamp, and the colonists had landed in late spring, well past the season for planting. Moreover, not all of the colonists—the "gentlemen," those who had paid cash to come to America and were indentured to no one—were willing or even able to do the hard work needed to start a farm, let alone with bare hands to hack a colony out of a wilderness. While many colonists worked tirelessly, just as many did not, and many died or disappeared. Within a few months of the landing, half of the settlers were dead or had run off into the woods, to meet whatever fate the local Indians might offer. Then things got worse. By 1609, famine drove some to cannibalism, even to looting fresh graves for food.

Jamestown would probably have met the fate of the "lost colony" of Roanoke had it not been for the soldier of fortune the Virginia Company had hired to look after the military defense of the colony. Captain John Smith ingratiated himself with the local Indians, people the English called the Powhatans, after the name they also applied to their aged but powerful chief. Smith was able to obtain enough corn and yams from the Powhatans to keep the surviving colonists from starving. Smith also assumed dictatorial powers over the colony, ruling it by martial law: Those who worked, he decreed, would eat. Those who did not work would starve. This dictum, combined with the charity of the Powhatans, saved Jamestown and established the English in America.

1608

Champlain Stakes France's Claim

Europe made its first significant contact with the New World in 1492, but it took many years before the Europeans began to see America for what it was and what it had to offer. When the search for cities of gold failed, some began looking for a "Northwest Passage" to Asia, a way to cut through the unknown continent to the known riches of the East. En route, many wanderers ended up farming. The French were even more immediately attracted by another resource: fur. By the early seventeenth century, fashion dictated the use of fur not only to line warm coats, but as trim on collars, cuffs, and fancy hats. People were willing to pay, and fur became an increasingly valuable commodity. Who needed gold? Who needed a passage to India?

Cardinal Richelieu (1585–1642), the strategist behind the throne of the weak-willed King Louis XIII, needed cash to finance his ongoing campaign to make France the dominant power in Europe. Seeing opportunity in America, Richelieu hired Samuel de Champlain (ca. 1570–1635) to probe the waters of North America and to explore inland. During the seven voyages he made between 1603 and 1616, Champlain mapped the northern reaches of the continent, accurately charting the Atlantic coast from the Bay of Fundy to Cape Cod. He also established settlements and got the French fur trade off to a most promising start. In July 1608, Champlain directed the digging of a ditch and the erection of a stockade. He called this Quebec, and it was the nucleus of French settlement in North America.

1609

Hudson Sails for the Dutch

enry Hudson was a British master mariner—such men proudly called themselves "sea dogs"—who sold his services to the Dutch and, in their employ, sailed his *Half Moon* out of Amsterdam, bound for the New World. Like so many other explorers before and after him, Hudson's primary mission was to find a "Northwest Passage," a watercourse through America and directly to the Pacific and the spice-rich Asian trade.

Hudson explored the Chesapeake Bay, then sailed north, encountering a great palisaded river that would be named for him. He sailed the Hudson as far as the location of present-day Albany, but, finding that the river was not subject to tides, he concluded that it was a dead end. He returned to Holland, then came back to the New World two years later to press on with the search for the Northwest Passage. His discouraged crew mutinied and cast him adrift in an open boat on what would be called Hudson Bay. He disappeared—without knowing that he had explored the site of what would become one of the great cities of the world, richer and more fantastic than any in Asia: New York.

1613

The Pocahontas Story

Once they were on their feet, the settlers of Jamestown proved remarkably ungrateful to the Indians who had been their salvation. In 1613, Captain Samuel Argall kidnapped the chief's daughter, presumably in a move intended to intimidate Chief Powhatan and his people. Her given name was Matoaka, but Powhatan and others called her Pocahontas, which the English translated as "Little Wanton," a description of her playful ways. Argall took her as a hostage to Jamestown and, later, to a new village, Henrico. Yet, unafraid, she never behaved like a hostage. Instead, fascinated by the English, she quickly learned their language and customs. Soon, she was no hostage, but an ambassador or, rather, a mediator between the English and her own people. Among Europeans, it was customary for the families of rival nations to marry in order to bring peace. In 1614, with the blessing of Powhatan, Pocahontas married John Rolfe, a tobacco planter. This brought eight years of uninterrupted peace between the colonists and the Powhatans, a period crucial to the growth of the colony, which became a thriving exporter of the New World's first cash crop, tobacco.

As for Pocahontas, Rolfe took his bride back to England, where she was an instant hit with London society and became a favorite of the royal court. She and Rolfe were genuinely in love, though, sadly, their bliss did not last long. Pocahontas, one of the most remarkable women in American history, succumbed to an illness and died in England on March 21, 1617, at the age of twenty-two.

Very little is known about Pocahontas, who has nevertheless fascinated generations of Americans. Most famous of the tantalizing stories concerning her is the tale of how she saved the life of Captain John Smith. The original version was related in *A History of the Settlement of Virginia,* by the early seventeenth-century Virginia merchant Thomas Studley and Smith himself:

At last they brought Captain Smith to Powhatan, their emperor. Here more than two hundred of those grim courtiers stood wondering at Smith as if he had been a monster. . . . Before a fire, and upon a seat like a bedstead, Powhatan sat covered with a great robe made of raccoon skins with all the tails hanging. . . .

At Captain Smith's entrance before the king all the people gave a great shout. The queen was appointed to bring him water to wash his hands, and another brought him a bunch of feathers, instead of a towel, on which to dry them. Having feasted him after the best barbarous manner they could, a long consultation was held. At last two great stones were brought before Powhatan. Then as many as could lay hands on Captain Smith dragged him to the stones, and laid his head on them, and were ready with their clubs to beat out his brains. At this instant, Pocahontas, the king's dearest daughter, when no entreaty could prevail, got his head in her arms, and laid her own head upon his to save him from death. . . .

1619

Slavery Comes to America

Almost immediately after Columbus "discovered" America in 1492, Europeans immersed themselves in the mythology of a *new* world, the notion that they had found a pristine place, a place for humanity to get a fresh start, a place that represented the future and yet also recalled Eden as it must have been before the fall. What those early mythologists failed to comprehend, however, is that simply traveling to a new world does not create new minds and new morality. In 1607, English men and women planted Jamestown, the first permanent English colony in America, and just twelve years later, in August 1619, Virginia tobacco farmers bought their first consignment of twenty slaves from Dutch traders.

While the twenty slaves brought to Virginia were the first introduced into what would become the United States, they were not the first brought to the New World. By 1619, Spanish and Portuguese slave traders had already transported more than a million Africans to their Caribbean and South American colonies.

The planters who came to the New World from Spain and Portugal were typically wealthy and could afford many slaves. In contrast, most of the English farmers who settled in Virginia and New England lacked the means to buy many African slaves. At first, indentured servitude, whereby English men and women bound themselves to a *limited*

During the 1600s, a slave could be purchased in Africa for about $25 and sold in America for $125.

period of service in return for passage to the New World, was a far more common source of cheap labor than African slaves. By the end of the seventeenth century, however, the price of slaves began to fall, even as the wealth of American planters increased. It now made economic sense to invest in a slave who, though he or she cost twice as much as an indentured servant, would yield not seven years of labor, but more than a lifetime; for the children of slaves were born slaves, and their children likewise.

1620

Voyage of the "Pilgrims"

The Spanish came to America in search of gold, empire, and souls to recruit for the Catholic Church. The English who settled Jamestown and the rest of Virginia were moved by commercial enthusiasm, but, farther north, in New England, English settlement was motivated mostly by a desire for religious freedom.

Not many years after Henry VIII, during 1536–1540, created a Church of England separate from the Roman Catholic Church, a growing minority of English Protestants began to criticize what they considered immoral compromises made with Catholic practice. These people felt that the mainstream Anglican church had not gone far enough in reforming worship, and when King James I ascended the throne in 1603, these religious reformers—called Puritans because they advocated a new purity of religious practice—clamored for major changes in the Anglican Church. James refused, and the Anglican archbishop, William Laud, initiated a campaign of persecution against the Puritans. Some Puritans chose to remain in England, where they formed an increasingly powerful political bloc and would ultimately fight a successful civil war against the crown. Others left England for Holland, celebrated for its religious toleration. These, called Separatists, were mostly farmers, poorly educated and of lowly social status; Puritanism appealed to few aristocrats.

The Separatist congregation of Scrooby, Nottinghamshire, was led by William Brewster and the Reverend Richard Clifton. They brought their flock from Scrooby to Amsterdam in 1608, then, the following year, moved to another Dutch town, Leyden, where they lived for a dozen years. Although treated with tolerance by the Dutch, these groups were beset by economic hardship and were disturbed by the prospect of their children growing up Dutch rather than English. Therefore, in 1617, some of them voted to strike out for America.

The Scrooby–Leyden congregation secured a pair of royal patents authorizing them to settle in the northern part of the American territory belonging to the Virginia Company. Somewhat less than half of the congregation finally decided to embark. One hundred two souls piled into a single vessel, the *Mayflower,* on September 16, 1620. Fewer than half of these passengers were Separatists. The rest, whom the Separatists referred to as Strangers, belonged to no particular religious group and simply sought new opportunity in the New World. After a sixty-five-day voyage, the Pilgrims (for so their first historian and early leader, William Bradford, would later label them) sighted land on November 19.

Here, the story gets a bit cloudy. The Pilgrims themselves claimed that rough seas off Nantucket forced the *Mayflower*'s skipper, Captain Christopher Jones, to steer away from the mouth of the Hudson River, where, according to the terms of their patent, the Pilgrims were supposed to establish their "plantation." He landed instead at Cape Cod, in present-day Massachusetts, *beyond* the Virginia Company's jurisdiction. This fact has led many modern historians to conclude that the "wrong turn" was no accident, but, rather, the result of a Pilgrim bribe. The Separatists *wanted* to ensure independence from the external authority of the Virginia Company. Whether by accident or design, then, the *Mayflower* dropped anchor off present-day Provincetown, Massachusetts, on November 21.

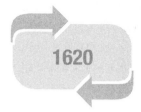

1620

The "*Mayflower* Compact"—
The First American Constitution

Small as it was, the band that rode at anchor off the Massachusetts coast was not united. There were the Separatists—the Pilgrims—but there were also the so-called "Strangers," who were not beholden to the Separatists and who were united

The *Mayflower* Compact, 1620

IN THE NAME OF GOD, AMEN. We, whose names are underwritten, the Loyal Subjects of our dread Sovereign Lord King James, by the Grace of God, of Great Britain, France, and Ireland, King, Defender of the Faith, &c. Having undertaken for the Glory of God, and Advancement of the Christian Faith, and the Honour of our King and Country, a Voyage to plant the first Colony In the northern Parts of Virginia; Do by these Presents, solemnly and mutually, in the Presence of God and one another, covenant and combine ourselves together into a civil Body Politick, for our better Ordering and Preservation, and Furtherance of the Ends aforesaid: And by Virtue hereof do enact, constitute, and frame, such just and equal Laws, Ordinances, Acts, Constitutions, and Officers, from time to time, as shall be thought most meet and convenient for the general Good of the Colony; unto which we promise all due Submission and Obedience. IN WITNESS whereof we have hereunto subscribed our names at Cape-Cod the eleventh of November, in the Reign of our Sovereign Lord King James, of England, France, and Ireland, the eighteenth, and of Scotland the fifty-fourth, Anno Domini; 1620.

among themselves by nothing more than a desire for economic opportunity. Moreover, neither the Pilgrims nor the Strangers had a *legal* right to settle here, beyond the boundary of their charter.

The two groups decided to resolve the first problem and, by declaring allegiance to King James I, clear the way to a resolution of the second problem. They gathered below decks and drew up the "*Mayflower* Compact," the first constitution written in North America. Very brief, its purpose was to create a "Civil Body Politic" and a set of laws for the good of the colony.

Plymouth Rock Landing

After the "*Mayflower* Compact" was signed, Captain Jones probed for a likely landing and found Plymouth Harbor, on the western side of Cape Cod Bay. An advance party set foot on shore—supposedly on a rock now carved with the year 1620 and enshrined in a modest tabernacle—on December 21. The main body of settlers disembarked on December 26.

Religiously inspired, they saw themselves as guided to this spot by God's providence. Yet whether Plymouth had been chosen by God, by accident, or by the Pilgrims themselves, the wayfarers could hardly have found a less favorable place or time for their landing. There were no ample harbors here—so trade would always be limited—and the flinty, ungenerous soil promised little fertility. As for the time of the landing, a characteristically bitter New England winter already had the land in its iron grip. During the first winter at Plymouth, more than half of the tiny colony would die.

1621

The First Thanksgiving

In contrast to the settlers of Jamestown, many of whom were "gentlemen" unaccustomed and unwilling to work, most of the Plymouth colonists were yeoman farmers, led by tough, able men. But hard work, a passion for liberty, and able leadership would not alone have brought the colony through its first dreadful winter. It was the charity of the neighboring Wampanoag Indians that saved the Pilgrims. Two Indians in particular, Squanto (a Pawtuxet living among the Wampanoags) and Samoset (an Abnaki), gave the newcomers hands-on help in planting crops and building shelters. Samoset also introduced the settlers to Massasoit, principal leader of the Wampanoags (with whom Edward Winslow negotiated an important treaty), and Squanto served as interpreter between the chief and the Pilgrim leaders.

In the fall of 1621, the Pil-

To this day, some Virginians lay claim to the first Thanksgiving, citing a collective prayer of thanksgiving offered on December 4, 1619, by members of the Berkeley plantation near modern Charles City, Virginia. George Washington proclaimed the first national Thanksgiving Day on November 26, 1789, but it wasn't until 1863 that Abraham Lincoln made Thanksgiving an official annual holiday, to be commemorated on the last Thursday in November. Between 1939 and 1941, by proclamation of Franklin D. Roosevelt, the day was celebrated on the third Thursday in November, but then was returned by act of Congress to the date set by Lincoln.

grims invited their Indian neighbors—and saviors—to a feast in celebration of the first harvest, the bounty of which was in no small measure due to Indian aid and expertise. It is this event that we usually identify as the first Thanksgiving.

Dutch Settlement Begins

Of all the peoples of Europe, the Dutch of the seventeenth century were perhaps the greatest traders. Their activities had made Amsterdam the busiest and wealthiest city in Europe, and in 1621 Dutch merchants incorporated the Dutch West India Company with the intention of dominating trade in the New World.

Holland soon displaced Portugal as the leading trader in sugar and slaves, and, in 1624, the Dutch penetrated the fur market by opening up a trading post, Fort Orange, at the site of present-day Albany, New York. Two years after this, Peter Minuit became governor-general of New Netherland, as the Dutch colony was called. He purchased from the Manhattan Indians, a local subtribe of the Delawares, the Hudson River island named for them, paying in trade goods valued at sixty guilders. The Dutch founded a village at the mouth of the Hudson, calling it New Amsterdam. This town would become not only a center of trade, but of immigration. Whereas the English Puritans of New England were loath to welcome strangers, the cosmopolitan Dutch of New Amsterdam threw open the settlement to all comers. Manhattan (such was the Indian name of the island on whose southern tip New Amsterdam had been settled) became home to a polyglot assortment of residents, even as New York City is today.

At the prevailing exchange rate, 60 Dutch guilders was the equivalent of 2,400 English pennies, and so it is traditionally said that Manhattan was purchased for the sum of $24. Even factoring in almost 400 years of inflation, it was a bargain.

1638

Individual Liberty—
Anne Hutchinson Takes a Stand

Born in Alford, Lincolnshire, England, in 1591, Anne Marbury married a merchant, William Hutchinson, in 1612. She sailed with him to Boston in 1634, eager to follow the Puritan minister she most respected, the Reverend John Cotton, who had recently left for New England.

Expecting religious enlightenment in the Massachusetts Bay Colony, what Hutchinson found were ministers devoted far less to affairs of the spirit than to the dry duty of prayer, fasting, and iron self-discipline. Hungry for something more, and noting that the male members of Boston's church met regularly after sermons to discuss the Bible, Hutchinson started to hold similar meetings for women in her own home. Although fully versed in the Bible and theology, Hutchinson espoused the radical point of view that mere conformity to religious laws was no proof of godliness. True spirituality derived not from ministers' sermons, from books, or even from the Bible itself, but came instead from an inner experience of the Holy Spirit. This gospel of inner revelation and total freedom of conscience began to draw a following, among men as well as women.

Perhaps inevitably, Hutchinson's growing popularity brought criticism from the church establishment. In time, what started as a difference in religious point of view became a gaping schism, one which threatened the political stability of the Massachusetts Bay Colony by challenging basic assumptions of religion and governance. As Hutchinson's opponents saw it, to question the church was to challenge the state. She was condemned as an "Antinomian," an adherent to the heretical doctrine that Christians are not bound by moral law. When the conservative John Winthrop became Bay Colony governor in 1637, he barred more "Antinomians" from settling in the colony, and he banned all private religious meetings. Hutchinson continued to hold her meetings and was charged with heresy. Winthrop described Hutchinson's meetings as "a thing not tolerable nor comely in the sight of God, nor fitting for your sex," and he accused her of breaking the Fifth Commandment by not honoring her father and mother—by which he meant, metaphorically, the magistrates of the colony.

At trial, Hutchinson proved more than the intellectual equal of Winthrop; however, she let her emotions get in the way. The Lord, she said, had revealed Himself to her, "upon a Throne of Justice." Take heed, she warned Winthrop, "God will ruin you and your posterity, and this whole State." With that, the governor pounced: "I am persuaded that the revelation she brings forth is delusion." The court voted to banish her from the colony, "as being a woman not fit for our society."

After another trial in the early spring of 1638, Hutchinson was excommunicated. Anne replied calmly: "The Lord judgeth not as man judgeth. Better to be cast out of the church than to deny Christ."

Fortunately for Anne Hutchinson, she was not the only spiritual outcast in New England. In 1636, Roger Williams, minister of the Puritan congregation in Salem, Massachusetts, was banished from the Bay Colony for having preached the ultimate authority of individual conscience—what he called "soul liberty"—for advocating toleration of all faiths, for seeking respect and fair treatment of the Indians, and for preaching the separation of church and state. "Forced religion," he said, "stinks in God's nostrils." Williams and his followers settled near Narragansett Bay, where they established the town of Providence in 1636, and then established the colony of Rhode Island, a haven of religious liberty.

Anne Hutchinson, with her husband, children, and sixty followers, moved to Rhode Island and purchased from the Narragansett chief Miantonomah the island of Aquidneck, which she called Peaceable Island. When her husband died in 1642, she took her children, except for the five eldest, to the Dutch colony in New Amsterdam, where she built a home on Pelham Bay (now in the Bronx, New York). Tragically, in August 1643, a band of Mahican Indians raided the house and slaughtered Anne Hutchinson and five of her youngest children, taking a sixth, Susanna, captive.

The murder of women like Anne Hutchinson was not an uncommon fate across the colonial frontier. Nevertheless, it was a sad end for the woman many credit as being among the first to lead the public fight for religious freedom, the sanctity of conscience, and women's rights.

1664

New Netherland Becomes New York

So much of the European settlement of the New World was wrapped in violence that the peacefulness with which Dutch New Netherland became British New York is rather astonishing. Toward the Indians, New Netherlanders had vacillated between friendly trade, barbaric cruelty (in the "Pavonia Massacre" of 1641, slaughtering Indian men, women, and children, then playing football in the streets of Manhattan with the severed heads of executed prisoners), and timid defensiveness. Relations with other colonies were similarly inconsistent, but relations between New Netherland and New England steadily deteriorated as the colonies competed for Indian loyalty and trade.

The Dutch military position was inferior to the English, but, even more important, the Dutch settlers were victims of the settlement scheme originally established by the Dutch West India Company. Dutch settlement was hampered by the patroon system, a policy that gave land ownership to absentee landlords who installed tenant farmers. Thus, New Netherland became mainly a colony of tenants, a fact that discouraged settlement and compromised patriotism, so that, by the 1660s, New Netherland was weak and torn by dissension. The irascible Dutch governor, Peter Stuyvesant, tried in vain to rally his countrymen when, on September 8, 1664, a fleet of British warships sailed up the Hudson. The Dutch colonists declined to offer resistance, and the frustrated Stuyvesant had no choice but to surrender.

The British renamed both the colony and its chief town New York to honor the Duke of York (the future King James II), and Stuyvesant retired peacefully to his farm, the Bouwerie.

Discovery of the Mississippi

For about two-thirds of the seventeenth century, New France, as the French territory in America was called, was practically the exclusive province of the explorer Samuel de Champlain. In 1642, on the death of his father, four-year-old Louis XIV ascended the throne under the regency of Cardinal Mazarin. When Mazarin died in 1661, Louis XIV began to rule in his own right. No longer content to let the fate of his North American possessions rest in the hands of a single individual, the king promoted not exploration, but the establishment of farms and cities in areas that had already been explored. However, in 1673, the French *intendant* (chief administrator) in Canada, Jean Baptiste Talon, couldn't resist going against this royal policy by hiring a fur trader named Louis Joliet to strike out into the unknown, following up on Indian tales concerning a "father" of all the rivers. This water source, Talon reasoned, might well prove to be the passage to the Pacific. The Indians called it the "Mesippi."

In company with a Jesuit priest, Jacques Marquette, Joliet went west and reported on many wonders, including herds of great buffalo and fish big enough to wreck a canoe. They also found the Mississippi, and while it was apparent that this was not a shortcut to the Pacific, it was grand enough. More important, its discovery established France's claim to a vast portion of what would one day be the United States. Joliet and Marquette named the realm Louisiana, in honor of their monarch, and figured that it encompassed everything between the Appalachian Mountains and the Rockies, which, they vaguely knew, lay far to the west. Neither the explorers nor Louis XIV had an inkling of the great commercial artery the Mississippi would become, and how it would one day demarcate East and West, the West becoming an immense magnet that drew millions. Indeed, by the end of Louis's long reign, New France remained nothing more than a few precarious settlements through Nova Scotia and along the St. Lawrence, with one or two isolated outposts huddled in "Louisiana."

1675–1676

King Philip's War

While today it is a conflict that mostly interests professional historians, in proportion to the region's population at the time, King Philip's War was the costliest war ever fought on American soil. Among New England colonists, one in sixteen males of military age was killed, and many others—old men, women, children—were also killed, starved, or captured. As for the Indians, at least 3,000 perished, and many who did not die were sold into slavery.

King Philip's War began on June 11, 1675, when a Massachusetts settler killed an Indian who was stealing his cattle. Led by the Wampanoag chief, Metacomet, known to the English as King Philip, a delegation of Indians demanded justice for the slain Indian. Rebuffed, they sought out the farmer and killed him, along with six others. This triggered reprisals, which, in turn, set off an uprising among the Wampanoags, Narragansetts, Nipmucks, and allied tribes. Murder, arson, and looting by Indians in the frontier regions of settlement became so widespread by the late spring of 1675 that colonists began retreating from the wilderness.

The colonists, poorly organized and more competitive than cooperative, fared very badly during the first months of the conflict. Only after they banded together as the United Colonies were they able to muster a substantial intercolonial army to counter King Philip and his allies. During the remainder of 1675 and well into 1676, the colonists fought a war of attrition against the Indians. In the course of the conflict, half the towns of New England were destroyed or severely damaged. It would require the work of a full generation to restore them. Disruption of the fur trade, of fishing, and of the West Indies trade devastated the fledgling colonial economy. Farm labor was greatly diminished, first by the absence of farmers gone to war, then by the fact that many never returned.

The cost to the Indians was even greater. The Wampanoag, Narragansett, and Nipmuck tribes were rendered forever subject to the English will. Many died. Many were sold into West Indian slavery, the profits of the sales used to help defray the direct costs of the war. If there is anything at all positive to be found in this war, it is that for the first time an effective (if temporary) union among the colonies was formed.

1681

The Pennsylvania Experiment

The New World appeared to the people of the Old as many things: a place of potentially vast wealth, a place of trade, a place for religious freedom, a place to conquer. To William Penn, prominent member of the then-radical Christian sect popularly called the Quakers, Pennsylvania appeared the perfect place to conduct an experiment in peace and toleration during an age of war and intolerance.

On March 14, 1681, King Charles II of England granted Penn a proprietary charter for the region encompassing present-day Pennsylvania and present-day Delaware as well. Here, Penn welcomed not only Quakers (victims of persecution elsewhere), but people of all creeds and nationalities. Upon this heterogeneous population, Penn imposed a mild government, which quickly fostered the development of something closely resembling our contemporary democracy: representative government. Pennsylvania and the great city that became its capital, Philadelphia, emerged as early models of free government, long before there was the slightest whiff of independence or softest whisper of revolution.

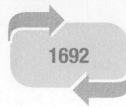

1692

Salem Punishes the Witches

On January 20, 1692, nine-year-old Elizabeth Parris (daughter of the Reverend Samuel Parris) and eleven-year-old Abigail Williams began to behave strangely, screaming out blasphemies, going into convulsions, slipping into trancelike states. Soon, other girls in the strongly Puritan settlement of Salem, Massachusetts, began to exhibit similar behavior. By mid-February, baffled Salem physicians, unable to find a physical cause for the girls' symptoms, concluded that they were possessed by Satan. In late February, after prayer services and community fasting failed to dispel the force of evil, and after a special "witch cake" (baked with rye meal and urine from the afflicted girls) failed to reveal the identity of Satan's agents, the girls themselves, under ceaseless interrogation, finally named three women, including Tituba, Parris's Caribbean slave, as witches. On February 29, warrants were issued for the arrest of Tituba, Sarah Good, and Sarah Osborne. Under examination, Osborne and Good maintained their innocence, but Tituba confessed to having seen the devil, and she went on to testify to a conspiracy of witches at work in Salem.

Over the next few weeks, townspeople came forward to testify that they had been harmed by certain people or had seen strange apparitions of those people. Soon, accusations were made against many Salem residents. Most frequently denounced were those typically accused of witchcraft in other communities: poor, elderly women or men who owned no property, the quarrelsome and disruptive, the social outcasts. But also accused were a number of upstanding members of the churchgoing community.

On May 27, after more than twenty persons were arrested and

interrogated, Governor Phips set up a special seven-judge Court of Oyer and Terminer. The judges weighed all manner of "evidence," ranging from direct confessions, stories of supernatural attributes, and the state and reactions of the afflicted girls themselves. Most controversial was "spectral evidence," which was based on the assumption that the devil could assume the "specter" of any person, no matter how innocent.

In 1692, more than 140 people were accused, 107 of them women. The first to be found guilty and condemned to death, on June 2, 1692, was Bridget Bishop, who was hanged on June 10. Through the summer and into the fall, fifty of the accused confessed to practicing witchcraft, twenty-six were convicted, and twenty, including Bishop, were executed. All were hanged, except for Giles Corey, who, on September 19, was pressed to death under heavy stones because he refused to stand trial.

A colonial merchant and voice of reason, Thomas Brattle, appalled at the pace of conviction and execution, wrote a letter on October 8 criticizing the trials. Governor Phips took heed and declared that reliance on spectral evidence and intangible evidence would no longer be allowed. Deprived of these legal weapons, the Court of Oyer and Terminer was dissolved, and Phips decreed that the Superior Court of Judicature would hear the remaining cases. From October until the end of the year, this court indicted twenty-one of the more than fifty remaining individuals accused. Subsequent trials resulted in only three convictions, which were overturned the following year. In 1693, individuals whose cases were still pending were given a pardon by the governor. Before 1693 was over, witchcraft was no longer regarded as a criminal offense.

The Salem witch trials have entered American history as well as American folklore, and they endure as cautionary tales about the dangers of superstition and guilt by suspicion. In 1953, when the nation was in the grip of the anticommunist hysteria orchestrated by the opportunistic Republican senator from Wisconsin, Joseph McCarthy, the playwright Arthur Miller used the Salem experience as the basis of a powerful play, *The Crucible*, which served as an allegory of the "witch hunt" over which McCarthy presided. By dramatizing the Salem trials, Miller reminded the nation of how political bullying and ideological hysteria could ruin lives and destroy democratic institutions.

1732

Georgia Is Chartered

The colony of Georgia began as a social experiment even more radical than Penn's Pennsylvania. In 1732, a high-minded entrepreneur named James Oglethorpe was granted a royal charter to found Georgia, last of the original thirteen colonies. Oglethorpe had leagued with other London-based philanthropists to create a colony that was to be populated by select inmates from English debtors' prisons. Not only would Georgia give these individuals new lives, the colony would serve the British empire by creating a buffer zone between England's Carolina colonies and Spain's colonial territory. But Oglethorpe's vision extended even beyond this. For Oglethorpe planned to install his colonists on fifty-acre farms, which they could neither sell nor transfer. Thus, they had no motives for greedy acquisition and envy. Both liquor and slavery—two great social evils—were to be banned from the colony.

Unfortunately for Oglethorpe's vision of utopia, only a few of the original colonists who came with the founder in 1733 were debtors. Most were speculators and land-hungry settlers. They quickly found loopholes that allowed them to amass great plantations far in excess of the stipulated fifty acres, and, with vast lands to work, slaves were soon imported as well. In 1752, Georgia was proclaimed a royal colony—no different from any of the others.

1734–1735

The Case of John Peter Zenger

Lewis Morris, chief justice of New York's provincial court, ruled against Governor William Cosby in a 1733 salary dispute. Cosby promptly responded by suspending Justice Morris, who appealed to the colony's only newspaper, the *New York Gazette,* to tell his story. Because the *Gazette* was wholly dependent on Governor Cosby's patronage, its editor declined to print anything Morris had to say. The justice joined several other lawyers and merchants in hiring a local printer, John Peter Zenger, to start up a new paper, the *New-York Weekly Journal,* which began publication on November 5, 1733.

As soon as Zenger published articles critical of Cosby, the governor had Zenger arrested on charges of "seditious libel." For ten months he was imprisoned without trial while his wife, Anna, kept publishing the paper. The case finally came to bench in 1735, and Zenger's attorney, Andrew Hamilton of Philadelphia, argued that Zenger was innocent of seditious libel because all that he had printed was true. The judge in the case did his best to block evidence to prove the truth of Zenger's articles, but the argument itself persuaded the jury, who acquitted the printer.

The Zenger case stands as a foundation of the freedom of the American press and established the sovereign defense against charges of libel: The truth cannot be defined as libelous and cannot, therefore, be stifled by legal prosecution.

1754

The French and Indian War Begins

Since the late seventeenth century, French and English colonists had been fighting one another over control of North America, often enlisting into the conflict the alliance of Indians. When, in 1749, England's King George II granted great tracts of the American wilderness to a cartel of entrepreneurs calling itself the Ohio Company, the governor of New France, the marquis de La Galissonière, responded by sending an expedition to lay claim to as much of the "Ohio country" (roughly, present-day western Pennsylvania, Ohio, Indiana, and Illinois) as could be encompassed in a round-trip of 3,000 miles. Over the next several years, a succession of French governors built a chain of forts from Montreal down to New Orleans and cultivated more and more Indian allies and trading partners. By the early 1750s, war fever had spread through the British American colonies. Virginia governor Robert Dinwiddie commissioned a twenty-one-year-old Virginia militia captain named George Washington to deliver to the French "invaders" an eviction notice. Washington confronted the commandant of Fort LeBoeuf (Waterford, Pennsylvania) on December 12, 1753. Captain Legardeur politely but firmly declined to depart, and Dinwiddie ordered the construction of a fort at the junction of the Monongahela, Allegheny, and Ohio rivers, site of present-day Pittsburgh. The French patiently watched construction, then, in April 1754, suddenly overran and took over the completed fort, christening it Fort Duquesne.

On the very day that the fort fell, Dinwiddie, quite unaware of what had occurred, sent Washington (now promoted to lieutenant colonel) with 150 men to reinforce it. En route, on May 28, Washington surprised a 33-man French reconnaissance party, attacked, and killed ten of the Frenchmen, including Ensign Joseph Coulon de Villiers de Jumonville, a French "ambassador." Thus, the English won the first battle of the French and Indian War.

But Washington did not let his victory go to his head. Realizing that the French would counterattack in force, he hurriedly built a makeshift stockade, aptly named Fort Necessity, at Great Meadows, Pennsylvania. On July 3, Major Coulon de Villiers, brother of the man Washington's detachment had killed, led a large force against Fort Necessity. After half his men had fallen, Washington, on the fourth of July, surrendered. He and the other survivors were permitted to leave, save for two hostages, who were taken back to Fort Duquesne. It was the English, not the French, who had been evicted from the Ohio country, and the French and Indian War began in earnest.

1755

Exile of the Acadians

While war between the French and English began in western Pennsylvania at the gateway to the Ohio country, up in Nova Scotia, British authorities demanded that the Acadians, French-speaking Roman Catholic farmers and fishermen who freely intermarried with the local Micmac and Abnaki Indians, swear loyalty to the British crown. French authorities countered not by threatening the English, but by warning the Acadians that the Indians would be turned loose against them if they caved in to British demands.

At last, during July 1755, the Acadians of Nova Scotia announced their refusal to submit to the loyalty oath, and, on July 28, 1755, Nova Scotia's newly appointed British governor, Charles Lawrence, ordered their deportation. On October 13, 1,100 Acadians were sent into exile. Many others followed—six to seven thousand in all—resettling throughout the colonies. But the Acadians made the best of it, and the many who settled in Louisiana immeasurably enriched the culture of the region. Through a contraction of the word *Acadians,* they became known as *Cajuns.*

British Defeat at the
Battle of the Wilderness

During 1754–1755, the French and Indian War escalated with the arrival of troops from the mother countries. From England, Major General Edward Braddock arrived with an army and sat down with the colonial commanders to lay out a grand strategy for the war. He proposed to send Brigadier General Robert Monckton against Nova Scotia, while he himself set about capturing Forts Duquesne and Niagara. Massachusetts governor William Shirley's army was assigned to reinforce Fort Oswego, in New York, and then to proceed to Fort Niagara. Another colonial commander, William Johnson, was detailed to capture Fort Saint Frédéric at Crown Point, on Lake Champlain.

Monckton and John Winslow (a colonial commander) successfully took Nova Scotia, but Braddock encountered great delay in starting his expedition to Fort Duquesne. Finally, two regiments of British regulars and a provincial detachment (under George Washington) marched out of Fort Cumberland, Maryland, 2,500 men in all, loaded down with heavy equipment. As French-allied Indians sniped at the slow-moving column, Washington advised Braddock to detach a "flying column" of 1,500 men to move swiftly for the initial attack on Fort Duquesne. By July 7, the flying column set up a camp ten miles from its objective. Two days later, French and Indian forces fell on the camp in a surprise attack that sent panic through the ranks of the British regulars. Some troops fired wildly at each other. Some simply huddled together like sheep. Braddock, dull but brave, had five horses shot from under him as he vainly tried to rally his men. He finally fell, mortally wounded. Of 1,459 officers and men who had engaged in the Battle of the Wilderness, only 462 survived. (George Washington, though unhurt, had two horses shot from under him, and his coat had been pierced by four bullets.) As he lay dying, Braddock remarked incredulously: "Who would have thought it?"

The disaster at the Battle of the Wilderness drove many more Indians into the camp of the French and laid open to attack English settlements all along the frontier. By June 1756, British settlers in Virginia had withdrawn 150 miles from the prewar frontier.

Chief Scarouady of the English-allied Oneida Indians said of Braddock: "He was a bad man when he was alive; he looked upon us as dogs, and would never hear anything that was said to him. We often endeavoured to advise him of the danger he was in with his Soldiers; but he never appeared pleased with us and that was the reason that a great many of our Warriors left him and would not be under his Command."

The First "World" War

For its first three years, the French and Indian War was a North American conflict. In 1756, it became truly a *world* war as Prussia invaded Saxony. The following year, the Holy Roman Empire (principally Austria) declared war on Prussia, which then invaded Bohemia. Through a complex of interests, intrigues, and alliances, the French, the British, the Spanish, and the Russians also joined the war, which eventually encompassed major fronts in Europe, India, Cuba, the Philippines, and North America. The world conflict was given the generic title of the Seven Years' War.

Committed now to an expanded war, France, on May 11, 1756, sent the dashing marquis de Montcalm to take charge of Canadian forces. The British still muddled along with mediocre commanders, who persisted in their haughty refusal to cooperate effectively with provincial forces. Montcalm easily took Fort Oswego, which yielded Lake Ontario to the French and made it impossible for the English to attack Fort Niagara. Even worse, Montcalm's victory brought the Iroquois into an alliance with the French. In all, 1756 was a very bad year for the British, but, at the end of it, in December, William Pitt became British secretary of state for the southern department, a post that put him in charge of American colonial affairs. He replaced incompetent commanders with more able ones, and he adopted a far more cooperative attitude toward colonial commanders. Although Fort William Henry fell to the French on August 9, 1757 (followed by the slaughter of the fort's garrison by Montcalm's Indian warriors), the tide began to turn in favor of the British.

Brigadier General John Forbes, one of Britain's best field commanders, prepared a new assault on the main French headquarters at Fort Duquesne. Despite many delays, Forbes attacked on November 24, 1757. The French abandoned Fort Duquesne and blew it up. No matter, the English had at last seized control of the gateway to the West.

1759

The Fall of Quebec and the Triumph of the English

f 1758 marked the turning of the tide in favor of the British, 1759 was appropriately dubbed "the year of French disaster." It culminated in the siege, battle, and loss of Quebec on September 18, 1759, which effectively brought to an end French power in North America. The British capture of Quebec was the long, arduous, frustrating work of British general James Wolfe, who made his first attack on the city on July 31, 1759. It wasn't until September 12, however, that Wolfe was able to deploy troops stealthily along the Plains of Abraham, which lay before Quebec, then mount a brilliantly executed attack, which took the city after a mere quarter-hour of fighting. Grievously wounded in the engagement, Wolfe lived just long enough to see the battle through to victory. By that time, Montcalm also lay dead. Quebec formally surrendered on September 18, 1759.

For all practical purposes, the Battle of Quebec effectively decided the French and Indian War, yet the fighting continued as the British steadily contracted the circle around French Canada. Combat between the English and the French diminished, while fighting between the English and Indians, who justifiably feared dispossession at the hands of the victors, intensified. Indian-held Detroit rapidly fell to English forces under Robert Rogers and his famed Rangers, but fighting along the southern frontier took two armies and two years to bring to an end. In the waning months of the war, Spain entered the picture on the side of France. England declared war on the new belligerent on January 2, 1762, and crushed it with sea power alone. On February 10, 1763, the Treaty of Paris ended both the French and Indian War in America and the Seven Years' War in Europe. Having given all of Louisiana to its ally Spain in compensation for what it had lost in the war, France ceded the rest of its North American holdings to Great Britain. England was now the supreme American power east of the Mississippi and throughout Canada.

1763

King George's Proclamation Line

For the British crown, the French and Indian War was a glorious victory, but an expensive one, and King George III was eager to prevent further costly conflict with the Indians. Therefore, at the close of the war, on October 7, 1763, he issued a royal proclamation forbidding white settlement west of the Appalachian Mountains. He trusted that this would effectively prevent settlers from encroaching on Indian territory.

In fact, the Proclamation Line did conciliate the Indians, but it proved impossible to enforce. Settlers generally ignored it and persisted in pushing settlement westward. This provoked Indian raids, which, in turn, sent settlers appealing to royal governors for aid. As often as not, colonial officials turned a deaf ear to the pleas of frontiersmen who had violated the Proclamation Line. This contributed to growing alienation between the frontier regions and the Tidewater—the thickly settled coast. Increasingly, over the years, officials in these coastal areas were forced to choose allegiance to the policies of the mother country or the demands of those who lived on the western fringes of the colonies. By the 1770s, the trans-Appalachian bonds between east coast and interior were growing stronger than the trans-Atlantic bonds between the colonies and England.

1765

The Stamp Act

Following the French and Indian War, at the behest of King George III, Parliament—for the first time in history—imposed a series of taxes on the colonies in an effort to defray some of the costs of the war. Each new tax was met with colonial protest, grounded in a concept articulated by Boston lawyer James Otis in 1761. "Taxation without representation," he declared, "is tyranny." And since the colonies were not represented in Parliament, Parliament had no right to tax them.

The passage of the Stamp Act, put into force on March 22, 1765, galvanized colonial opposition, unified the colonies to an unprecedented degree, and pushed them closer to rebellion. The Stamp Act taxed all sorts of printed matter, including newspapers, legal documents, and paper itself, all of which required a government stamp as proof that the tax had been paid.

Opposition took three principal forms. First, colonists simply refused to buy the stamps. Second, militant organizations, such as one led by a Boston agitator named Samuel Adams, formed to intimidate the stamp agents (those responsible for selling the stamps and enforcing their use) into resigning. These groups, known collectively as the Sons of Liberty, proved highly effective. Finally, on October 7, 1765, a Stamp Act Congress convened in New York City and brought together representatives from South Carolina, Rhode Island, Connecticut, Pennsylvania, Maryland, New Jersey, Delaware, and New York. The congress drafted a Declaration of Rights and Grievances and masterminded a boycott of English goods. Not only did the boycott result in the repeal of the Stamp Act, but the congress also proved a major step in unifying the colonies, which began to develop a national identity separate from that imposed by the mother country.

1769

Daniel Boone Traverses the Cumberland Gap

Where the borders of the present-day states of Tennessee, Kentucky, and Virginia meet, millennia of wind and water carved a major break in the great Appalachian Mountain barrier that divides the Atlantic seaboard from the vast lands to the west. Like many other Americans of the mid- to late eighteenth century, Daniel Boone hankered after those lands, but, unlike most of his contemporaries, he was not only a frontiersman, but a natural-born leader. He didn't discover the Cumberland Gap—white hunters had been using it for years, Indians for untold centuries, and, doubtless, herds of migratory animals before both of these groups—but, on June 7, 1769, the Cumberland Gap took Boone to Kentucky, changed his life, and changed the course of American history.

"We found every where abundance of wild beasts of all sorts, through this vast forest," Boone—or, rather, a ghostwriting land promoter, John Filson—wrote in 1784. Boone saw Kentucky as a new Garden of Eden. Financed by a colorful and influential North Carolina entrepreneur, Judge Richard Henderson, Boone would hew out the first readily passable road through the Gap, the Wilderness Road, and in 1775 led the first substantial group of settlers into Kentucky, where he founded Boonesborough.

The settlement suffered mightily through the American Revolution (Boone himself was captured by the Shawnee and lived among them for several months before making a break for it), but it stuck, and by the end of the Revolution, 12,000 persons had migrated to Kentucky. In 1792, when the territory's population hit 100,000, it was admitted to the Union. The trans-Appalachian West was on its way to being settled.

1770

The Boston Massacre

In 1770, times were hard for American colonists as well as for the British troops sent to police them. The British were paid so poorly that many looked for off-duty work just to make ends meet. Hard-pressed colonists resented this, and when an off-duty soldier sought employment at Grey's Ropewalk (a Boston wharf-side rope maker) on the evening of March 5, 1770, he was mobbed. By nine o'clock that night, the situation had escalated into a near riot as Bostonians confronted Redcoats.

The mob threw insults, then ice balls, and, finally, a wooden club. This elicited a musket shot from a soldier, then another. A Bostonian named Samuel Gray lay mortally wounded, and Crispus Attucks, a runaway slave, was killed instantly. Crispus Attucks is traditionally counted as the first American to die in the struggle for independence.

More shots were fired, two more citizens fell dead, and a third, wounded, would die later. But at this point, the British commander regained control of his men, and the melee ended.

Samuel Adams and others did their best to propagandize the "Boston Massacre" and elevate it to an immediate cause for revolution. However, two brilliant colonial attorneys, Josiah Quincy and future president John Adams, intervened to defend the British captain and six Redcoats who had been indicted for murder. Although both Quincy and Adams were partisans of independence, they believed that mob rule was fatal to a people who craved democracy. Thanks to their skill, Captain Preston and four men were acquitted, and two others were found guilty of the lesser charge of manslaughter.

Sam Adams and other Sons of Liberty were frustrated that the Boston Massacre did not produce an instant revolution. However, the fair trial and the verdict that followed demonstrated that the people of Boston were both worthy of and ready for liberty.

1773

The Boston Tea Party

By 1773, the colonists had succeeded in forcing the crown to repeal most of the taxes levied on them. However, King George insisted on keeping a tax on tea, primarily because he believed that "there must always be one tax" in order to preserve Parliament's right to tax the colonies. Colonists evaded the tax by smuggling Dutch tea, which worked a hardship on the financially ailing British East India Company. If the company couldn't soon ship to America some of the 17 million pounds of Indian tea lying in its London warehouses, the whole lot would go rotten. The company asked prime minister Lord North for help. He understood that the East India Company paid two taxes: one when it landed tea in Britain, whether for sale or shipment elsewhere, and another tax when it landed a shipment in America. The Tea Act of May 10, 1773, forgave the first tax and retained the lesser three-penny-a-pound duty due on landing in America. This would price East India tea below the smuggled tea.

But instead of prompting American consumers to buy British tea, the Tea Act was seen as a government-enforced monopoly and yet another affront to colonial rights. Throughout the colonies, Sons of Liberty and other activists intimidated into resignation East India Company consignees in Philadelphia, New York, and Charleston, and American captains and harbor pilots refused to handle the East India Company cargo. Tea ships were turned back to London from Philadelphia and New York. In Boston, when three Tea Act ships landed at Boston Harbor, the Sons of Liberty prevented their being unloaded—even as the royal governor refused to allow the ships to leave the harbor and return to London.

At the height of this standoff, on the night of December 16, a group of protestors dressed as Mohawk Indians boarded the ships and dumped 90,000 pounds of tea overboard.

"The flame is kindled, and like lightning it catches from soul to soul." —letter from Abigail Adams to her husband, John, as the tea ships stood in Boston harbor

Parliament's response to this outrage was to punish Massachusetts by passing the Port Act, which blocked trade in and out of Boston until the tea had been paid for; the Administration of Justice Act, which allowed crown officials to be tried outside of the colony; and the Massachusetts Government Act, which increased the power of the royal governor at the expense of the colonial assembly. In addition, the Quartering Act allowed royal governors throughout the colonies to seize privately owned buildings as barracks and billets for British troops.

The colonists branded these laws the "Intolerable Acts," and the colonies united in solidarity with Massachusetts. In its effort to break the colonial will and force obedience to the crown, the British government pushed the colonies ever closer to union. Leaders of rebellion called for a "Continental Congress" to convene.

1774

The First Continental Congress

Spurred by the Boston Tea Party and the "Intolerable Acts" that followed, delegates from every colony except Georgia converged on Philadelphia in September 1774 for the First Continental Congress. Whereas the concept of taxation without representation had been the focus of most colonial protest, the delegates now held that Parliament had no right to make *any* laws for the colonies. Some delegates believed that reform of the colonial system was still possible, but the majority were radicals who would settle for nothing short of independence. What moderates and radicals did agree on was the creation of a Continental Association to conduct boycotts of British goods and to enforce an embargo on exports to England. Beyond this, the Congress endorsed a call by Massachusetts delegates for citizens to recognize their right to take up arms in defense of their liberties.

> "The revolution was complete, in the minds of the people, and the Union of the colonies, before the war commenced." —John Adams, recalling the significance of the First Continental Congress

Although opinion in the First Continental Congress was by no means unanimous, colonial solidarity and identity had reached an unprecedented level of intensity.

1775

Patrick Henry Demands Liberty—
or Death

By 1775, acts of disorder and rebellion were breaking out all over New England. At midnight on February 25, 1775, General Thomas Gage, British commander in chief and military governor of the American colonies, sent 240 men of the 64th Foot Regiment from Boston to Salem, Massachusetts, where, he had heard, the rebels stored cannon and munitions stolen from the royal arsenal. But the well-developed colonial network of spies and informers warned the people of Salem, who managed to move to safety the nineteen cannon and other munitions that had, indeed, been stored there.

The following month, when Virginia's House of Burgesses, barred by royal order from their official place of assembly, met at Raleigh Tavern on March 23, 1775, Patrick Henry made an electrifying speech alluding to the outbreaks in New England:

> There is no retreat but in submission and slavery! Our chains are forged. Their clanking may be heard on the plains of Boston! The war is inevitable—and let it come! I repeat it, sir, let it come!
>
> It is in vain, sir, to extenuate the matter. Gentlemen may cry, "Peace! Peace!"—but there is no peace. The war is actually begun! The next gale that sweeps down from the north will bring to our ears the clash of resounding arms! Our brethren are already in the field! Why stand we here idle? What is it that gentlemen wish? What would they have? Is life so dear, or peace so sweet, as to be purchased at the price of chains and slavery? For-

bid it, Almighty God! I know not what course others may take, but as for me, give me liberty or give me death!

His speech instantly united South and North, providing just enough momentum to ensure that a great American revolution would begin to roll, then rush forward.

1775

The Midnight Ride of Paul Revere

Unlike Virginia's Patrick Henry, Paul Revere of Charlestown, Massachusetts, was no politician. He was a silversmith by trade, the son of a silversmith, Apollos Rivoire, who had come to America as one of thousands of Huguenots (French Protestants) fleeing the deadly religious persecution they suffered at home. Paul Revere prospered in his profession and fathered a large family—eight children by his first wife and eight more by his second. With many mouths to feed, it was a good thing that Revere did so well, but he was not content merely to earn money. The son of a man who had known persecution firsthand, Revere was drawn to the political movers and shakers of Boston, members of the Sons of Liberty, including Sam Adams and his distant cousin John Adams, John Hancock, James Otis, and Dr. Joseph Warren. Revere served the Sons of Liberty as a courier, and on April 16, 1775, it was Revere who rode to Lexington, Massachusetts, to warn Sam Adams and John Hancock that they were in imminent danger of arrest. Shortly after this mission, on April 18, 1775, Revere was one of three riders who alerted the citizen militia of the Massachusetts countryside to the approach of the British, who were determined to capture an important cache of Patriot arms at Concord.

The British troops stepped off at 10:30 P.M. Revere had stationed a friend, John Pulling, in the steeple of Charlestown's North Church, his task to signal whether the British were marching out by land or using whaleboats to cut across the Back Bay. A one-lantern signal meant they were coming overland; two, via the Back Bay.

As soon as Revere saw two lanterns in the steeple, he and another Sons of Liberty courier, William Dawes, raced ahead of the advancing British column. Thanks to Revere, Dawes, and a third courier, Samuel Prescott, the British lost the element of surprise, and the Minutemen—the citizen militia so-called because they claimed combat readiness on a minute's notice—were prepared to fight.

1775

Battle of Lexington

A t Lexington, Massachusetts, which lay squarely in the line of march between Boston and Concord, militia captain Jonas Parker formed up the ranks of seventy or so citizen-soldiers on Lexington's green, which fronted the Concord road.

"Stand your ground," Captain Parker ordered. "Don't fire unless fired upon. But if they want to have a war, let it begin here!"

Such brave words, tailor-made for history, were probably concocted long after the fact by some historian. No one knows what Parker actually said. Whatever it was, though, it failed to inspire all of the militiamen. Some, staring at the unbroken line of advancing Redcoats, shook their heads, shrugged, and walked away.

"So many of them, so few of us. It is folly to stand here." —one of the Minutemen, at the approach of battle, Lexington, Massachusetts

For his part, the British second in command, John Pitcairn, restrained his own men while calling out to the Americans, "Lay down your arms, you rebels, and disperse!"

Parker ordered his men to disband—but he told them to take their weapons with them. After Pitcairn repeated his demand that they lay down their weapons, shots rang out. A Redcoat was wounded slightly in the leg, and two balls grazed Pitcairn's horse.

Were the shots American or British? No one knows. But they were enough to prompt a British officer to command, "Fire, by God, fire!"

When the Battle of Lexington was over, eight militiamen, including Captain Parker, lay dead on Lexington green. Ten more were wounded. A single British soldier was slightly hurt. Then the British resumed their march on Concord.

1775

Battle of Concord

No one knows just how many Americans were ultimately involved in the Battle of Concord. Wild guesses have run as high as 20,000, but, most likely, a total of 3,763 Americans fought—though never more than half this number at any one time. However, at the moment of the British arrival in Concord—which was unopposed—only about 400 militiamen, under the command of local resident "Colonel" James Barrett, had assembled on a ridge overlooking the town.

Not one to be hurried, British Lieutenant Colonel Francis Smith dined at a local tavern while his grenadiers searched the town for hidden munitions. When the grenadiers set fire to some gun carriages they found, one of Barrett's officers turned to him: "Will you let them burn the town down?" At this, Barrett ordered the militia to march to the defense of Concord.

And so the battle began. The captain of the British light infantry ordered his men to form two ranks for firing. It was the standard maneuver, drilled countless times, but, this time, something went wrong. The volleys of the first British rank fell short—hitting only two marks, militia captain Isaac Davis and Abner Hosmer, a little drummer boy who marched bravely at the head of the American column.

"Fire, fellow soldiers!" an unidentified American officer called to his men. "For God's sake, fire!"

Years later, the poet-philosopher Ralph Waldo Emerson would call this the "shot heard 'round the world": Three British soldiers were killed, nine more wounded, and the Redcoats retreated into the town. The American Revolution had truly begun.

Had the Americans been more disciplined soldiers, they would have pursued the retreating British. Instead, Colonel Smith was permitted to withdraw from Concord, although his troops were sniped at all the way back to Boston. In the twin engagements at Lexington and Concord, which opened the American Revolution, seventy-three Redcoats were confirmed dead and twenty-six were reported missing and presumed dead. One hundred seventy-four British solders were wounded. The Americans suffered forty-nine deaths, as well as five missing and thirty-nine to forty-one wounded.

1775

Battle of Bunker Hill

The British military chief and governor of Massachusetts, General Thomas Gage, received reinforcements from England on May 25 and was also joined by three additional generals, John Burgoyne, William Howe, and Henry Clinton. Thus fortified, he believed he could now intimidate the colonists into giving up the revolution. He offered amnesty to all, save Sam Adams and John Hancock, the two chief troublemakers. In response, the Massachusetts Committee of Public Safety, the body that was now running the war, ordered General Artemus Ward to fortify Bunker Hill on Charlestown Heights, overlooking Boston harbor.

It was a good defensive plan, but Ward chose instead to send Colonel William Prescott with 1,200 men to occupy nearby Breed's Hill, which was lower and more vulnerable than Bunker. Seeing that the colonists intended to fight, Gage directed a naval bombardment against Breed's Hill at dawn on June 17. He followed this with an amphibious attack by 2,500 men under General Howe. Twice, this superior British force attempted to take Breed's Hill. Twice they were repulsed with heavy losses. A third assault—this one with bayonets—succeeded chiefly because the defenders were exhausted and out of ammunition.

Misnamed for Bunker Hill—the position that *should* have been defended—the battle was certainly a tactical defeat for the colonists, but it was also a psychological victory for them. As they saw it, a shortage of ammunition, not the British army, had defeated them. Besides, although the Americans were pushed off Breed's Hill and Bunker Hill, of the 2,500 British troops engaged,

1,000 had died—a devastating casualty rate of 42 percent and the heaviest loss the British were to suffer during the long war. Inspired, the Americans would fight on, would lay siege to Boston, and would drive the British army out.

1775–1776

Early Victories, Early Defeats

The first year of the American Revolution was marked by great success in Boston. The American army, pushed out of the city by the loss of the Battle of Bunker Hill, regrouped and laid siege to the British in Boston. By March 1776, the British had had enough. Evacuating by sea, they moved their headquarters all the way to Halifax, Nova Scotia. Boston was in Patriot hands.

In the South, the Americans also successfully repulsed a British invasion under Sir Henry Clinton. Clinton bombarded the harbor fortifications of the South's chief city, Charleston, South Carolina, but was driven off by June 28, 1776. This effectively neutralized the British in the South for the next two years.

While the Patriot cause fared far better in the first year of the war than anybody could have expected, an American attempt to persuade British Canada to join the revolution was rebuffed, and an American attempt to invade Canada proved a costly failure. Worse, by the summer of 1776, the British began to wrest the initiative from the Americans. The Continental Army led by George Washington was defeated on Long Island on August 27, 1776, but fought a brilliant rearguard action in Manhattan from August through November. Although the Americans relinquished this key city to the British, it cost the Redcoats time, money, energy, and men.

General William Howe pushed Washington into and across New Jersey. Had he been more determined and Washington less skillful, Howe could have destroyed the Continental Army and ended the Revolution. Instead, Washington and his forces escaped across the Delaware River and into Pennsylvania on December 7, 1776.

1776

Thomas Paine's *Common Sense*

The "shot heard 'round the world" was fired on April 19, 1775, and the misnamed Battle of Bunker Hill and the successful siege of Boston followed. Although a revolution had begun, many Americans were still not certain that outright independence from the mother country was a good idea. Even as the war was fought during 1775, individuals and entire colonies wavered. What finally crystallized popular opinion in favor of complete and immediate independence was a modest forty-seven-page pamphlet published on January 9, 1776, and written, according to the title page, "by an Englishman." It was *Common Sense* by Thomas Paine, a newly arrived immigrant from England. After a clear and eloquent argument advocating not merely the desirability of independence, but its very necessity, Paine concluded:

> Ye that dare oppose not only the tyranny but the tyrant, stand forth! Every spot of the old world is overrun with oppression. Freedom hath been hunted round the globe. Asia and Africa have long expelled her. Europe regards her like a stranger, and England hath given her warning to depart. O receive the fugitive, and prepare in time an asylum for mankind!

In less than three months, 120,000 copies of *Common Sense* were sold. Before the end of the Revolution, more than half a million copies had been distributed. As John Adams wrote on May 20, 1776, following the publication of *Common Sense* and George Washington's victory in the siege of Boston: "Every post and every day rolls in upon us Independence like a torrent." One after the other, the colonies now voted for independence.

The Declaration of Independence

The final debate over independence got under way in the Continental Congress on July 1, 1776, with Pennsylvania's John Dickinson counseling delay, while John Adams and others passionately urged immediate action. By July 2, eleven of the twelve colonies represented at the Second Continental Congress—Georgia sent no delegate, and the New York delegation abstained—voted for independence. Earlier, in anticipation of this moment, the Congress had appointed a committee to draft a declaration of independence, naming to it John Adams, Benjamin Franklin, Robert Livingston, Roger Sherman, and Thomas Jefferson.

In 1825, writing to his fellow Virginian and revolutionary colleague Henry Lee, Jefferson explained what he had intended to accomplish in writing the Declaration. He was not trying to be particularly original, to "find out new principles, or new arguments, never before thought of," but, rather, "to justify ourselves in the independent stand we are compelled to take" and to "appeal to the tribunal of the world . . . for our justification."

The choice of committee members was logical. Adams was a prime mover of revolutionary activity in the cradle of the Revolution, Massachusetts. Franklin was a figure of international reputation, renowned as a scientist, inventor, writer, editor, politician, and now emerging as a brilliant statesman. Livingston, son of an old New York family, represented the more conservative wing of the Congress. Sherman, from Connecticut, was a self-educated legislator and economic theorist, as well as a skilled writer. Jefferson, the junior member of the committee, had already written in 1774 *A Summary View of the Rights of British America*. It was to Jefferson that the committee turned for the first draft.

Jefferson drew from the philosophy of the seventeenth-century British philosopher John Locke, who had enumerated the basic rights of human beings as life, liberty, and property. Jefferson borrowed the rights to life and liberty, but for Locke's *property* he substituted the "pursuit of happiness," as if to declare that America offered an opportunity to aspire to a level of satisfaction and self-fulfillment unavailable elsewhere in the world and at any other time in history.

After editing by the Second Continental Congress—antislavery passages were cut so as not to alienate the South—the document was signed by the members of the Congress on July 4, 1776. A nation was born, and the American Revolution now had a unified direction, an international standing, and a bold inspiration.

The Articles of Confederation

N o sooner did the United States declare its independence in 1776 than Pennsylvania's John Dickinson (1732–1808) set to work drafting a constitution for the new republic, the Articles of Confederation. Dickinson favored a strong national government, but the states demanded more rights—especially the power of taxation—and, between 1777 and its ratification in 1781, Dickinson's original was watered down to create not a nation, but a "firm league of friendship" among thirteen essentially sovereign states. There was no president, no federal judiciary, and Congress had no real power, because, while it could enact laws, it could not enforce them. The states chose either to comply—or not. Most important, Congress had no authority to impose taxes.

The Articles went into effect even before the Revolution ended, but their fatal weakness was demonstrated almost daily. Congress, for example, was powerless to aid Massachusetts in 1786 when a farmer named Daniel Shays led a popular "rebellion" against the lawful authority of the state judicial system. Nor could Congress intervene when Rhode Island printed a ruinous torrent of entirely worthless paper money. These crises motivated a 1786 convention at Annapolis, Maryland, which, in turn, called for a constitutional convention to revise the crumbling Articles.

1776

Triumph at Trenton

From the historical perspective of more than 200 years, Washington's long retreat looks less like a defeat than a strategic withdrawal. But, at the time, Washington understood that wars are not won in retreat, and he also understood that Howe viewed his army as defeated and the Revolution all but over. Washington decided on a bold move.

In the dead of a very bitter winter, a season in which armies traditionally avoided battle, Washington collected his scattered militia and regular forces, rallied them, and led them back across the half-frozen Delaware on Christmas night. Back on the New Jersey bank, he stealthily marched his men to confront in battle a force not of Redcoats, but of Hessians, German mercenary troops in the employ of the British. These soldiers, perhaps the finest in Europe, were justly feared for their discipline and cruelty. To oppose them, Washington had an inferior number of ill-equipped, ill-clothed amateurs. But, he knew, he also had the element of surprise. The Hessians and their commander, Colonel Johann Rall, would be groggy from Christmas feasting, and a ragtag American army was certainly the last thing they expected to encounter on December 26.

The battle was short and sharp. Washington's army suffered no casualties, whereas the Hessians lost 106 men killed or wounded. More than 900 became prisoners of war. Colonel Rall was mortally wounded.

This victory, followed by another at Princeton on January 3, 1777, moved the Continental Congress to reject the latest British peace terms and to press ahead with the fight for independence.

1777

Victory at Saratoga,
Defeat in Philadelphia

The defeat the Hessians suffered at Trenton was a profound shock to the British. Even more shattering were the results of two battles near Saratoga, New York. American commanders Horatio Gates, Benedict Arnold, and the quasi-guerrilla leader Daniel Morgan twice inflicted heavy losses on the army of British general John Burgoyne, at Bemis Heights on September 19, 1777, and at Frayer's Farm on October 7. Cut off after these defeats, Burgoyne found himself in the unenviable position of surrendering an entire British army—6,000 regulars plus various auxiliary forces—to the Patriots on October 17.

Simultaneously with this great American victory, however, came a dispiriting defeat. General William Howe made an amphibious landing on the upper Chesapeake Bay, then advanced on the capital of the Revolution, Philadelphia, the seat of the Continental Congress and the very place where the Declaration of Independence had been signed.

Washington led an inept defense at the Battle of Brandywine on September 11, 1777, but the British overran Philadelphia, and the Continental Congress fled to York, Pennsylvania.

The British had a right to gloat over the capture of the rebel capital. But what, exactly, had they gained? Congress, in exile, continued to function, and the war went on. Washington made an unsuccessful attempt to retake Philadelphia by attacking the British in the Battle of Germantown on October 4. Yet even this Patriot defeat gained something for the Americans. The French, who had been pondering whether or not to aid the Americans in their fight against the British, were thrilled by the Patriot victory at Saratoga, but even more impressed by the American gallantry displayed at Germantown—despite defeat there. A Franco–American alliance was formally concluded on February 6, 1778, and France became the first foreign power to recognize the United States of America.

Yorktown

After initial frustration in the South, the British returned to the region in 1778 and racked up one victory after another along the coast, only to suffer some notable defeats inland. Lord Charles Cornwallis led British triumphs along the seaboard, but then found himself pinned down by frontier guerrillas. Although he broke free, Cornwallis made the tactical blunder of withdrawing into Virginia, where he established a headquarters at the port of Yorktown. His idea in settling his army on this peninsula was to have ready access to an evacuation by sea; however, the fleet of French admiral François de Grasse blocked the British fleet and thereby cut off any supply or escape by water. Cornwallis had penned himself into the tip of the peninsula.

In collaboration with the French army of the comte de Rochambeau, George Washington laid siege to Cornwallis at Yorktown on October 6, 1781. On October 19, the British commander surrendered to the allies with 17,000 men. Although peace would not formally come until the conclusion of the Treaty of Paris, ratified on April 15, 1783, the American Revolution was suddenly ended. The United States emerged an independent nation, and Cornwallis's regimental band, at the surrender ceremony, played a popular tune of the time: "The World Turned Upside Down."

1787

The Writing of a Constitution

The Annapolis convention, convened in 1786 to revise the Articles of Confederation, instead called for a full-scale constitutional convention to meet in Philadelphia. The fifty-five delegates who convened in May 1787 began to fashion a document that would create a genuine national government rather than a merely hopeful confederation of states. The delegates unanimously elected George Washington president of the convention. Soon, the proposals boiled down to two rival plans: The "Virginia Plan" proposed the creation of a central federal government consisting of a bicameral legislature (House and Senate), an executive branch, and a judicial branch. The chief executive was to be elected by the members of the legislature, who, in turn, would be elected by the citizens. Representation in the two-chambered legislature would be proportionate to state population—a provision that greatly worried and even enraged representatives of the smaller states. The "New Jersey Plan" retained most of the Articles of Confederation, but gave all of the states equal representation in the legislature. There would be no executive branch, but there would be a Supreme Court, separate and independent from the legislature.

It was Roger Sherman, delegate from Connecticut, who formulated the "Great Compromise" between the two plans. It called for a bicameral legislature; however, the Senate would provide each state with equal representation, whereas the House of Representatives would provide representation proportionate to each state's population. There would be a chief executive, the president, who would be elected not directly by the people, but by an electoral college, the members of which were voted into office by the state legislatures.

William Johnson (secretary of the Convention), Alexander Hamilton, James Madison, Rufus King, and Gouverneur Morris wrote the actual Constitution document, the product of three and a half months of debate. When thirty-eight of the fifty-five Convention delegates approved the Constitution, it was sent to Congress, which submitted it to the states for ratification. Now the real battle would begin.

1787

The Three-Fifths Compromise

Unlike many political compromises, the "Great Compromise" between the rival plans for the Constitution was genuinely satisfying. However, it did not resolve the most complex and rancorous outstanding issue, the matter of slavery.

There was no serious movement to abolish slavery outright in this new land dedicated to liberty, but there was serious dispute over how slaves should figure in the calculation of each state's representation in the federal government. The more representatives a state could claim, the more influential it would be in that government. Therefore, the South wanted its slaves counted as population—even though slaves were property rather than people. Northerners objected, arguing that the slaves should be excluded entirely from the calculation. After much debate, Article I, Section 2 of the Constitution was hammered out, a compromise calling for "Representation and direct taxes [to be] apportioned among the several states according to respective numbers determined by adding to the whole number of free persons including those bound to service for a set number of years and excluding Indians not taxed three-fifths of all other persons." In other words, for purposes of levying taxes and apportioning representatives, each slave was counted as three-fifths of a person.

The notorious "Three-Fifths Compromise" was the first of many jury-rigged stopgaps that would be cobbled together in an increasingly desperate effort to keep the fact of slavery from blowing the nation apart.

1787–1788

The Struggle for Ratification

Those who supported the Constitution that Congress approved and submitted for ratification by the states were called Federalists. Those who opposed it—who feared the creation of a strong, perhaps tyrannical federal government—were called Anti-Federalists.

Delaware, Pennsylvania, and New Jersey immediately ratified the proposed Constitution, but ratification by a total of nine states was required to enact the document. The process was hotly contested in many states and nowhere more so than in the key states of Virginia and New York. To persuade New Yorkers to ratify the proposed Constitution, Alexander Hamilton, James Madison, and John Jay collaborated on a series of essays collectively called *The Federalist Papers* and published during 1787–1788 in various New York newspapers under the joint pseudonym "Publius."

One of history's great political treatises, *The Federalist* argued that people were chiefly motivated by self-interest and, therefore, the establishment of a representative government, while valuable, was dangerous. Inherently selfish representatives might betray their trust, one faction might oppose and oppress another, and passions might well overcome rational decision. Investing certain central authority in the government was presented as a means of defending against these dangers. Of particular significance was the tenth *Federalist* essay, written by James Madison. Rejecting the common belief that republican government was possible only for small states, Madison argued that liberty, justice, and stability were actually more likely to be attained in a large area with a numerous and varied population.

The Federalist presented a strong enough case in favor of the new Constitution to tip the balance in New York, thirty delegates voting for ratification, twenty-seven against. The vote in Virginia was also close—eighty-nine to seventy-nine—and that came about when the Anti-Federalist protest that the Constitution failed to address the rights of individuals was answered by a promise that a "Bill of Rights" would be added. When New Hampshire became the ninth state to ratify the Constitution on June 21, 1788, the document became law, and was put into effect officially on March 4, 1789.

Election of George Washington

One of the many innovations the new Constitution introduced into the United States government was the office of president, and in April 1789, a month after the document had been put into effect on March 4, the new Senate convened to count ballots cast by members of the electoral college for the first president of the United States. The result surprised no one and pleased just about everyone. George Washington was elected unanimously, with John Adams as his vice president.

In effect, that first election was rigged. For it was with the implicit understanding that Washington would be elected that the framers of the Constitution created a strong executive branch. The thought of having fought a long and painful revolution to get free of King George III only to embrace some new tyrant was a chilling one. Washington, however, had not only demonstrated a genius for leadership in commanding the Continental Army, he had also exhibited great skill as a statesman in presiding so productively over the contentious Constitutional Convention. Perhaps most important of all, he possessed the character of a true republican. Such was his popularity after the Revolution that, had he so chosen, Washington could have become absolute dictator of the United States or even the new nation's new king. Instead, he eagerly withdrew to his beloved Virginia plantation, Mount Vernon, and only with considerable reluctance did he answer his country's call to office.

Washington was inaugurated in New York City on April 30, 1789. Although the Constitution was in place, Washington's immediate task was to create much of the American government and, most important of all, to give shape to the office of president. He rapidly created key executive departments, naming Thomas Jefferson as secretary of state, Henry Knox as secretary of war, Alexander Hamilton as secretary of the treasury, Samuel Osgood as head of the post office, and Edmund Randolph as attorney general. Certain of these departments Washington organized into a close body of presidential advisors, the Cabinet.

Washington understood that his administration would set the pattern for future presidents. The chief quality he introduced was restraint. He studiously avoided conflict with Congress, believing it was not the chief executive's duty to propose legislation. He also opposed the formation of political parties—although, by the time of his second term, two competing parties had, indeed, been formed: the conservative Federalists, headed by John Adams and Alexander Hamilton, and the liberal Democratic-Republicans, headed by Thomas Jefferson.

Washington could have been president for life, but it is powerful evidence of his unwillingness to become a tyrant that he declined to stand for a third term, and the two-term presidency thereafter became a hallowed tradition until the twin crises of the Depression and World War II prompted the nation to elect Franklin Delano Roosevelt to a third and a fourth term.

> FDR was a beloved president, to whom the nation was intensely grateful, but Congress and the people were fearful of allowing any other man or woman in the future to become president for life. On February 26, 1951, Congress approved the Twenty-second Amendment to the Constitution, restricting future presidents to no more than two terms.

In classical times, Romans set one honor above all others, reserving it for their greatest leaders: the title of "*Pater Patriae*," Father of His Country. Almost immediately, the free citizens of a new nation bestowed this epithet on George Washington.

The Bill of Rights

The framers of the Constitution aimed to create as concise and elegant a document as the needs of government would permit. They believed it unnecessary to provide an explicit guarantee of individual rights because the Constitution clearly stated that the government is one of "enumerated powers" exclusively. That is, the government can take no action and can assume no authority except those actions and that authority explicitly provided for in the Constitution. Anti-Federalists and many others regarded this as an insufficient safeguard against tyranny and clamored for a "bill of rights."

At the behest of Congress in 1789, James Madison painstakingly examined, weighed, and synthesized the rights already included in several state constitutions, especially the Virginia Bill of Rights, which had been adopted in 1776. He then produced a set of twelve amendments to the Constitution. The first two—which had to do with an adjustment to the proportion of congressional representatives to population and the regulation of compensation for legislators—were rejected, but the other ten, enumerating and guaranteeing individual rights, were ratified on December 15, 1791, as the Bill of Rights.

The First Amendment protects freedom of religion, freedom of speech, freedom of the press, and the right of popular assembly for the purpose of petition for redress of grievances. The Second Amendment guarantees the right to bear arms, and the Third Amendment strictly limits the quartering of soldiers in private homes. The Fourth Amendment forbids unreasonable searches and seizures and requires search-and-seizure warrants to be specific—not blanket documents—and to be issued only upon probable cause. The Fifth Amendment mandates grand jury indictments in major criminal prosecutions, prohibits "double jeopardy" (being tried more than once for the same crime), and guarantees that no one need testify against himself or herself. This amendment also forbids taking private property for public use without just compensation and prohibits deprivation of life, liberty, or property without due process of law. The Sixth Amendment guarantees a speedy public trial by jury. It further specifies that the accused must be fully informed of the charges, must be confronted with the witnesses against him or her, must have the power to subpoena witnesses for his or her defense, and must have access to legal counsel. The Seventh Amendment guarantees jury trials in civil cases, and the Eighth prohibits excessive bail, unreasonable fines, and "cruel and unusual punishments."

The Ninth and Tenth amendments are special. The Ninth explicitly provides that the enumeration of rights in the Constitution does not nullify or deny other rights, which are retained by the people. The Tenth Amendment expresses the "doctrine of reserved powers": All powers not explicitly delegated to the United States are reserved to the states or the people.

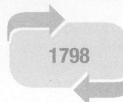

Trouble with Citizen Genêt

The Treaty of Paris, which ended the American Revolution in 1783, stipulated (among many other things) that all British interests were to evacuate the frontier forts of the "Old Northwest" (roughly the region encompassing the present states of Ohio, Indiana, Illinois, Michigan, and Wisconsin). Despite the treaty, many British traders remained in the region and, in some cases, incited the local Indians against American settlers. Simultaneously, on the high seas, Royal Navy ships periodically stopped and boarded American merchant vessels and abducted sailors who were—often arbitrarily—deemed British subjects; these individuals were then "impressed" into service on British men-o'-war. For their part, the British also had grievances, complaining that the United States breached the terms of the Treaty of Paris by failing to pay prerevolutionary debts owed to British creditors and by refusing to compensate Loyalists for property seized during the Revolution.

President George Washington did not want a new war with Britain, and so commissioned Chief Justice John Jay to negotiate a new treaty to secure evacuation of the frontier forts and to see to the settlement of debt and boundary disputes. The so-called Jay Treaty, concluded on November 19, 1794, mollified the British, but greatly alarmed the French, who feared that their erstwhile ally, the United States, was about to join forces with their greatest rival.

These fears were not entirely unjustified. Most Americans recoiled from the bloody excesses of the ongoing French Revolution (1789–1799), and, just a year before the Jay Treaty was concluded, Washington had coolly rebuffed the overtures of Edmond Charles Edouard Genêt, a French diplomat sent to the United States to secure U.S. aid for France in its war with England. Although Washington gave him the cold shoulder, "Citizen Genêt" (as French revolutionary etiquette styled him) was warmly greeted by some of the American public, and Genêt chose to interpret this reception as a show of universal popular support. In defiance of the president, he hired American sea captains to raid British vessels in U.S. coastal waters. To Washington's stern warning that he was violating U.S. sovereignty, Citizen Genêt replied with a threat to make a direct appeal to the American people. At this, Washington asked the French government to recall him.

In France, by this time, a new revolutionary party, the Jacobins, had replaced the Girondists, the party to which Genêt belonged. The Jacobin government sent a new foreign minister to the United States and asked Washington to send Genêt back—under arrest. Observing strict neutrality, Washington refused to compel Genêt to return to a Jacobin guillotine. Grateful, Genêt chose to become a U.S. citizen and settled into quiet respectability as the husband of New York governor George Clinton's daughter. It was a happy ending for Genêt and for the sovereignty of the fledgling American republic, but this episode, in combination with the Jay Treaty, brought France and the United States to the brink of war.

The XYZ Affair

I n an effort to heal the growing breach between the United States and France, President Washington sent a new foreign minister, Charles Cotesworth Pinckney, to France, but the French legislative body known as the Directory refused to receive him. Washington's successor, John Adams, dispatched to Paris a commission, consisting of Pinckney, John Marshall, and Elbridge Gerry, in the hope of averting outright war by concluding a new Franco–American treaty of commerce. This time, in October 1797, French prime minister Charles Maurice de Talleyrand-Perigord sent three agents to greet the American commissioners in Paris. The agents told them that before a treaty could even be discussed, the United States would have to loan France $12 million *and* pay Talleyrand a personal bribe of $250,000. Indignant, on April 3, 1798, Adams submitted to Congress the correspondence from Pinckney, Marshall, and Gerry, which designated the French agents as "X," "Y," and "Z." Congress, in turn, published the entire portfolio, and in this way the public learned of the "XYZ Affair."

The XYZ Affair ignited a small-scale, undeclared, but perilous naval war between the United States and France, and, even more dangerous, created a counterrevolutionary, antidemocratic backlash in American government, which threatened some of the liberties so recently won in the War of Independence.

1798

The Alien and Sedition Acts

assed during the staunchly Federalist administration of President John Adams in an atmosphere of deteriorating relations with radically revolutionary France, the Alien and Sedition Acts consisted of the Naturalization Act (June 18, 1798), which required immigrants seeking U.S. citizenship to have been resident in the country for fourteen years instead of the originally mandated five; the Alien Act (June 25), which authorized the president to deport any alien he deemed dangerous; the Alien Enemies Act (July 6), which authorized the president, in time of war, to arrest, imprison, or deport nationals of any enemy power; and, most infamous of all, the Sedition Act (July 14), which banned any assembly convened "with intent to oppose any measure . . . of the government." The act also outlawed printing, uttering, or publishing anything "false, scandalous, and malicious" concerning the government.

The Sedition Act alone was an outrageous infringement of the Constitutional rights to peaceable assembly and to free speech. But even the legislation relating to naturalization and the status of aliens was a bold affront to democracy. The fact was that a great many of the leading Democratic-Republicans—the liberal party opposed to the conservative Federalists—were relatively recent refugees from turbulent Europe. They had not been resident in the United States for anything approaching fourteen years, and to postpone citizenship for them would greatly erode the power base of the fledgling opposition party. Thus, Adams and his party mounted a blatant assault on their Democratic-Republican opposition, with the tyrannical object of legislating it out of existence.

The Virginia and Kentucky Resolutions

When John Adams was elected president in 1796, the election law at the time provided that the runner-up would become vice president. This meant that Adams, a Federalist, had his Democratic-Republican arch rival, Thomas Jefferson, as his vice president. Jefferson declared that if the Alien and Sedition Acts were permitted to stand, "we shall immediately see attempted another act of Congress, declaring the President shall continue in office during life, reserving to another occasion the transfer of the succession to his heirs, and the establishment of the Senate for life." Fearing the transformation of a revolutionary democracy into a pseudo-monarchy, Jefferson drew up a set of resolutions attacking centralized governmental authority and promoting the sovereignty of the states. As vice president, however, he thought it inappropriate and disloyal for him personally to make the resolutions public, so he persuaded the legislature of Kentucky (which had become a state in 1792) to publish them on November 22, 1799. Jefferson's friend and political protégé James Madison had drafted a similar set of resolutions, which were published by Virginia on December 24, 1798.

The Virginia and Kentucky Resolutions argued that the Alien and Sedition Acts were unconstitutional and, therefore, not binding on the states. Jefferson's original draft maintained that a state not only had the right to judge the constitutionality of acts of Congress, but also to "nullify"—declare invalid—any acts it determined to be unconstitutional. The outright statement of nullification authority was too radical for the Kentucky legislature to accept, and so the passage was suppressed in the final draft of the resolutions.

Nevertheless, nullification was unmistakably implied in both the Kentucky and Virginia documents. Seeking to restore democracy to American government, Jefferson had articulated the position that the United States was a compact among the states, not among the people. While Jefferson did not contest with the federal government the powers specifically given it by the Constitution, he did hold that federal acts outside of the federal government's constitutionally enumerated powers were inherently unconstitutional and, therefore, had no binding force on the states.

The Virginia and Kentucky Resolutions galvanized opposition to repressive Federalism in the United States, and while they did not secure the immediate repeal of the Alien and Sedition Acts, they ensured that, for the most part, the laws would be short-lived. Moreover, the electorate repudiated Federalism and endorsed Jefferson's Democratic-Republican position by electing Jefferson over Adams in 1800.

1803

The Louisiana Purchase

I n his first inaugural address, Thomas Jefferson, third president of the United States, remarked the nation's great good fortune in possessing "room enough for our descendants to the thousandth and thousandth generation."

But did it really *possess* such room?

As much territory as the new nation had, it was also hemmed in. There was British Canada to the north and the vast Louisiana Territory of France to the west. Or did that land belong to Spain? Following the French and Indian War, France had ceded the territory to Spain, but in 1800, Napoleon secretly reacquired Louisiana in exchange for parts of Tuscany, which he pledged to conquer on behalf of Spain. No sooner was the Secret Treaty of San Ildefonso concluded, however, than Napoleon abandoned his plan to conquer Tuscany, and Spain reneged on the treaty. While France asserted possession of Louisiana, *Spanish* officials closed the Mississippi River to American trade in 1802. President Jefferson could not tolerate the disruption of western trade, but he was reluctant to support France's claims on the territory against those of Spain. The thought of aiding a rapacious conqueror like Napoleon to establish himself in America was appalling—and even if Napoleon did not choose to menace the United States, the ongoing warfare between France and England would, sooner or later, motivate Britain to seize Louisiana for itself.

Searching for a solution to the Louisiana crisis, Jefferson sent James Monroe to France and Spain to make an offer for the purchase of the port city of New Orleans and Spanish Florida. This would secure the Mississippi River for trade and would neutralize the Spanish along the East Coast. However, even as Monroe sailed to Europe, Napoleon pondered the fate of one of his large armies, which was bogged down in the disease-infested West Indies, fruitlessly tangling with rebels led by Haitian freedom fighter Toussaint Louverture. With little to be gained and much to be lost, Napoleon decided to withdraw from the Americas altogether and to focus exclusively on his European campaigns. In light of this decision, Louisiana became more of a French military liability than an asset, and Napoleon's minister, Talleyrand, asked the resident U.S. foreign minister, Robert R. Livingston, what Jefferson might be willing to pay, not for New Orleans alone, but for the entire Louisiana Territory. In the days before instantaneous communication, Livingston had to stall until Monroe arrived. When he did arrive, he made the greatest real estate deal the world has ever seen. For 60 million francs—about $15 million—he purchased 90,000 square miles of trans-Mississippi territory for the United States. The "Treaty for the Cession of Louisiana" was formally concluded on May 2, 1803, and antedated to April 30.

One of the conditions of the purchase was that the United States assume all financial claims of American citizens in Louisiana against France. If we discount from the purchase price the amount of this assumption, $3,750,000, then the territory was purchased at three cents an acre!

The Louisiana Purchase instantly expanded the territory of the United States by 140 percent. Eventually, the region of the purchase would contain Missouri, Nebraska, Iowa, Arkansas, North and South Dakota, Kansas, Minnesota, Montana, Wyoming, most of Louisiana, and portions of Colorado and Wyoming.

The Expedition of Lewis and Clark

Thomas Jefferson's most immediate reason for making the Louisiana Purchase was to put vast distances between the United States and its European colonial neighbors. His next thought was that a great western territory could serve for the eventual peaceful—but mandatory—relocation of Indians currently living east of the Mississippi. But, deeper in his imagination, the American West meant much more to Jefferson than a solution to certain domestic and international problems. As early as 1792, Jefferson had written about the desirability of mounting a scientific expedition to explore the wonders of the West. Early in 1803, when he contemplated nothing more than the purchase of New Orleans, Jefferson twisted congressional arms to obtain $2,500 to finance such an expedition. He sold the project to Congress as a search for the fabled Northwest Passage, a water route connecting the Atlantic and the Pacific. Whether or not the president actually expected the expedition to find such a passage remains an open question, but what he had no doubt about was the scientific importance of the trek.

When he took office, Jefferson had hired his cousin, army captain Meriwether Lewis, as his private secretary. He became virtually a surrogate father to the twenty-seven-year-old Lewis, whose own father had died when he was eighteen. Seeing in the young man intelligence, courage, and resourcefulness, Jefferson appointed him to lead the "Corps of Discovery" through the vast West. As cocaptain of the expedition, Lewis chose his close friend William Clark, another very able army officer.

The Lewis and Clark expedition left St. Louis on May 14,

1804, and reached central North Dakota in November. The Corps wintered among the friendly Mandan Indians, from whom they gathered information on what lay ahead. Accompanied by a remarkable young Shoshoni woman, Sacagawea, who served as translator and guide, the Corps explored the Rockies and reached the Continental Divide on August 12, 1805. The expedition reached the Columbia River and the Pacific Ocean in November 1805. The second winter of the Corps of Discovery was spent exploring the Northwest coast, and the return trip east began in March 1806 and ended at St. Louis on September 23.

True, Lewis and Clark did not bring home news of a Northwest Passage, but their twenty-seven-month, 8,000-mile odyssey yielded a trove of geographical, biological, geological, and anthropological observations all meticulously and eloquently recorded in Lewis's journals. The explorers had discovered 122 animal species and subspecies, as well as 178 previously unknown plants. They made valuable and peaceful contact with great Indian tribes, thereby establishing the basis for profitable trade. They raised the curtain on the momentous drama of western settlement, a drama that would prove, at times, a tragedy, but also a great American epic that profoundly shaped the nation's subsequent history.

1803

Marbury v. *Madison*
Empowers the Supreme Court

The philosophical and political paths of John Adams and Thomas Jefferson, boon collaborators on the American Revolution, diverged sharply during the early days of the republic. Adams was a conservative Federalist, who believed in building a powerful central government, whereas Jefferson was a liberal who created the Democratic-Republican Party to promote a government in which most of the power rested with the states and the people. In the election of 1800, Jefferson defeated Adams in Adams's bid for a second term. Just two days before Jefferson was inaugurated, Adams, acting under the Judiciary Act of 1801, which he had championed, sought to ensure a Federalist judiciary by appointing a slate of conservative judges, marshals, and other judiciary officials. Moreover, although the Judiciary Act increased the number of federal circuit courts, thereby enabling Adams to appoint more judges, it limited the Supreme Court to five members, blocking Jefferson from appointing a Democratic-Republican to the high court.

President Jefferson lobbied for the repeal of the Judiciary Act, which was finally repealed on March 8, 1802, and replaced by a new Judiciary Act restoring the sixth Supreme Court seat and slashing the number of federal circuit courts. Prevented by the 1801 act from dismissing Federalist judges, Jefferson, acting on the new law, simply pulled the offices out from under many of Adams's "midnight appointees." But he was not completely successful in removing Federalists from government. Just two days before Jefferson's inauguration, Adams appointed William Marbury justice of the peace for Washington, D.C. Rushing headlong to complete his last-minute appointments, Adams failed to distribute—that is, actually issue—Marbury's and other appointments. Thus, when Jefferson entered office, Marbury, although *appointed* justice of the peace, had yet to *receive* his appointment. After spending months deftly dodging Marbury's attempts to secure his appointment, in February 1803, Jefferson formally directed his secretary of state, James Madison, to withhold the appointment, which, he claimed, was invalid because it had not been distributed before the repeal of the 1801 Judiciary Act.

An outraged Marbury petitioned the United States Supreme Court for a writ of mandamus, a court order to the secretary of state demanding that he distribute the commission. As a staunch Federalist, Chief Justice John Marshall might have been expected to sympathize with Marbury's plight. But Marshall was also a statesman determined to be a good steward of what was, after all, a branch of a government still evolving. He understood that if he simply issued the writ, he would put the court in direct opposition to the president, a situation he believed harmful to the fledgling government. Yet, if he denied the writ, he would forever diminish the authority of the Supreme Court by appearing to defer to the will of the chief executive.

Marshall plotted a third course. Ruling that Marbury had been wrongfully deprived of his commission, Marshall also declared that Section 13 of the Judiciary Act of 1789, the act that empowered the Supreme Court to issue writs of mandamus and under which Marbury had filed suit, was unconstitutional. The reason was this: Section 13 added to the Supreme Court's "original jurisdiction" by improperly giving the high court jurisdiction in a case that should be heard by a lower court. Thus, Marbury's suit was thrown out. However, the victory was not for Jefferson and his party, but for the Supreme Court. Marshall's ruling in the case of *Marbury* v. *Madison* forever established the momentous authority of the Supreme Court to perform "judicial review"—

that is, to review particular cases from lower courts and, if necessary, make decisions regarding them on the basis of a judgment on the constitutionality of the laws that apply in the case. This gave the Supreme Court the awesome power to set aside any statutes of Congress the court judged unconstitutional.

1807

Jefferson's Embargo

The end of the eighteenth century and the early years of the nineteenth saw the wars of the French Revolution followed by the Napoleonic Wars. The United States struggled to remain neutral in these great conflicts, but when neither the French nor the English could score a decisive victory, they began to prey on the commerce of neutral nations, including the United States. The British even resumed the practice of "impressment," boarding American commercial vessels, examining their crews, and pressing into Royal Navy service any men judged on the spot to be British subjects. British warships also seized U.S. vessels attempting to enter French ports.

Jefferson did not want to go to war with Britain over these violations of sovereignty. Instead, he pushed through Congress the Non-Importation Act, which barred the importation of many English goods. But, on June 22, 1807, the ongoing crisis exploded when a British warship, the *Leopard,* fired on the U.S. Navy frigate *Chesapeake* off Norfolk Roads, Virginia. British officers boarded the *Chesapeake* and seized four men they claimed to be deserters from the Royal Navy. Amid national outrage and a clamor for war, Jefferson instead championed passage of the Embargo Act of December 22, 1807. This legislation sought to punish Britain and other European powers economically by prohibiting all exports to Europe and severely restricting imports from Britain.

The search for an alternative to war was admirable, but the embargo proved to be a self-inflicted economic wound. It severely crippled the American economy and created, in effect, a nation of smugglers and lawbreakers. In the meantime, relations between the United States and Britain continued to deteriorate, and calls for war grew louder.

1812

Rise of the War Hawks

From the perspective of today, the War of 1812 seems a particularly obscure conflict. Many assume that it was fought primarily over the issue of "impressment," the British practice of abducting sailors from U.S. merchant ships and, if they were unilaterally deemed British subjects, pressing them into service aboard Royal Navy warships. In fact, shortly before the United States declared war on June 18, 1812, Britain agreed to end its impressment policy.

The real cause of the War of 1812 was land hunger. Western congressional representatives—dubbed War Hawks—pushed for war with Britain because doing so would provide two important opportunities to acquire new territory. Spanish Florida, which encompassed modern Florida, but which extended as far west as the Mississippi, was a possession of Britain's ally Spain. War with Britain would mean war with Spain, and American victory in that war would mean the acquisition of Spanish Florida. War with Britain would also give the United States another opportunity to invade Canada and, perhaps, add that vast territory to the nation's continental empire. Finally, in the "Northwest" (that is, the upper Midwest), British interests, some Canadian-based, were arming Indians against American settlers. Westerners wanted to put a stop to that.

And so war was declared—with precious little thought given to just how unprepared the United States was for it. The nation's regular army consisted of about 12,000 men in widely scattered outposts, led mainly by inexperienced officers who were, in effect, political patronage appointees. Its navy included no more than a handful of ships. The British, in contrast, had the greatest army and navy in the world.

1812

American Defeats

A merican military planners drew up a grandiose strategy to invade Canada in three places: from Lake Champlain to Montreal, from New York across the Niagara frontier, and from Detroit into so-called Upper Canada.

On July 12, 1812, sixty-year-old William Hull, governor of Michigan territory, led a militia force across the Detroit River into Canada, his objective to capture Fort Malden, which defended the entrance to Lake Erie. Believing himself outnumbered, Hull delayed his assault on the fort, which gave the British commander, Isaac Brock, ample time to get his regulars into position. In the meantime, the great Indian warrior Tecumseh, allied with the British, led an attack that chased Hull out of Canada and back to Fort Detroit. There Hull and his 1,500 men hunkered down until Brock's and Tecumseh's troops showed themselves. Hull surrendered Fort Detroit without firing a shot.

On the Niagara frontier, New York militia general Stephen Van Rensselaer led 2,270 militiamen and 900 regulars in an assault against Queenston Heights, Canada. On October 13, Brock, newly arrived from victory in Detroit, pinned down the portion of Van Rensselaer's force that had crossed into Canada. The rest just looked on, refusing to cross the international boundary. American defeat here was total.

This left the principal U.S. force, 5,000 men under General Henry Dearborn, waiting to invade Canada via Lake Champlain. On November 19, however, just as the invasion was about to step off, the militia contingent of Dearborn's force declared fighting across international boundaries a violation of the Constitution.

The men refused to fight, and Dearborn had no choice but to withdraw.

The collapse of these early offensives laid the West open to British invasion and to devastating raids by British-allied Indians. Fortunately, they did not take full advantage of their own early victories, but the war that the War Hawks had begun to gain new territory for the United States now greatly imperiled the continued existence of America's western frontier.

1813

Battles of Lake Erie and the Thames

During the summer of 1813, William Henry Harrison, territorial governor of Indiana, assembled an army of some 8,000 men while a bold young naval officer, Oliver Hazard Perry, built, from scratch, an armed flotilla on Lake Erie. On September 10, Perry engaged the British fleet in a fierce battle that resulted in nothing less than the destruction of the British naval presence on Lake Erie. He conveyed to Harrison one of the most famous military messages in American history: "We have met the enemy, and they are ours."

Perry's victory at the Battle of Lake Erie cut off supplies to British land forces and sent them in a general retreat from Detroit. Harrison overtook the retreating army on October 5, 1813, and fought the British and their Indian allies at the Battle of the Thames. Not only did this result in a decisive British defeat in the West, but it also brought the defeat and death of Tecumseh, in whose leadership was the last real hope of halting the American invasion of Indian lands in the West.

1814

Burning of Washington, D.C.

The American victories of 1813 brought relief to the West, but, on the East Coast, British forces continued to prosecute the war vigorously. By 1814, the British plan was to campaign in New York, along Lake Champlain and the Hudson River, with the object of severing New England from the rest of the country; simultaneously, the British planned on taking New Orleans, thereby blocking the vital Mississippi artery. Finally, while these operations were being executed, an army would attack along the Chesapeake Bay, keeping U.S. military forces occupied and preventing them from interfering at New York and New Orleans.

Late in the summer of 1814, U.S. resistance to the Chesapeake Bay attack collapsed as Major General Robert Ross led British forces to victory in the Battle of Bladensburg, Maryland, on August 24. Sweeping aside the feeble remnants of American resistance, Ross invaded Washington, D.C., and set fire to most of the public buildings, including the Capitol and White House. President James Madison and most of the government fled into the countryside.

1814

"The Star-Spangled Banner"

With Washington in flames, Robert Ross marched against Baltimore. During this, the low point of American fortunes in the War of 1812, a young Baltimore attorney, Francis Scott Key, was detained in Baltimore Harbor aboard a British warship. He watched anxiously through the night of September 13–14, 1814, as Ross bombarded Fort McHenry, the principal defense of the city. To Key's great astonishment and relief, he saw, "by dawn's early light," that the American flag, the "star-spangled banner," yet waved. Fort McHenry had held out against the British onslaught, Baltimore remained in American hands, and Ross soon withdrew. On September 14, Key penned the words to what would become the United States national anthem.

The words of "The Star-Spangled Banner" were original, but the tune they were later set to had been written in 1777 by the Englishman John Stafford Smith. Composed as a setting of a tavern verse, "To Anacreon in Heaven," the tune was applied to Key's verse by about 1820. It did not become the official national anthem until President Herbert Hoover proclaimed it so on March 3, 1931.

1814

Battle of Lake Champlain

While Washington burned and Baltimore resisted attack, a large force of 10,000 British soldiers, all veterans of the just-concluded Napoleonic Wars, marched south from Montreal. Their objective, ultimately, was New York City, and they intended, en route, to cut off New England from the rest of the country. The United States had no land forces sufficient to resist such an invasion, but, on September 11, 1814, American naval captain Thomas MacDonough engaged, defeated, and destroyed the British fleet on Lake Champlain. This spectacular victory was sufficient to send into retreat the 10,000-man land force, which rightly feared being entirely cut off from any source of supply.

The victory on Lake Champlain gave the American negotiators considerable strength as they hammered out a treaty with their British counterparts in the Flemish city of Ghent. That treaty, which ended the War of 1812, was signed on December 24, 1814. It restored the "status quo ante bellum"—the situation as it had been before the war. The War of 1812 had been dangerous and very costly for the United States, which gained no territory or other consideration as a result of it. Yet many judged it nothing less than a "a second war of independence." For better or worse, the United States had stood up to the greatest military power in the world—and had not lost.

1814

Battle of Horseshoe Bend

L ike the American Revolution before it, the War of 1812 was not just a conflict between Americans and British, but also involved the Indian allies of these powers. Most Indian tribes that did not remain neutral sided with the British during the War of 1812 in the belief that a British victory would curb American incursions into Indian lands.

On March 27, 1814, Andrew Jackson, at the time a minor frontier political figure, led a successful campaign against the hostile "Red Stick" Creek Indians and defeated them at the Battle of Horseshoe Bend, in present-day Alabama. This brought an end to a phase of the War of 1812 sometimes referred to as the Creek War. The treaty that resulted forced the Creeks to yield to the United States about two-thirds of their tribal lands, a massive cession that instantly pushed American settlement from the Tennessee River out to the Gulf of Mexico. The victory also thrust Jackson into national prominence. A second victory would prime him, ultimately, for the White House.

1815

Battle of New Orleans

I n 1814, even the most momentous news traveled at the stately pace of wood and sail, and so neither Andrew Jackson nor British major general Edward Pakenham received word of the Treaty of Ghent before they met in battle at New Orleans.

Pakenham led 7,500 British veterans from Jamaica to attack New Orleans, which was defended by 3,100 Tennessee and Kentucky volunteers, in addition to local militiamen and hangers-on, all under the command of Jackson, fresh from his triumph at Horseshoe Bend.

Jackson's outnumbered forces repulsed two British attacks. Then, on January 8, 1815, having suffered severe losses—including the fatal wounding of Pakenham—the British withdrew. Although the battle came after the war had ended, it gave Americans the sweet taste of victory, and it let them feel that the War of 1812, for the most part a costly mistake, had been an American triumph. As for Jackson, his fortune was made. Catapulted to national prominence, he was destined to become a two-term president who brought to the federal government the common touch and was the first representative of the American frontier to hold the reins of national power.

1817

The Rush–Bagot Agreement

n 1817, President James Monroe's acting secretary of state, Richard Rush, and British minister to the United States, Charles Bagot, negotiated the Rush–Bagot Agreement, definitively establishing the U.S. border with Quebec, which had been a sore spot in relations with British Canada. Even more important, the agreement established a precedent of a nonfortified, open border between the United States and Canada.

These days we take our cordial relations with our northerly neighbor for granted, but things didn't start out that way: Americans had invaded Canada during the Revolution and, again, during the War of 1812. Ever since Rush–Bagot, however, we've been on the most cordial of terms, with border relations the friendliest in the world. The relationship is certainly rare in history, perhaps even unique.

The Erie Canal Is Built

During the administration of James Monroe (1817–1825), westerners pushed for federal assistance in building the roads the West urgently needed in order to foster its commerce and economy. The president consistently vetoed such projects, however, for he did not believe in showing federal favor to any particular region. His attitude did not kill the projects, but, on the contrary, spurred development of an alternative link between the East Coast and the nation's vast inland realm.

As early as 1699 a French engineer named Vauban advocated building a canal between Lake Erie and Lake Ontario. By the beginning of the nineteenth century, when the Allegheny Mountains were effectively the western frontier, many Americans were coming to realize that the so-called Northwest Territories—the region that would later become Illinois, Indiana, Michigan, Wisconsin, and Ohio—were extremely rich in timber, minerals, and fertile farmland. The problem was transporting the produce and resources of this region back to markets in the East. In 1800, Gouverneur Morris, U.S. senator from New York, proposed building a great canal from the Hudson River to Buffalo, a growing commercial center on Lake Erie. As usual, the federal government would have none of it, but Governor De Witt Clinton of New York was excited by the prospect of a water link from Buffalo to Albany, on the upper Hudson River, which would thereby connect New York City, principal metropolis of the Northeast coast, with the great West.

Such a canal would be no small undertaking, since the distance between Buffalo and Albany was almost 400 miles. Yet, as

Clinton wrote in 1816, "As an organ of communication between the Hudson, the Mississippi, the St. Lawrence, the Great Lakes of the north and west and their tributary rivers, the canal will create the greatest inland trade ever witnessed," transforming New York City into "the granary of the world, the emporium of commerce, the seat of manufactures, the focus of great moneyed operations. . . . And before the revolution of a century, the whole island of Manhattan, covered with inhabitants and replenished with a dense population, will constitute one vast city." The following year, Clinton persuaded the state legislature to authorize $7 million for construction of a canal 363 miles long, 40 feet wide, and 4 feet deep.

After eight years of intensive labor, the canal was completed and, on October 26, 1825, Governor Clinton set out from Buffalo in the canal boat *Seneca Chief* along with two other boats to formally open the Erie Canal. The journey into New York Harbor took nine days—much faster than freight could be carted overland. Some 150 vessels and thousands of New Yorkers greeted the arrival, and Clinton emptied two barrels of Lake Erie water into the ocean at New York City in a ceremony contemporary publicists grandiosely dubbed the "Marriage of the Waters" between the Great Lakes and the Atlantic.

Before the canal, overland freight rates from Buffalo to New York City were $100 per ton. After the canal, rates dropped to $10 per ton. In 1829, 3,640 bushels of wheat traveled down the canal from Buffalo. By 1837, the figure was 500,000 bushels, and in 1841 the number of bushels topped one million. The success of the Erie Canal ignited a spectacular canal-building boom. By 1840, the United States was veined by 3,326 miles of canals.

Boundaries Settled, Territories Acquired

The Convention of 1818, hammered out by President Monroe's secretary of state John Quincy Adams and the British government, tackled the thorny issue of the Oregon Territory—the land west of the Rocky Mountains, extending from the forty-second parallel north to 54 degrees 42 minutes. The War of 1812 had failed to settle the boundary between the United States and British Canada here, and the 1818 convention called for joint U.S. and British occupation. True, this was nothing more than a temporary solution to ultimate possession of a very hotly contested region, and it by no means put the boundary dispute to bed, but it *was* a solution—a peaceful solution—and it showed that England was now quite willing to take American sovereignty seriously.

On February 12, 1819, Secretary Adams concluded another treaty, this one with Luis de Oñis, Spain's minister to the United States. It secured possession of both western and eastern Florida for the United States. With the acquisition of this territory, a principal objective of the War of 1812 was belatedly realized.

More difficult, however, was figuring out the precise border between the United States and Mexico, which was, until the Mexican Revolution of 1822, a colonial possession of Spain. Adams wanted a border that would pull Texas into American territory, but Spain was unwilling to relinquish both Texas and Florida to the United States, so the secretary of state finally agreed on a boundary at the Sabine River—the western boundary of the present-day state of Louisiana—and renounced any claim to Texas. This renunciation survived into the era of Mexican independence; however, after Texas won its independence from Mexico in 1836, the border issue would flare up again and, ultimately, become a cause for war between Mexico and the United States.

The busy Department of State concluded yet one more key treaty, this one with the czar of Russia, who had laid claim to the California coast as far south as San Francisco Bay. Adams managed to persuade his ministers to settle for a position north of the 54-degree-42-minute line, so that Russia would no longer be a third contender for the Oregon Territory. The czar retained his claim to Alaska—but, at the time, no one in the United States could imagine a use for that frozen wasteland.

1820

The Missouri Compromise

Since the ratification of the Constitution in 1787, the people of the United States had lived a lie, namely that a democratic nation could exist half free and half slave. That lie raised its ugly head whenever the balance between slave and free states was threatened. In 1818, the United States Senate consisted of twenty-two senators from free states and twenty-two from slave-holding states. Ever since independence, the balance between the non-slaveholding North and the slaveholding South had been precariously preserved with the addition of each state. But now the territory of Missouri petitioned Congress for admission to the Union—as a slaveholding state. The balance was in jeopardy, and Congress scrambled to find a new way to perpetuate the same old lie.

New York representative James Tallmadge introduced an amendment to the Missouri statehood bill allowing persons who were slaves in the present Missouri Territory to remain slaves after statehood, but banning the introduction of new slaves into the state. Furthermore, all slaves born in the state would continue as slaves until they reached twenty-five years of age, whereupon they would be automatically emancipated. In this way, slavery would be gradually eliminated from Missouri. The House of Representatives, which contained a free-state majority, passed the Tallmadge amendment, but the Senate, evenly divided between slave states and free, rejected it—and then promptly adjourned without reaching a decision on Missouri statehood. Only after the Senate reconvened did a long and agonizing debate begin.

The northern senators held that Congress possessed the authority to ban slavery in new states. The southerners countered that new states had the same right as the original thirteen: to determine for themselves whether they would allow slavery or not. After much wrangling, a compromise was reached in March 1820. It was grudgingly agreed that Missouri would be admitted to the Union as a slave state, but, simultaneously, that Maine (which had been a part of Massachusetts and was now seeking statehood in its own right) would be admitted as a free state.

Thus, the balance was preserved—for the present. But the Missouri Compromise also looked toward the future, stipulating that a line be drawn across the Louisiana Territory at a latitude of 36 degrees 30 minutes, north of which slavery would be forever banned—except in the case of Missouri. No one was truly pleased with the Missouri Compromise, but it did hold together the increasingly fragile Union for three more decades.

1821

Texas Colonized

The Louisiana Purchase of 1803 added a large amount of territory to the United States, and many poured in to settle it. Yet, vast as the Louisiana Territory was, it seemed only to whet the appetite for more land. In the 1810s, Augustus Magee, a U.S. army officer stationed in the Louisiana Territory, befriended one Bernardo Gutierrez, who had been fighting for Mexican independence from Spain. Together, Magee and Gutierrez led an expedition into Texas, where they captured the lightly held villages of Nacogdoches, Goliad, and San Antonio. But then Magee died—no one knows why—and the expedition abruptly ended. Shortly after this, in 1819, Dr. James Long of Natchez, Mississippi, led another expedition to Texas, hoping to carve out of the region an independent state; he was soon defeated by Spanish colonial forces.

In 1820, Moses Austin, a Missouri lead miner, took a different tack. He traveled to San Antonio—in peace—and sought government permission to establish an American colony in the area. The Spanish government responded with a modest grant, but Moses Austin fell ill and died in 1821 before he could actually begin the project of settlement. On his deathbed, he asked his son, Stephen F. Austin, to carry out his plans. The young man was bookish and introverted—hardly a born leader—but he promised his dying father that he would do his best.

In the meantime, Mexico had won independence from Spain and made to Stephen Austin an even more generous grant than the Spanish government had offered his father. Soon, Austin led more than 1,200 American families to Texas, and by 1836 the American population of Mexican Texas had exploded to 50,000.

1823

The Monroe Doctrine

The Napoleonic Wars, which spanned 1803 to 1815, were, in significant measure, *world* wars. Combat reached the American hemisphere, particularly South America, where, by overthrowing old regimes in Europe, the Napoleonic Wars sparked widespread revolution in the colonies. After Napoleon's final defeat in 1815, Spain started making noises about reclaiming the South American colonies it had lost. Britain, which now enjoyed highly profitable trade relationships with the new South American republics, asked the United States to join it in a stand against Spanish interference in South America. But instead of joining hands with the British in protesting any Spanish incursion into South America, President James Monroe included in his 1823 state of the union message to Congress the four principles we now call the Monroe Doctrine. He declared, in the first place, that the Americas were no longer available for colonization by any power. Second, he pointed out that the political system of the Americas was basically and essentially different from that of Europe. Third, he warned that the United States would consider any interference by European powers in the affairs of any of the Americas a direct threat to United States security. Finally, he pledged that the United States would not interfere with existing colonies, nor with the internal affairs of European nations, nor would it participate in any European wars.

It was a bold doctrine for a nation that, in 1823, possessed no standing army and a navy of minuscule proportions. But the Monroe Doctrine has endured into the present, exerting a powerful influence on our nation's foreign policy as the United States fashioned itself the guardian of the hemisphere. A stance of great strategic importance, it has also served, at times, to justify imposing the American will on smaller republics, especially in Central America and the Caribbean.

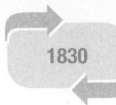

1830

Congress "Removes" the Indians

"An Act to Provide for an Exchange of Lands with the Indians Residing in Any of the States or Territories, and for Their Removal West of the River Mississippi"—known more simply as the Indian Removal Act—was signed into law on May 28, 1830 by President Andrew Jackson, and, for that reason, the policy of "Indian removal" has always been associated with him. However, the idea of relocating Indians living east of the Mississippi River to specially reserved Indian Territory in the West did not originate with Jackson. The very first president of the United States, George Washington, talked of finding some equivalent of a "Chinese Wall" to separate Indians and whites, and Presidents Jefferson, Madison, and Monroe all contemplated the issue. It was President John Quincy Adams who laid the administrative groundwork for the legislation that was finally enacted during the Jackson administration.

The Indian Removal Act was not a government-decreed land grab, nor did the law itself mandate the *forcible* eviction of the Indians. Rather, it provided for land exchanges supplemented by re-settlement funds, subsidies, and annuities. Nor was the law overtly motivated by government-sanctioned racism—although racism certainly played a part in Indian removal. As John Quincy Adams saw it, the legislation was key to averting a constitutional crisis. On December 20, 1828, the legislature of Georgia enacted a law to bring all Indian residents of the state under state jurisdiction within six months. Like Georgia, other southern states, desirous of appropriating Indian lands, contemplated similar legislation aimed at circumventing federal laws protecting Indian lands and

Indian rights. The state legislation came after President Adams repeatedly denied southern requests for the federal removal of the Indians. The president was even prepared to send federal troops into Georgia and other southern states in which Indian rights were being violated and lands confiscated. A showdown between federal authority and states' rights was brewing, and civil war loomed. Adams decided to defuse the issue by resettling the Indians of the Southeast in the West.

While the 1830 law outlined a fundamentally voluntary exchange of eastern lands for western lands, in practice Indian removal was tragically very different. Most often, Indians were coerced or duped into making land exchanges. Typically, government officials would secure an agreement from compliant individual Indians, then would hold the agreement as binding, regardless of whether or not a majority of the tribe concurred. Once even a dubious agreement was concluded, the government believed itself entitled to remove *all* Indians of the tribe, by force, if necessary.

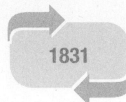

1831

Rebellion of Nat Turner

Throughout history, wherever slavery was practiced, fears of slave rebellion loomed, and, in the American South, such anxieties were occasionally justified. Nat Turner was a slave and charismatic lay preacher. He assembled a band of fellow slaves on the Southampton County, Virginia, plantation of Joseph Travis and, just before dawn on August 22, 1831, led them in killing every white member of the Travis household. After this, they raked the countryside, killing every white they encountered during the next twenty-four hours—fifty-five in all. The white response was equally swift and terrible. Not only were Turner and fifty of his followers captured and tried, twenty were summarily hanged, and white avengers then launched out on a rampage of indiscriminate killing and torture of whatever blacks were unfortunate enough to cross paths with them.

Horrific as the Turner rebellion and its aftermath were, equally destructive was the widespread panic created throughout the South, which hardened southern antagonism to growing antislavery efforts in the North. The lines of coming battle were being drawn.

Abolitionists Lose Patience

The very year that saw Nat Turner's Rebellion also witnessed the emergence of a new newspaper in the North. William Lloyd Garrison was a liberal New Englander from Newburyport, Massachusetts, who became coeditor of a moderate abolitionist newspaper called the *Genius of Universal Emancipation.* But Garrison soon abandoned moderation and, on January 1, 1831, published the first issue of the *Liberator,* a radical abolitionist periodical that demanded nothing less than the immediate emancipation of all slaves.

The eloquent and impassioned *Liberator* electrified the abolitionist movement. Garrison became the most powerful white voice in support of abolition, and he was among those who pushed the slavery issue beyond compromise.

Nullification Crisis

By the early nineteenth century, cotton, in the American South, was king, and the biggest customer for southern cotton was England, which spun the crop into cloth, then exported the finished cloth to the United States. Because of its higher quality, British fabric was more eagerly sought after in the United States than domestic-milled cloth. The result was that northern textile industries increasingly suffered. Through the first twenty-five years of the nineteenth century, the South enjoyed almost completely free trade with England and its other European customers. U.S.-imposed tariffs and duties were all but nonexistent. This was a great boon to the agricultural economy of the South, but it was a drag on the fledgling industrial economy of the North. To prod Americans into buying American-made goods, such as domestic cotton cloth, Congress passed a strongly protective tariff law in 1828, levying a heavy duty on all imported manufactured goods. Northerners welcomed the tariff, while southerners took to cursing it as the "Tariff of Abominations."

In response to the 1828 tariff, John C. Calhoun, from South Carolina and, at the time, vice president under John Quincy Adams, became the architect of a profound crisis. He composed an anonymous pamphlet entitled *South Carolina Exposition and Protest,* which argued that any state could pronounce the federal tariff "null and void" if that state deemed it unconstitutional.

Now, the notion of nullification was not original with Calhoun. No less than two founding fathers, James Madison and Thomas Jefferson, had introduced the nullification concept in their Virginia and Kentucky resolutions of 1798 and 1799 opposing the

Alien and Sedition Acts. Despite this precedent, Calhoun had a hard time recruiting support for nullification; most of the southern states repudiated the doctrine. In any case, the timely election of Andrew Jackson, who had campaigned, in part, on a platform of tariff reform, stole Calhoun's thunder. But the promised reform was slow in coming and, when it came, it proved deeply disappointing to the South. The Tariff Act of 1832, passed during the Jackson administration, so offended Calhoun that he promptly resigned as Jackson's vice president and stood for election to the Senate. He won, and, at his instigation, the state of South Carolina called a convention that, on November 24, 1832, enacted an Ordinance of Nullification forbidding collection of tariff duties in the state. Another South Carolina senator, Robert Y. Hayne, upped the ante to an even more dangerous level when he embellished Calhoun's nullification theory with the additional argument that not only could a state nullify an unconstitutional law, it could also, as a last resort, withdraw from the Union itself. In response, Massachusetts senator and legendary orator Daniel Webster delivered his most famous speech, defending the powers of the federal government versus the alleged rights of the states: "Liberty and Union, now and forever, one and inseparable!"

Nullification brought the nation to a crisis, a stark showdown between the will of a single state and the law of the land. The scope of the crisis reached far beyond the Tariff of 1832. Underneath it all, Calhoun and his cohorts were fighting for the perpetuation of an economy based on slavery. They clearly saw that slavery would, someday, be abolished by a northern majority in Congress. Calhoun was quite capable of doing the math, and he understood that such a majority, someday, was inevitable. The nullification doctrine seemed the only means of circumventing the democratic principle of majority rule, especially if the doctrine was linked to the threat of secession.

Calhoun took heart in the belief that Andrew Jackson, a southerner after all, would now certainly back down on the tariff. Instead, Jackson responded to nullification on December 10, 1833, with a declaration that not only asserted the constitutionality of the tariff, but denied the power of any state to prevent enforcement of a federal law. The president vowed to use federal troops to enforce the collection of duties, and he secured from Congress passage of a Force Act, which empowered him to do so.

The Force Act might well have brought on civil war, not in 1861 but in 1833. However, having made his point, Jackson then supported a compromise tariff, which mollified the South. War had been averted—for the present—but nullification and the concepts of states' rights and secession would not go away. Even after the South had fought and lost the Civil War, the doctrine of states' rights would resurface in the twentieth century as an excuse for dodging the force of federal civil rights legislation.

Fall of the Alamo

By 1836, the Texas colony Stephen Austin had founded in 1821 had grown to 50,000 Americans. The local Mexican population was only 3,500. During the 1830s, the burgeoning American majority chafed under Mexican rule. Many objected in particular to Mexican laws forbidding slavery. Many were disturbed by cultural and religious differences with the Mexicans: The colonists were predominantly Protestant while the Mexicans were overwhelming Catholic. Austin, believing his colony was hardly prepared to fight a war of independence, repeatedly negotiated terms of peaceful coexistence with the ever-tumultuous Mexican government. He drafted a proposed constitution to make Texas a full-fledged Mexican state, and in 1833 traveled to Mexico City to seek an audience with Antonio López de Santa Anna, the country's new president. Austin waited five months before he was granted an audience; then Santa Anna rejected the plea for statehood. As Austin rode back to Texas, he was arrested, returned to Mexico City, and imprisoned there for the next two years. At last released in 1835, Austin was broken in health and returned to Texas sufficiently embittered to urge Texans to support an internal Mexican revolt against Santa Anna. It was this that triggered the Texas Revolution.

Against the advice of Sam Houston, who became the de facto leader of the Texas revolution, a small force of Texans under militia colonel William B. Travis took a defensive stand behind the walls of the decayed Spanish mission called San Antonio de Valero, but nicknamed the Alamo because it was close to a grove of cottonwoods (*alamos* in Spanish). Santa Anna entered San Antonio on February 25, 1836. A number of noncombatants, mostly women and children, now took refuge with the Alamo garrison, and, at the last minute, reinforcements arrived, bringing the number of the Alamo defenders to 189 (some recent scholars believe the number was over 250).

Santa Anna unleashed a weeklong artillery bombardment, which—quite incredibly—failed to kill a single Texan, even as the defenders' grapeshot and rifle fire took a heavy toll among the attackers. However, the artillery did batter down the Alamo walls faster than the defenders could repair them, and, on March 6, Santa Anna deployed 1,800 men to storm the fortress. It was a clumsy attack that cost the Mexicans about 600 killed, but sheer numbers prevailed. After an hour and a half of fighting, almost all of the Alamo's defenders had fallen, and the old mission was in Santa Anna's hands. Davy Crockett—the legendary Tennessee frontiersman who had volunteered to defend the Alamo—and the few other prisoners Santa Anna took were summarily executed. The women and children who had sought refuge in the Alamo were released, however, and Santa Anna charged one of their number, Susannah Dickerson, to tell all of Texas what had happened at the Alamo. He was confident that her tale of horror would extinguish any further rebellion. He was, of course, mistaken.

1836

Independence for Texas

L ed by Sam Houston, a small army of Texans rallied to the battle cry of "Remember the Alamo!" Houston mustered only about 800 Texans against 1,250 Mexicans under Santa Anna at the Battle of San Jacinto, west of the San Jacinto River, just off Galveston Bay, on April 21, 1836. But he led them brilliantly, advancing on Santa Anna's forces as they were settling in for their afternoon siesta. He ordered his men to hold their fire until his main column was just sixty yards from the Mexicans. Then, with a shout of "Remember the Alamo!" Houston ordered the attack.

The battle, which gained Texas its independence, was over in fifteen minutes. Six hundred thirty Mexican troops were killed—many frankly slaughtered in revenge for the Alamo and for the earlier execution of prisoners at Goliad, Texas. Texan forces lost nine killed and thirty-four wounded, including Houston, who had taken a musket ball in the right leg. Santa Anna temporarily escaped, but was soon captured. Houston spared his life in exchange for his signature on the Treaty of Velasco on May 14, 1836, whereby Mexico granted the full and complete independence of Texas.

1837

"The American Scholar": Milestone in American Culture

I n an age before movies, radio, and television, the public lecture was a popular form of entertainment, and even speeches delivered before special audiences—such as the Harvard chapter of the Phi Beta Kappa Society—sometimes received wide attention. In 1837, Ralph Waldo Emerson, who would soon gain a reputation as the dean of American men of letters, was just getting his literary start. When he spoke before the Phi Beta Kappa audience on August 31 of that year, he made an impact that is difficult to appreciate or even understand today. People listened—and they were changed by what they heard. The author and physician Dr. Oliver Wendell Holmes, Sr. (father of the famed Supreme Court justice), called the speech "our intellectual Declaration of Independence."

The title of the speech, "The American Scholar," was hardly one to set the world on fire, but the message electrified and inspired not only American intellectuals, but Americans in general. By the late 1830s, Americans were justly proud of their international and historical standing as political pioneers, but in matters cultural, intellectual, and aesthetic, they remained the vassals of old Europe, slavishly adhering to European standards of art, of literature, of philosophy, and thereby stunting the development of American creativity. In his speech, Emerson called on the rising generation of the nation's cultural creators to strike out on bold new intellectual and artistic paths, just as the founding fathers had dared to blaze new political and moral trails. Democracy demanded a democratic art and science and philosophy. And just as a government dedicated to liberty was a vast improvement on ancient governments shackled by kings and queens and deference to them, so an art, literature, science, and philosophy produced with true independence by a democratic people was bound to be an improvement on the cultural pursuits of the outmoded continent across the sea. If American writers and artists complained that, in contrast to Europeans, they had no rich native history to draw on—no great myths and legends—Emerson countered that Americans did not *suffer* from the absence of such a history, but were blessed by *freedom* from it. Nothing of an outworn past need retard intellectual and aesthetic progress in America. Instead, Americans were in an enviable and unique position to be pioneers not just of human settlement, but also of the human spirit and the human mind. Soon, Emerson argued, it would be Europe that followed the American lead.

Between Emerson's 1837 speech and the Civil War in 1861, American arts and letters enjoyed a sudden and spectacular renaissance that stunned and continues to stun the world. The naturalist philosopher-poet Henry David Thoreau began writing, the poet Walt Whitman published his *Leaves of Grass,* Edgar Allan Poe raised the horror tale to a height of uncanny psychological penetration, Nathaniel Hawthorne created profound allegories of the soul tormented by personal history, and Herman Melville expanded the novel into a book about the universe within each of us and beyond each of us. The literary and philosophical works of this "American Renaissance" (as later literary historians called it)— triggered, it seems, by Emerson's message—transported America from the backwaters of world culture to a leading position in the thought and art of the nineteenth and twentieth centuries and of our present day.

The Trail of Tears

Pursuant to the Indian Removal Act of 1830, some northeastern tribes were peacefully resettled in Indian Territory. However, many of the Indians of the Southeast, members of the so-called Five Civilized Tribes—Chickasaw, Choctaw, Seminole, Cherokee, and Creek—militantly resisted removal. The army was called out and, under extreme coercion, about 100,000 of these people were marched off to Indian Territory (the present state of Oklahoma and some surrounding territory) during the 1830s. About one-quarter of this number died en route.

Most infamous among the removals was the Cherokee trek of 1838–1839 along what generations of Cherokees have called the "Trail of Tears." Concentrated in Georgia, the Cherokee tribe was politically sophisticated. The tribe's majority, organized into the Nationalist Party, appealed to the U.S. Supreme Court in 1832 to protest abuse and land swindles suffered at the hands of Georgia. In *Worcester* v. *Georgia* (1832), Chief Justice John Marshall declared the state's actions unconstitutional, but President Jackson refused to use federal power to enforce the high court's decision. Instead, he advised the Indians to resolve their difficulties by accepting removal. At Jackson's direction, a removal treaty, the Treaty of New Echota (December 29, 1835), was negotiated with a minority Cherokee party, called the Treaty Party, which represented perhaps 1,000 out of 17,000 Cherokees. Although, then, the treaty was rejected seventeen to one, the government held it as binding on all of the Cherokees, and, during the summer of 1838, Major General Winfield Scott began a mass roundup of Cherokees and confined them for the rest of the summer in what were, in fact, concentration camps. During the fall and winter of 1838–1839, Scott marched them under armed escort 1,200 miles to Indian Territory. They were cold, short of food, and often abused by their military guards, who raped women, robbed everyone, and killed anyone who made trouble. Four thousand of the 15,000 who started on the journey perished.

A Georgia soldier recalled years after the Trail of Tears trek: "I fought through the Civil War and have seen men shot to pieces and slaughtered by thousands, but the Cherokee removal was the cruelest work I ever saw."

1844

Invention of the Telegraph

I n the nineteenth century, space, vast space, was the great American blessing—and curse. There was plenty of land to accommodate a burgeoning population, and yet how could a nation—one nation—be held together over such a vast territory? How could Americans communicate with one another?

The answer, it turned out, was technological rather than political, but the person who supplied the solution was no technologist. He was a painter. Born in Charlestown, Massachusetts, in 1791, Samuel F. B. Morse earned a solid reputation as an artist. He twice studied abroad, and, on the return voyage from his second trip, he struck up a conversation with another passenger, a British scientist named Thomas Jackson. These chats literally sparked an idea in Morse's imagination: Why not use electrical current as a medium through which communication might be transmitted?

Once home, Morse laid aside his brushes and set about inventing what he called the telegraph. That word was not his invention. It had been used to describe any number of signaling systems, typically employing semaphore flags or lanterns displayed on hilltop towers, at least as early as the beginning of the nineteenth century, and the word itself was compounded of two Greek roots—the "tele" portion meaning distant, and the "graph" part signifying writing: distant writing. But the idea of harnessing the still highly novel (and, thus far, pretty useless) phenomenon of electricity to transmit intelligible speech was groundbreaking.

Morse read the scientific journals of his day and learned that, in 1819, the Danish scientist Hans C. Oersted (1777–1851) had discovered the principle of "induction" when he noticed that a wire carrying an electric current deflected a magnetic needle. Several scientists had followed up on this discovery by experimenting with deflecting-needle telegraphs. Two men, William F. Cooke and Charles Wheatstone, actually installed a working deflecting-needle telegraph along a railway line in England in 1837—but the technology was too fragile and unreliable to be developed much further. Morse read that, in 1825, William Sturgeon had invented the electromagnet—a coil of wire wrapped around an iron core, which magnetized the core only as long as current flowed through the coil. Building on this, and further inspired by the electromagnetic experiments of Michael Faraday and Joseph Henry, Morse began working on a telegraph receiver based on the electromagnet. When energized by a current from the line—that is, when the remote operator pressed a switch ("telegraph key")—Morse's electromagnet attracted a soft iron armature, which was designed to make marks on a moving piece of paper. Depending on the duration of the electrical impulse received, the armature would inscribe a dot (if the remote telegraph key had been depressed for a fraction of a second) or a dash (if it had been held down a bit longer). Not only did Morse invent a robust electromagnetic telegraphic transmitter and receiver, he also created a logically coded system of short *dots* and longer *dashes* for transmitting the alphabet with the device.

Once Morse was confident that he had perfected a practical device, he persuaded Congress to finance the world's first long-distance telegraph line, between Washington, D.C., and Baltimore, a distance of about forty miles. On May 24, 1844, he transmitted the first telegraphic message over that wire: "What hath God wrought?"

Within a decade of Morse's first message, the nation's original forty miles of wire stretched to 23,000, and the telegraph was well on its way to annihilating distance itself.

Black America Gains a Voice

Frederick Douglass was born into slavery in 1817 on a Maryland plantation. His master sent him to Baltimore to learn the skill of ship caulking. The young man had already been taught the alphabet by his master's wife, and, while apprenticing in Baltimore, he taught himself how to write by tracing the letters of the names of ships painted on their prows. In 1838, Douglass obtained seaman's papers from a free black. Using these, he made his escape to New Bedford, Massachusetts, and freedom. Ever since he had learned to read and write, Douglass was a voracious reader and soon discovered William Lloyd Garrison's *Liberator.* By 1841, he had added eloquence to literacy, and he found himself in great demand as a lecturer under the auspices of the Massachusetts Anti-Slavery Society. Douglass was so impressive an orator that many whites, even those who meant well, simply refused to believe that he had ever actually been a slave. As this skepticism became increasingly persistent, Douglass was moved to write, in 1845, his autobiography, the *Narrative of the Life of Frederick Douglass,* an unflinching account of slavery and liberation, which not only portrayed the inhumanity of slavery, but, even more important, exhibited to the world the intense humanity of the slaves.

Five thousand copies of *Narrative* were sold within four months of its first printing, and six new editions were published between 1845 and 1849. Douglass published two later versions, *My Bondage and My Freedom* (1855) and *The Life and Times of Frederick Douglass* (1881).

The "Great American Pastime"

Games resembling baseball had been played in England and America for years. They were called "one o'cat," "rounders," "base," and even "baseball." By the mid-nineteenth century, social-athletic clubs were formed in American cities to play these games. One such club, a Manhattan group calling itself the Knickerbocker Base Ball Club, wrote down the rules of their game in 1845—and to this event may be assigned the birth of "professional" baseball in the United States.

Within twenty years of the Knickerbockers' codification of the rules, baseball became the most popular game in America, and before the end of the nineteenth century, it was being called the "great American pastime."

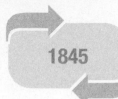

1845

Texas Statehood and a California Revolution

Having won its independence from Mexico in 1836, Texas existed as a republic while United States legislators argued over admitting it to the Union as a new state. There was the usual problem over upsetting the legislative balance between slave and free states by admitting a slave state, and there was also the near certainty that taking on Texas would mean war between the United States and Mexico. For expansionists, who saw such a war as a means of acquiring much southwest territory, the prospect of the conflict was both necessary and inviting. For others, especially those in the Northeast, picking a fight with Mexico seemed both unwise and immoral.

As both England and France made overtures of alliance to the Republic of Texas, the president and Congress at last acted, and Texas was admitted to statehood on December 29, 1845. As predicted, this brought the United States and Mexico to the verge of war. Then, when President James K. Polk saw that England and France were now hungrily eyeing California—which was held so feebly by Mexico that it looked ready to drop into the hands of whoever was there to catch it—he offered Mexico $40 million for the territory. Not only did the Mexican president turn down the offer, he also rebuffed President Polk's emissary, refusing even to see him. This provoked Polk to authorize the U.S. consul at Monterey (California), Thomas O. Larkin, to organize California's small but powerful American community into a movement for U.S. annexation. At the same time, John Charles Frémont—a daring and headstrong western explorer surveying prospective transcontinental railroad routes for the U.S. Bureau of Topographical Engineers—marched into California and took over the incipient independence movement, the so-called Bear Flag Rebellion, proclaiming the Bear Flag Republic on June 14, 1846. After a skirmish or two, California independence was secured. By this time, however, the short-lived Bear Flag Rebellion had dissolved into the events of the U.S.–Mexican War. For, as Mexico saw it, the rebellion in California only added insult to the injury inflicted by the annexation of Texas, whose border with Mexico the Mexican government disputed.

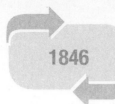

1846

The U.S.–Mexican War Begins

A fter the United States admitted Texas to the Union and precipitated a rebellion in California, Mexican troops laid siege to Fort Texas—present-day Brownsville—on May 1. President Polk dispatched troops to the new state and, on May 13, 1846, declared war on Mexico. General Zachary Taylor, marching to the relief of the fort, faced 6,000 Mexican troops with a mere 2,000 Americans, but nevertheless defeated the enemy in the May 8 Battle of Palo Alto.

That contest established the pattern for the rest of the war. Typically, American forces were significantly outnumbered by the Mexican troops, which, however, were so poorly led and indifferently equipped (chronically supplied with faulty gunpowder and ammunition) that the Americans, enthusiastic and commanded by highly competent officers, almost always prevailed. On May 9, Taylor was victorious at Resaca de la Palma, a dry riverbed just north of the Rio Grande, and he advanced onto Mexican soil.

In the meantime, early in June, *official* U.S. action got underway against the Mexicans in California as Stephen Watts Kearny led the "Army of the West" from Fort Leavenworth, Kansas, to California via New Mexico. Along the way, Kearny captured Santa Fe on August 15 without firing a shot. Before Kearny even reached California, he was intercepted by the legendary Indian fighter Kit Carson, who told him that, on August 17, Commodore Robert F. Stockton had announced the annexation of California. A brief spasm of resistance was put down in December and January, and California was secure.

In New Mexico, during the winter of 1846–1847, resistance

was more violent. On January 19, 1847, the citizens of Taos killed the local sheriff and a deputy, then murdered Governor Charles Bent as well as any other Americans they could find. Colonel Sterling Price—who would later serve the Confederacy as a general—made short work of the so-called Taos Rebellion.

"Civil Disobedience"

I n the American West and South, the war with Mexico was so popular that recruiting offices had to turn applicants away. In the Northeast, however, especially in New England, many saw the war as an unjust display of naked aggression, and they protested it.

Henry David Thoreau, the American naturalist, philosopher, and essayist, protested the U.S.–Mexican War by refusing to pay a poll tax used, he claimed, to help finance the conflict. In July 1846, Sam Staples, the Concord, Massachusetts, constable and tax collector, personally demanded payment. Thoreau refused and was clapped into the local jail. The next morning a still-unidentified woman, probably Thoreau's aunt, paid the tax on his behalf (and without his permission), and Thoreau was released.

In 1849, Thoreau used this episode as the subject of an essay, "Civil Disobedience." He wrote: "Under a government which imprisons any unjustly, the true place for a just man is also a prison." There is, he declared, a higher law than the civil one, and only those who follow this higher law are truly free. When civil law and higher law conflict, the only appropriate choice is civil disobedience.

Although the essay was little read in the nineteenth century, it received widespread attention in the twentieth, and it inspired and instructed such leaders of nonviolent revolution as Mohandas Gandhi and Martin Luther King, Jr.

1846–1848

Victory Against Mexico

As the U.S. "Army of the West" conquered California—what had been Mexico's northern provinces—and the "Army of the Center" secured the Texas–Mexico borderlands, the "Army of Occupation" marched deep into Mexico itself. Monterrey (Mexico) fell to General Zachary Taylor on September 24, 1846, but, in the meantime, the astoundingly resilient Antonio López de Santa Anna, who had been living in Cuban exile after a popular rebellion ended his dictatorship of Mexico, offered to help the United States rapidly win the war in return for $30 million and safe passage to Mexico. American officials declined to pay him, but he was allowed to return to his homeland, and, no sooner did he arrive than he mustered an army intended to defeat Zachary Taylor. By January 1847, Santa Anna had assembled 18,000 men, about 15,000 of whom he sent against Taylor's 4,800-man force at Buena Vista. After a two-day battle, Taylor defeated the far superior force on February 23.

At this point, however, President Polk, worried that Taylor would become a military hero and, therefore, a political rival, replaced him with General Winfield Scott, an apolitical veteran of the War of 1812. Scott launched an invasion of Vera Cruz on March 9, 1847, and fought a daring advance all the way to Mexico City. On September 13, Chapultepec Palace—the seemingly impregnable fortress guarding the capital—fell to Scott, and on September 17, 1847, Santa Anna surrendered.

Peace terms were hammered out in the Treaty of Guadalupe Hidalgo (ratified by the U.S. Senate on March 10, 1848). In exchange for a payment of $15 million and a U.S. pledge to assume various claims against Mexico, the Mexican government ceded to the United States New Mexico (which also included parts of the present states of Utah, Nevada, Arizona, and Colorado) and California and renounced claims to Texas above the Rio Grande. Five years later, with the $10-million Gadsden Purchase, the United States acquired more territory from Mexico, thereby completing the acquisition of the land that makes up the continental United States today.

The Mormon Trek

From the beginning, one of the cornerstones of American liberty has been freedom of religion, yet no religion in American history has been more persecuted than the Church of Jesus Christ of Latter-Day Saints, the Mormons. Founded as a result of a mystical visitation upon fifteen-year-old Joseph Smith, Jr., in 1820, the church grew rapidly, but Smith and his followers were hounded out of each place in which they attempted to settle—upstate New York, Ohio, and Missouri. The Mormon town finally founded as Nauvoo, Illinois, prospered, but after Smith and his brother were lynched in 1844, church leader Brigham Young made plans to resettle the Mormons in the Far West, in a place so remote that the people would finally be free of persecution.

During the winter of 1845–1846, all of Nauvoo built wagons and other necessities for the great trek. With the logistical brilliance of a great general, Young planned and executed a 1,400-mile overland migration of successive waves of several hundred Mormon "Saints" (as the people called themselves) at a time. They settled in the Salt Lake valley of present-day Utah, where Young laid out a utopian city, built around a central Temple Square.

The Mormon Trek was one of the first of the great mass migrations to the West, and it was unique in that it resulted in the establishment of a "theo-democracy," which, ultimately, was integrated into the United States and came to coexist with neighbors and government alike.

1848

Seneca Falls Convention
Addresses the Rights of Women

Well before the middle of the nineteenth century, thoughtful women—and plenty of men, too—awoke to the realization that the United States Constitution disenfranchised not only black slaves, but also women. Indeed, most of the early feminists in the United States were active on behalf of both women's rights and abolition; they saw both slavery and the oppression of women as essential issues of human rights that deserved to be linked. While attending the World Anti-Slavery Convention in London in 1840, Elizabeth Cady Stanton met Lucretia Mott, at the time the most outspoken and most visible American female abolitionist. In 1833, Mott had founded the Philadelphia Female Anti-Slavery Society, but, astoundingly, the organizers of the World Anti-Slavery Convention denied her a seat as an official delegate because she was a woman. This moved Mott to broaden her human rights focus to the cause of equality for women.

After returning to the United States from England, Stanton and Mott became energetic leaders of a women's suffrage movement, and organized a conference at Seneca Falls, New York, held during July 19–20, 1848. Attended by 240 women and men, it was the first public meeting in the United States devoted to women's rights. The Seneca Falls Conference produced the "Seneca Falls Declaration of Sentiments," which, modeled on the Declaration of Independence, catalogued the abuses women commonly suffered in a male-dominated society, government, and nation.

We hold these truths to be self-evident: that all men and women are created equal. . . .

The history of mankind is a history of repeated injuries and usurpations on the part of man toward woman, having in direct object the establishment of an absolute tyranny over her. . . .

Now, in view of this entire disfranchisement of one-half the people of this country . . . we insist that they have immediate admission to all the rights and privileges which belong to them as citizens of the United States.

1849

The California Gold Rush

On January 24, 1848, James Wilson Marshall, a foreman on the northern California ranch of German immigrant Johann Augustus ("John") Sutter, rode out to inspect the race (a channel for waterflow) of a new mill that had been built on the property. He was suddenly attracted by something shiny in the sediment collected at the bottom of the race. He looked at it. He felt it. It was gold.

Surprisingly enough, Marshall's discovery did not immediately set the countryside on fire, but, after a matter of weeks, word spread, and Sutter found that his employees were deserting him to pan for gold. Ranch operations fell apart, and, even worse, Sutter had failed to purchase the property *before* he built the mill, so his land claims were invalidated. Around John Sutter, everyone (it seemed) was getting rich while he himself faced financial ruin.

While Marshall's discovery caused a big stir in California's central valley during 1848, it was neither Sutter nor Marshall who broadcast the discovery to the world. Sam Brannon, a renegade Mormon living near San Francisco (called at the time Yerba Buena), saw the discovery of gold as an opportunity to prosper— not from grubbing for the ore, but by supplying hordes of hopeful prospectors with pans, picks, shovels, tents, clothing, food— everything they needed, and at prices he could virtually dictate. Brannon used the local newspaper he owned to publicize the discovery of "Gold! Gold from the American River!" Within two weeks, Yerba Buena emptied out, plummeting from a population of a few thousand to a few dozen, as men dropped their tools and left their jobs to prospect on the south fork of the American River.

As word of gold spread east, similar scenes played out in city after city, town after town, farm after farm. Men dropped their tools where they worked, bid farewell to employers—and often to families as well—and set out on the long trek to California.

For some few of the hundreds of thousands who made the California trek over the next several years, the danger, the cost, and the effort were well worth it. But most prospectors found in California nothing more than hard lives, mean spirits, and perhaps just enough gold to pay for meals, shelter, and clothing, all at extravagantly inflated prices. Some found much less than even this, and died, like Sutter himself, ruined. Still others—most of those who came—soon gave up prospecting and took up farming or some other occupation. In this manner, the population of California and the Far West grew.

There were still others, men like Brannon, who decided that the real money in the Gold Rush was not on a riverbed or in the ground, but in the pockets of those who came in quest of ore. Collis Huntington and Mark Hopkins, for example, made a fortune selling miner's supplies. Charles Crocker grew so rich from his expanding dry goods mercantile operation that he started the bank that still bears his name. Leland Stanford parlayed his own mercantile pursuits into a political career that culminated in the California state house and in the founding of the great Palo Alto university named for him. And one Levi Strauss hit upon the idea of using denim reinforced with metal rivets to make pants even a prospector couldn't destroy. They were called blue jeans.

1850

The Compromise of 1850

The territory of California had been officially transferred to the United States by the Treaty of Guadalupe Hidalgo, which ended the Mexican War on February 2, 1848. But on January 24, 1848, just a few days before the treaty was signed, gold was discovered in the territory, and by 1849, tens of thousands of prospectors were pouring into California. The explosion of population suddenly made statehood an urgent issue—and that, of course, raised a familiar question: Would the territory be admitted as a slave state or free?

Back in 1846, Congress, seeking a means of bringing the U.S.–Mexican War to a rapid conclusion, had debated a bill to appropriate $2 million to compensate Mexico for "territorial adjustments." To this bill, Pennsylvania congressman David Wilmot proposed an amendment, which became known as the Wilmot Proviso. It would have barred the introduction of slavery into any land acquired by the United States as a result of the U.S.–Mexican War. This provoked South Carolina's John C. Calhoun to formulate, once and for all, the South's opposition to federal intervention in the slavery issue. Calhoun proposed four resolutions:

First: Territories, including those acquired as a result of the war, are to be deemed the common and joint property of the states.

Second: With respect to the territories, Congress acts as agent for the states and, therefore, can make no law discriminating among the states or depriving any state of its rights with regard to any territory.

Third: Any national law governing slavery violates the Constitution and the doctrine of states' rights.

Fourth: The people of a state have the right to form their state government as they wish, provided it is republican in form.

Having loudly and clearly laid down his resolutions on behalf of the South, Calhoun issued a stern warning: Fail to maintain a balance between the conflicting demands of the North and the South, and a "civil war" would surely ensue.

Partly in response to Calhoun's resolutions, the Wilmot Proviso was scrapped, and a new compromise was reached in 1850, which enunciated the principle of "popular sovereignty," an enactment of the fourth of Calhoun's resolutions, allowing the people of a territory to determine by popular vote whether they would seek admission to the Union as a free state or a slave state. In the immediate case, California was admitted as a free state, and the territories of Utah and New Mexico were created, each to be subject to popular sovereignty on the issue of slavery.

The Kansas–Nebraska Act

In 1854, when the territories of Nebraska and Kansas applied for statehood, Congress looked at the Compromise of 1850 and decided to repeal and replace it. Whereas the 1850 compromise applied popular sovereignty (the right of citizens of a state to decide whether or not their state would be slave or free) to some of the territory acquired as a result of the U.S.–Mexican War, the 1854 legislation extended popular sovereignty beyond this territory and, in the process, rubbed out the geographical barrier to slavery created by the Missouri Compromise of 1820. The situation had been explosive in 1820 and was explosive again in 1850. Now, the Kansas–Nebraska Act was as a match applied to a fuse.

There was never any doubt that Nebraskans, who were free-soil northerners, would vote themselves a free state. But Kansas, south of Nebraska, was an entirely different matter. On the eve of statehood, pro-slavery Missourians and antislavery Iowans streamed into the territory, each side vying to create a majority for the popular sovereignty vote. The Missourians proved faster and more numerous than the Iowans and elected a pro-slavery territorial legislature to ensure that Kansas would enter the Union as a slave state. Once this was done, many returned to Missouri, whereas the Iowans remained. Thus, Kansas became a slave territory with an abolitionist majority, and the result was a chronic condition of bitter civil warfare between the slavery and free-soil factions: a prelude to civil war on a national scale.

1854–1860s

Bleeding Kansas

I n the wake of the Kansas–Nebraska Act of 1854, intimidation, ambush, arson, murder, and aggression followed by retribution and revenge—all over the issue of whether Kansas would be free-soil or slave—became so commonplace that the nation dubbed the emerging state "Bleeding Kansas."

This was typical: In 1856, pro-slavery "border ruffians" raided the abolitionist town of Lawrence, Kansas, setting fire to a hotel and several houses, destroying a printing press, and then killing a number of townspeople. By way of payback, one May night, John Brown, a radical abolitionist who had taken command of the Kansas Free Soil Militia, led four of his sons and two other followers in an attack on pro-slavery settlers along the Pottawatomie River. Brown and his men used sabers to kill five unarmed settlers.

In 1861, Kansas would be admitted to the Union, not as a slave state, but a free one. This hardly brought peace. As "Bleeding Kansas" was a prelude to the Civil War, the Civil War itself, once under way, brought to Kansas a particularly ugly brand of guerrilla violence. As for John Brown, he would go on, in 1859, to lead a raid on the federal arsenal at Harpers Ferry, Virginia, with the object of arming the slaves for a general revolt. He thus became a radical martyr to the cause of abolitionism and his action a curtain raiser on the drama that broke and then transformed the United States of America.

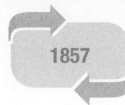

The Dred Scott Decision

Dred Scott was a Missouri slave who belonged to a U.S. Army surgeon, John Emerson, of St. Louis. As a military officer, Emerson served in several posts. Transferred first to Illinois and then to Wisconsin Territory, he took Scott with him to each new assignment. When Emerson died in 1846, Scott returned to St. Louis, where, at the urging of abolitionist lawyers who volunteered their services to him, he sued Emerson's widow for his freedom, arguing that he was now legally a citizen of Missouri, having been made free because of his long residence in Illinois, where slavery was banned by federal law (the Northwest Ordinance), and in the Wisconsin Territory, where the provisions of the 1820 Missouri Compromise made slavery illegal. When a Missouri court ruled against Scott, his lawyers appealed to the United States Supreme Court, which handed down its decision in 1857.

The Supreme Court's antislavery northern justices sided with Scott, while the pro-slavery southerners upheld the Missouri court's decision. Chief Justice Roger B. Taney, native of the slave-holding state of Maryland, wrote the majority opinion, which held that neither enslaved blacks nor, for that matter, free blacks were citizens of the United States; therefore, they had no right to sue in federal court. This point, outrageous though it was, would have been sufficient to settle the case, but Taney wanted the decision to go further, much further. He held that the Illinois law banning slavery had no force on Scott once he returned to Missouri, a slave state. Furthermore, he concluded that the law that applied in Wisconsin was also without force, because the Missouri Compromise was unconstitutional in that it violated the Fifth Amendment, which bars the government from depriving an individual of "life, liberty, or property" without due process of law—and slaves were manifestly property.

Anyone who abhorred slavery found the Dred Scott decision nothing less than obscene. Had the United States come to this? That the highest court in the land was emboldened to use the Bill of Rights to *deny* freedom to a human being? This outrage alone was sufficient to galvanize abolitionist sentiment throughout the nation. But the implication of the Dred Scott decision went beyond even moral outrage. Because Taney had defined slavery as nothing more or less than an issue of property, a Fifth Amendment issue, a constitutional issue, his decision made it incumbent on the federal government to protect slavery in every state, whether or not slavery was practiced in a particular state. That is, even in a free state, a slave remained the property of his or her owner, and, like any other item of property, could not be taken from the owner without due process of law. Thus, the decision put slavery beyond any further compromise. The constitutional rights of slaveholders had to be universally upheld. In this there was no choice—so long as slavery itself legally existed. To free even a single slave—legally—slavery itself had to be abolished, and not just in some states, but nationally. Without the possibility of a middle course, Taney's decision made civil war all but inevitable.

1859

Oil Boom

Before the middle of the nineteenth century, Americans used oil distilled from whale blubber to fill their oil lamps. Unlike so-called rock oil—a kerosene product distilled from surface shale rocks—whale oil burned clean and bright. The trouble was that the demand for whale oil had caused the mammal to be hunted to near extinction. Fortunately, a new type of Austrian lamp was just beginning to appear in the United States, which was designed to burn the shale oil—and burn it cleanly. Suddenly, there was a substantial market for petroleum from the ground.

By the late 1850s, a number of oil companies were formed, including the Rock Oil Company of Connecticut. The company's founders heard that oil was seen floating on water near Titusville, Pennsylvania. They purchased property there and hired Edwin Drake to find the underground source of the oil. Drake consulted a drilling expert, William Smith, and the two men sunk a well, which, on August 27, 1859, at a depth of sixty-nine feet, struck oil. The Titusville well was the first that tapped oil at its source, and it almost immediately launched a great industry. By the 1880s, drilling for oil became a nationwide enterprise.

John Brown's Raid on Harpers Ferry

I n 1857, John Brown moved to Boston from Kansas, where he had led militant—and extravagantly violent—antislavery forces. In Boston, capital of the northern abolition movement, Brown gained the financial backing of leading abolitionists. He laid plans to raid the federal arsenal at Harpers Ferry, Virginia (today West Virginia), with the intention of arming local slaves and fomenting a massive uprising.

Brown and his small band of raiders, which included four of his sons, invaded the town of Harpers Ferry, cut telegraph lines, and occupied the arsenal on October 16. Some of Brown's men rode through the countryside, menacing plantation owners and freeing slaves;

> "I, John Brown, am now quite *certain* that the crimes of this *guilty land* will never be purged *away* but with Blood." —John Brown, note intended to be read after his execution

however, the massive, spontaneous slave rebellion Brown had anticipated did not materialize, and, on October 17, U.S. Marines, under the operational command of U.S. Army colonel Robert E. Lee, marched into Harpers Ferry. When Brown refused to give up the arsenal, Lee's troops rushed the facility, killed ten of Brown's men, and took the rest, four men, including Brown, prisoner.

John Brown, tried for treason, conspiracy, and murder, was found guilty and hanged on December 2, 1859. Abolitionists were quick to paint him as a martyr to the cause of freedom, and certainly his violent example made any further talk of compromise on the issue of slavery seem pale, weak, and useless.

1860

Susan B. Anthony Wins Key Rights for Women

After the Seneca Falls Conference of 1848, some delegates continued to work toward the twin causes of abolition of slavery and women's suffrage. But another leading delegate, Susan B. Anthony, decided to focus exclusively on the cause of women's rights. Anthony organized grassroots female suffrage organizations throughout New York state, and she became the first-ever political lobbyist on behalf of a social cause, successfully persuading New York state legislators to pass the Married Women's Property Act of 1860. This landmark law secured for women the basic rights of holding property, of earning wages and retaining the wages they earned, and of petition for custody of children in cases of divorce. In no other state at the time did women have these rights.

Anthony succeeded in transferring the topic of women's rights from the arena of moral theory directly into law, politics, and the economy. The New York legislation became a model for the other states.

1861

The Fall of Fort Sumter

South Carolina became the first state to secede from the Union on October 20, 1860. Six more quickly followed; then, shortly afterward, another four. War did not begin, however, until the following year. Discounting a signal gun fired a few moments earlier, the first shot of the Civil War came at 4:30 A.M. on the morning of April 12, 1861, when Edmund Ruffin, a choleric South Carolina pro-slavery newspaper editor, pulled the lanyard on one of the many cannon trained on Fort Sumter. Major Robert Anderson, commandant of the fort located in Charleston Harbor, held out for two days of continuous bombardment, during which some 4,000 rounds fell on the fort, before he finally surrendered on April 14. Miraculously, no one, in all that fire, had been hurt. As for Anderson and his command, the chivalrous Louisiana general P.G.T. Beauregard allowed him and his command to withdraw with full military honors. At West Point, years earlier, Anderson had been Beauregard's artillery instructor.

From the moment the war began, similar ironies were seen. Brother officers, comrades at arms, now found themselves on opposite sides of a geographically defined conflict. Sometimes, members of the same family suddenly became enemies. People understood this right away. What almost no one saw, however, was that Fort Sumter would be the only battle without casualties. Before it was over, four long years in the future, at least 618,000 Americans, most of them very young, would be dead.

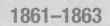

The Civil War Goes Badly for the North

A t the outset of the Civil War, the South didn't seem to have a chance of winning independence. Its population, economy, and industrial base were dwarfed by those of the North. Yet the South did have a leg up in military leadership. The cream of the U.S. Army officer corps was predominantly southern and felt allegiance to their home states. Thus, the Confederate forces were better led than those of the North, especially early in the war. The southern war strategy was, for the most part, defensive, which meant that troops would be defending their homeland against the equivalent of foreign invaders. That conferred a great advantage of morale. And the North? What was the North fighting for? As some saw it, it was to free the slaves—and relatively few white northerners were willing to lay down their lives for that. As President Abraham Lincoln saw it, the fight was not to free the slaves, but to save the Union. But there were many northerners who didn't even believe this was worthwhile. As General Winfield Scott said of the states that had left the Union, why not simply "let the wayward sisters depart in peace"?

Perhaps, then, northerners shouldn't have been stunned (as they were) when the Confederates won victories at Bull Run (July 21, 1861), the battles of the Seven Days (during the Peninsula Campaign of Union commander George B. McClellan), the Second Battle of Bull Run (August 29–30, 1862), Fredericksburg (December 13, 1862), and Chancellorsville (May 2–4, 1863). Despite its superiority of resources, the North had all it could do just to stay in the fight through the early summer of 1863.

1862

The Homestead Act

With the nation torn North from South, President Lincoln was eager to bind East and West closer together. He signed into law, on May 20, 1862, the Homestead Act, a piece of legislation that immediately began to shape the American destiny. The act gave 160 acres of public land in the West as a homestead to "any person who is the head of a family, or who has arrived at the age of twenty-one years, and is a citizen of the United States, or who shall have filed his declaration of intention to become such." This wasn't a free gift, but it required very little cash—something westerners and would-be westerners were always short of. For a modest filing fee, the homesteader obtained his 160 acres, and then, to "perfect" his claim (establish permanent ownership), he had to live on the land for five years and make certain improvements, the most important of which was the construction of a dwelling. After these requirements were met, the homesteader was granted clear title to the land. There were also alternatives to this process. A homesteader could "preempt" the land after a mere six months' residence by purchasing it at the bargain rate of $1.25 per acre, and if the settler could scrape together $50—no mean sum in the 1860s—he could add an additional 40 acres to his original 160 and even purchase additional lots of 40 acres each, at $50, up to a maximum of 160 added to his original grant.

As public policy, the Homestead Act was unprecedented in nothing less than the history of the world. To begin with, few of the world's "civilized" nations had any free land to distribute, but those that did typically distributed territory at the whim and prejudice of some ruler. By the close of the nineteenth century, under the Homestead Act, about 600,000 farmers had received clear title to some 80 million acres of formerly public land. It opened the West to tens and then hundreds of thousands.

1862

The Emancipation Proclamation

On a personal level, it is clear that Lincoln abhorred slavery. "As I would not be a slave, so I would not be a master," he once wrote. But, as president, he believed himself bound by his oath of office to uphold the Constitution, which clearly protected slavery in the slave states. Of more immediate concern was Lincoln's fear, in the midst of civil war, that any attempt simply to declare the slaves free would drive the four slaveholding border states—Maryland, Delaware, Kentucky, and Missouri—still nominally loyal to the Union, into the Confederate fold, while in those portions of the Confederacy currently under Union military occupation, such a declaration might well incite renewed rebellion. So Lincoln moved slowly, so slowly that, on August 19, 1862, Horace Greeley, the highly influential editor of the *New York Tribune,* published an open letter to the president on behalf (he said) of the 20 million citizens of the loyal states. He called for immediate emancipation. Lincoln replied:

> My paramount object in this struggle *is* to save the Union, and is *not* either to save or destroy Slavery. If I could save the Union without freeing *any* slave, I would do it; and if I could save it by freeing *all* the slaves, I would do it; and if I could do it by freeing some and leaving others alone, I would also do that. What I do about Slavery and the colored race, I do because I believe it helps to save this Union; and what I forbear, I forbear because I do *not* believe it would help to save the Union.

Nevertheless, Lincoln did edge closer to an emancipation proclamation, but he decided to issue it only on the heels of some Union army victory. Coming after a string of Union defeats, it would only ring hollow and desperate. While the Battle of Antietam on September 17, 1862, resulted in something of a bloody draw, it could at least be *construed* as a Union victory. So Lincoln chose the moment to issue, on September 23, 1862, the Preliminary Emancipation Proclamation.

The document freed no slaves; instead, it merely served warning on slaveowners living in states "still in rebellion on January 1, 1863," that their property would be declared, after that date, "forever free." Only after the January 1 deadline had passed—and the Civil War continued—did Lincoln issue the "final" Emancipation Proclamation. Even that document gave freedom only to those slaves living in areas of the Confederacy that were not under the control of the Union army. In the Union-occupied South, owners still held their slaves, as did owners in the border states.

Timid as the Emancipation Proclamation may strike us from a twenty-first-century perspective, the document did much to galvanize the North's resolve to see the war through to total victory. It elevated the struggle to the highest possible moral plane, and it made the abolition of slavery the single most visible issue of the war. It also laid the legal foundation for subsequent constitutional amendments that abolished slavery, that ensured full citizenship for freedmen, and that enfranchised all persons "regardless of previous condition of servitude."

The Emergence of General Grant

The principal focus of the Civil War was on its eastern theater. Here, until Gettysburg, the Union's performance was a heartbreaking disappointment. In the meantime, in the war's western theater, an obscure Union general named Ulysses S. Grant was scoring the kind of major triumphs sorely missed in the battles of the East. Shiloh (April 6–7, 1862) was the usual bloody struggle, but Vicksburg, which yielded to Grant's long siege on the day after Meade's victory at Gettysburg, July 4, 1863, and Chattanooga, which fell to the North on November 25, 1863, were signal victories that gave the Union control of large territories. Coupled with U.S. Navy flag officer David Farragut's capture of New Orleans in April 1862, Grant's victory at Vicksburg gave the Union control of the Mississippi River, thereby cutting the Confederacy in two and denying it a major source of transport and supply.

In 1864, after having appointed and fired a series of mediocre (or worse) commanding generals, Lincoln recognized Grant as the dogged, relentlessly aggressive commander the Union Army so badly needed. Appointed general in chief, Grant set about inexorably forcing Lee's army back toward the Confederate capital of Richmond, Virginia. Grant's secret? He was a superb tactician, but, most of all, he understood the grim equation of this war: The North had more men than the South, more money than the South, more railroads than the South, and more industry than the South. The North could afford to "spend" more of all these resources—paramountly, the men—than the South. If the North stayed in the fight, Grant understood, the Confederacy would inevitably exhaust itself.

1863

Gettysburg

During the early summer of 1863, the South's principal commander, Robert E. Lee, boldly abandoned the defensive strategy that had served the Confederate forces so well and took the offensive by invading Pennsylvania. During July 1–3, 1863, at a Pennsylvania crossroads town called Gettysburg, Confederate and Union forces clashed. The first day went badly for the North, but General George G. Meade's field subordinates managed to hold their positions and prevent a rout. On the second day, the tide turned, and on the third day, following a massed charge by the Confederates—so-called Pickett's Charge—which was as dashing as it was desperate, Lee's army was defeated.

Had the Union lost the engagement, it is quite possible that the northern will to continue the fight would have been broken, leading to some negotiated, compromise settlement with the secessionist states. But Meade not only turned back the Confederate army at Gettysburg, his forces also dealt the South a defeat that discouraged both England and France, which had been courting the Confederacy at least to some degree, from supporting the rebel cause. Undeniably, Gettysburg marked the turning point of the war. At the same time, that war was hardly over. While the Union army had achieved much, Meade failed to pursue the defeated Lee, whose army was allowed to escape, beaten but intact, back to the South.

1864–1865

The Fall of Atlanta and the March to the Sea

Grant bore down steadily on Lee's Army of Northern Virginia. Lee sometimes out-generaled him, but even when he was defeated, Grant continued to advance, always forcing Lee to spend precious blood against him. While Grant fought the bitter Wilderness Campaign in Virginia through May and June of 1864, his chief lieutenant, William Tecumseh Sherman, advanced through Tennessee and Georgia to Atlanta, a key rail hub, which he captured, occupied, and finally burned (September–November 1864) before continuing on his infamously destructive "march to the sea."

Grant concentrated on destroying Lee's Army of Northern Virginia while Sherman made real the most terrifying kind of modern combat—"total war," war waged not just against an opposing army but against the entire "enemy" population. It was war intended to kill the people's will to fight by attacking their means of sustenance and survival. Sherman cut a swath of destruction from Atlanta to Savannah, then worked his way north, aiming to catch Lee in a great pincers between his forces and those of Grant.

1864

The Thirteenth Amendment

C ongress did not wait until the war was won to formalize and extend the provisions of the Emancipation Proclamation with the Thirteenth Amendment to the Constitution. As with most amendments, its language was simple:

> *Section 1.* Neither slavery nor involuntary servitude, except as a punishment for crime whereof the party shall have been duly convicted, shall exist within the United States, or any place subject to their jurisdiction.

> *Section 2.* Congress shall have power to enforce this article by appropriate legislation.

But its implications were profound. The Senate passed the amendment on April 8, 1864. Representatives argued in the House but they, too, passed it, on January 31, 1865. The measure was ratified on December 18, 1865.

1865

The War Ends

Under the grinding pressure of "total war," the South fought on, hoping to salvage some possibility of a negotiated peace in preference to abject surrender.

Union general Philip Sheridan defeated Confederate general George E. Pickett at Five Forks (April 1, 1865), and, after an almost yearlong siege, Grant took heavily fortified Petersburg, Virginia, key to the Confederate capital city of Richmond. On April 2, 1865, Richmond—from which the Confederate government had fled—fell to him. Then, one week later, at Appomattox Court House, General Robert E. Lee surrendered his Army of Northern Virginia to General Grant, effectively, if not officially, ending the Civil War.

The great and daunting task that remained was, in the words of President Lincoln's Second Inaugural Address, to "bind up the nation's wounds" and restore the Union. Lincoln, who proposed a policy of "malice toward none and charity for all," was perhaps the only national leader capable of successfully guiding such a task.

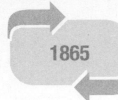

1865

Assassination of Abraham Lincoln

On the evening of April 14, 1865, with the Civil War all but over, an unimaginably careworn Abraham Lincoln sought a few hours' diversion at a Ford's Theater performance of a popular comedy, *Our American Cousin.* At about 10 P.M., John Wilkes Booth, a popular matinee idol and well-known southern sympathizer, entered the theater, approached the door of the president's private box, found that the lock was broken (he may well have known that it would be), opened the door, and calmly leveled his derringer between Lincoln's left ear and spine. He squeezed the trigger.

Among the 1,675 members of the audience, few heard the report of the tiny weapon. The dull pop made little impression on Mrs. Lincoln, seated next to her husband, nor on Major Henry Rathbone, seated in the presidential box with his fiancée, Clara Harris. Booth was familiar with the script of *Our American Cousin,* and he had timed his shot to coincide with the play's biggest laugh—just after Harry Hawk, playing Mr. Trenchard, says, "Wal, I guess I know enough to turn you inside out, you sockdologizing old mantrap."

When Rathbone realized an intruder was present, he tangled with Booth, who stabbed him in the shoulder, then leaped down from the box to the stage. He caught his right spur in the Treasury Regiment flag that festooned the box. As a result, his left leg took the full impact of his fall, and a bone snapped just above his instep. Turning to the audience, the actor shouted the state motto of Virginia: "Sic semper tyrannis!"—Thus ever to tyrants!—then limped into the wings, fell, recovered, and ran, lopingly, out of the theater. No one in the bewildered audience thought to give chase.

Booth was on the loose twelve days before he was run to ground, about midnight on April 26, at a tobacco farm near Port Royal, Virginia. Shot and fatally wounded, he was never brought to trial. On the very day of Booth's death, General Kirby Smith surrendered the last Confederate military unit to General E.R.S. Canby. It was, officially, the final day of the Civil War.

1866

The First Cattle Drive

I n large numbers, Texans went off to fight in the Civil War, leaving behind their homes—and their cattle. By the end of the war, millions of head of Texas cattle ranged freely across the state. With the Texas economy in ruins, the cattle offered wealth on the hoof. Strays abounded, and if a man could round up a stray and brand him, that animal was his. In this way, large herds were accumulated after the war, and the profession of cowboy came into its own.

Charlie Goodnight had been mustered out of the Texas Rangers after the war and, with old-time cattleman Oliver Loving, he put together a postwar herd of some 5,000 head and decided to make a fortune by driving 2,000 of them from Texas to the new Indian-fighting army outposts in Colorado. Soldiers demanded beef, and government provisioning contracts were highly lucrative. Together, Goodnight and Loving pioneered the Goodnight–Loving Trail, which became one of four principal cattle trails and marked the beginning of the trail-drive industry. That business produced more than beef, of course. It gave rise to the cowboy, certainly the most celebrated and beloved worker in American history; the subject of legend, of dime novels, and of film—a national icon.

1866–1868

Reconstruction Begins

The tragedy of Abraham Lincoln's violent death was even worse than probably anyone at the time could have imagined. John Wilkes Booth had killed perhaps the only man capable of beginning and fostering the healing of the nation. Lincoln had been determined to fight the war to absolute victory, but, once the war had been won, he did not want the South punished. He favored amnesty and other steps to heal the nation. As a healing gesture, in 1864, he had chosen a Democrat, a Tennessean, as a running mate. Now, thanks to Booth, that man, Andrew Johnson, was president. Loud, boorish, abrasive, and given to drink, Johnson was universally unloved. Like Lincoln, he favored amnesty and healing, but he lacked Lincoln's charisma, eloquence, intelligence, and moral force. His clumsy efforts to jam down congressional throats generous treatment for the former Confederacy resulted in a legislative rebellion. Congress both feared and resented an amnesty that restored power to the very individuals who had brought about the rebellion. Moreover, while the Republican Party was the majority party of the North, the Democratic Party was the majority party of the South, and the Republican Congress had no desire to allow the Democratic Party to revive. Finally, there was genuine moral outrage over the manner in which the former Confederate states, while ostensibly freeing the slaves in compliance with the Thirteenth Amendment, actually kept them in bondage, denying them the vote and their other rights.

So Congress and President Johnson always found themselves on opposite sides concerning "Reconstruction," the process of reincorporating the former Confederate states into the Union. In

1866, over Johnson's veto, Congress passed the Freedman's Bureau Act and the Civil Rights Act to assist blacks in their transition from slave life to freedom and to assure that African Americans would be deemed full citizens of the United States. Congress pushed through the Fourteenth Amendment, which explicitly extended citizenship to everyone "born or naturalized in the United States," forbidding states to enact laws "which shall abridge the privileges or immunities of citizens of the United States," and guaranteeing the voting rights of all citizens. All of this was noble and just, but, typical of Reconstruction in the absence of Lincoln, the Fourteenth Amendment also included measures of naked vengeance: Section 3 barred former Confederates from holding federal—*or state*—offices unless individually pardoned by a two-thirds vote of Congress, and Section 4 repudiated debts incurred by the former Confederate government and also repudiated compensation for "the loss of emancipation of any slave."

The only former Confederate state to ratify the Fourteenth Amendment was Tennessee, and when the others refused, Congress passed a series of harsh Reconstruction Acts, which put all of the former Confederacy, save Tennessee, under military government. Only after the states drafted and approved acceptable state constitutions, fully enfranchising blacks, were the military governments removed. But, even then, Reconstruction was not finished. More federal laws were passed, intended, on the one hand, to assure equal rights for African-American citizens, to establish state-supported free public schools, to provide more equitable conditions for labor, and to apportion taxes more equitably, but also clearly intended to punish and keep punishing the South. Burdensome taxes were levied. Corruption became universal and crippling. In a vengeful frenzy, those who administered Reconstruction thrust illiterate former slaves into high-level positions in state and local governments. The result, of course, was only to increase chaos and corruption, and to trigger self-righteous bitterness, acts of defiance against the federal government, and, worst of all, brutal acts of terror against blacks.

In the absence of Lincoln, Reconstruction created a climate of sectional division and resentment that endured well into the twentieth century and, by casting southern blacks into the unwilling role of scapegoat, fostered in the South a new kind of racism, founded not, as slavery had been, on mindless assumptions of black racial inferiority but on naked racial hatred.

1868

Impeachment of Andrew Johnson

No one thinks Andrew Johnson was an effective president. His efforts to prevent Congress from punishing the South with harsh Reconstruction measures were well intended, but clumsy, inept, ineffectual, and alienating. As the Civil War had challenged the basic democratic concept of national union, the rapidly escalating war between Johnson and Congress challenged the equally basic democratic concept of separation of powers and the system of checks and balances. Congress sought to seize executive powers, even as President Johnson tried to thwart Congress by interfering in the execution of the Reconstruction laws it had passed.

The struggle between the two branches of government reached its point of greatest crisis on March 2, 1867, when, over Johnson's veto, Congress passed the Tenure of Office Act. This law barred the president from dismissing, without senatorial approval, any civil officeholder who had been appointed with senatorial consent. Part of the general effort to usurp as many executive prerogatives as possible, the act was immediately and specifically aimed at preventing Johnson from removing a member of his own cabinet, Secretary of War Edwin Stanton, who was strongly allied to the cause of the Radical Republicans. With typical absence of understanding or finesse, Johnson defied the law by dismissing Stanton in 1868. This moved the House of Representatives to vote the impeachment of Andrew Johnson.

Under the Constitution, only the House of Representatives may bring impeachment charges against the president, who is then tried before the Senate. The charges brought against Johnson were weak and transparently motivated by partisan politics. The Tenure of Office Act was dubious at best, and Johnson's defiance of it, though heavy-handed, was intended to bring the law to a constitutional challenge before the Supreme Court. Congress prevented this by voting articles of impeachment, and, from March through May 1868, the Senate held a trial. The key votes, on May 16 and 26, 1868, fell only one short of the two-thirds majority required for conviction and removal from office. Seven Republicans, all men of conscience, voted with Johnson's supporters. What would have been, in effect, a coup d'etat was averted, but the gulf between Andrew Johnson and Congress was so deep and wide that the president, though he continued to hold office, was effectively neutralized as a political leader at a time when the wounded nation required leadership above all else.

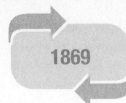

1869

A Golden Spike Defeats Distance

The idea of building a transcontinental railroad was discussed seriously just two years after the very first American railroad, the Baltimore and Ohio, began operation in 1830. In 1832, Hartwell Carver, a physician from Rochester, New York, published some articles in the *New York Courier and Enquirer* proposing the construction of a railroad on 8 million acres of government land from Lake Michigan to Oregon Territory. Over the years, many more schemes were proposed, even the most feasible of which became political footballs and resulted in nothing but talk.

As often happened with great American enterprises, it took the exertions of a single inspired individual to transform visions into reality. Theodore Dehone Judah, the son of a Bridgeport, Connecticut, Episcopal priest, turned to engineering instead of the Good Book, and became a builder of railroads. He tirelessly publicized, raised money, and lobbied Congress. Then, in 1860, he discovered a relatively easy pass through the formidable California Sierra. With a partner, a mining town druggist named "Doc" Strong, he recruited seven backers, including four whose names and fortunes would be forever linked with the transcontinental railroad: Collis P. Huntington and Mark Hopkins, partners in a hardware store; Leland Stanford, a wholesale grocer; and Charles Crocker, a dry goods merchant. Now backed by real money, Judah secured passage of the Pacific Railway Act of 1862, authorizing two companies—the Union Pacific, starting from the east (Omaha, Nebraska) and building west, and the Central Pacific, moving eastward from Sacramento, California—to begin construction. Judah then traveled back to California to light a fire under his backers. When they balked over laying track farther east than the California–Nevada state line, he set off back to Washington in search of new backers. He took the quickest route available at the time: a ship to Panama, a difficult overland trek through the isthmus jungle, and another ship up the east coast of Central and North America. In Panama, however, he contracted typhoid fever and, weeks later, died.

But by this time, the Civil War had made construction of the railroad a top priority for the Lincoln administration. The Pacific Railway Act was only the first of several pieces of legislation that granted huge tracts of land to the railroads, not only for laying track but as parcels that could be sold to finance construction. This scheme was given momentum with liberal government loan packages, and yet, even with finance and authorization in place, the project stalled. Finally, in 1865, President Lincoln called on Oakes Ames, a prominent industrialist who made his first fortune manufacturing shovels (he was therefore nicknamed the "ace of spades"), and asked him to "take hold" of the project.

Ames instantly recruited investors in a corporation created by Union Pacific vice president Thomas Durant and named after the company that had financed the French railway system a decade earlier, Crédit Mobilier. For major investors, it was the mother of all sweetheart deals. Run by the directors *of* the Union Pacific, Crédit Mobilier was paid *by* the Union Pacific to *build* the Union Pacific. The scheme culminated in a spectacular scandal—yet it did get the transcontinental railroad moving.

Led by a U.S. Army engineer, Grenville Mellon Dodge, the Union Pacific began laying prodigious lengths of track—266 miles in 1866 alone. The Central Pacific, which had to lay track in the mountains, carving paths out of slopes and bridging vast chasms, advanced more slowly. The bulk of work on both railroads fell to immigrant laborers. Irish hands built most of the Union Pacific, while Chinese "coolies" endured racial slurs and even racial violence to build the Central Pacific.

The cost of the railroad was in the millions, of course, but the amount of graft paid out by the tycoons to government officials and others is incalculable. And local governments themselves were liberal with bribes of their own. A town could be made or ruined, depending on whether or not the railroad passed through it. Western municipalities ponied up huge sums to bend the advancing line this way or that. As for the workers—the Irish, the Chinese, and the others—they were regarded as little more than expendable commodities. The politics, the graft, the exploitation, the racism, the waste, all were part of the transcontinental railroad—and yet, so were the dreams, the will, the muscle, the vision, and the courage of many men.

On May 10, 1869, at Promontory Summit (often mistakenly identified as Promontory Point), Utah, railroad tycoon Leland Stanford—aided by workers—wielded a sledgehammer to drive home a ceremonial "golden spike" to join the rails of the eastbound Central Pacific with the westbound rails of the Union Pacific. From sea to shining sea, the nation was now bound by bands of iron.

The Telephone

Born in Scotland, Alexander Graham Bell became a distinguished teacher of the deaf, first in England and then in the United States, where, in Boston, he opened a school for the deaf in 1872. His interest in sound and speech led to experiments with two devices: a harmonic telegraph (an instrument to transmit multiple telegraph messages simultaneously over a single line) and a device to record sound waves graphically (so that the deaf might *see* sound). In 1874, the two ideas suddenly merged in Bell's imagination, and he began to think that if he could "make a current of electricity vary in intensity precisely as the air varies in density during the production of sound," then he could "transmit speech telegraphically."

It was a brilliant insight into converting one form of energy, sound, into another, electricity, and Bell spent the next two years intensively working on it. He was tinkering with a version of the device when he accidentally spilled battery acid in his lap. In pain, he called to his assistant, Thomas Watson, who was in the next room, stationed at the receiver. Watson heard Bell's call—"Mr. Watson, come here; I want you"—not through the door, but through the receiver. The telephone had been born, and within a very few years, it became a ubiquitous and indispensable feature of modern civilization.

Yellow Hair Falls at the Little Bighorn

ate in the spring of 1876, Philip Sheridan, in overall command of army operations against the Indians, laid out the
latest of many campaigns to force the Sioux onto reservations. He ordered General Alfred Terry, leading a force from the
east, Colonel John Gibbon from the west, and General George
Crook from nearby Fort Fetterman to converge on the Yellowstone River, where major Sioux camps were believed to be. Among
Terry's command was the Seventh Cavalry, led by George Armstrong Custer.

Custer had graduated from West Point in 1861 at the very bottom of his class, but in the Civil War he had commanded troops
with a combination of heroism and utter disregard for their lives
and his. This catapulted him to promotion as brigadier general of
volunteers at age twenty-three, then, two years later, to the same
rank in the regular service—at twenty-five, the youngest general in
the history of the U.S. Army. Like many other officers, Custer re-
verted to lower rank after the Civil War, but he soon climbed back
to colonel, was given the Seventh Cavalry, and sent to fight Indians—who, in reference to his flamboyantly long blond locks,
dubbed him "Yellow Hair." Courageous, to be sure, Custer was
also hungry for glory—at the expense of the Indians as well as the
men of his command.

On the morning of June 17, 1876, Crook, with more than
1,000 men, halted for a rest at the head of the Rosebud Creek in
Montana. Sitting Bull led Sioux and Cheyenne against Crook's position, and the cavalry was forced into retreat after a fierce six-

hour fight. After the Battle of the Rosebud, the Sioux established a camp. In the meantime, Terry's column linked up with Gibbon's at the mouth of the Rosebud, both commanders unaware of Crook's retreat. Gibbon's and Terry's officers, including Custer, convened in the cabin of the Yellowstone River steamer *Far West* to lay out a campaign strategy. They believed they would find a Sioux encampment on the stream the Indians called the Greasy Grass and the whites called the Little Bighorn. Their plan was to attack. Custer was to lead his Seventh Cavalry up the Rosebud, cross to the Little Bighorn, then advance down the Bighorn valley from the south as Terry and Gibbon marched up the Yellowstone and the Bighorn to block the Indians from the north. Thus, Sitting Bull would be caught in the jaws of a pincer.

What none of the officers knew was that the "camp" was really a large village, populated by perhaps as many as 7,000 Sioux, including many warriors.

On June 25, when his scouts sighted a Sioux camp and warriors, Custer resolved to attack immediately, before the always-elusive enemy could flee. He did not pause to determine just how many Sioux were present. Instead, he led his men across the divide between the Rosebud and the Little Bighorn, dispatching Captain Frederick W. Benteen with 125 men to the south to make sure the Sioux had not moved into the upper valley of the Little Bighorn. As Custer drew nearer to the Little Bighorn, he spotted about 40 warriors and sent Major Marcus A. Reno, with 112 men, after them. Reno was to pursue the warriors back to their village, while Custer, with his remaining men, more than 200, charged the village from the north.

Reno's 112 men, in pursuit of the 40 warriors seen earlier, were soon engulfed by masses of Sioux. In the meantime, Custer had ascended a bluff, saw now that the Sioux encampment was vast—later estimates vary wildly, from 1,500 to 7,000, but certainly far in excess of the Seventh Cavalry's 600 men—and he saw that Reno had advanced right into it. Custer summoned his bugler, Giovanni Martini, and handed him a note to deliver to Benteen, ordering him to bring the ammunition packs and join the fight. The errand would save Martini's life. He was the last surviving cavalryman to see Custer alive.

Warriors led by Gall, a Hunkpapa Sioux chief, charged across the Little Bighorn and waded into the knot of cavalry troopers. While Gall pressed in from the south, Crazy Horse pushed in from the north. For Custer and his command, it was over in less than an hour. They died, all of them.

More than 200 men, including Custer, were killed on the Little Bighorn battlefield. Congress authorized an increase in the army's strength, but the defeat so demoralized the army that no attempt at reprisal was made until November. Nevertheless, the defeat of George Armstrong Custer, a brilliant tactical victory for the Sioux warriors, was, ultimately, a strategic disaster for the Native Americans. Before the Little Bighorn, white public opinion wavered between hatred of and sympathy for the Indians. Afterward, most American citizens were prepared to let the army do whatever it deemed necessary to confine the Indians to their reservations.

1876

The Disputed Hayes–Tilden Election

On election night, 1876, Republican presidential candidate Rutherford B. Hayes, governor of Ohio, went to bed believing he had lost to the Democratic governor of New York, Samuel J. Tilden. But dawn brought a different story—and an election dispute that would go on for four months amid charges of voter fraud, intimidation and even murder of black voters in the South, manipulation of ballots by partisan election judges, the threat of lawsuits, and a recount of votes in contested states.

The popular vote gave Tilden a 250,000-ballot lead over Hayes. This fact did not discourage Hayes supporter Daniel Edgar Sickles from pointing out that the fate of Hayes could yet be determined by contesting electoral votes in Oregon, Louisiana, South Carolina, and Florida. If at least some of these disputed electoral votes could be delivered to Hayes, he would win.

The resulting electoral battle raged wildly and with no end in sight before the March 4, 1877, inauguration date. There was talk of authorizing the current secretary of state to serve as interim chief executive. Many in the South were actually discussing secession, and some were already setting up rival governments. Just two days before the inauguration deadline, Congress authorized a bipartisan Electoral Commission even as legislators negotiated a behind-the-scenes deal to decide the issue. In essence, the deal was this: The South would give the election to Hayes in return for his pledge to bring full home rule to the southern states and an immediate end to the military-enforced Reconstruction governments that had been established in the wake of the Civil War. If this meant that the rights of African-American citizens were to be sacrificed, well—so be it.

The southern legislators agreed to a commission composed of eight Republicans and seven Democrats, who voted straight down party lines to rule in favor of Hayes. As for the country, it held together—after a fashion; for the rift between North and South was wide, and the gulf between white and black Americans deepened. As for Hayes, he bore throughout his single presidential term the mocking title of "His Fraudulency."

1879

Edison's Incandescent Electric Lamp

Born in Milan, Ohio, in 1847 to a family of modest means, Thomas Edison was an intensely curious and always restless boy, who so exasperated his teachers that he soon left school, although he continued to read voraciously. His maverick ways and his continual questioning, tinkering, and experimentation vexed his conventional father, who worried that his son was "addlepated," but his mother, always supportive, encouraged Edison and did the best she could to further his education by tutoring him at home. In his teens, Edison secured a job as an itinerant railway telegrapher and, in his twenties, embarked on a career as an inventor, beginning with devices that built on, improved, and extended the telegraph in various ways. By the time of his death, in 1931, he held 1,093 patents, a still-unbroken record for any individual.

The most famous of his inventions was, of course, the incandescent electric light. Edison spent many months of exhausting experimentation and failure. Electric arc lighting already existed, but it was intensely brilliant and impractical for widespread domestic and industrial use. Edison saw that the task before him was (as he put it) to "subdivide the light," and he further saw that finding just the right material to use as a filament was the key to solving this problem of subdivision. As he worked on this, he also envisioned a whole new industry—an industry devoted to generating electrical power for the masses, for the world.

But finding the filament, this little bit of material, proved to be a daunting task. Edison set about collecting thousands of candidate items, from exotic metal wires to a hair plucked from the beard of one of his assistants, and he tediously tried each, observing and evaluating how each worked—and failed to work. At long last, he discovered the virtues of carbonized cotton, which glowed brightly in a vacuum and had a reasonably long life—forty hours, at first. He told a reporter that he had tried some ten thousand materials before he hit upon carbonized cotton. When the reporter marveled that he had never become sufficiently discouraged to quit, Edison replied in a manner that revealed his brute-force approach to technology: "I didn't fail ten thousand times. I successfully eliminated, ten thousand times, materials and combinations which wouldn't work."

On December 31, 1879, he offered a public demonstration of the lamp and was awarded a patent the next month. Shortly after this, Edison oversaw the first commercial installation of electric lights, on the steamship *Columbia,* belonging to the Oregon Railroad and Navigation Company. By 1881, he had built the world's first central electric power plant, the Pearl Street Station in lower Manhattan.

Very soon, all of urban America—and much of the urban world—was being electrified. Rural areas followed more slowly, but follow they did, and by the end of Edison's life electric lighting and electric appliances were part of the very tissue of modern civilization. This American inventor had transformed life itself.

1881

Tuskegee Institute Founded

Like many African Americans of the nineteenth century, Booker T. Washington, born in 1856 at Rocky Mount, Virginia, had a future with precious little to hope for. He was a slave, and the emancipation that came after the Civil War brought scarcely brighter prospects. At the age of nine, Washington moved with his family to Malden, West Virginia, where he worked at a salt furnace and, later, in a coal mine. His primary education was virtually nonexistent, but he prepared himself sufficiently to enroll in the Hampton Normal and Agricultural Institute at the age of sixteen while working as a janitor to support himself. Washington graduated three years later, taught for two years, studied theology for another year, then decided on a full-time career as a teacher. He joined the staff of Hampton Institute, where he created a program for educating American Indians.

In 1881, Washington answered the call to head a new school for blacks in remote Tuskegee, Alabama. As with his own early life, there was little promising about the place, which consisted of two run-down buildings and very little else. Washington christened the place Tuskegee Normal and Industrial Institute, and decided that he would of-

During a speech given at the Atlanta Cotton States and International Exposition on September 18, 1895, Booker T. Washington spread out the fingers of his hand and raised it in front of his face: "In all things that are purely social, we can be as separate as the fingers, yet one as the hand in all things essential to mutual progress."

fer young black Americans a broad but vocationally practical education. For what he believed in was not theoretical equality for African Americans, but hard-nosed, practical economic self-determination. Achieve that, he declared, and political and civil rights would—in the fullness of time—come.

Many whites, even southerners, were willing to work with Washington, who politely assured would-be donors, southern white employers, and southern governors that young black men would get from Tuskegee an education that would keep them down on the farm and in the basic trades. But as the civil rights movement began to grow and develop, and especially with the founding of the National Association for the Advancement of Colored People (NAACP) in 1909, the "accommodationist" and "compromise" view of Booker T. Washington came under increasing attack by progressive African Americans. Still, for blacks whose early twentieth-century horizons rarely extended further than the poverty of a sharecropper's field, Tuskegee offered hope—real hope that could be counted in the dollars of a decent wage. For better or worse, Booker T. Washington became the leading spokesman for African-American "social progress" at the turn of the century. He offered a hard compromise: black acceptance of disfranchisement and segregation in exchange for white encouragement of black progress in economic and educational opportunity.

1890

How the Other Half Lives

Like many other New Yorkers of the late nineteenth century, Jacob August Riis was an immigrant. He had come from Denmark in 1870 and had spent his first seven years in the city struggling with poverty until, at last, he found his calling as a newspaper reporter. Riis worked in lower Manhattan, in offices adjacent to some of the most notorious slums in the city. Where others were repulsed by these neighborhoods, Riis was fascinated, and he appointed himself the chronicler—with pen and camera—of the slums.

He observed and wrote for two decades, finally producing in 1890 a masterpiece of sociology and journalism, *How the Other Half Lives*. As political reformer Theodore Roosevelt put it, the book was "an enlightenment and an inspiration," revealing to more fortunate Americans a world they had chosen to ignore and allowing them to ignore it no more. How effective was Riis's book? The evidence is clear. Prior to its publication in 1890, there were no serious efforts to rebuild the slums. After 1890, such efforts swept the nation.

1890

The Death of Sitting Bull

During the 1880s, a Native American religious movement the whites called the Ghost Dance began spreading through many of the western Indian reservations. It was essentially a peaceful movement, the Indians' stoic and highly spiritual acceptance of defeat in this world and a hope for victory in the next. Yet, among the Teton Sioux, the Ghost Dance took on militant overtones that white authorities found ominous and menacing. So, on November 20, 1890, cavalry and infantry reinforcements were sent to the Pine Ridge reservation in Dakota Territory. Their arrival only fanned the flames of rebellious discontent, and some 3,000 Indians defiantly gathered on a plateau at the northwest corner of Pine Ridge dubbed the Stronghold.

Brigadier General John R. Brooke, commander of the Pine Ridge area, held talks with the militants, but the anger continued to simmer, and Brooke's commanding officer, Major General Nelson A. Miles, transferred his headquarters to Rapid City, Dakota Territory. In the meantime, the most revered and influential of Sioux leaders, Sitting Bull, a figure who combined military skill with profound moral and religious force, began actively espousing the Ghost Dance at Standing Rock Reservation, also in Dakota Territory.

The government agent in charge of Standing Rock, James McLaughlin, understood that, for many Indians, Sitting Bull was the very embodiment of their cultural and spiritual identity. A major uprising could easily form around such a man. McLaughlin decided to neutralize Sitting Bull by arresting him—as quietly and as quickly as possible. Instead of calling in troops to do the job, he deployed Native American reservation policemen. But on December 15, 1890, the arrest went terribly wrong, a riot broke out, and, in the melee, the legendary Sitting Bull was shot dead. The death of Sitting Bull symbolized the eclipse of Native American culture by the forces of Euro-American culture.

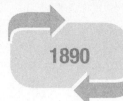

Massacre at Wounded Knee
Ends the Indian Wars

The killing of Sitting Bull during a botched arrest attempt on December 15, 1890 created an explosive situation on the Sioux reservations. Fearing an uprising, army commander Nelson A. Miles decided to arrest Chief Big Foot of the Miniconjou Sioux, a well-known leader of the Native American Ghost Dance movement, which whites believed was at the heart of the incipient rebellion. What Miles did not know was that Big Foot, having decided that the Ghost Dance offered nothing but desperation and futility, had abandoned the faith. Miles was also unaware that Chief Red Cloud, a Pine Ridge reservation leader friendly to the whites, had invited Big Foot to travel from his home on the Cheyenne River to Pine Ridge to exercise his considerable influence in persuading the would-be leaders of uprising to surrender.

Miles deployed troops in a dragnet across the prairies and badlands to intercept all Miniconjous and, in particular, Big Foot. On December 28, 1890, a squadron of the Seventh Cavalry, the outfit of the slain George Custer, tracked down Big Foot—who was seriously ill with pneumonia—and about 350 Miniconjous camped near a Dakota stream called Wounded Knee Creek.

The troops waited and watched. That evening, reinforcements arrived, and, by morning, 500 cavalrymen, under Colonel James W. Forsyth, surrounded Big Foot's camp. Determined to take no chances, Forsyth positioned on the surrounding hills four Hotchkiss guns, rapid-firing Howitzer-like artillery pieces. With these in place, he ordered his men to disarm the Indians in an orderly fashion and take them to the rail line, where a train would "remove them from the zone of military operations." The procedure was routine; the soldiers quietly entered the Indian camp and began their search for guns.

During the search, a medicine man named Yellow Bird, outraged by the presence of the troops, began dancing wildly and urging the others to resist. He reminded them all that they wore sacred "ghost shirts," which would protect them against the white men's bullets. Next, Black Coyote, described by another Indian as "a crazy man, a young man of very bad influence and in fact a nobody," menacingly lofted his Winchester above his head as the cavalrymen moved about the throng, collecting weapons. Black Coyote loudly protested that the rifle had cost him dearly and that nobody was going to take it from him. The soldiers responded provocatively, crowding around him, shoving him, taking him by the shoulders and spinning him around.

While attention was focused on Black Coyote, a rifle was fired. Was it Black Coyote's? Was it another Indian's? Was it the carbine of a trooper? Was it fired on purpose? Was it fired by accident? Whoever fired and for whatever reason, it was enough to unleash rifle fire on both sides. However, at this point, few of the Indians were still armed, and hand-to-hand combat broke out. Almost as soon as the fighting began, it ended, with the Indians making a break.

To prevent the escape of the Miniconjous, Forsyth ordered the Hotchkiss guns to open up. They fired at a rate of almost a round a second, targeting men, old men, women, and children. In less than an hour, Big Foot and 153 other Miniconjous were dead. So many others staggered, limped, or crawled away that no one knew or knows just how many died at Wounded Knee. Probably, some 300 of the 350 who had been camped at the creek finally perished. Casualties among the Seventh Cavalry were twenty-five killed and thirty-nine wounded, most of them victims of Hotchkiss rounds.

The U.S. Army called the event the "Battle of Wounded Knee," but the public, even those hardened against the Indians, called it a massacre. On December 30, a combination of hostile and hitherto friendly Sioux factions ambushed the Seventh Cavalry near the Pine Ridge Agency. Elements of the Ninth Cavalry came to the rescue, and General Miles marshaled 3,500 troops around the Sioux who had assembled along White Clay Creek, fifteen miles north of the Pine Ridge Agency. Chastened by Wounded Knee, Miles moved with patient restraint, gradually contracting the ring of troops around the Indians, all the while asking for their surrender and pledging good treatment in return.

Even the most determined among the Sioux leaders were persuaded now that their cause was lost, and, on January 15, 1891, the Sioux formally surrendered to the army.

1892

Opening of Ellis Island

I n his message to Congress on December 1, 1862, Abraham Lincoln called the United States the "last, best hope of earth." Before and after that day, millions proved him right. From all over the Earth, from places that failed humanity politically, economically, or spiritually, people have poured into America, a nation of immigrants.

The greatest waves of immigration came in the late nineteenth and early twentieth centuries, when the demands of burgeoning American industry began to outweigh the concerns of those who wanted to bar entry to "foreigners." The labor of the immigrant was cheap, and employers looking for unskilled and semiskilled workers to feed newly emerging assembly lines and do the heavy lifting required to build bridges and to raise the nation's first skyscrapers welcomed, first and foremost, the Irish, then people from southern and eastern Europe as well. The end of that century saw the coming of Italians, Greeks, Turks, Russians, and Slavs. With these came, for the first time, large numbers of Jews, who added a distinctive new element to the nation's blend of ethnic identities and religious faiths.

The urban centers of the East Coast and the Midwest had little trouble assimilating the new immigrants, although their lives in these cities were by no means easy. Many immigrants had been promised a land whose streets were paved with gold. More often, the reality was a dark and crowded slum. Yet no slum could screen the world of promise and opportunity that did, indeed, lay beyond this street or that. If there were no golden nuggets to pick off the American pavement, there was plenty of hope. But if the cities of the East and Midwest accepted immigrants, the West and Southwest resisted. Employers in these regions had no scruples against hiring "foreigners," but they didn't want them to enjoy the benefits of citizenship. In the Southwest, migrant labor from Mexico provided a cheap source of temporary farm workers, and, farther north, Asians—especially Chinese—were prized for their efficiency, determination, and endurance. Yet naturalization laws barred them from attaining U.S. citizenship, and, by 1882, anti-Asian prejudice resulted in passage of the first of a series of Chinese Exclusion Acts, which blocked even the temporary immigration of Chinese laborers. As for the Mexican migrants, authorities winked. Big farmers—agribusiness—wanted cheap labor, and federal legislators as well as local authorities were willing to oblige.

As the nineteenth century drew to a close, American authorities recognized the need for a centralized immigration processing facility—a doorway, as it were, to America. Chinese exclusion meant that this portal would not be built on the Pacific coast, but on the Atlantic. In 1890, the United States Bureau of Immigration was created. In New York City, the chief point of immigrant entry was Castle Garden, a disused military fortress at Battery Park, on the southern tip of Manhattan. It was woefully inadequate to handle the immigrant flood, and the new immigration bureau decided to move operations to Ellis Island in upper New York Bay. Named for Samuel Ellis, who owned the island in the 1770s, it had been purchased by the federal government from the state of New York in 1808 for use as an arsenal and fort. The Bureau of Immigration saw it as an ideal immigration facility, a *cordon sanitaire,* separated from the mainland by water, so that immigrants could be received, examined for disease, quarantined if need be, then admitted to the mainland—or deported.

The first of the Ellis Island immigration station buildings was opened on January 1, 1892. During the fifty-two years of its operation, from 1892 to 1943, Ellis Island processed more than 12 million immigrants; during the height of its operation, it sometimes did so at rates of a million people a year.

Explosion of the *Maine* Provokes the Spanish–American War

By the close of the nineteenth century, the people of the Spanish colony of Cuba, just ninety miles off the coast of Florida, hungered for independence from Spain. Sentiment in the United States was mostly friendly to the independence movement. After all, since 1823, with proclamation of the Monroe Doctrine, the United States had regarded itself as the chief steward of the Americas and didn't like the imperial presence of European powers in its hemisphere. Despite popular sentiment, which was whipped up and shaped by leading "yellow journalists," paramountly Joseph Pulitzer and William Randolph Hearst, President Grover Cleveland and his successor, William McKinley, resisted intervening in Cuban affairs. But in February 1896, Spanish general Valeriano Weyler began to take particularly brutal steps to "restore order" in Cuba. He set up "reconcentration camps" for the incarceration of known rebels as well as other citizens accused of supporting or sympathizing with the rebels. Hearst's papers branded the Spanish general "Butcher Weyler," and correspondents reported in graphic detail a host of acts of violent repression.

In the heat of growing war fever, President McKinley ordered the battleship *Maine* into Havana Harbor for the purpose of protecting American citizens and interests there. Those "interests" were not exclusively ideological, but also financial. By the late nineteenth century, great American business concerns had invested heavily in Cuba, especially its highly productive sugar plantations. While revolutionary unrest posed a threat to those investments, the prospect of a *successful* revolution, bringing independence from Spain, was most promising to business. If the United States could ensure the establishment of an independent Cuban government that was nevertheless beholden to the United States and that was inclined to make provisions favorable to business, U.S. investors stood to profit handsomely. To some, even more inviting was the prospect not of an independent Cuba, but of a Cuba formally annexed to the United States.

On February 15, 1898, with war fever running high in the United States, the battleship *Maine* suddenly blew up, with the loss of 266 crewmen.

A naval court of inquiry hurriedly concluded that the ship had struck a Spanish mine. (Modern analysts agree that no such thing happened; the ship's powder magazine spontaneously exploded,

Telegram from Charles Dwight Sigsbee, captain of the U.S.S. *Maine*:

HAVANA, February 15, 1898.

SECRETARY OF THE NAVY,
Washington, D.C.:

Maine blown up in Havana Harbor at 9.40 tonight, and destroyed. Many wounded and doubtless more killed or drowned. Wounded and others on board Spanish man-of-war and Ward Line steamer. Send light-house tenders from Key West for crew and the few pieces of equipment above. No one has clothing other than that upon him. Public opinion should be suspended until further report. All officials believed to be saved. Jenkins and Merritt not yet accounted for. Many Spanish officers, including representatives of General Blanco, now with me to express sympathy.

Sigsbee.

and no hostile action had been involved.) The American people raised the cry of "Remember the *Maine* . . . to hell with Spain!"— a deliberate echo of the battle cry of Texas independence three-quarters of a century earlier: "Remember the Alamo!"

Spain did its best to avert war by accelerating the withdrawal of its troops from Cuba, but the U.S. Congress voted a resolution to recognize, immediately, Cuba's independence. This left Spain no choice. It declared war on the United States on April 24, 1898.

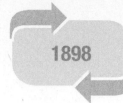

1898

A "Splendid Little War"

The first American military action of the Spanish–American War took place not in Cuba, but in the Spanish-occupied Philippine Islands. At the outbreak of war, Commodore George Dewey sailed the U.S. Asiatic Squadron from Hong Kong to Manila Bay, where, on May 1, he attacked the Spanish fleet and, in a spectacular battle, sank all ten warships in the bay. Following this, 11,000 U.S. troops landed at Manila and, coordinating their operations with the guerrilla forces of Filipino rebel leader Emilio Aguinaldo, rapidly defeated the Spanish army in the islands. In July, Spanish Guam also fell to the United States, which picked up Wake Island as well, at the time claimed by no one—other than the people living there. Congress quickly passed a resolution annexing to the United States the commercially important Hawaiian Islands.

In the meantime, action got under way on Cuba. On May 29, an American naval fleet blockaded and bottled up the Spanish fleet at Santiago Harbor while, in June, 17,000 American soldiers landed at Daiquiri and assaulted Santiago. The war's great make-or-break land battle, at San Juan Hill on July 1, included a magnificent charge up adjacent Kettle Hill by the all-volunteer Rough Riders, led by Theodore Roosevelt, who had resigned as assistant secretary of the navy to accept a colonelcy of the volunteers.

On July 3, after the American victory at San Juan Hill, Spanish admiral Pasqual Cervera decided to run the U.S. naval blockade of Santiago Harbor. After four hours of battle, almost all of Cervera's fleet was at the bottom of the harbor. On July 17, 24,000 Spanish troops surrendered, and Madrid sued for peace nine days later. John Hay, McKinley's secretary of state, summed up the ten-week conflict by calling it a "splendid little war."

The Course of American Imperialism

By the terms of the peace settlement that ended the Spanish–American War in 1898, Spain withdrew from Cuba and ceded to the United States Puerto Rico and Guam. It also sold the Philippines to the United States for $20 million. Immediately, America established a territorial government in Puerto Rico, but it was less sure about what to do with Cuba. In April 1898, Senator Henry M. Teller of Colorado, like many others alarmed by the prospect of unbridled United States imperialism, proposed an amendment to the U.S. declaration of war against Spain. It stipulated that the United States "hereby disclaims any disposition or intention to exercise sovereignty, jurisdiction, or control over said island except for pacification thereof, and asserts its determination, when that is accomplished, to leave the government and control of the island to its people." The United States established a military government on the island "to restore order" while Cubans drafted their own constitution. In the meantime, however, the Teller Amendment was succeeded by the Platt Amendment, introduced by Senator Orville Platt of Connecticut in February 1901. This gave the United States "the right to intervene for the preservation of Cuban independence, the maintenance of a government adequate for the protection of life, property, and individual liberty. . . ." The Platt Amendment was used as the basis by which an "independent" Cuba became a virtual puppet of U.S. interests. This relationship persisted even after the Platt Amendment was abrogated on May 29, 1934, and continued until the 1959 revolution led by Fidel Castro.

As for the Philippines, Aguinaldo proclaimed Filipino independence in defiance of the Treaty of Paris, by which Spain sold the islands to the United States, and a guerrilla war broke out between Filipino freedom fighters and the U.S. army of occupation. Only after World War II would the United States grant the Philippine Islands full and complete independence.

Despite the moral and political conflicts associated with the Spanish–American War and its outcome, the episode established the United States as an emerging world power, a status that U.S. participation in World War I and then World War II would confirm and enlarge in the twentieth century.

1903

Birth of the Movie Industry

Cinema is one of those complex inventions that never really was "invented," at least not at any single moment and by any one person. What was the first movie? We could go back to the shadow plays of fifteenth-century Europe, which used a lantern to project the shadows of puppets and was a technique borrowed from Java via the Middle East. We could go back to various experiments exploiting the persistence of vision phenomenon, most famously the zoetrope, patented almost simultaneously in 1867 in England and the United States, a device that used thirteen slots and thirteen pictures spinning around in a metal cylinder. By varying the number of pictures, figure movement was simulated. Then there was the work of British photographer Eadweard Muybridge, who developed the zoopraxiscope, which combined sequenced still photographs to create a "moving picture" representing the events of specific periods of time. In 1889, using a film base devised by American photography pioneer George Eastman, Thomas A. Edison invented the first movie film. It was not until 1891 that he patented a movie camera to expose the film and 1894 that he came up with the kinetoscope, a means of viewing the developed motion picture.

Edison's kinetoscope was not a projector, but a single-viewer "peep" device. The Lumiere brothers, Auguste and Louis, produced what most film historians consider the first real movie show with the presentation of their Lumiere Cinematographe to a paying audience at the Grand Café in Paris on December 28, 1895. After seeing the Lumiere Cinematographe, another Frenchman, Georges Méliès, magician-owner of the Theatre Robert-Houdin in

Paris, decided to purchase filmmaking equipment and turned out a series of extraordinary short films, including early experiments with color, and at least one film incorporating "special effects," the 1902 *A Trip to the Moon,* which was also the world's first science fiction movie.

Despite the great success of *A Trip to the Moon* and other films, Méliès was soon driven out of business by pirates and swindlers. Thomas Edison did not intend to suffer a similar fate. In 1893, he built the world's first movie studio. Christened the "Black Maria" because it looked like a police paddy wagon, it was an ungainly building on the grounds of his Menlo Park, New Jersey, workshop and could be rotated 360 degrees to take advantage of available sunlight. Here was produced the earliest surviving copyrighted film, *Fred Ott's Sneeze, January 7, 1894,* which was nothing more or less than a portrayal of an Edison employee sneezing. In 1896, the Edison Company began turning out minute-long "shorts" and ten-minute "one-reelers" on a regular basis.

In 1903, Edwin S. Porter, a former Edison Company cameraman, directed for the Edison Company *The Great Train Robbery,* a ten-minute, fourteen-scene "epic" that was advertised as "a faithful duplication of the genuine 'Hold Ups' made famous by various outlaw bands in the far West." In fact, the plot was inspired by a real event, which occurred on August 29, 1900, when four members of Butch Cassidy's famed Hole-in-the-Wall gang stopped the Union Pacific's No. 3 on its way to Table Rock, Wyoming. The robbers forced the conductor to uncouple the passenger cars from the rest of the train and then blew up the safe in the mail car. They made off with some $5,000 in cash.

To tell the story, Porter introduced innovative techniques that would become cornerstones of filmmaking, including parallel editing—cuts that show chronologically parallel as well as overlapping action, minor camera movement for added realism, and shooting on loca-

The Great Train Robbery can be viewed online, for free, at memory.loc.gov/ammem/edhtml/gtr.html.

tion (parts of New Jersey made to look like the Wild West). Editing was complex and exciting, and, for the first time in movie history, the camera was allowed to pan.

The Great Train Robbery was tremendously successful. Movies became the poor man's theater, then quickly evolved into the first truly mass medium, not only entertaining America, but helping the nation, as the preeminent exporter of movies, to become an international cultural capital.

Invention of the Airplane

Before the end of the eighteenth century, people were flying in hot-air balloons, but the true dream of flight had always been to emulate the birds—not just to float in air, but to soar, at will, swiftly, and in whatever direction one chose. Gliding dates back to at least the year 1000, when a Benedictine monk named Elmer of Malmesbury launched himself from the tower of Malmesbury Abbey, England, and soared for some 600 feet before crashing to Earth and breaking both legs. Some 900 years later, in 1892, the two sons of a bishop—this one of the Church of the United Brethren of Christ—started making and selling bicycles in Dayton, Ohio. The "Bishop's boys," as townspeople called them, made a fine living from their shop, with plenty of money left over to finance what soon became their real passion: aeronautics. In 1896, the Bishop's boys—Wilbur and Orville Wright—avidly read an account of the death of Otto Lilienthal, a German builder of gliders, who had been killed in the crash of one of his own machines. From this point on, they bought every aeronautical book and magazine they could find. By 1899, when they had completed their first man-carrying biplane kite, they had already methodically consulted the Weather Bureau—precursor of today's National Weather Service—to determine the best location for testing flying machines. Following the bureau's advice, the Wrights took their aircraft to the beach at Kitty Hawk, North Carolina. Here they perfected the most efficient manned gliders ever produced to that time. Then, in December 1903, they fitted a 170-pound, twelve-horsepower gasoline-fueled motor to a 750-pound gossamer craft fashioned of fabric and wood. On the morning of December 17, the boys flipped a coin. When it came up heads, Orville, without further discussion, assumed his position at the controls. It was not a seat in a cockpit, for there was no seat and there was no cockpit. Orville Wright lay on his belly across the bottom wing, the engine coughed into life, and the aircraft rolled down a rail track the Wrights and a handful of assistants had laid on the sand. It took off and flew for twelve seconds, over a distance of about 120 feet.

That first day, the Wrights made three more flights, Wilbur managing to keep the aircraft aloft for almost a minute and over a distance of 852 feet. Then they returned quietly to Dayton, where they continued their experiments at Huffman Prairie, a local cow pasture, until, by 1905, they had achieved a flight of thirty-eight minutes' duration over a distance of twenty-four miles. Securing necessary patents in 1906, they toured a flabbergasted world during 1908–1909, the year in which they began manufacturing aircraft commercially. Just more than 900 years had passed since the flight and crash landing of Elmer of Malmesbury. Sixty-six years after Kitty Hawk, three Americans would fly to the moon, and two would walk on it.

> "Success. Four flights Thursday morning. . . . Inform press. Home Christmas." —Orville and Wilbur Wright, telegram to their father

1908

The Model T

Henry Ford was born on a Dearborn, Michigan, farm, but it was machines, not crops, that interested the boy, who soon apprenticed himself to the owner of a machine shop. After working as an itinerant farm-machinery repairman and a sawmill operator, Ford became chief engineer for the brand-new Edison Illuminating Company generating station in Detroit.

Electricity wasn't the only cutting-edge technology that intrigued Ford. "Horseless carriages" had started to appear on the streets of a few cities, and Ford tinkered together his first automobile in 1896. He went to work for a builder of custom-made cars, then designed and built a racer—the 999, capable of an astounding sixty miles per hour—and, at last, organized the Ford Motor Company in 1903.

By the beginning of the twentieth century, there were hundreds of small automobile manufacturers in the United States. At first, Ford's company was no different from these. But, in 1908, he hit on something to set his operation apart. Cars were expensive, hand built for the wealthy. Ford saw that the materials were not costly, but the skilled labor to fashion them into an automobile was. He set about designing a car that could be mass produced, and he created the assembly line to mass produce it.

The car was the Model T, which, in 1908, sold for $850, cheaper than any custom-built car, but still more expensive than most people could afford. Between 1908 and 1913, Ford perfected his assembly line, thoroughly breaking down, streamlining, and standardizing the production process. In 1908, he manufactured 10,607 cars. By 1916, when the assembly line was in full swing, he turned out 730,041, not priced at $850, but at $360—within the reach of the average American.

The Model T gave its owner unprecedented freedom and mobility. It triggered a demand for roads, which, in a remarkably short time, stitched the nation together as never before. It promoted as well the suburbanization of America, for the most part greatly improving the quality of life available to the average man and woman. Equally profound was the effect of the assembly line, which, for better or worse, forever changed the relationship between labor and management and, indeed, changed the nature of labor itself.

The NAACP Is Founded

Booker T. Washington, founder of the Tuskegee Institute in Alabama, and, at the end of the nineteenth century, America's most famous African-American leader, was not a fighter for civil rights or social equality. He advocated setting such issues aside and instead focusing black energy on achieving economic self-determination in the belief that, as this was achieved, social equality would follow. Washington's "gradualism" appalled many more progressive African Americans, and to hasten the process of racial equality, in 1909, a group of New York–based intellectuals and social activists—black as well as white—decided to create an organization to counter gradualism. They called it the National Association for the Advancement of Colored People (NAACP) and used it as a platform for public lectures, political lobbying, and popular social publishing. Its most effective organ, a magazine called *The Crisis,* was edited for many years by the distinguished writer, sociologist, and historian W.E.B. DuBois, the nation's first African-American Ph.D., with degrees from Fisk University, Harvard, and the University of Berlin.

The NAACP used its public programs and publications to raise the social consciousness of blacks as well as whites, to make them aware that there were alternatives to passive patience and gradual change. Added to its outreach and educational programs were well-financed and carefully planned legal efforts aimed at testing and ultimately overturning in the nation's courts discriminatory state and local legislation. By 1920 the NAACP claimed 90,000 members, nearly half of whom were southerners, and it was clear that this organization was the leading voice of African-American social progressivism.

Income Tax Enacted

I n February 1913, after ratification by the states, the Sixteenth Amendment gave the federal government the authority to levy taxes on personal income. In principle, there was nothing new about an income tax. The Old Testament speaks of tithing, the payment to the state of the tenth part of what one earns, and the U.S. government enacted a temporary income tax—from 3 to 5 percent—during the Civil War, beginning in 1862. Even earlier, back in 1812, when the government needed cash to finance the War of 1812, the Treasury Department thought seriously of adopting what was then the new British practice of taxing income, a tax Parliament used to finance the seemingly ceaseless Napoleonic Wars.

The first U.S. income tax was repealed after the Civil War, but the agency that had administered it, the Internal Revenue Service, remained in existence, and in 1894 Congress enacted the tax again. It was a popular measure, urged by the nation's farmers and urban laborers, who believed that the wealthy should pay more in taxes than the ordinary working man. Tested in the Supreme Court the following year in *Pollock* v. *Farmer's Loan & Trust Co.*, however, the 1894 income tax was ruled unconstitutional.

It was now clear to progressive reformers that public sentiment was high for the income tax and that the only way around the constitutional roadblock was to amend the Constitution. Progressive political thinkers were sufficiently alarmed by the concentration of wealth among a coterie of industrialists to prompt them to form an unlikely alliance with arch conservatives, who were always looking for a dependable way to raise money for national emergencies. This unique progressive–conservative coalition pushed the legislation through Congress and into the hands of the states for ratification.

The demands of the federal income tax began modestly enough. The law laid claim to 1 percent of taxable income above $3,000 for individuals or $4,000 for married couples. The rate was *graduated and progressive,* rising with income level. It hit its maximum—7 percent—for those with annual incomes in excess of $500,000. War brought a dramatic increase in the income tax. At the height of United States involvement in World War I, rates on the top income bracket temporarily shot up to 77 percent. With the Great Depression, the high-end rates increased sharply again, and when World War II bound federal revenue to national survival, the top rate reached a stratospheric 91 percent. Over the years, the tax code has been patched, shored, plugged, and punched through with a stupefying array of deductions, credits, subsidies, and exemptions. It is now the most complex body of public law ever enacted, and while most people agree (however reluctantly) that the income tax has become essential to financing the nation, there is absolutely no doubt about its effectiveness in having financed a multibillion-dollar tax-accounting industry.

1917

The Zimmermann Telegram

Woodrow Wilson was elected president of the United States in 1912 on a promise to improve government and to lead Americans to better lives. His many progressive reforms came swiftly and proved remarkably successful. Less than two years into his first term, on June 28, 1914, the assassination of the Austro-Hungarian Archduke Franz Ferdinand and his wife, the Grand Duchess Sophie, in Sarajevo, propelled Europe and the colonial empires associated with it into the bloodiest war fought on Earth up to that time. Initially, the German armies made a spectacular drive through France, sweeping all resistance before them. On the Eastern Front, the Germans and Austro-Hungarians held off, then repeatedly defeated the armies of mighty Russia. But after a month of ceaseless advance in the west, the German commander in chief was seized by a spasm of strategic uncertainty. He turned his southern forces, then dug in less than thirty miles outside of Paris. France was saved—or, at least, reprieved—and for the next four years, the flower of Europe's young manhood slaughtered each other along opposing lines of static trench works extending from the English Channel coast in the north to the Swiss border in the south.

Early in the war, most Americans were thankful that President Wilson managed to keep the United States neutral. In February 1915, he did warn Germany—whose U-boats glided under the Atlantic, targeting mostly British merchant and passenger vessels—that the United States would hold it strictly accountable for the loss of American lives in the sinking of neutral or passenger ships. Just four months later, on May 7, 1915, a U-boat torpedoed the

British passenger liner *Lusitania,* killing 1,200 people, including 128 Americans. This outrage elicited from many in America a clamor for war, but Wilson stayed the neutral course, and, in 1916, was reelected in large part on the strength of the campaign slogan, "He Kept Us Out of War!"

The *Lusitania* sinking brought United States diplomatic pressure on Germany to end unrestricted submarine warfare. The German kaiser yielded and ordered all U-boats to surface and warn passenger liners before attacking them, so that passengers and crew might abandon ship. Nevertheless, relations between the United States and Germany continued to deteriorate until, in February 1917, with the situation increasingly desperate on the Western Front, Germany announced the resumption of unrestricted submarine warfare—attack by submerged U-boats and without warning. Almost immediately, on February 3, the U.S.S. *Housatonic* was torpedoed and sunk. President Wilson responded by severing diplomatic relations with Germany. The next month, on March 1, the American public learned of the "Zimmermann Telegram," a coded message sent on January 19, 1917, from German foreign secretary Arthur Zimmermann to his nation's ambassador to Mexico outlining the terms of a proposed German–Mexican alliance against the United States. Publication of the telegram left little public sentiment for continued neutrality, and, on April 2, 1917, Woodrow Wilson asked Congress for a declaration of war. It was voted up on April 6.

1917

The United States Mobilizes for War

President Wilson made it clear that America's entry into the "Great War" was not merely in retaliation for violations of U.S. neutrality, but "to make the world safe for democracy." With this statement, the president elevated the United States to the status of a world power. The U.S. Navy was already a reasonably formidable force, but the U.S. Army was downright puny. It numbered only about 200,000 men in 1917. Wilson led a spectacular mobilization that, by the end of the war in November 1918, would swell the army to four million men. The president directed the creation of a welter of war agencies, which essentially put private industry entirely under government control. He pushed through Congress, in May 1917, a Selective Service bill, by which 2.8 million men were drafted. In command of the AEF (Allied Expeditionary Force) was the highly capable General John J. Pershing. The navy sailed under the command of Admiral William S. Sims.

Pershing's arrival in Paris on June 14, 1917, with nothing more than a small staff, came at the nadir of Allied fortunes. One after the other, each major Anglo–French offensive had failed. Thoroughly demoralized, much of the French army mutinied. On the Eastern Front, the giant Russian army had folded, and the broken nation was tumbling headlong into a revolution that would end centuries of czarist rule, introduce communism into the world, and take Russia out of the war, instantly freeing up masses of German troops for service on the Western Front.

Despite the rapid pace of American mobilization, it would be October 21, 1917, before U.S. strength in Europe was sufficient to commit even a few units to battle. Not until the spring of 1918 did large masses of Americans make a significant impact on the fighting. But before he could even begin to command his forces against the Germans, Pershing found himself at war with his French and British allies, who demanded that U.S. troops be placed under their control. Wilson backed Pershing's resistance to this, and the American general retained full authority over U.S. troops. At home, Wilson conducted a campaign of his own, creating a powerful propaganda machine to generate tremendous support for what was, after all, a "foreign war." In instances where propaganda failed, the Wilson government used emergency war powers to censor the press and to silence critics. All of this contributed to the patriotic pressure put on America's young men, who enlisted in great numbers. Those who failed to enlist or, even worse, sought to avoid the draft, were branded as "slackers" and subjected to public humiliation. American idealism and democratic ideals were bolstered by commercially slick propaganda and repressive laws.

World War I: The American Battle Record

The American Expeditionary Force was not committed to battle in truly large numbers until June 1918, but once it was in the war, it fought exceedingly well, with great gallantry, and at a terrible cost in life. Between June 6 and July 1, 1918, the "Yanks" recaptured for the allies Vaux, Bouresches, and, after a hellish struggle, Belleau Wood, while also managing to hold the key Allied position at Cantigny against a crushing German offensive launched between June 9 and June 15.

As the spring of 1918 became summer, during July 18–August 6, 85,000 Americans ended the endless Western Front stalemate by defeating the Germans' last major offensive at the Second Battle of the Marne. This was followed throughout August by a series of Allied offensives—at the Somme, Oise-Aisne, and Ypres-Lys—in which U.S. troops played important roles.

In one great offensive, against the St. Mihiel salient during September 12–16, the Americans acted independently in a deployment of some 1.2 million men against the German supply lines between the

It was called the "Great War," and it was bigger and more terrible than any war that had come before it. A total of 65 million men and women served in the armies and navies of combatant nations during World War I. Of this number, at least 10 million were killed and 20 million wounded. Of the 2 million U.S. troops actually committed to combat, 112,432 died, and 230,074 were wounded. In monetary terms, the war cost the United States the equivalent of $32,700,000,000 in current dollars.

Meuse River and the Argonne Forest. The campaign, which continued until the very day of armistice, November 11, 1918, was both highly successful and terribly costly.

As it became apparent to Germany that American troops not only fought fiercely and well, but were available in seemingly inexhaustible numbers, pouring out of a nation that also ground out the weapons and matériel of war, the German government agreed to an armistice, which was set for the eleventh hour of the eleventh day of the eleventh month of 1918.

The Treaty of Versailles and the League of Nations

World War I had cost America dearly, but it also gave the nation new prestige as a great world power. This was enhanced by the leadership role President Woodrow Wilson took in hammering out the peace in what he hoped would be a "war to end all wars." Tragically, the other three of the "Big Four"—as the heads of state of Great Britain, France, Italy, and the United States were called—were less interested in creating a new world of universal peace than in claiming immediate vengeance on Germany and disabling it from ever threatening the West again. Despite Wilson's valiant efforts, the Treaty of Versailles emerged as a relentlessly punitive document that, far from bringing world peace, created in Germany the desperate climate that, within a few years, produced Hitler and Nazi militarism.

As disappointed as Wilson was with most of the Treaty of Versailles, he believed he had triumphed in integrating into it the League of Nations, which he had reason to believe would become a credible force for preventing war. But Wilson, negotiating in Europe, was out of touch with the postwar temper of his own nation. The last thing most Americans wanted was further involvement with Europe and its destructive problems. When isolationist Republicans, led by Senator Henry Cabot Lodge, chairman of the Foreign Relations Committee, blocked United States participation in the League of Nations, Wilson, home again, decided to take his appeal directly to the American people. Despite his profound exhaustion, he embarked on a speaking tour of the West, only to collapse after a speech at Pueblo, Colorado, on September 25, 1919.

This was followed by a debilitating stroke after he returned to Washington, and, while he was incapacitated, chances for Senate approval of the League of Nations died. Confirming the nation's new mood of isolationism, the bland Warren G. Harding was elected to the presidency in 1920 and promised Americans nothing more or less than a "return to normalcy." The League, he announced, was "not for us." With that, the nation turned its back on developments in Europe, blithely ignoring the conditions and acts that, within two decades of the "war to end all wars," would produce a second world war.

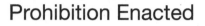

1919

Prohibition Enacted

When the Eighteenth Amendment was passed by Congress on December 18, 1917 and ratified by two-thirds of the states on January 29, 1919, America was more than ripe for Prohibition. Typical of constitutional amendments, the language was brief and straightforward, its principal article stating, "After one year from the ratification of this article the manufacture, sale, or transportation of intoxicating liquors within, the importation thereof into, or the exportation thereof from the United States and all territory subject to the jurisdiction thereof for beverage purposes is hereby prohibited." The background history of Prohibition was, however, long, and its implications profound.

In the years leading up to the Civil War, the rural United States was swept by fundamentalist Christian religion that spawned a "Temperance Movement," which campaigned so successfully against the manufacture and sale of liquor that, by 1855, thirteen of thirty-three states had voted themselves dry. After the Civil War, the Woman's Christian Temperance Union and, in 1895, the Anti-Saloon League became increasingly powerful lobby organizations on local, state, and federal levels. Candidates for virtually every office were obliged to declare themselves "wet" or "dry" and, often, voters made their choices solely on this distinction. By 1916, twenty-one states outlawed saloons, and voters across the country, but principally in rural states, sent a dry majority to Congress. It was this majority that enacted the Eighteenth Amendment, passing it over the veto of Woodrow Wilson, who feared that Prohibition could never be enforced and would, in his words, create "a nation of lawbreakers."

And so it did.

At first, there was a kind of innocence about it all. Urban folk never wanted Prohibition, and now that they had it, they brewed up moonshine, bathtub gin, wine, and beer at home, often in the seclusion of their cellars. It was also not a very difficult matter to smuggle liquor across the borders with Canada or Mexico. Soon, neighborhood people started making or importing—bootlegging, it was called—the stuff for friends and neighbors and, later, for distribution by neighborhood restaurants, drug stores, and former saloon keepers. As for the cop on the beat, alienating the neighborhood by making a raid or an arrest just wasn't worth the trouble. And if he *was* inclined to enforce the law, a few dollars—or bottles—were usually sufficient to generate benign neglect.

Increasingly, however, people turned to professional criminals to slake their thirst. The immigrant experience in the United States was typically a hard road, and streetwise second-generation immigrants were always on the lookout for a shortcut. Crime held allure as the shortest cut of all. Moreover, often excluded from mainstream American society, ethnic immigrants found the fellowship and society they needed in *organized* crime, including the Irish gangs that sprang up in New York and other cities and the Italian Mafia, which, transplanted from its Sicilian seedbed, took root on American shores late in the nineteenth century. Prohibition, an opportunity to turn crime into big business by controlling the supply and distribution of an illegal substance much in demand, brought the American Mafia into full bloom. Far from producing a nation of hardworking, sober, reverent citizens, Prohibition created organized crime, which, in many cities, came to figure as a shadow government and terrorized, drained, and plagued the nation for decades to come—long after Prohibition was repealed by the Twenty-First Amendment, passed on February 20, 1933, and ratified on December 5 of that year.

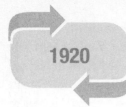

1920

Women Get the Vote

Back in 1777, New Jersey, embroiled in the American Revolution, made a mistake in drafting its voting law. The statute specified that all "individuals" worth fifty pounds or more could vote. So, New Jersey *women* who met the fifty-pound criteria voted in 1777, and they were the only women who voted in the United States of America. Assuming the matter of gender was self-evident, New Jersey lawmakers failed to specify the word *men* when they drew up the law. The embarrassing oversight was soon corrected, and the loophole plugged. It was not until 1848, with the Seneca Falls Conference, that the organized women's suffrage movement began.

Before the Civil War, the women's suffrage movement was closely tied to the abolition movement. But, after the war, women suffragists became divided over whether or not to bind the campaign for women's right to vote with the campaign to ensure the enfranchisement of former slaves. Elizabeth Cady Stanton and women's rights activist Susan B. Anthony fought hard for constitutional amendments that would enfranchise both blacks and women, and Lucretia Mott was elected chair of an Equal Rights Association. But when the Fourteenth and Fifteenth Amendments, extending the vote to black men, failed to address women's rights, Stanton and Anthony broke with Mott's group to form the National Woman Suffrage Association, which opposed the Fifteenth Amendment because it enfranchised slaves, but not women. Yet another splinter group, the American Woman Suffrage Association, supported the Fifteenth Amendment as a necessary first step in the broadening of voting rights.

The fragmentation of the women's suffrage movement slowed progress on the issue until, in 1890, the National Woman Suffrage Association and the American Woman Suffrage Association merged under the leadership of Anna Howard Shaw and Carrie Chapman Catt to become the National American Woman Suffrage Association. It was this group that made the final, long push toward getting the vote for women. Under unrelenting political pressure, individual states began to give women the vote—in nonfederal elections. Wyoming was the first, in 1890, and several other western states followed suit. Nationally, Theodore Roosevelt's Progressive ("Bull Moose") Party endorsed women's suffrage in 1912, and, during World War I, President Woodrow Wilson endorsed a constitutional amendment granting women the right to vote as what he called "a vitally necessary war measure," for so many adult males were away at war.

With such a broad base of support, the Nineteenth Amendment was passed by Congress on June 4, 1919, and ratified by the states on August 18, 1920. Its principal clause, so long and difficult in coming to birth, could not have been simpler: "The right of citizens of the United States to vote shall not be denied or abridged by the United States or any State on account of sex."

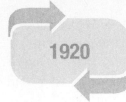
1920

Birth of Commercial Broadcast Radio

The basic radio had been developed at the end of the nineteenth century by the Irish-Italian Guglielmo Marconi, but it was an American, Reginald Fessenden, who invented the first practical radio voice transmitter in 1906 and another American, Lee De Forest, who developed the vacuum tube, the heart of pre-transistor electronics. De Forest made a few stabs at broadcasting musical programming between 1907 and 1909, but it wasn't until November 2, 1920, that Pittsburgh's KDKA broadcast returns from the presidential election, thereby inaugurating the first regular commercial broadcasting. Over the next three years, 556 commercial radio stations went into operation nationwide, and by the end of the decade, radio had become a genuine mass medium, a viable alternative to newspapers and magazines for the mass dissemination of entertainment and information.

1923–1982

The Equal Rights Amendment

For the most part, the campaign for women's suffrage worked within the system: by lobbying, by selectively supporting candidates for elective office, and by generally raising public consciousness. At the radical fringe, however, was the Congressional Union's National Woman's Party, organized by Alice Paul, a University of Pennsylvania Ph.D. and Quaker activist. Paul, a militant advocate of women's suffrage and women's rights, was jailed three times in England and three times in the United States. In prison, she waged a hunger strike, was pronounced insane, and force-fed. Her followers picketed, also staged hunger strikes, and engaged in other forms of civil disobedience to support passage of a constitutional amendment that would not only give women the right to vote, but would explicitly confer on them equal rights with men.

The Equal Rights Amendment

Section 1. Equality of rights under the law shall not be denied or abridged by the United States or by any State on account of sex.

Section 2. The Congress shall have the power to enforce, by appropriate legislation, the provisions of this article.

Section 3. This amendment shall take effect two years after the date of ratification.

Paul drew up what she called the Equal Rights Amendment, which, even after women were granted the right to vote by the Nineteenth Amendment, languished for decades in Congress. When finally passed in the 1970s, the amendment failed to achieve ratification by the requisite two-thirds majority of states. An extension of the ratification deadline was given, but "ERA" died in 1982. The amendment was reintroduced during the 107th Congress (2001–2002), but has yet to gain passage.

1927

Lindbergh Flies the Atlantic

By 1927, the airplane had come a long way since the Wright brothers' first flight at Kitty Hawk, North Carolina, in 1903. Nevertheless, through the early 1920s, most people still regarded flying as something for daredevils and certainly not as an alternative to the train or the ship. Charles Augustus Lindbergh—University of Minnesota dropout; son of a Minnesota congressman; one-time stunt flier; former second lieutenant in the 110th Observation Squadron, 35th Division, Missouri National Guard; and sometime airmail pilot—loved the thrill of flight, but, even more, was determined to bring flying into the mainstream. When hotel owner Raymond Orteig put up a $25,000 prize—to be awarded to the first person or persons who crossed the Atlantic by plane, nonstop, between New York and Paris—Lindbergh saw an opportunity to demonstrate the potential of transoceanic flight.

Armed with the prospect of the Orteig prize, Lindbergh persuaded a group of St. Louis businessmen to finance construction of a suitable aircraft. Lindbergh researched several models before he commissioned the Ryan Aeronautical Company of San Diego, California, to customize a single-engine airplane especially for the flight. More cautious aviators would have chosen a twin-engine plane for the hazardous crossing. In case one engine failed, the pilot could reach land and bring the plane down on the other. But a twin-engine plane burned more fuel than a single-engine craft, and it generally required a two-man crew. Lindbergh wanted to save fuel, and he wanted to fly with the only person whose aviation skills he thoroughly trusted: himself. So the Ryan aircraft, christened *The Spirit of St. Louis,* was designed as a kind of flying fuel tank, with a single, large engine. Lindbergh even put a fuel tank in front of the cockpit, where, ordinarily, the windshield would be. He reasoned that he would encounter no obstacles over the water, that fuel was more important than a continuous straight-ahead view, and if he needed to see what was in front of him, he could poke his head out the window or use a small built-in periscope. The plane cost $10,580.

The 1920s loved daring deeds, and all eyes were focused on the tall, unassuming, boyishly handsome Lindbergh, dubbed by all the papers "The Lone Eagle." There was a very good chance that he'd go the way of earlier competitors for the Orteig prize. They crashed and burned or simply disappeared.

The night before his takeoff, from Long Island's Roosevelt Field (today the site of a shopping mall), the incessant clatter of reporters' typewriters kept Lindbergh awake. He had had almost no sleep when, at 7:52 on the morning of May 20, 1927, he began to roll down an unpaved airstrip turned to mud by a night of heavy rain. Lindbergh had stripped the plane of all unnecessary weight. "Unnecessary," as he saw it, included a parachute. Lindbergh reasoned that one would do him little good over the icy Atlantic anyway. However, loaded with fuel and mired in the mud, the stripped-down *Spirit of St. Louis* barely cleared the treetops at the end of the field.

For the next thirty-three hours twenty-nine minutes, an already sleep-deprived Lone Eagle battled fatigue, the elements, and the vagaries of dead-reckoning navigation as he made his way, alone, across the ocean.

On May 21, when he touched down at Le Bourget Field outside of Paris at 10:22 P.M. (local time), a groggy but elated Lindbergh was overwhelmed by the reception he was accorded. Thousands thronged him in Paris, and later, back home as well, in all the major cities of the United States. He was elevated to a heroic status that recalled, if anything, the champions of ancient Greece. Lindbergh, it seemed, had not only defied death, but had annihilated time and nullified distance. If those who acclaimed young Lindbergh envied his eagle-like freedom, they also felt that his feat had won a part of that freedom for everyone. In economic terms, Lindbergh's transatlantic flight raised a groundswell of commercial interest in aviation. In less than a dozen years, airlines inaugurated regularly scheduled transatlantic service, and life itself was, quite simply, transformed.

1929

The Stock Market Crash

The roar of the "Roaring Twenties" was not fueled exclusively by bootleg liquor, but also by money or, more precisely, by spending. During the decade, many Americans had a go-for-broke attitude and speculated in stocks in unprecedented numbers, frequently overextending themselves by purchasing securities "on margin," putting down as little as ten cents on the dollar in the hope that the stock price would rise fast and far enough to cover loans few could truly afford. So much stock was bought on margin—backed by dimes, not dollars—that much of it amounted to little more than paper. Well-financed industries poured cash into production, machinery, and plants to turn out more and more products that, however, were priced beyond the means of most consumers. Goods piled up and the prices fell, and industry laid off workers. If people with average incomes couldn't afford many of the goods being produced in profusion, people without incomes could afford even less. The marketplace continued to shrink, and as that happened, companies found themselves unable to make new hires. And this represented just the industrial sector of the economy. Long before the vicious cycle of increased production and reduced demand began, farmers were suffering from chronically low farm prices and high transportation costs.

There were warning signs of instability during the autumn of 1929, one of the most obvious being wildly fluctuating stock prices. On October 24, the market was caught up in a selling spree, which culminated five days later, on October 29. It was called "Black Tuesday," the day the bottom fell out.

Prices disintegrated. Value evaporated. Brokers "called" their margin loans, demanding immediate payment in full on loans used to purchase stocks that were now worthless. The investors didn't have the money. Many were ruined. The brokers collected the stocks—collateral for the margin loans they had made—but who was there to buy them? So brokers and brokerages went belly up, too.

On Black Tuesday, stocks lost an average of 40 points. This was at a time when the Dow-Jones Industrial Average peaked at 380. By the close of business on October 29, 1929, the Dow was at 230. In 1930, 1,300 banks failed. By 1933, another 3,700 would fail, and one out of four workers was jobless.

The "Bonus Army" Marches on Washington

Herbert Hoover had been elected president in 1928, when most Americans felt good about the economy and were pleased with the hands-off-business approach taken by government under Hoover's predecessor Calvin Coolidge. Known as "Silent Cal," Coolidge was notoriously tight-lipped, but he is remembered for having declared, "The business of America is business." And now, as the nation descended into economic depression, his fellow Republican, Hoover, came across as stunned and as fearful as his fellow Americans, assuring them unconvincingly that "prosperity was just around the corner."

Hoover did propose a number of relief programs, but he steadfastly insisted that it was up to the states and local governments to finance and administer them. In principle, this was prudent, but Hoover's policy was doomed for the very simple reason that state and local governments had no money. Hoover, who had made his reputation as a great humanitarian, brilliantly administering international relief efforts following the devastation of Europe after World War I, also cleaved to the steadfast belief that federal aid must not be given directly to individuals. Big-government intervention in private lives, he feared, would compromise the liberty, integrity, and initiative of the individual citizen.

The policies of Herbert Hoover were not callous, but they were ineffectual. Shantytowns constructed of boxes and crates bloomed like evil flowers across the American landscape to house the jobless and homeless. They were called "Hoovervilles," and the desperation they housed bred something approaching revolution. Already, revolutionary unrest had swept much of the world (for this depression was worldwide), especially Germany, badly crippled by the punitive Treaty of Versailles. In Italy and Germany, totalitarian government—fascism in Italy, National Socialism, and Nazism in Germany—offered some hope for recovery. Most Americans clung to democracy, but democracy was not putting beans on the table, and among intellectuals and some radical working men and women, communism seemed to offer a viable alternative.

How close did the United States come to revolution? One indication was the fate of the "Bonus Army" in 1932. Veterans of World War I were entitled by law to a cash payment, a so-called "bonus," payable in 1945. With conditions desperate in 1932, however, a movement arose to secure immediate payment of the bonuses. In May 1932, some 15,000 to 20,000 unemployed veterans marched on Washington in an effort to compel Congress to release their bonuses. This "Bonus Army" camped in the city and just outside it, at Anacostia Flats, Maryland. The House of Representatives took notice and did pass a bonus bill on June 15, only to have it voted down by the more conservative Senate. By the time this happened, the marchers' makeshift camp had grown into a sprawling "Hooverville" of crates, shacks, and shanties. When rioting broke out on July 28, President Hoover ordered General Douglas MacArthur to clear Pennsylvania Avenue of demonstrators. Although he also ordered MacArthur *not* to cross into Anacostia Flats, the general did just that, advancing against the unarmed Bonus Army—which included women and children—with units of cavalry, infantry, and armor, and making liberal use of tear gas and the flat of cavalry officers' sabers.

The assault on the Bonus Army was a national disgrace, and President Hoover, whipped by a storm of protest, managed to make matters worse by calling the Bonus Army nothing more than a "pack of criminals." Of what, the nation asked in response, were they guilty? Poverty? Joblessness? Despair?

Fortunately for the American democracy, 1932 was an election year. The people had available to them the same opportunity for revolution that had been available every four years since the election of George Washington. They could vote in a whole new government. And that is what they did.

FDR Is Elected on the Promise of a "New Deal"

I n 1921, the career of a promising young New York politician, Franklin Delano Roosevelt, seemed to have been ended by a crippling attack of polio, but, with buoyant optimism and smiling determination, FDR refused to give up, became the dynamic governor of New York, and in 1932 was elected president of the United States, earning 22.8 million votes to Herbert Hoover's 15.8 million.

He had promised the Depression-burdened nation a "New Deal," and in the first "Hundred Days" of his administration ushered through Congress radical and sweeping legislation aimed at relieving suffering, and at transforming the economic policies of the United States. New Deal measures included a Federal Deposit Insurance Corporation and tight federal regulation to prevent the devastation of bank failures; a Home Owners' Loan Corporation to help Americans buy—and keep—their homes; a Federal Securities Act to curb the kinds of careless activities that had contributed to the stock market crash of 1929; and a host of federally subsidized employment programs to give Americans jobs.

The New Deal introduced unprecedented government regulation of private enterprise, including aid to industry and price controls on the products produced. The federal government forged a close alliance with business through the National Industrial Recovery Act, which also protected the rights of labor and guaranteed collective bargaining. Farmers were the particular focus of FDR's New Deal. Programs subsidized farm prices and helped farmers secure credit. Great public works—most notably Boulder (now Hoover) Dam—harnessed the forces of nature itself to irrigate arid lands and to furnish raw power in the form of electricity.

But, most of all, there was the presence of Roosevelt himself. His courage, his vision, and his ability to communicate confidence and hope worked political magic in sustaining the nation through the worst economic crisis in its history. "We have nothing to fear," he declared in his first inaugural address, "but fear itself." And most Americans proved willing to take him at his word.

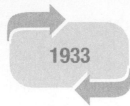
1933

World's First Television Broadcast

A s with motion pictures, the technology of television is so complex that we can't point to any one person as the "inventor" of TV. But if any individual comes close, it's Vladimir Zworykin, a Russian immigrant who, while working as an electrical engineer for Westinghouse, invented the "iconoscope" in 1924. A specially treated vacuum tube, the iconoscope transformed light into electrical impulses and electrical impulses back into light—in the form of an image projected electronically onto a phosphor-coated screen. Because it was capable of a two-way transformation—light to electricity, electricity to light—the iconoscope became the basis for the television camera as well as the familiar TV "picture tube," the heart of the television set.

Although technicians and scientists were excited by the iconoscope, it found no immediate commercial application. While working at RCA Laboratories in the 1930s, Zworykin developed the iconoscope into a genuine television system and, in 1933, demonstrated his invention by transmitting a television picture from New York to Philadelphia—the world's first TV broadcast.

And yet Zworykin hardly became a household name. No one—none of the great radio networks and not even RCA—leaped at the revolutionary technology. Half a dozen years crawled by before the first *public* television broadcast was made: In 1939, NBC aired live video of President Franklin D. Roosevelt addressing the nation as he opened the New York World's Fair. The broadcast caused a stir, including predictions that a great new medium had been born, but the sudden onset of World War II diverted most of America's technological effort to the war. Television, destined to revolutionize civilized life, had to be put on hold.

1940

The Mark I Computer

IBM, the International Business Machine corporation, a leading manufacturer of calculating machines since 1924, joined forces with a team from Harvard University to create the Mark I, an electro-mechanical device that is generally acknowledged as the world's first genuinely programmable computer. The Mark I saw service during World War II as a device capable of making intensely complex calculations of the speed and trajectory of artillery shells.

Mark I was a gargantuan machine, eight feet high and fifty feet long. It was rendered obsolete in 1946 by ENIAC, which replaced all mechanical parts with vacuum tubes and was therefore the first fully electronic computer. Like Mark I, however, it was enormous: 3,000 cubic feet in volume, thirty tons in weight, and equipped with 18,000 vacuum tubes, which had to be changed almost continually.

Together, Mark I and ENIAC ushered in the electronic age, in which computers would become increasingly powerful and would play an ever larger role in daily life. By the 1970s and 1980s, with the advent of integrated circuits, miniaturization reduced the enormous volume of these early machines to a size that could be set upon a desk. The "personal computer," especially linked to the Internet, redefined computing and extended its reach into virtually every American life.

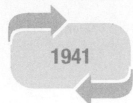

1941

Attack on Pearl Harbor

The United States remained neutral as a volatile situation developed in Europe, with Nazi Germany and fascist Italy hammering out the Rome–Berlin Axis in 1936 and the Empire of Japan concluding an alliance with Germany the same year. In 1938, Adolf Hitler annexed Austria to his Third Reich and then carved the Sudetenland out of Czechoslovakia, followed by all of Czechoslovakia and a part of Lithuania. Germany's military actions went unopposed in Europe, until on September 1, 1939, it invaded Poland. England and France declared war and World War II had begun.

American attention was nervously focused on Europe while Japan, having violated a 1922 international agreement, established the puppet state of Manchuko in Manchuria in 1932 and, by 1937, was engaged in a full-scale war of aggression against China. On September 27, 1940, Japan signed the Tripartite Pact with Italy and Germany, thereby creating the Berlin–Rome–Tokyo Axis. Relations between the United States and Japan deteriorated when President Franklin Roosevelt embargoed the export of scrap metal, oil, and other commodities to that country. Instead of curbing Japanese aggression, as Roosevelt had hoped, the embargo pushed the empire to attack. On Sunday, December 7, 1941, at 7:50 in the morning, carrier-launched Japanese aircraft struck without warning at Pearl Harbor, Hawaii, where some seventy-five major U.S. Navy ships were moored. The attack was over by ten o'clock, leaving eighteen U.S. ships sunk or badly damaged and more than 200 aircraft destroyed on the ground. The battleships *Arizona*, *West Virginia*, *Oklahoma*, and *California* were among those sunk, and the *Nevada* was badly damaged. Some 2,400 U.S. servicemen were killed, 1,300 wounded, and 1,000 missing, while the Japanese suffered fewer than 100 casualties, losing only twenty-nine planes and five midget submarines. The only bright spot in this military disaster was that the U.S. aircraft carrier fleet was not in port. It would form the powerful nucleus of the American response to Japanese aggression in the Pacific.

On December 8, President Roosevelt asked a joint session of Congress for a declaration of war, calling December 7, 1941, a "day which will live in infamy." The attack on Pearl Harbor was a spectacular tactical victory for Japan, but, strategically, it was a military blunder. It brought an end to the Great Depression in the United States as well as instant unity of purpose. The nation was forged into a weapon the likes of which the world had never before seen.

1941–1942

The Fall of the Philippines

In the days and weeks following Pearl Harbor, Imperial Japanese forces attacked Wake Island and Guam (both U.S. possessions), British Malaya, Singapore, the Dutch East Indies, Burma, Thailand, and the Philippines (at the time a U.S. commonwealth territory). On Guam, the small U.S. garrison was quickly overwhelmed and surrendered. On Wake Island, grotesquely outnumbered marines repelled a first Japanese attack, but were forced to yield to a second. Britain's crown colony of Hong Kong folded, as did Singapore, and then the Dutch East Indies. Burma, lifeline to China, fell—although Claire L. Chennault, a former U.S. Army Air Service captain now working as air advisor to China's Generalissimo Chiang Kai-shek, led his American Volunteer Group, the famed Flying Tigers, and their outnumbered and outclassed Curtiss P-40s in crippling action against the Japanese.

The cruelest blow in the Pacific came in the Philippines, where, despite a gallant defense through May 6, 1942, U.S. and Filipino forces under Lieutenant General Jonathan M. Wainwright surrendered and were subject to unspeakable brutality at the hands of their Japanese captors. The infamous Bataan Death March, in which prisoners were forced on foot from Corregidor to POW camps in Bataan, caused the deaths of 10,000 prisoners from abuse and starvation. Fortunately, the senior American commander in the Pacific, General Douglas MacArthur, escaped to Australia, promising those left behind on the Philippines, "I shall return." His pledge would not be redeemed until 1944.

1942

Japanese-American Internment

At the time of the Japanese attack on Pearl Harbor, some 120,000 persons of direct Japanese descent were living in the United States. Of these, about 80,000 had been born in this country and were citizens. As early as December 11, 1941, just four days after Pearl Harbor, the FBI rounded up and detained 1,370 Japanese Americans as "dangerous enemy aliens"—although they were, in fact, Americans. The first public call for putting Japanese Americans "under federal control" came on December 22, 1941, from the Agriculture Committee of the Los Angeles Chamber of Commerce. The source was significant. For years, Japanese-American farmers had enjoyed great success in California, Oregon, and Washington, running their farms so efficiently that many Anglo farmers couldn't compete. Doubtless, many Americans were very fearful of Japanese Americans and the acts of sabotage they might commit, but it is also true that the war provided a convenient means for sweeping away years of agricultural competition.

On January 5, 1942, U.S. draft boards classified all Japanese-American selective service registrants as enemy aliens. On January 29, U.S. Attorney General Francis Biddle established "prohibited zones," forbidden to all enemy aliens. German and Italian as well as Japanese aliens were ordered to leave San Francisco waterfront areas immediately. The next day, Earl Warren, at the time California's attorney general, but destined to gain fame beginning in the 1950s as a liberal chief justice of the Supreme Court and eloquent voice of civil liberties, declared that, "unless something is done," the presence of Japanese Americans on the West Coast "may bring about a repetition of Pearl Harbor." Early in February, the entire West Coast congressional delegation appealed to President Franklin D. Roosevelt to order the removal of "all persons of Japanese lineage . . . aliens and citizens alike, from the strategic areas of California, Oregon and Washington." On February 19, President Roosevelt signed Executive Order 9066, authorizing the secretary of war to define military areas "from which any or all persons may be excluded as deemed necessary or desirable." As carried out by Secretary of War Henry Stimson and the man he put in charge of the operations, Lieutenant General John DeWitt, this meant that Japanese Americans, citizens and noncitizens alike, living within 200 miles of the Pacific Coast had to evacuate.

More than 100,000 persons were moved to internment camps in California, Idaho, Utah, Arizona, Wyoming, Colorado, and Arkansas. The camps were spartan, and many of the internees suffered great financial hardship and loss. Worst of all, the forced removal of Americans—the deprivation of liberty and property without due process of law—seemed flatly unconstitutional. Yet the only significant opposition to the removal came from Quaker activists and the American Civil Liberties Union. Suits brought before the Supreme Court, including *Hirabayashi* v. *United States* and *Korematsu* v. *United States,* failed. The high court upheld the constitutionality of the executive order.

Some young Japanese men—about 1,200—won release from the camps by enlisting in the United States Army. They were segregated in the 442nd Regimental Combat Team (which also consisted of some 10,000 Japanese Hawaiian volunteers—the Hawaiians had not been confined to camps), and they fought in Italy, France, and Germany. The 442nd amassed a remarkable record of heroism, becoming the

"**You fought not** only the enemy, but you fought prejudice—and you have won." —President Harry S Truman, addressing the 100th Battalion, 442nd Regimental Combat Team, on its return from Italy, July 1946

most decorated unit for its size and length of service in American military history.

On December 17, 1944, Major General Henry C. Pratt issued Public Proclamation No. 21, which, effective January 2, 1945, allowed the "evacuees" to return to their homes. Some were able to take up their lives where they had left them; others found themselves financially and emotionally devastated. All court cases seeking recompense from the government failed until 1968, when the United States reimbursed many who had lost property because of their relocation. In 1988, Congress appropriated funds to pay a lump sum of $20,000 to each of the 60,000 surviving Japanese-American internees.

1942

The Doolittle Raid on Tokyo

During the early months of World War II, the news from the Pacific was bleak. In a spectacular effort to raise American morale, Lieutenant Colonel James Doolittle of the U.S. Army Air Forces led an extraordinary surprise bombing raid against Tokyo on April 18, 1942, using sixteen twin-engine B-25 bombers launched from the aircraft carrier *Hornet*. The pilots were well aware that the bombers could not carry sufficient fuel to return to any American base, nor were they designed to land on an aircraft carrier. The plan was to bomb Tokyo, then find landing places in China and seek safe haven among Chinese resistance fighters. From here, it would be up to each crew somehow to find a way home.

The raid was launched, and although the damage inflicted on Tokyo was minor, the psychological effect was incalculable—both upon the shocked Japanese and upon the elated American public, signaling the intention of the U.S. military to take the offensive as soon as possible.

1942

Battle of Midway

E arly in May 1942, the U.S. Navy sank or disabled more than twenty-five Japanese ships in action that prevented Japan from extending its conquests deep into the south Pacific and, equally important, checked Japanese efforts to sever supply lines to Australia. Seeking to recover from its losses, the Japanese Imperial Navy staged a major offensive by attacking the island of Midway, some 1,100 miles northwest of Hawaii. If the Japanese could knock out this U.S. outpost, all American hope for regaining control of the Pacific would be lost.

In one of the most momentous battles of the war, beginning on June 3, 1942, U.S. aircraft launched from the *Hornet, Yorktown,* and *Enterprise* sank four Japanese carriers and inflicted other losses. Reeling from this blow, the Imperial Navy withdrew its fleet, which was pursued by American forces that sank or disabled two heavy cruisers and three destroyers and shot down 322 Japanese planes. The U.S. Navy also took heavy losses—the carrier *Yorktown* and a destroyer were sunk, and 147 aircraft lost—but not only did Midway Island remain under U.S. control, the Japanese suffered losses from which they would never recover, and they were unable to resume the offensive in the Pacific. If any single engagement can be called the turning point of the war in the Pacific, Midway was it.

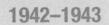

1942–1943

Battles of Guadalcanal and the Bismarck Sea

Having been defeated at Midway, the Japanese prepared to invade Australia and, as a stepping-off place for the invasion, began building an airstrip on Guadalcanal in the southern Solomon Islands. To stop this, on August 7, 1942, U.S. Marines landed at Guadalcanal and began a six-month battle, ultimately defeating the Japanese contingent.

Guadalcanal was the first step in an American strategy of "island hopping," a plan to take Japanese-held islands selectively, gradually closing in on the Japanese mainland itself, while isolating and cutting off certain Japanese outpost islands.

After Guadalcanal came Rabaul, on the eastern tip of New Britain Island, just east of New Guinea. It was the largest of the Japanese naval and air bases. General Douglas MacArthur led U.S. and Australian troops in a campaign through the Solomons and into New Guinea. When the Japanese rushed to reinforce their position on the islands of Lae and Salamaua, on March 3–4, 1943, American bombers attacked Japanese troop transports and their naval escorts with devastating results. This Battle of the Bismarck Sea cost the Japanese 3,500 men, while the Allies lost only five planes, and by the end of 1943, Rabaul was neutralized, cutting off some 100,000 Japanese troops from any hope of supply, support, or reinforcement.

Action in the Central Pacific

Simultaneously with the Battles of Guadalcanal and the Bismarck Sea in the south Pacific was a massive offensive in the central Pacific, beginning with U.S. assaults against Tarawa and Makin islands. While Makin fell quickly, the Tarawa battle, begun on November 20, 1943, did not end until November 26. Of the 5,000 Japanese troops defending the island, only 17 were taken prisoner at battle's end.

Invasion of Italy

L argely at the behest of Britain's prime minister Winston Churchill, the Allies adopted a strategy of invading Europe via what Churchill called its "soft underbelly." After defeating the Italians and Germans in North Africa, Anglo–American forces invaded Sicily, landing there on July 9–10, 1943. The Italian army crumbled before them, but German resistance was much stiffer. Nevertheless, the invasion of Sicily culminated in the fall of Messina to the Allies on August 17, 1943. The month before, Italy's fascist dictator, Benito Mussolini, had been overthrown, and the new Italian government, under Marshal Pietro Badoglio, made secret peace overtures to the Allies. The Germans, however, were determined to defend the Italian peninsula at whatever cost.

At first, the invasion of the Italian mainland went well. British and U.S. forces left Messina on September 3, 1943, and, within a month, southern Italy had fallen to the Allies, but the Allied progress northward was heartbreakingly slow and costly. On January 22, 1944, 50,000 U.S. troops landed at Anzio, just thirty-three miles south of Rome, but were pinned down by German forces, and Rome did not yield until June 4. From this point on, the Germans steadily retreated northward, fighting a bloody campaign in that retreat.

1944

D-Day

From Europe's "soft underbelly," the British and Americans advanced northward through Italy, while the Soviets, who had turned the tide against the Nazis with the monumental Battle of Stalingrad (present-day Volgograd), fought from July 17 to November 18, 1942, pressed from the east. The decision was at last taken to begin the major Allied invasion from the west, and on June 6, 1944—"D-Day"—approximately 5,000 Allied ships, 11,000 Allied aircraft, and more than 150,000 troops assaulted what Adolf Hitler liked to call Fortress Europe. Under the overall command of General Dwight David Eisenhower, the greatest invasion force ever assembled anytime, anywhere landed on the beaches of Normandy.

At some landing points, German resistance was surprisingly light—the Germans having been deceived into expecting the invasion at Pas de Calais—but at others, most notably the sector code named Omaha Beach, the defense was brutal. Still, the invasion was an overwhelming success. Beachheads were established, and, over the next weeks and months, Allied troops and supplies poured into Europe.

1944

The G.I. Bill

As victory began to appear on the horizon during World War II, Congress looked forward to the return of millions of soldiers and began to think about their reintegration into society. At the urging of President Roosevelt, legislators passed the Servicemen's Readjustment Act, more popularly known as the "G.I. Bill of Rights" or, simply, the "G.I. Bill." This unprecedented piece of legislation established veterans' hospitals, made low-interest mortgages available, and provided financing for vocational and college education. In these ways, the legislation did not merely reintegrate returning troops into American society, it reshaped that society, creating a postwar generation that was better educated, better trained, and better housed than any other in history.

Victory in Europe

From the beaches of Normandy and other, secondary landing
areas, Allied troops poured into Europe. On August 25,
1944, Paris was returned to Allied hands, and the Allies continued to sweep through France. By early September, British forces
liberated Brussels, and American troops crossed the German frontier at Eupen. On October 21, the U.S. First Army captured
Aachen, the first German city to fall to the Allies.

It was clear to all rational leaders that Germany had lost the
war, but Adolf Hitler was hardly rational and ordered a fight to
the last man. On December 16, 1944, General Gerd von Rund-
stedt mounted a desperate surprise counteroffensive that drove
a wedge into Allied lines through the Ardennes on the Franco–
Belgian frontier. Because German forces distended the Allied line
westward, the contest that followed was called the Battle of the
Bulge. Despite heavy losses, the U.S. First and Third armies—the
latter led brilliantly by Lieutenant General George S. Patton—
pushed back the "bulge" and crushed the last great German offensive. In February 1945, Patton led his armored units to the
Rhine River and, on March 7, captured the bridge at Remagen,
near Cologne. Allied armies streamed across this bridge and other
points along the Rhine.

Although Anglo–American forces were now poised to take
Berlin, General Eisenhower, believing Hitler would make his last
stand in the German south, chose to head for Leipzig instead and
to leave the German capital to the Soviet Red Army. On April 16,
1945, Soviet marshal Georgy Zhukov entered the city, fought for
it street by street, and finally took Hitler's underground bunker

VICTORY IN EUROPE   261

headquarters, only to discover that the Führer had committed suicide. On May 7, 1945, senior representatives of Germany's armed forces surrendered to the Allies at General Eisenhower's headquarters in Reims. An unconditional surrender was concluded the next day. This left the war in the Pacific still to be won.

1945

Death of Franklin Roosevelt

The terrible news broke over the nation's radios at 5:47 P.M., Eastern War Time, on April 12, 1945. Less than an hour earlier, Franklin Delano Roosevelt, haggard, exhausted, but ever gallant, had died of a cerebral hemorrhage at the "Little White House" in Warm Springs, Georgia.

Not since the assassination of another war president, Abraham Lincoln, had the nation felt the sudden loss of its leader so keenly. FDR had served an unprecedented three full terms and was embarked on his fourth. He had guided the nation through the Great Depression and had led it to the verge of victory in World War II. His vice president, Harry S. Truman, took the oath of office two hours twenty-four minutes after the president's death. What he said the next day to a group of reporters expressed his frank understanding of the burden that had become his: "Boys, if you ever pray, pray for me now. I don't know whether you fellows ever had a load of hay fall on you, but when they told me yesterday what had happened, I felt like the moon, the stars, and all the planets had fallen on me."

1945

Atomic Bombings of
Hiroshima and Nagasaki

On April 25, 1945, less than two weeks after the death of Franklin Roosevelt, Secretary of War Henry L. Stimson handed the new president, Harry Truman, a typewritten memorandum: "Within four months," it began, "we shall in all probability have completed the most terrible weapon ever known in human history, one bomb of which could destroy a whole city."

President Roosevelt had confided very little in his vice president. Stimson's note was the first time Truman heard about the "Manhattan Project," code name for one of the biggest scientific and technological projects ever undertaken by any nation at any time in history. Begun in 1941, the entire project had one objective and one purpose. The objective was to liberate the enormous energy that holds together atomic nuclei, to liberate that energy in a split second as an explosion more terrible than any humankind had ever before created. The purpose was to use this explosion to win World War II.

Overall direction of the Manhattan Project was assigned to Brigadier General Leslie R. Groves, an army engineer. While Groves commanded the logistics of the Manhattan Project, the charismatic American physicist J. Robert Oppenheimer directed the science, brilliantly coordinating the efforts of a civilian army of the most prominent physicists, chemists, and mathematicians in the world. As vast a scientific undertaking as it was, the Manhattan Project was also a tremendous manufacturing enterprise. Two radioactive isotopes, uranium 235 and plutonium 239, undergo fission most readily—if present in sufficient quantity to constitute critical mass. Enormous processing facilities are required to produce enough of these isotopes to build bombs. Groves oversaw construction of giant, but completely secret, plants at Oak Ridge, Tennessee, for the separation of uranium 235 from its natural companion isotope, uranium 238, and at Hanford, Washington, for the production of plutonium 239, while Oppenheimer supervised creation of a laboratory on a remote mesa at Los Alamos, New Mexico. Here is where theoretical physics had to be transformed into a bomb. Methods had to be found to reduce the fissionable products produced at Oak Ridge and Hanford to pure metal, to fabricate that metal into shapes suitable for bringing the chain reaction to an explosive level, and to instantly bring together sufficient amounts of the fissionable material to achieve a supercritical mass—an explosion.

In a remarkably short time, all of the problems were solved, and the first test of the bomb, code named Trinity, took place in the Alamogordo desert at Los Alamos at 0529:45 on July 16, 1945. Everyone who witnessed the detonation said it was like the creation of a sun on Earth.

On August 6, 1945, a lone B-29 Superfortress took off from an airfield on Tinian Island. The pilot, Colonel Paul Tibbets, named it after his mother, Enola Gay. At 8:15 in the morning, local time, the uranium-235 bomb, nicknamed "Little Man," was released from *Enola Gay*'s bomb bay. It detonated 1,900 feet above the city of Hiroshima, instantly destroying two-thirds of the city and killing, wherever they stood or sat or lay, 78,000 of Hiroshima's

"We waited until the blast had passed, walked out of the shelter and then it was extremely solemn. We knew the world would not be the same. A few people laughed, a few people cried. Most people were silent. I remembered the line from the Hindu scripture, the *Bhagavad Gita:* Vishnu is trying to persuade the Prince that he should do his duty . . . and says, 'Now I am become death, destroyer of worlds.' I suppose we all thought that one way or another." —J. Robert Oppenheimer in 1965, recalling the 1945 Trinity test

350,000 residents. By the end of 1945, about 62,000 more suc-cumbed to injuries or radiation sickness.

On August 9, a plutonium-239 bomb, called "Fat Man," was loaded aboard another B-29, *Bock's Car,* bound for Kokura. Dense cloud cover over that target sent the crew to Nagasaki, and, at 11:02 A.M. local time, Fat Man detonated at 1,650 feet. Half the city was flattened by the blast. Of 270,000 people there, about 70,000 would be dead before the end of the year.

Now, at last, Japan's emperor, Hirohito, overruled the military dictatorship that had long wielded the real power in Japan. At noon on August 15, 1945, he broadcast his first-ever radio mes-sage to his people, announcing his acceptance of the Allied surren-der terms and citing as his reason the explosion of a "cruel new bomb." World War II was over, and the Atomic Age, in two terri-ble flashes of universal death, had been born.

The Marshall Plan

World War II devastated Europe more thoroughly than had any previous calamity, natural or human made. In a commencement address delivered at Harvard University on June 5, 1947, Secretary of State George C. Marshall, army chief of staff during World War II, proposed a plan by which the United States would finance much of the rebuilding of Europe, giving aid to allies and former enemies alike.

The Marshall Plan was a bold humanitarian step—as Winston Churchill said of it, the "most unsordid political act in history"—and a means of countering the spread of communism. For Marshall and the other diplomats had learned the lessons of the Treaty of Versailles, which punished Germany after World War I, creating the desperate economic and social conditions in which disastrous dictatorship took root and flourished. By supplying economic assistance, the United States sought to foster the development of democracy in Europe.

1947

Branch Rickey and Jackie Robinson Cross the "Color Line"

Nineteenth- and twentieth-century American history is punctuated by a number of momentous laws—from the Emancipation Proclamation and the Thirteenth, Fourteenth, and Fifteenth Amendments to the Civil Rights Act of 1964 and the Voting Rights Act of 1965, among others—all intended to bring an end to racial inequality in the republic. Ultimately, however, it has been the people—individuals, one by one—who have created the most meaningful changes.

One of these changes came in 1947 when Branch Rickey, president and general manager of the Brooklyn Dodgers, boldly crossed the "color line" by hiring the great African-American athlete Jackie Robinson for his team. Robinson was the first black player in major league baseball, and America's "national pastime" was now integrated.

Long excluded from the white professional leagues, African Americans formed their own teams, which, during the 1920s, were loosely organized as the Negro League. It soon became obvious to anyone who watched a Negro League game that segregation was depriving white baseball of some great talent, but it wasn't until the post–World War II era, a time of social ferment, that Branch Rickey, influenced by advanced social thought on race and looking for the best players he could find, felt emboldened to recruit Robinson.

Robinson was unusual for a black man and for a baseball player of the period. He had gone to college and had been a star player on the UCLA team. He was serious about being an athlete, but he was also serious about being a black man in America. In the army, he faced a court-martial for having challenged the illegal segregation to which he was subjected on an army bus. In hiring Robinson, Rickey did not quite jump in with both feet. He relegated Robinson to a year on the farm team before moving him up to the Dodgers, and then Rickey extracted from Robinson a pledge to endure, silently and without protest, any abuse he might receive from fans. That abuse came in the form of jeers, insults, hate mail, and a series of death threats. Through it all, for two years, Robinson honored his pledge, even refusing comment to the press. During this time, under great stress, he played magnificently and soon became a household name. At last, in 1949, he began to speak out against racial discrimination, Jim Crow laws, and the slow pace with which professional baseball moved forward with integration. By this time, Rickey and most fans were more than willing to hear Robinson speak out.

Jackie Robinson retired from baseball in 1957. While it is true that the National Football League had been integrated the year before Robinson became a Dodger, it was the combination of Robinson's talent as a ball player, his personality, his decency, and his dignity that captured the imagination of the nation and heightened the social consciousness of many ordinary Americans, of all races and origins.

The Berlin Airlift

Throughout World War II, the United States and Britain were allied with the Soviet Union against Nazi aggression. Immediately following the end of the war, this alliance between the democracies and the Soviets disintegrated, as occupied Germany was divided into sectors controlled by the United States, France, England, and the Soviet Union. By the end of March 1948, the Soviets had become wary of the strong alliances being formed among the Western democracies to combine the German sectors they controlled into a separate, independent, capitalist state: West Germany. In an effort to block the creation of this state, Soviet forces began detaining troop trains bound for West Berlin, the U.S.–French–British sector of the divided German capital, which lay deep within Soviet-controlled eastern Germany. Unintimidated by Soviet harassment, on June 7, 1948, the western nations publicly announced their intention to create West Germany. Slightly more than two weeks after this announcement, on June 24, Soviet forces blockaded West Berlin. The Soviets protested that West Berlin, a mere enclave within the Soviet sector of Germany, could not serve as the capital of West Germany.

United States president Harry S Truman declared his belief that to yield West Berlin to Soviet threats would mean ultimately relinquishing all of Germany to the Soviets. His administration was guided by a policy newly developed by the State Department. "Containment" it was called, and its object was to counter Soviet expansion wherever it occurred in the world. The blockade of Berlin was the first test of the new policy.

Truman ordered the U.S. Air Force, itself newly independent

from the U.S. Army, to organize a massive emergency airlift to keep West Berlin supplied with food and, equally important, fuel (mostly coal for heating and generating purposes) for as long as necessary. Truman did not want to start a war with the Soviets, but he was determined to defy and defeat the Soviet blockade. Responding to the president's orders, on June 25, 1948, U.S. Army general Lucius D. Clay telephoned Lieutenant General Curtis E. LeMay, commander of United States Air Forces–Europe (USAFE), and asked: "Curt, can you transport coal by air?" LeMay did not hesitate: "Sir, the Air Force can deliver anything."

On the very next day, June 26, LeMay called in all available transport aircraft, and on June 27 "Operation Vittles" began. Through September 30, 1949, the USAF made 189,963 flights over Soviet-held territory into West Berlin, and cooperating British forces made 87,606 flights. The Air Force flew in a total of 1,783,572.7 tons of food, coal, and other cargo; the Brits, an additional 541,936.9 tons. In addition, some 25,263 inbound and 37,486 outbound passengers were flown (British pilots flew in 34,815 and flew out 164,906). The pilots flew twenty-four hours of every day in all kinds of weather. Extremely hazardous, the Berlin Airlift was a logistical and political triumph for the West. Recognizing that the blockade had failed, the Soviets lifted it on May 12, 1949. The separate nations of East and West Germany were formally created later that month.

The United States and Great Britain had taken a key stand against Soviet aggression and had won the first battle in what would be more than four decades of "Cold War" between the "free world" and the Soviet-dominated communist bloc. In more immediate terms, the Berlin Airlift became the basis for NATO (North Atlantic Treaty Organization), the West's principal alliance against the Soviet Union and its satellite states.

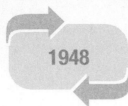

A Powerful New Medium Emerges

A practical television system had been developed by 1933, but the conservatism of radio broadcasters and the demands of World War II put the commercial development of the medium on hold. While it was true that, in 1944, regularly scheduled programs were broadcast a few hours out of the week to a handful of New York–area subscribers (mostly electrical engineers), television was caught in the chicken-or-egg dilemma. Television receivers were costly and very temperamental. Few people could afford to buy a set, and even fewer wanted to buy one when there was almost nothing to watch. The early programming that developed immediately after the war included one or two lame variety shows, a couple of quiz shows, and, soon, professional boxing. What TV desperately needed was compelling programming, but the radio-broadcast networks were in no hurry to invest the necessary money in a medium for which an audience barely existed. But, without programming, there would never be such an audience. A jump-start was needed, and it was administered by a most unlikely individual.

Mendel Berlinger, the son of immigrants, was born on July 12, 1908, in New York City and, after changing his name to Milton Berle, struggled to eke out a living as a dime-a-dozen stage comic in the waning days of vaudeville. He was the kind of low-rent talent early television producers could afford, and, in 1948, when NBC approached Berle to emcee a show called the "Texaco Star Theater," almost no major star would be caught dead on this gimmick called television.

From the moment Berle debuted on September 21, 1948,

something clicked. Berle was outlandish, silly, inventive, and yet ordinary—the classic Everyman figure (albeit often dressed in very homely drag, sporting enormous falsies, a dyed rag mop for hair, and a frumpy housedress). "Uncle Miltie," he called himself, but he was soon far more accurately dubbed "Mr. Television." His presence rapidly came to dominate the new medium. All over the nation, people dropped whatever they were doing every Tuesday evening at eight o'clock to watch the hour-long program.

The seven days of a week consist of 168 hours, of which at least 40 are consumed by earning one's daily bread and another 56 are devoted to sleep. Of the 72 hours that remain, according to the ACNielsen company, the leading compiler of TV statistics, Americans currently dedicate an average of 28 hours to television viewing.

At first as the "Texaco Star Theater" and then as the "Milton Berle Show," the program was broadcast from 1948 to 1956, was resurrected from 1958 to 1959, and again from 1966 to 1967. In its early days, viewers hurriedly assembled in the parlor of whatever neighbor happened to be doing well enough to be able to afford a TV set. The weekly presence of Berle motivated many of these people to buy sets of their own, and as more sets were purchased, broadcasters programmed more shows, which drove sales of more sets. The price of TV sets began to drift lower, pushing more people toward a purchase. By and by, many families bought more than one set, so that each family member could watch whatever interested him or her. On American roofs, TV antennas sprouted like some spidery forest, and by the mid-1950s, television was more influential than books, movies, and radio—combined.

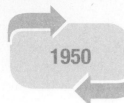

1950

U.S. Responds to a Communist Invasion of South Korea

The world took little notice when Japan annexed Korea in 1910. But immediately after the Japanese attack on Pearl Harbor, December 7, 1941, American politicians and diplomats acknowledged, among many other things, that Japan had made Korea one of its first victims of imperialist aggression, and that was enough to connect the Korean cause with that of the United States and its western allies. After World War II came to an abrupt end with the atomic bombings of Hiroshima and Nagasaki, the United States proposed that the Soviets receive Japan's surrender in Korea north of the thirty-eighth parallel while the United States accept surrender south of this line. Thus, a partition of Korea was created, but only as a strictly temporary administrative expedient until Korea could be fully restored to peace and independence was introduced. The Soviets, however, seized on the "temporary" division to bring northern Korea into the communist fold. Red Army troops erected fortifications along the thirty-eighth parallel and refused to cooperate with the United States on the establishment of a Korean provisional government. America appealed to the United Nations, which, over Soviet objections, decided that a unified government should be established for Korea after a general election and that the UN would provide a security force to protect Korean independence.

Yet the country was hardly unified. The north was dominated by communists, the south by capitalists with democratic leanings. Egged on by the Soviets, the North Korean communists prevented the UN commission from holding elections north of the thirty-eighth parallel. South of the parallel, the elections proceeded on May 10, 1948, creating the Republic of Korea (ROK) under President Syngman Rhee. Twice the UN affirmed the ROK as the only lawful government of Korea. The Soviets responded by setting up a rival government in North Korea under the leadership of Kim Il Sung, a Soviet-trained Korean communist. The UN refused to recognize the northern government as legitimate, but Korea was now effectively divided into two countries, each driven by an ideology hostile to the other. The United States, determined to block the postwar spread of communism wherever it could, resolved to train and equip a security force for the South and to provide economic aid while also pressing through the UN for reunification.

The situation was extremely delicate. America wanted to arm South Korea for defense, yet it did not want to give the appearance that it was sponsoring South Korean aggression, which might lead to full-scale war involving the North Koreans as well as the Soviets. But, on June 25, 1950, units of the North Korean People's Army crossed the thirty-eighth parallel, brushed aside inferior South Korean forces, and marched on Seoul, the South Korean capital, about thirty-five miles below the thirty-eighth parallel. Smaller communist forces simultaneously moved down the center of the Korean peninsula and along the east coast. Seoul quickly fell, and President Truman was caught between the objectives of containing communist aggression yet avoiding a major war. He ordered the U.S. 7th Fleet to proceed toward Korea, but then sent most of it to Taiwan, to prevent the Chinese Communists on the mainland from attacking the Chinese Nationalists' Taiwanese stronghold. In the meantime, Truman gave General Douglas MacArthur the desperate assignment of using the modest U.S. air and land forces immediately available to strike at North Korean positions below the thirty-eighth parallel.

With the situation critical in Korea, there came the terrifying news that the Soviets had entered into a treaty of alliance with Communist China. However, the USSR also announced that it would boycott all UN organizations and committees on which Nationalist—noncommunist—China participated. The Soviet boycott meant that it was not present to veto the UN Security Council resolution authorizing military action against North Korea. Backed, then, by UN sanctions, President Truman named MacArthur commander of U.S. and UN forces, and America and other nations girded for another war, just five years after World War II had ended.

The McCarthy "Witch Hunt"

A s 1950 began, the colorless, thoroughly undistinguished, hard-drinking Republican senator from Wisconsin, Joseph R. McCarthy, found his popularity flagging. He needed to make a bold play on a vital issue, and at the February 9, 1950, meeting of the Women's Republican Club of Wheeling, West Virginia, he seized his chance. Addressing this audience, he suddenly held aloft a piece of paper on which—he said—was a list of 205 known communists currently employed in the United States Department of State.

The audience was electrified. The United States was caught in the grip of a Cold War against communism. From the Soviet Union, the anticapitalist, antidemocratic ideology spread in a red stain across eastern Europe, while, in Asia, all China went red, and communism pushed at the borders of such nations as Korea and Vietnam. Americans were thoroughly prepared to take McCarthy at his word. Indeed, no one even bothered to examine the list McCarthy exhibited to the women Republicans of Wheeling. Had anyone done so, they would have made the disquieting discovery that it was blank, a mere prop—though in the climate of the nation at the time, even such a discovery probably would not have prevented what happened next.

McCarthy's Wheeling speech was reported nationally, and the junior senator from Wisconsin suddenly became famous. Over the next four years, he spearheaded a legislative crusade to "root out" communists in government and in other positions of influence and power. Many Americans believed McCarthy was leading a great *crusade,* whereas others—a minority at first—called it what it ultimately was: a *witch hunt,* reckless and destructive, destructive of reputations, of careers, and even of lives.

McCarthy gained chairmanship of the powerful Senate Subcommittee on Governmental Operations and, from this post, launched investigations into the Voice of America broadcasting service and the U.S. Army Signal Corps. His method of operation was merely to point fingers, make accusations, and raise suspicions. The constitutional guarantees of due process of law, the rules of evidence, and the presumption that a person is innocent until *proven* guilty were discarded in what he deemed a war against internal subversion. In the prevailing climate of fear and disillusionment, however, a pointed finger was more than sufficient to ruin a reputation or destroy a career. McCarthy and his followers hauled before the committee suspects who, to exonerate themselves, were asked to "name names," to expose other individuals with communist affiliations. Those who refused, typically resorting to the Fifth Amendment guarantee against self-incrimination, were charged with contempt of Congress and, often, imprisoned.

McCarthy spawned a legion of followers, some earnest—at least at first—but most, like McCarthy himself, opportunistic seekers after power and influence. The most prominent of McCarthy's acolytes was an oily young attorney named Roy Cohn, who was the prime mover of perhaps the most sensational phase of the witch hunt, an inquisition into "communist influence" in the Hollywood film industry. Paraded before the Senate committee was a succession of movie executives, producers, directors, and stars, some of whom eagerly "named names," while others refused. Cohn rarely bothered to charge these "noncooperative witnesses" with contempt of Congress. He had a much more powerful weapon at hand. Those who did not name names or who simply stood accused were blacklisted. This was not an official procedure, let alone a legal one. It was simply a way of letting the studios and other powers that be know that to hire a certain actor or writer or director invited the wrath of the United States government and, more particularly, Joseph McCarthy. The blacklist proved highly effective. Studios dutifully refused to hire "tainted" individuals, and a host of careers were crippled or killed.

1950

"Containing" Communism in Korea

The objectives of World War II had been clear-cut: Do or die, a commitment to total victory. But, in fighting the Korean War, an all-out effort could bring on World War III and the end of civilization. Of course, an overly cautious approach would produce nothing more than defeat. Not that the United States was even immediately capable of an all-out effort. Demobilization after World War II had been swift and deep, so that the once mighty U.S. military was now both undermanned and underequipped.

With objectives unclear and prospects dim, American ground forces began arriving in Korea just six days after the June 25 Communist invasion. The news was consistently bad. By July 13, the North Koreans had pushed South Korean and U.S. forces to Taejon, in south central South Korea. That city fell on July 20. As disheartening as the defeats were, General MacArthur understood that the rapid advance of the North Koreans had stretched their lines of communication and supply to the breaking point. While U.S. ground troops were badly outnumbered, the U.S. Air Force quickly mastered the air and began hitting communist supply lines. Bidding for time to bring in more forces, MacArthur ordered the U.S. 8th Army to hold a line north of Pusan, the 140-mile-long "Pusan perimeter," extending in an arc from the Korea Strait to the Sea of Japan. While this desperate defense was being fought, MacArthur decided on a high-stakes, high-risk move. He would land major forces at Inchon, an ideal point for launching a surprise assault against the tenuously supplied communist invaders, but also an inlet with highly variable tides, creating terrible hazards for landing craft. Moreover, assuming the landing craft successfully negotiated the treacherous Inchon channel, the troops, once ashore, would immediately have to scale a high seawall, then fight through an extensively built-up, thickly settled area. MacArthur rolled the dice, leaving nothing in reserve. Should the landing fail, there would be no reinforcements available to rescue the troops.

As it happened, everything went right on September 15, 1950. Planners had predicted the treacherous tides accurately, the ships steered safely through the perilous straits, and the troops encountered nothing but light resistance—for no one (except MacArthur) had thought a landing possible here. Within two weeks, Seoul had been retaken, and, soon afterward, the North Korean army had been pushed back beyond the thirty-eighth parallel.

Now it was necessary to decide whether or not to cross the thirty-eighth parallel and invade North Korea. The reasons for doing so were ample: Some 30,000 NKPA troops had escaped to the North, which harbored at least another 30,000, making for an effective military force of 60,000, which posed a continuing threat to the South. Furthermore, defeating North Korea on its own territory would greatly advance the cause of reunification. Yet there was also a single compelling reason not to invade: Both Communist China and the Soviet Union had declared their intention to defend against such an invasion. President Truman agonized, then decided to take the risk. On September 27, he ordered MacArthur to pursue the North Korean forces across the thirty-eighth parallel, but to steer well clear of the Yalu River (the Manchurian border) and the Tumen River (the Soviet border). The invasion was swift and highly successful, so that by October 24, 1950, UN forces were close to the Chinese border.

United States and Red China Face Off in Korea

By the fall of 1950, under the brilliant tactical command of Douglas MacArthur, U.S.-dominated United Nations forces had driven the North Korean invaders out of the South and, indeed, had pushed them close to the Yalu River, the border with China. When China threatened to intervene, President Truman conferred with MacArthur on Wake Island. The general declared his certainty that the Chinese threats were empty, but by November, it had become clear that Chinese troops were in the battle. MacArthur insisted that Chinese operations were strictly defensive and that, in fact, few Chinese troops had actually crossed into North Korea. Accordingly, he ordered the UN advance to continue, and, on November 24, U.S. forces reached the Yalu. The next night, massive numbers of Chinese troops attacked the U.S. 8th Army hard on its center and right. Two days later, even more powerful Chinese attacks overran units of X Corps on its left flank. By November 28, UN positions were caving in. On December 15, after suffering severe losses, UN forces had pulled back to the thirty-eighth parallel and were now establishing a defensive line across the breadth of the Korean peninsula.

MacArthur responded to the Chinese entry into the war by lobbying for authorization to expand the war into China. Seeing the specter of World War III, Truman and his advisors said no. In the meantime, a massive Chinese attack on New Year's Eve sent the 8th Army into retreat toward Seoul, which fell on January 4, 1951. Yet the Chinese did not pursue the 8th Army south of Seoul, and within weeks, all Chinese advances had halted. MacArthur continued to demand permission to attack China, but Truman and his advisors ordered 8th Army commander Matthew Ridgway to pound away at the stalled Chinese troops within South Korea, which he did in a methodical and excruciating offensive, dubbed the "meatgrinder" by frontline G.I.s, beginning on January 25, 1951. By the middle of March, Ridgway had regained Seoul, and by March 21, UN troops were back at the thirty-eighth parallel.

1951

Truman Fires MacArthur

After U.S.-dominated UN forces regained their positions at the thirty-eighth parallel dividing North and South Korea, the UN member nations agreed that securing South Korea below the thirty-eighth parallel was an acceptable outcome for the Korean War. But when General MacArthur was informed that President Truman would announce his willingness to commence negotiations with the Chinese and North Koreans on the basis of current positions, he made an unauthorized announcement of his own, declaring that, if the UN would expand the conflict to North Korea's coastal areas and interior strongholds, the Chinese would back down. Worse, on April 5, 1951, Representative Joseph W. Martin read into the *Congressional Record* a letter from MacArthur stating the necessity of opening up a second front against China itself, using Nationalist Chinese troops. MacArthur wrote that he could not stomach a war without victory.

For Truman, this was the last straw. In a showdown between the civilian commander in chief and a five-star general, Truman was determined that the president must prevail. In an act of great courage, on April 11, 1951, President Truman removed MacArthur, one of the most venerated and popular heroes of World War II, and replaced him as supreme commander of UN forces in Korea with General Matthew Ridgway. This occasioned from Mac-Arthur a sentimental and stirring farewell speech to a joint session of Congress, in which the general quoted an "old barrack ballad": "Old soldiers never die, they just fade away." Many—mistakenly, it turned out—wrote off Harry Truman as a political dead man.

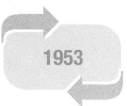

1953

An Ambiguous End to the Korean War

Truman relieved MacArthur of command in Korea because the general was insubordinate and because the president feared that his actions would expand a limited, if brutal, war into a thermonuclear World War III. Peace talks between the Chinese and North Koreans on one side and the UN, U.S., and South Koreans on the other side began at the end of June 1951 and dragged on, with frequent breakdowns and impasses, for the next two years. During this period, the war ground on, mostly along the thirty-eighth parallel. At last, in April 1953, it was agreed that the war would end with a cease-fire along that parallel.

The only individual who remained adamant in his dissatisfaction with this arrangement was Syngman Rhee, the president of South Korea. He would settle for nothing less than Korean unification under his leadership, and when the armistice was signed on July 27, 1953, it did not formally include South Korea. Still, the shooting war was over, and, since July 27, 1953, North and South Korea have existed in a kind of limbo, suspended between war and peace, a coexistence neither peaceful nor overtly hostile, but at all times threatening, as evidenced by North Korea's apparent reactivation of a nuclear weapons program in 2003.

It is not known how many Chinese and North Korean troops were killed in the Korean War, but guesses range from between 1.5 and 2 million, in addition to at least a million civilians. The UN command lost 88,000 killed, of whom 23,300 were American.

1953

The Rosenberg Case

arly in 1950, federal investigators arrested David Greenglass, who had served in the U.S. Army in World War II and
had been stationed near the atomic laboratory at Los
Alamos, New Mexico. By this time, British agents had already
picked up Klaus Fuchs, a German-born British atomic scientist
and communist sympathizer, who confessed to having transmitted
to the Soviets not only atomic secrets but also secrets relating to
the far more powerful hydrogen bomb, a device that uses nuclear
fission to trigger a much more energetic nuclear fusion explosion.
Fuchs implicated as his accomplice Harry Gold, an American
chemist whom Greenglass had supplied with information pilfered
from Los Alamos. Greenglass told investigators that his brother-
in-law, a New York machine-shop owner named Julius Rosenberg,
acted as a go-between in his exchanges with Gold. Based on this
information, which was extracted, in part, on a promise not to ask
for the death penalty against Greenglass, federal agents arrested
Rosenberg and his wife, Ethel, on July 17, 1950.

There is no doubt that the Rosenbergs had a history of communist affiliation. They did not deny this, but they pleaded not
guilty to the charges of having conspired to obtain national defense information for the Soviet Union. The subsequent trial riv-
eted the attention of the nation, which became deeply divided over
the question of the Rosenbergs' guilt or innocence. The proceedings were made more poignant by the fact that the couple had two
young children, who defense lawyers liberally paraded before
newsreel and press cameras. Today, historians continue to debate
the degree of the couples' involvement in espionage. Although

most scholars now believe that Julius Rosenberg at least dabbled in passing information, some also point to the fact that the major item he was accused of passing, Greenglass's sketches of a bomb component, were too crude and vague to be of any practical use. Others, however, point out that memoirs written by several Soviet leaders after the collapse of the USSR specifically mention the great value of atomic information that came via Julius Rosenberg.

What is clear is that the Rosenbergs' liberal intellectual leanings, their connection with socialism and communism, and, perhaps most of all, their being Jews hurt them at least as much as any evidence prosecutors presented against them. Disturbing even to those who believed the Rosenbergs were guilty was the self-serving nature of Greenglass's testimony against them. Although he was certainly more deeply involved than the Rosenbergs in passing atomic secrets, he was sentenced only to a fifteen-year prison term, of which he served ten. The Rosenbergs, in contrast, found guilty, were sentenced to death.

The Rosenberg trial, verdict, and sentence deeply divided America. Many regarded the proceedings as symptoms of an anti-Semitism that lay under the surface of democratic America. Others saw it as the product of the Cold War and McCarthyism. Still others thought the couple had reaped what they had sown. The Rosenberg lawyers unsuccessfully appealed the sentence to the Supreme Court, and, on June 19, 1953, Julius and Ethel Rosenberg were put to death in the electric chair.

1954

The Army–McCarthy Hearings

The dangerous Cold War era did produce an army of spies, including insiders in the American military, government, and technology industries. It was bona fide American traitors who communicated U.S. atomic secrets to the Soviets, which enabled the USSR to develop an atomic bomb in 1949 and a hydrogen bomb in 1954. Yet the "witch hunts" of Senator Joseph McCarthy did not turn up such spies, and McCarthy made no serious, sustained effort to separate fact from fantasy in his accusations. He thrived on the creation of national hysteria and was, in fact, little interested in the nuts and bolts of actual espionage. Just how irrational McCarthyism was became apparent when the senator stepped up his investigation even *after* his own Republican party had captured the White House in 1952. He brought the proceedings to a crescendo in 1954, when he accused the entire United States Army of being not just infiltrated, but positively riddled with communists. This reckless accusation was enough to provoke President Dwight D. Eisenhower, a career army officer and former supreme commander of all Allied military forces in Europe during World War II, to encourage Congress to form a new committee, one focused on investigating McCarthy himself.

The committee looked into the senator's illegal and self-serving attempts to coerce army brass into granting preferential treatment for a former McCarthy aide, Private G. David Schine. The "Army–McCarthy Hearings" were conducted from April to June 1954, and, perhaps most important of all, were broadcast on the still-infant medium of television. On camera, before the nation, Joseph McCarthy was exposed for the heedless demagogue he

On June 9, 1954, the Army–McCarthy hearings reached a dramatic high point in an exchange between McCarthy and Joseph N. Welch, special counsel for the U.S. Army. In an effort to interrupt Welch's persistent cross-examination of his chief counsel, Roy M. Cohn, McCarthy suddenly injected into the hearings a charge that one of Mr. Welch's Boston law firm associates, Frederick G. Fisher, Jr., had been a member of the National Lawyers Guild, "long after it had been exposed as the legal arm of the Communist Party."

MR. WELCH: . . . Until this moment, Senator, I think I never really gauged your cruelty or your recklessness. Fred Fisher is a young man who went to the Harvard Law School and came into my firm and is starting what looks to be a brilliant career with us. When I decided to work for this committee, I asked Jim St. Clair, who sits on my right, to be my first assistant. I said to Jim: "Pick somebody in the firm to work under you that you would like." He chose Fred Fisher and they came down on an afternoon plane. . . . I . . . said to these two young men: "Boys, I don't know anything about you except I've always liked you, but if there's anything funny in the life of either one of you that would hurt anybody in this case, you speak up quick." And Fred Fisher said: "Mr. Welch, when I was in the law school and for a period of months after I belonged to the Lawyer's Guild," as you have suggested, Senator. . . . And I said, "Fred, I just don't think I'm going to ask you to work on the case. If I do, one of these days that will come out and go over national television and it will hurt like the dickens." So, Senator, I asked him to go back to Boston. Little did I dream you could be so reckless and so cruel as to do an injury to that lad. . . . If it were in my power to forgive you for your reckless cruelty, I would do so. I like to think I'm a gentle man, but your forgiveness will have to come from someone other than me. . . . Senator, may we not drop this? We know he belonged to the Lawyer's Guild. . . . Let us not assassinate this lad further, Senator. You've done enough. Have you no sense of decency, sir? At long last, have you left no sense of decency?

was. The hearings ended the witch hunt and McCarthy's career. Censured by action of the Senate later in 1954, he lost all power and influence. A chronically heavy drinker, he retreated further into the bottle and died, in 1957, at the age of forty-nine. Few mourned his passing. Perhaps worse still, few noted it.

1954

The "Domino Theory"

World War II interrupted France's colonial hold on Vietnam, at the time called French Indochina. After the surrender of Japan, the United States, seeking to block the spread of communism in Asia—it would soon engulf China and divide Korea—supported French attempts to reassert control of Vietnam and to fight against guerrillas led by Ho Chi Minh, a Soviet-trained nationalist. On August 3, 1950, the first contingent of U.S. military "advisors" arrived to aid the French, and by 1953, the United States was funding 80 percent of the cost of France's war effort. The French attempted to strike a decisive blow against Ho's forces on the strategically situated plain of Dien Bien Phu, near Laos. But, in a stunning development, Dien Bien Phu fell to the forces of Ho Chi Minh on May 7, 1954. The military disaster completely demoralized French forces, which suffered a string of defeats that prompted France to seek peace. At a July 1954 conference, the French and Ho's provisional government, the Viet Minh, agreed for the time being to divide Vietnam along the seventeenth parallel. A cease-fire was declared.

While the French were still struggling in the Dien Bien Phu campaign, on April 7, 1954, U.S. president Dwight D. Eisenhower explained to reporters why he thought it important to aid France, a foreign power, to fight against communism in another foreign country, Vietnam. "You have a row of dominoes set up," he explained, "you knock over the first one, and what will happen to the last one is the certainty it will go over very quickly." It was an offhanded figure of speech, but the press took it up and dubbed it the "domino theory." It would become the leading rationale for escalating America's involvement in the Vietnam War.

Brown Versus the Board of Education

D uring the Depression and World War II, increasing numbers of African Americans left the rural South to settle in cities, both in the North and South, in search of employment. More and more, the issue of racial integration came to the fore in American society. In the North, no laws enforced segregation, but all-black and all-white neighborhoods were nevertheless the norm in northern cities. In the South, segregation was typically enforced by law. In the early 1950s, while racial segregation in public schools was common in the North, it was universal in the South and protected by law. Authorities defended its legality by referring to the "separate but equal" doctrine, which had been annunciated in a late-nineteenth-century Supreme Court decision in the case of *Plessy* v. *Ferguson*. The legal theory was this: Maintaining separate schools for blacks and whites was constitutional, provided that, in any given district, the schools were equal in quality and resources offered. For years, bolstered by *Plessy* v. *Ferguson*, the "separate but equal" doctrine endured, southern schools remained segregated, and segregation in this arena was used to justify segregation in other public accommodations, such as restaurants, hotels, bus and train stations and waiting rooms, public restrooms, and so on.

At the start of the 1950s, African-American legal activists mounted a determined challenge against *Plessy* v. *Ferguson* and the segregation doctrine it upheld. In Topeka, Kansas, an African-American third-grader named Linda Brown had to walk a full mile—and through a hazardous railroad switchyard—to get to her segregated, all-black elementary school. A white elementary school was a safe seven-block walk from her house. When the principal of the white school refused to enroll Brown, the girl's father, Oliver Brown, approached the Topeka branch of the NAACP (National Association for the Advancement of Colored People). Other African-American parents indicated their willingness to join Brown in forcing the integration of the Topeka schools. In June 1951, the NAACP filed for an injunction to accomplish exactly this. The U.S. District Court for the District of Kansas listened to the argument of the NAACP, which was, in essence, that segregated schools sent the message to black children that they were inferior to whites; therefore, the schools were inherently unequal, regardless of whatever physical facilities or teaching faculty they might offer. In defense of its segregation policy, the Topeka Board of Education argued that because segregation in Topeka and elsewhere in the United States was pervasive—the norm—segregated schools realistically prepared black children for the segregation they would experience as adults. Therefore, the argument went, a segregated education was actually a valuable developmental service!

The district court concurred with the NAACP position that segregation "has a detrimental effect upon the colored children," instilling in them a "sense of inferiority" that negatively "affects the motivation of a child to learn"; however, the court decided that the firmly established legal precedent of *Plessy* v. *Ferguson* allowed separate but equal school systems for blacks and whites. Without a ruling from the Supreme Court overturning *Plessy,* the district court believed its hands were tied and, in the court's language, it was "compelled" to rule in favor of the Board of Education. Although ostensibly a legal defeat, the district court decision conspicuously threw open the door to a Supreme Court appeal, which Brown and the NAACP made on October 1, 1951. Their case was combined with other cases that challenged school segregation in South Carolina, Virginia, and Delaware. On May 17, 1954, the high court handed down a decision declaring segregated public schools unconstitutional because they were inherently unequal as a result of intangible social factors. Two years later, the court issued detailed guidelines to be used in a nationwide program of desegregation of America's schools.

Brown v. *Board of Education* not only achieved integration of public schools, it also encouraged African Americans—and socially conscious white Americans—to challenge all laws and traditions that segregated society and that violated civil rights. Indeed, if we wish to fix the birth date of the modern civil rights movement, no date is more significant than May 17, 1954—with the possible exception of December 1, 1955.

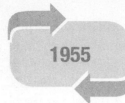

1955

Montgomery Bus Boycott

On December 1, 1955, in Montgomery, Alabama, an African-American department-store tailor did what any other person would do at the end of a long workday. She settled into a bus seat, intending to ride home. It was an ordinary act by an ordinary woman—but it was performed in what seems today the extraordinary context of legally sanctioned racial segregation. When the bus driver, James F. Blake, ordered Mrs. Rosa Parks to give up her seat in the white-only front of the segregated city bus and relinquish it to a white man who had boarded, she refused. Blake called the police, who arrested Parks for violating the city's segregation ordinance.

Leaders of Montgomery's black community seized the incident as an opportunity for launching a high-profile protest against the city's segregation laws. During the weekend of December 3–4, Rev. Ralph Abernathy and Rev. Martin Luther King, Jr., prominent Montgomery pastors, met with Jo Ann Robinson, head of the Women's Political Council, and E. D. Nixon, of the local chapter of the National Association for the Advancement of Colored People (NAACP), to plan a nonviolent response to Mrs. Parks's arrest: a boycott against the Montgomery city bus lines. Forty thousand handbills were quickly printed and circulated throughout Montgomery's black neighborhoods, and, on December 4, African-American ministers included the boycott in their Sunday sermons.

The message and the movement electrified the black community. On Monday, December 5, as revealed by bus company receipts, some 90 percent of the blacks who routinely rode the buses found other means of transportation. That evening, black leaders created the MIA (Montgomery Improvement Association), with Martin Luther King, Jr., as president. The MIA directed the boycott day after day, week after week, month after month, well into 1956. Police frequently harassed black carpoolers. Bombs were set off at the houses of both King and Nixon, and King was arrested on an inconsequential traffic offense. Unintimidated, the leaders continued to lead, and the community continued the boycott, even as the nation began to pay attention and watch. Using an Alabama statute against boycotts, conspiracy charges were brought against King as well as the other leaders of the MIA. This only served to accelerate the U.S. Supreme Court decision, in November of 1956, declaring that segregation on public buses was unconstitutional.

The boycott, sparked by the refusal of a forty-two-year-old seamstress to move to the back of the bus, changed American law and launched the modern civil rights movement, propelling Martin Luther King, Jr., to its forefront. The boycott also set the pattern of nonviolence, which would dominate the civil rights movement under King, giving to that movement the full measure of moral force.

1961

Bay of Pigs

I n 1959, Fidel Castro, a charismatic leftist guerrilla leader, suc- cessfully led a revolution in Cuba, overthrowing the government of Fulgencio Batista, corrupt but friendly to the United States. Over the succeeding two years, Castro, the new dictator, allied his nation more and more closely to the Soviet Union. Communism was coming perilously close to American shores, so, toward the end of the administration of Dwight David Eisenhower, the U.S. Central Intelligence Agency (CIA) devised a plan to overthrow Castro. Incoming president John F. Kennedy bought into the scheme, which was to assemble a force of anti-Castro Cuban ex- iles now living in the United States and land them in Cuba, at a place called the Bay of Pigs, from which they would invade the is- land. The CIA was confident that this would be sufficient to spark a great popular uprising against Castro.

As it turned out, the CIA couldn't have been more wrong. It was a disaster from the moment the operation stepped off on April 17, 1961. Not only did the Cuban people fail to rally to the in- vaders, the United States failed to provide promised air support, and, within three days, the invasion had been crushed by Castro's small army and even smaller air force. This was a major disaster for the brand-new Kennedy administration, and it served only to heighten tension between Cuba and the United States. Convinced that another invasion attempt would come, Castro agreed to allow the Soviets to build nuclear missile bases on the island. A crisis of potentially doomsday proportions was in the making.

Into the Vietnam Quagmire

L ike Korea before it, Vietnam was divided into a communist-controlled north and noncommunist south after the defeat of French colonial forces in 1954. A key condition of the armistice agreement between France and the Viet Minh nationalists was that the divided Vietnam would hold popular elections with the object of reunifying under whatever regime the people chose. Because South Vietnam's president, Ngo Dinh Diem, was well aware that the charismatic Ho Chi Minh would win any popular election, he abrogated the peace agreement and refused to hold the promised elections. More concerned to stem the communist tide than to uphold the principles of democracy, the United States backed Diem's refusal, and John F. Kennedy, who succeeded Dwight Eisenhower in 1961, progressively increased the number of military "advisors" sent to Vietnam.

Throughout the Kennedy years, American policy makers did their best to overlook the profound unpopularity and corruption of the Diem regime. Not only did Diem's cronies control top government positions, but Diem, a Catholic, was unstinting in his support of the nation's Catholic minority at the expense of its Buddhist majority. The world was shocked by newsreel images of protest demonstrations in which Buddhist monks soaked themselves in gasoline and set themselves ablaze in the streets of Saigon. Deciding at long last that the Diem regime was a liability, President Kennedy secretly allowed the CIA to arrange the assassination of Diem in a U.S.-backed military coup of November 1, 1963. This led only to more coups, as South Vietnam became increasingly unstable, a situation that encouraged the communists, now drawing aid from the Soviets and Chinese, to escalate the war.

1962

Cuban Missile Crisis

I n October 1962, a United States U-2 spy plane, on one of the surveillance flyovers that had become routine over Cuba, photographed Soviet nuclear missile bases under construction. President Kennedy presented the photographic evidence to the American people in a televised broadcast on October 22, and he demanded of Soviet premier Nikita Khrushchev the immediate withdrawal of the missiles. Still reeling from the Bay of Pigs debacle, the Kennedy administration was faced with a crisis of unprecedented gravity. Do nothing, and the Soviet Union would have nuclear missiles in America's backyard, capable of hitting virtually any United States city. Act rashly, and a confrontation could be triggered in that other Cold War flashpoint, Berlin, which might well engulf Europe in a thermonuclear World War III. Delay or act ineffectively, and a nuclear strike could be launched directly at the United States.

Before addressing the nation and after brainstorming with the finest minds in his administration, Kennedy decided on his course of action: to order a naval "quarantine" of Cuba—he avoided the word "blockade," since a blockade is technically an act of war—on October 24. All incoming ships were to be stopped, boarded, and inspected. Any carrying nondefensive military hardware would be turned back. With each day that the quarantine was in place, an armed confrontation between American and Soviet vessels seemed more likely. Thermonuclear Armageddon was an intensely real possibility.

Yet the quarantine never developed into a shooting war, and the standoff in the waters surrounding Cuba was ended on October 28, when Soviet premier Nikita Khrushchev, approached by Kennedy indirectly via quasi-diplomatic back channels, proposed to remove the missiles under United Nations supervision. Quietly, in exchange, JFK offered to remove obsolescent U.S. missiles stationed in the NATO nation of Turkey and, even more important, made a pledge never to attempt an invasion of Cuba.

On October 29, President Kennedy suspended the quarantine, and by November 2 the missile bases were being dismantled. The showdown was a triumph for American diplomacy, but the Cuban missile crisis also demonstrated just how dangerous the thermonuclear world had become.

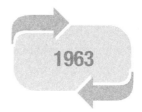

1963

Assassination of John Kennedy

P artisans and historians will long continue to argue the merits of the Kennedy presidency. There was plenty that went wrong with it. There were the tragically bungled Bay of Pigs invasion and the early escalation of American involvement in Vietnam. While JFK was popular with youth and intellectuals, he was never able to put together much support in Congress, especially where his efforts to improve civil rights and to provide a program of medical care for the elderly were concerned. Yet there was an undeniable magic about the Kennedy years. He introduced important, forward-looking programs, such as the Peace Corps, an American space program targeting the moon, and the Alliance for Progress with Latin American countries, and, of course, there was his masterful handling of the Cuban Missile Crisis. Perhaps most magical of all was the general tone of the Kennedy White House, as a gathering place for the very best in American art and culture and thought, presided over not only by JFK, but also by his incomparable wife, the elegant Jacqueline Bouvier.

However one evaluates the Kennedy years, his assassination, during a visit to Dallas, Texas, on November 22, 1963, seemed to rob America, at gunpoint, of youth, of idealism, of hope, and it underscored the essential fragility that underlay the vigor of democracy. In more immediate terms, Kennedy's death came as a kind of martyrdom. His successor, Lyndon B. Johnson, used the Kennedy aura to usher through Congress all of the great social legislation Kennedy had been unable to pass—and then some. Civil Rights and Medicare became the cornerstones of LBJ's "Great Society" program of social reforms. More enduringly, the Kennedy legend—the melancholy romance of a youthful, courageous, vigorous man cut down in his prime—made it impossible for many to believe that he could have been shot by a lone malcontent, the misfit Lee Harvey Oswald, whose own story we never heard, because he himself was gunned down, in the garage of Dallas police headquarters, by a local mob-connected nightclub owner, Jack Ruby.

Hoping to lay to rest a welter of conspiracy theories, President Johnson named a commission, headed by Chief Justice Earl Warren, to investigate the assassination. After a ten-month investigation, the Warren Commission concluded that Oswald was, in fact, the lone assassin. But the conspiracy theories continued to survive and to proliferate, and in 1976, no less a body than the United States Congress issued startling new revelations concerning the activities of the CIA and the FBI, and a special committee concluded that, the Warren Commission notwithstanding, an assassination conspiracy was likely. The speculation has never stopped.

1964

The Civil Rights Act of 1964

The years following World War II saw a slow but inevitable march toward making racial equality the law of the land in the United States. In 1947, Harry S. Truman ordered the integration of the U.S. armed services, a step that gave many whites and blacks their first opportunity to live and work together. In 1954, the U.S. Supreme Court ruled that segregated public schools were unconstitutional, and in 1956 that same court declared segregated public transport unconstitutional as well. For many, the culminating event of the first great phase of the modern civil rights movement was the August 1963 March on Washington, when more than 200,000 converged on the capital—peacefully—to demand racial equality. In this atmosphere, President John F. Kennedy hoped to gain passage of a civil rights act, which would give desegregation the full force of federal law. Discrimination on the basis of race would be banned in employment, in unions, and in all enterprises that drew federal funding of any kind. All public places—hotels, theaters, restaurants, and the like—would be, by law, integrated. Yet Kennedy was never able to get the legislation past a strong southern congressional bloc, and it fell to his successor, Lyndon Johnson, to invoke the memory of the "martyred" JFK, the idealist and fighter for social justice, cut down in his prime, to gain passage of the momentous Civil Rights Act of 1964.

Although it gave equality the full measure of federal law, the act did not immediately or miraculously provide true social equality to the nation's African Americans and other minorities. Many state and local governments defied the federal government and continued to act from motives of racism and racial segregation.

Within hours of its passage, on July 2, 1964, President Lyndon B. Johnson signed the Civil Rights Act of 1964 into law in a nationwide television broadcast from the White House. He spoke:

"We believe that all men are created equal—yet many are denied equal treatment. We believe that all men have certain inalienable rights. We believe that all men are entitled to the blessings of liberty—yet millions are being deprived of those blessings, not because of their own failures, but because of the color of their skins.

"The reasons are deeply embedded in history and tradition and the nature of man. We can understand without rancor or hatred how all this happens. But it cannot continue. Our Constitution, the foundation of our Republic, forbids it. The principles of our freedom forbid it. Morality forbids it. And the law I sign tonight forbids it. . . ."

Even some federal institutions, most notoriously the FBI, retained racist policies; FBI director J. Edgar Hoover, who looked upon Martin Luther King, Jr., as a menace to the stability of the nation, covertly ordered illegal wiretaps and other surveillance aimed at embarrassing and discrediting him. Violence within the black community became especially heated during the 1960s, a period in which America's urban ghettoes routinely flamed into riot during a series of "long, hot summers." Violence against black activists descended to its most tragic depths with the assassinations of Malcolm X in 1965 and Martin Luther King, Jr., in 1968.

The changes wrought by the Civil Rights Act of 1964 were profound and have left a lasting mark on American culture and society. Certainly, the most blatant and overt forms of racial discrimination have greatly diminished. The social acceptance of expressed bigotry is no longer the norm. And all officially sanctioned segregation of public establishments, schools, and facilities has come to an end. Black politicians occupy many top offices throughout the United States. Yet no one looking at American society today can honestly say that the mass of black Americans and the mass of white Americans enjoy equally all of the benefits our society offers. If *de jure* (law-based) segregation has disappeared, *de facto* (actual) segregation remains strong in many places, and true racial harmony is still enough of a rarity to merit feature stories on TV news programs or in the magazine section of the Sunday paper. The struggle continues.

1964

The Gulf of Tonkin Resolution

The American destroyer *Maddox,* conducting electronic surveillance in international waters, was attacked by North Vietnamese torpedo boats on August 2, 1964. Undamaged, it was joined by a second destroyer, the *C. Turner Joy.* On August 4, it was reported that both ships had been attacked. Evidence of the second attack was thin (later, it was discovered that the second attack had not even occurred), but President Lyndon B. Johnson ordered retaliatory air strikes, and he asked Congress for support. That support came, on August 7, when the Senate passed the so-called Gulf of Tonkin Resolution, which gave the president virtually unlimited authority to expand United States involvement in what was a long-standing war in a part of the world few Americans knew, much less cared, about. The Vietnam War would devastate Vietnam, and it would nearly tear apart the United States.

The Gulf of Tonkin Resolution:

Joint Resolution of Congress H.J. RES 1145 August 7, 1964
Resolved by the Senate and House of Representatives of the United States of America in Congress assembled,

That the Congress approves and supports the determination of the President, as Commander in Chief, to take all necessary measures to repel any armed attack against the forces of the United States and to prevent further aggression. . . .

1965

Vietnam War—LBJ Commits the Nation to Combat

In February 1965, Lyndon Johnson sent his personal advisor, Mc-George Bundy, on a fact-finding mission to Saigon in an effort to decide whether or not to commit more troops to defend an unpopular and corrupt South Vietnamese regime. At this very time, on February 7, the Viet Cong—the popular military front of the communist North—attacked U.S. advisory forces and the headquarters of the U.S. Army 52d Aviation Battalion near Pleiku, killing 9 Americans and wounding 108. U.S. forces retaliated against North Vietnam, which made a counterstrike on February 10 against a barracks at Qui Nhon. On the next day, U.S. forces struck back with a long program of air strikes deep into the North, a campaign dubbed Rolling Thunder. The operation formally began on March 2, 1965, and marked the first great U.S. escalation in Vietnam, as 50,000 new ground troops were sent into the country, ostensibly to "protect" U.S. air bases.

LBJ had sent Bundy to find facts, but the facts found the president. Pleiku and its aftermath prompted escalation of the war and the commitment of U.S. forces for the long haul.

1968

The Tet Offensive and
the Antiwar Movement

President Johnson's aim in prosecuting the Vietnam War was to fight a war of gradual escalation, wearing down the North Vietnamese without provoking overt intervention from China or the Soviets. It was, in fact, a no-win strategy, for the North Vietnamese were willing to make tremendous sacrifices and were not about to be worn down. As the North's apparently inexhaustible will to fight became increasingly apparent, LBJ embraced a strategy of "Vietnamization," giving the South Vietnamese ARVN (Army of the Republic of Vietnam) the tools and training to take over more and more of the fighting, so that American forces could ultimately disengage. Despite this, the numbers of Americans "in country" continued to rise. In 1965, 75,000 Americans were fighting in Vietnam. In 1966, the number jumped to 375,000, and, by 1968, more than half a million American troops were at war there.

By 1968, the war had become intensely unpopular with a growing majority of Americans, and a full-blown antiwar movement developed, first on college campuses (after all, it was the nation's college-age men who were subject to the draft), and then throughout all sectors of American activity. Increasingly, Americans became divided into pro-war supporters of the administration and antiwar detractors, who had lost trust and faith in the administration. Demonstrations and "confrontations," sometimes escalating into riots, became commonplace.

On January 30, 1968, the communists unleashed a series of massive offensives, first along the border with South Vietnam, attacking the U.S. base at Khe Sanh, and then against South Vietnamese provincial capitals and principal cities. The offensives coincided with Tet, a Vietnamese lunar holiday, and while they were costly to U.S. and ARVN forces, they were far more costly to the Viet Cong. Yet, psychologically, it was an unalloyed victory for the communists. It was the Tet Offensive that finally persuaded many Americans, including politicians and policy makers, that the Vietnam War was unwinnable.

On March 31, President Johnson made two surprise television announcements. He declared that he would restrict bombing above the twentieth parallel, a gesture that opened the door to a negotiated settlement of the war, and he announced that he would not seek another term as president. He recognized that his advocacy of the war was tearing the nation apart.

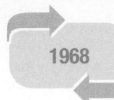

1968

Assassination of Martin Luther King, Jr.

The year 1968 saw more internal turmoil in the United States than at any other time since the Civil War. The Tet Offensive, a massive communist military campaign throughout South Vietnam, began the year and, in the United States, triggered new waves of antiwar protests. These tended to merge with growing racial unrest in the country. For one thing, a disproportionate number of African-American draftees served in Vietnam, and, for another thing, it was quite justifiably believed that the economic demands of the war had drained the funding for LBJ's vaunted "Great Society" social programs. On February 29, the large, black ghetto neighborhood of Watts in Los Angeles erupted into riot, the most destructive since the Draft Riots of the Civil War era.

Against this background of national upheaval, Martin Luther King, Jr.—the most prominent of the nation's civil rights leaders, winner of the Nobel Peace Prize, the champion and master of nonviolent protest—continued to do what he did best: work at the grassroots of the movement for social justice. He went to Memphis, Tennessee, not to launch some great public initiative or address some august group of philosophers and political leaders, but to talk to the city's striking sanitation workers and to encourage them in their cause. In a show of solidarity with the African-American community of Memphis, King chose accommodations at the black-owned Lorraine Motel. At 6:01 on the evening of April 4, Dr. King prepared to get dinner. He stepped out of his room and onto a balcony. As he leaned over the railing to speak to his driver, a single shot rang out from a high-powered rifle. It found its mark, and Martin Luther King, Jr., lay dying of a wound to the head. He was thirty-nine years old.

Arrested for the assassination was a small-time thief named James Earl Ray, who allegedly shot King from the bathroom of a flophouse across from the Lorraine Motel. No witness saw Ray shoot, but a bag found in front of a store near the flophouse contained a rifle, which bore Ray's fingerprints. Although he subsequently confessed to the crime, was convicted (without public trial), and was sentenced to life imprisonment, Ray retracted his confession. Many, including the family of Dr. King, continue to doubt that Ray was the murderer and suspect that King had been the target of a broader conspiracy, perhaps even involving the federal government. (In 1998, Ray died, in prison, of cancer, still professing his innocence.)

Grief and outrage came in the immediate aftermath of the assassination, and many inner cities erupted into riot. Even after these outbreaks had been quelled, there remained the depressing, anxious sense that all hope for racial equality and harmony in the nation had been extinguished. However, it soon became apparent that Dr. King's example had not been in vain. The struggle for Civil Rights continued, and, beginning in 1986, King's birthday was commemorated as a national holiday.

Assassination of Robert Kennedy

The Tet Offensive in Vietnam at the beginning of 1968 raised the antiwar movement in America to a new pitch. Senator Eugene McCarthy, most eloquent and popular of Congressional "doves" (as legislators who opposed the war were called), very nearly defeated incumbent Lyndon B. Johnson in the crucial New Hampshire Democratic primary, a fact that encouraged the charismatic brother of the slain JFK, Robert Kennedy, to declare, on March 16, his candidacy for the Democratic nomination. Less than two weeks later, on March 31, President Johnson announced in a televised address to the nation that he would not run for re-election. Change was in the air, some violent, some hopeful, all unsettling.

Appointed attorney general in the administration of his brother, Robert F. Kennedy had continued to serve in that post briefly under Johnson, but soon left the LBJ administration and embraced the antiwar movement. RFK proved an effective vote-getter by winning primaries in Indiana and Nebraska. After this, Lyndon Johnson withdrew, and Kennedy went on to the all-important California primary. A win here would show that an antiwar candidate had a strong chance of becoming president and, indeed, ending the war in Vietnam. For if the election pitted a "dove" against a "hawk," it would be nothing less than a national referendum on the war.

Just before midnight on June 5, 1968, the California results were in. Kennedy had won. Shortly after midnight, on June 6, Kennedy made an informal speech to campaign workers, then, at a quarter past twelve, he left the ballroom of the Ambassador Hotel in Los Angeles to give a press conference. By prearrangement, his route cut through a food service pantry. As he passed through, a Palestinian immigrant, Sirhan Sirhan, stepped forward and fired a .22 revolver. In the close quarters of the passageway, Sirhan was quickly subdued, but Kennedy and five others lay wounded. Kennedy, shot in the head, died shortly afterward. Arrested at the scene, Sirhan was charged and convicted of first-degree murder. He continues to serve a life sentence.

As with the assassination of Martin Luther King, Jr., and, for that matter, the 1963 assassination of John F. Kennedy, many believed and many continue to believe that Robert Kennedy was not the victim of a lone, twisted gunman, but the target of a conspiracy. We may never learn the full truth, or, perhaps, we already know all there is to know. What cannot be known is what would have happened had Robert Kennedy lived to oppose Richard M. Nixon in the 1968 race. Would he have won? And would the Vietnam War have ended in 1969, perhaps, or very soon afterward? We cannot know the answers to these questions. What is certain is that the assassination of Robert Kennedy robbed mainstream, middle-class America of a chance in 1968 to embrace the movement against an unwinnable war.

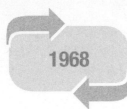

The Democratic National Convention

By August 26–29, 1968, when the Democratic Party held its national convention in Chicago, Americans had lived through the aftershock of the Tet Offensive, which turned increasing numbers against the war in Vietnam; they had also lived through the Watts Riots in Los Angeles and the assassinations of Martin Luther King, Jr., and Robert F. Kennedy. The nation became more profoundly divided politically and racially. Many liberals and young people, including young voters, turned their backs on "the system," and the 1968 Democratic National Convention nominated Hubert H. Humphrey, who was not opposed to the Vietnam War and who, in fact, offered no real alternative to Republican candidate Richard M. Nixon.

The convention had become the focal point of a massive youth, leftist, and antiwar protest that turned violent and led to what witnesses described as a "police riot" as Chicago officers unleashed their rage indiscriminately against protesters and residents of African-American neighborhoods south and west of Grant Park, the lakefront site of the protesters' makeshift tent camps.

It was not Chicago police officers who were tried in the aftermath of the convention and riot, but, instead, the so-called "Chicago Seven"—seven of the most visible leaders of the antiwar movement. During a five-month proceeding, David Dellinger (National Mobilization Against the War), Tom Hayden and Rennie Davis (Students for a Democratic Society, SDS), Abbie Hoffman and Jerry Rubin (Youth International Party, YIPPIEs), John Froines and Lee Weiner (local Chicago protest leaders), and Bobby Seale (Black Panther Party) were tried on charges of conspiracy to incite rioting. Five were found guilty in a trial presided over by the grotesquely biased Judge Julius Hoffman—who, at one point, ordered Seale bound and gagged—although their convictions were subsequently overturned on appeal.

The entire sequence of events—protest, police overreaction, the trial, the appeal—epitomized a decade of protest and suggested to many that the United States was on the verge of revolution if not dissolution. Some found this prospect enormously liberating. Others found it terrifying. Most were simply bewildered and demoralized.

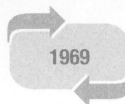

1969

Americans Land on the Moon

The year 1968 had been harrowing and dispiriting, a year of assassination, riot, and escalation in war. There was little to suggest that 1969 would be much better. Then, on July 20, 1969, at 4:17 P.M. (EDT), the nation—and much of the world—suddenly united in a moment of supreme achievement for the human race: Two men, Neil Armstrong and Buzz Aldrin, visitors from the planet Earth, walked on the surface of the moon.

As many saw it, the lunar landing was the culmination of the "space race" that had begun on October 4, 1957, when the Soviet Union successfully launched and orbited a thirty-eight-pound metal sphere containing nothing more than a simple radio transmitter. *Sputnik I* was the first human-made object to orbit the Earth, and it sent America into a frenzied game of catch-up with the communist dictatorship. It wasn't until January 1958 that America successfully orbited *Explorer I,* but, on April 12, 1961, the Soviets sprinted far into the lead by orbiting the first man in space, cosmonaut Yuri Gagarin. About three weeks later, on May 5, 1961, U.S. Navy commander Alan B. Shepard was sent on a fifteen-minute *suborbital* flight, a great day for Americans, but a distant second to the Russians' orbital achievement. Nevertheless, just twenty days later, with the American manned space program very much in its infancy, President John F. Kennedy addressed Congress: "I believe this nation should commit itself to achieving the goal, before the decade is out, of landing a man on the moon and returning him safely to earth. No single space project in this period will be more impressive to mankind, or more important for the long-range exploration of space, and none will be so difficult or expensive to accomplish."

Throughout the 1960s, the Soviets and the Americans continued to send men (and, in the case of the Soviets, a woman as well) into space. The United States did so with the goal of creating the technology and techniques for the eventual lunar mission: the *Apollo* program, nothing less than the biggest, most daring scientific and technological venture in the history of humankind. A giant *Saturn V* multistage booster would start the three-man *Apollo* spacecraft on a two-and-a-half-day voyage to the moon. The craft would assume lunar orbit, then the Lunar Excursion Module, with two men aboard, would separate from the orbiting Command Module and land on the moon. After a period of exploration on the lunar surface, the astronauts would climb back into the Lunar Excursion Module, lift off, and dock with the orbiting Command Module, which would blast out of lunar orbit and carry the three astronauts back to Earth.

The technological choreography involved in so complex a set of procedures was daunting, and the entire program got off to a tragic beginning when a fire broke out inside the *Apollo 1* spacecraft during a routine launchpad test on January 27, 1967. Astronauts Virgil I. "Gus" Grissom, Edward H. White, and Roger B. Chaffee were killed, and there was serious talk of scrapping or, at least, greatly delaying the entire lunar program. Yet NASA (the National Aeronautics and Space Administration) was able to persuade a wary Congress to proceed, and, after a series of Earth- and moon-orbital flights, *Apollo 11* was launched on July 16, 1969, manned by Neil A. Armstrong, Edwin E. "Buzz" Aldrin, Jr., and Michael Collins. As planned, Armstrong and Aldrin left the Command Module and entered the Lunar Excursion Module while the spacecraft was in lunar orbit. The Lunar Excursion Module, called *Eagle,* separated from the Command Module and took the pair to the surface. Touchdown came at 4:17 Eastern Daylight Time (8:17 P.M. Greenwich Mean Time) on July 20.

Leaping off the module's ladder into the unreality of one-sixth

Earth gravity, Armstrong declared: "That's one small step for [a] man, one giant leap for mankind."

For the next twenty-one hours thirty-six minutes, Armstrong and Aldrin explored the moon, collecting lunar soil and "moon rocks" and setting up various scientific experiments. All of this was important, to be sure, but it was the fact itself—the realization of human imagination and national will in aiming at, flying toward, and landing on the moon—that reached far beyond science to speak eloquently of and to the human spirit. That landing and the televised images of two men, no longer earthbound, walking, leaping, and skipping across the face of an alien world brought our own nation and our own world together in a joyous passage of human triumph during a time marked so deeply by bitterness, doubt, and despair.

> "Here men from the planet Earth first set foot on the moon, July 1969 A.D. We came in peace for all mankind."
> —plaque left on the moon to mark the site of the first lunar landing

Nixon's Vietnam Policy

I n the wake of President Johnson's announcement that he would not seek reelection, cease-fire negotiations with the North Vietnamese began in May 1968, but broke down repeatedly. Republican Richard Milhous Nixon won election to the presidency in 1968 on a platform that promised a plan to end the war. However, he began his administration by expanding the war into neighboring Laos and Cambodia, pursuant to a grand strategy he had worked out with his foreign policy advisor (and, later, secretary of state), former Harvard political science professor Henry Kissinger. This called for improving relations with the Soviets (through trade and an arms-limitation agreement) in order to disengage Moscow from Hanoi, and for normalizing relations with China. Once the USSR and China had cut the North Vietnamese loose, Kissinger believed, the United States could negotiate what Nixon called "peace with honor" in Vietnam.

As this strategy proved ineffective, however, Nixon decided to accelerate the "Vietnamization process," only to find that, as U.S. troops were withdrawn, the South Vietnamese were unable to take up the slack. The war was being lost, and Nixon turned from diplomacy to force, by striking at Communist supply and staging areas in Cambodia. This incursion into an ostensibly neutral Buddhist nation brought angry protests at home, including a demonstration at Kent State University in Ohio on May 4, 1970, which resulted in the killing of four unarmed students and the wounding of nine more when inexperienced National Guardsmen opened fire on them. After Kent State, 100,000 demonstrators descended on Washington, and Congress registered its own protest by rescinding the Gulf of Tonkin Resolution. Under pressure, Nixon withdrew ground troops from Cambodia, but stepped up bombing raids.

Yet the Nixon administration also continued to withdraw U.S. ground forces from Vietnam. While this eased dissension on the home front, it destroyed military frontline morale. Drug and alcohol abuse assumed epidemic proportions among troops, some of whom were openly rebellious and even mutinous. When peace talks faltered, President Nixon, freshly reelected to "four more years," ordered massive B-52 bombing raids north of the twentieth parallel, which forced the North Vietnamese back to the conference table. On January 31, 1973, the United States and North Vietnam signed the Paris Accords, which finalized U.S. withdrawal and the return of prisoners of war, some of whom had been languishing in North Vietnamese prisons for nearly a decade.

The Nixon administration continued to send massive amounts of aid to South Vietnam, and it even resumed bombing Cambodia to intimidate the North Vietnamese into observing the cease-fire. Congress, however, was war weary and had turned against President Nixon, whose administration was now deeply mired in the Watergate Scandal. In November 1973, the War Powers Act was passed, precisely to prevent another Gulf of Tonkin Resolution. The act required the president to inform Congress within forty-eight hours of deployment of U.S. military forces abroad and mandated troop withdrawal within sixty days if Congress did not approve. Congress also ruthlessly slashed aid to South Vietnam. Whatever hopes South Vietnam's President Nguyen Van Thieu held out for support from the Nixon administration were extinguished when Nixon, facing impeachment, resigned in August 1974.

The Pentagon Papers

I n 1967, Lyndon Johnson's Secretary of Defense, Robert Mc-Namara, commissioned a top-secret study by members of the Rand Corporation, an ultra-high-level political and policy "think tank." Officially titled *The History of the U.S. Decision Making Process in Vietnam,* the forty-seven-volume study traced the history of America's involvement in and conduct of the Vietnam War. The fully documented, excruciatingly detailed story was one of deliberate deceit, illegal covert action, and simple confusion, extending from the administration of Harry S. Truman to that of Lyndon Johnson and hopelessly miring the United States in a tragic war.

Daniel Ellsberg, an MIT professor who had collaborated on the study, leaked the massive work to the *New York Times,* which, on June 13, 1971, began publishing a series of articles based on it. Popularly dubbed *The Pentagon Papers,* it created a national sensation. At the behest of the Nixon White House, the U.S. Department of Justice obtained a court injunction against further publication on national security grounds, but, on June 30, the Supreme Court ruled that constitutional guarantees of a free press overrode other considerations, and allowed further publication. The government indicted Daniel Ellsberg in 1971 and a colleague, Anthony J. Russo, on charges of espionage, theft, and conspiracy, but, in 1973, a federal judge dismissed all charges against them due to improper government conduct.

The vindication of the *New York Times,* Ellsberg, and Russo were all triumphs of the U.S. Constitution and, therefore, heartening. But the revelations of *The Pentagon Papers* were profoundly disturbing, creating a picture of what had been, in effect, a shadow government operating outside of the Constitution virtually since the end of World War II.

1972

The Watergate Break-in

June 17, 1972, should have been like any other day in the re-election campaign of Richard M. Nixon—upbeat, since the president's victory seemed a sure thing. But that night, Washington, D.C., police officers were summoned by a security guard to the prestigious Watergate apartment and office complex to stop a burglary in progress. The target was the headquarters of the Democratic National Committee.

At first, the story was buried in the local news—until it was revealed that the five burglars were employees of the Nixon campaign's Committee to Re-elect the President, an organization better known by its remarkable acronym: CREEP. As burglars, they were amateurs, but as espionage agents they were, in varying degrees, pros, members of an unofficial White House unit dubbed the "Plumbers," because they had been formed in 1971, at the behest of Richard Nixon himself, to plug "leaks"—not the kind of leaks that might pose a national security risk, but the kind that might be embarrassing to the president and his administration. The Plumbers' first mission, in 1971, had been to burglarize the office of Daniel Ellsberg's psychiatrist. Ellsberg was the man who had leaked *The Pentagon Papers* to the *New York Times,* and the Nixon White House was desperate to obtain material that might discredit him. The following year, at the Watergate, the Plumbers attempted to tap the telephones of Democratic leaders and to obtain documents outlining the Democratic campaign strategy.

The five Watergate burglars included three anti-Castro Cuban refugees, all veterans of the ill-fated Bay of Pigs invasion, and James McCord, Jr., a former CIA agent and now "security" officer for CREEP, who reported directly to CREEP's director, John Mitchell, who had resigned as attorney general to become Nixon's campaign manager. In a lapse of security, one of the burglars carried in his pocket an address book with the name of E. Howard Hunt. A former CIA agent, Hunt had planned the Bay of Pigs operation and, by 1972, was a writer of pulpy spy novels as well as an assistant to Charles Colson, special counsel to President Nixon. What address did the burglar's little black book give for E. Howard Hunt? "The White House."

As the Watergate story gained national exposure, Mitchell declared that the "White House has had no involvement whatever in this particular incident," and President Nixon himself would later try to dismiss the episode as a "third-rate burglary." All through the summer and fall of 1972, elements of an ominous scandal broke in the press, mainly in the *Washington Post,* through the efforts of two dogged reporters, Bob Woodward and Carl Bernstein. Each revelation pointed more sharply to a conspiracy at the very highest levels of government. At last, in September, the burglars and two co-plotters—Hunt and former FBI agent G. Gordon Liddy (another CREEP operative, known for his almost flamboyant right-wing extremism)—were indicted on charges of burglary, conspiracy, and wiretapping. As each Nixon associate was convicted, each (except for Liddy) began to talk, and each word led investigators higher up the ladder of the executive branch of government.

1973

The Watergate Year

Despite the arrests and early revelations surrounding the Watergate burglary, Richard Nixon won election to a second term. No sooner had that term begun, however, than the unraveling of the Watergate conspiracy accelerated. In February 1973, the Senate created an investigative committee headed by North Carolina Senator Sam Ervin, Jr., and, as the Army–McCarthy Hearings had done two decades earlier, the televised Watergate Hearings commanded the rapt attention of the nation. A bizarre routine set in: After each shattering disclosure the committee produced, the president announced the resignation of another key aide. John Ehrlichman and H. R. Haldeman, his closest advisors, fell. The White House counsel, John W. Dean III, was dismissed. In the end, Senator Ervin, going about his questioning with the drawling, cunning persistence of a "country" lawyer educated at Harvard, elicited testimony uncovering malfeasance and crimes that reached far beyond a "third-rate burglary" at the Watergate. It was revealed that John Mitchell, while still attorney general, controlled secret monies used to finance a campaign of forged letters and false news items intended to damage the Democratic party. These were known as "dirty tricks," and the Nixon campaign used them extensively. The nation learned that major U.S. corporations had made illegal campaign contributions amounting to millions of dollars, that Hunt and Liddy were the burglars who had looted the office of Daniel Ellsberg's psychiatrist in order to discredit the *Pentagon Papers* whistle-blower and that they had plotted to assault Ellsberg physically. It was revealed that President Nixon had promised the Watergate burglars clemency and even bribes in return for their silence, and that L. Patrick Gray, Nixon's nominee to replace the recently deceased J. Edgar Hoover as head of the FBI, illegally surrendered FBI records on Watergate to White House counsel John Dean. The Ervin committee discovered that two Nixon cabinet members, Mitchell and Maurice Stans, took bribes from John Vesco, a shady financier with ties to organized crime. Witnesses testified that illegal wiretap tapes were in the White House safe of Nixon advisor John Ehrlichman, that Nixon had directed the CIA to instruct the FBI not to investigate Watergate, that Nixon used $10 million in government funds to improve his personal residences, and—not least of all—that during 1969–1970, the United States had secretly bombed Cambodia without the knowledge, let alone the consent, of Congress.

As if Watergate weren't debacle enough, in the midst of it all, Vice President Spiro T. Agnew was indicted for bribes he had taken as Maryland governor. He resigned as vice president in October 1973 and was replaced by Congressman Gerald Ford of Michigan. Then came the final blows. When it was revealed that President Nixon not only had wiretap tapes, but also covert tapes of White House conversations, the committee subpoenaed them. The president sought to evade the subpoena by asserting "executive privilege" and withheld the tapes. He then ordered Attorney General Elliot L. Richardson to dismiss special Watergate prosecutor Archibald Cox. Richardson refused and resigned in protest. When his deputy, William Ruckelshaus, also refused to fire Cox, he, too, was dismissed. Nixon's solicitor general, Robert H. Bork, did not share the scruples of Richardson and Ruckelshaus. Bork discharged Cox. All of this—the resignation of Richardson, the firing of Ruckelshaus, and the dismissal of Cox—took place on the evening of October 20, 1973, and was dubbed by the press the "Saturday night massacre." It spoke volumes about a man who had much to hide.

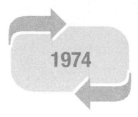

1974

President Nixon Resigns

By the summer of 1974, President Richard Nixon had run out of legal options for blocking the release to Congress of secret audiotapes made in the White House. He released transcripts of some of the tapes—except for a suspicious eighteen and a half minutes—and, after reviewing the material during July 27–30, the House Judiciary Committee delivered its recommendation that the president be impeached on three charges: obstruction of justice, abuse of presidential powers, and attempting to impede the impeachment process by defying committee subpoenas.

Nixon released the remaining tapes on August 5, 1974, which revealed unequivocally that he had taken steps to block the FBI's inquiry into the Watergate burglary. Four days later, on August 9, 1974, in a televised announcement, Richard Milhous Nixon became the first president in American history to resign from office.

In the end, all of the Watergate conspirators, save Nixon, were convicted, and all of them, save Nixon, went to jail. Nixon's successor, President Gerald Ford, presented the former chief executive with a preemptive pardon, for all crimes committed or that "may have been" committed.

In the decades following the scandal, Richard Nixon persisted in attempts to minimize the gravity of Watergate, protesting that he had neither planned nor ordered the "third-rate burglary," and that his political enemies had used it as a pretext for hounding him out of the White House. Indeed, to a remarkable degree, the Nixon of later years did rehabilitate his image and was viewed by many as an elder statesman. Even those who deplored Watergate and the White House policies that had spawned it, were inclined to remind their fellow Americans that, whatever else he may have done, it was Nixon who started down the road to détente with the Soviets, who inaugurated nearly cordial relations with Communist China, and who led the United States to the conclusion of the war in Vietnam. Yet it is impossible to overlook the Richard Nixon whose imperious contempt for the Constitution and solemn oath to uphold it drove him to corrupt the legitimate electoral process, to seek the expansion of executive power far beyond constitutional limits, and to subvert nothing less than the American legal system.

1975

Evacuation of Saigon

The year 1975 brought one South Vietnamese defeat after another. President Thieu resigned, leaving the presidency to Duong Van Minh, whose single official act was unconditional surrender to the North on April 30, 1975. This was followed by a frenzied evacuation of remaining U.S. personnel, and the American television audience was stunned by the spectacle of hundreds being airlifted by helicopter from the roof of the U.S. embassy in Saigon. It was a humiliating and heartbreaking end to a war that had cost the nation more than $150 billion and 58,000 American lives, not to mention a degree of faith in the righteous might of the United States. By any tactical measure, the Vietnam War was actually a victory for United States forces. If almost 60,000 Americans had been killed, millions of North Vietnamese, Viet Cong, and other hostile troops had died. Yet, strategically and—even worse, as many Americans saw it—morally, Vietnam stood as the only major military defeat in the history of the United States.

1979

Three Mile Island

The close of the 1970s was a time of discontent throughout America. The nation was suffering a prolonged recession aggravated by inflation—an economically distressing situation dubbed "stagflation"—and there was a growing, dispiriting sense that the nation's best days were behind it. The infrastructure of America, especially in the cities, seemed to be crumbling—roads in poor repair, bridges abandoned as unsafe—crime was on the rise, and even that great symbol of American industrial know-how and American personal freedom, the automobile, was under attack. The domestic auto industry was rapidly losing ground to Japanese imports, which were better built, more reliable, more efficient, and cheaper than many of their American counterparts.

One of the most frightening events of this period not only forced Americans to question their faith in made-in-the-U.S.A. technology, but seemed symbolic of the decline of American power and competence. On March 28, 1979, a nuclear reactor at the Three Mile Island electric generating plant, near the Pennsylvania capital of Harrisburg, lost coolant water, which initiated a partial "meltdown" of the reactor's radioactive core. A badly shaken Pennsylvania governor Richard Thornburgh appeared on television to warn residents to remain indoors, and he advised pregnant women to evacuate the area, because the partial meltdown had already released some radioactive gases into the atmosphere. For several days, Pennsylvania and the nation watched with great anxiety as efforts to correct the problem slowly succeeded and the danger of a nuclear "meltdown" receded.

In retrospect, there is ample evidence that plant officials improperly delayed notifying public authorities of the accident, and it is clear that a combination of human and mechanical error nearly created a catastrophe of a magnitude unprecedented in the United States. Yet it is also true that backup safety features in the plant functioned as they were supposed to. That, however, was not sufficient to keep Three Mile Island from looking like yet another in a train of dismal failures of American industry, technology, and competence. The accident all but killed the nuclear power industry in the United States, and it deepened the already yawning credibility gap between the officers of big business and ordinary Americans.

Iran Hostage Crisis

The radical Islamic cleric and political leader Ayatollah Ruhollah Khomeini successfully led a revolution in Iran that ousted longtime U.S. ally Muhammad Reza Shah Pahlavi, the shah of Iran, who fled into exile in January 1979. In October, critically ill with cancer, the shah was invited to travel to the United States to receive specialized medical treatment. This invitation inflamed the leading radical element in Iran and, on November 4, some 500 Iranians stormed the U.S. embassy in Tehran. There they took 66 U.S. embassy employees hostage, demanding for their release nothing less than the return of the shah.

The policy of the United States was not to bargain with terrorists, and, besides, President Jimmy Carter was not about to deliver to certain death a leader who had been a faithful ally. The shah left the United States on his own initiative in early December, but this did not end the crisis. Except for thirteen hostages, who were black or female, released on November 19–20, the others remained in captivity. Stalemated, President Carter authorized a U.S. Army Special Forces unit to attempt a rescue. The mission was hurriedly cobbled together and launched on April 24, 1980. After a series of mishaps, culminating in a disastrous collision between a helicopter and a transport plane, the mission was aborted. Fortunately, the failure did not result in reprisals against the hostages, but it seemed just one more humiliating defeat for a superpower unaccountably rendered impotent.

Day after day, week after week, month after month, the hostage crisis dragged on. It was not until November 1980 that the Iranian parliament proposed new conditions for the release of the hostages. These included an American pledge to refrain from meddling in Iranian affairs, the release of Iranian assets frozen in the United States by President Carter, the lifting of all U.S. sanctions against Iran, and the return of the shah's property to Iran. An agreement was concluded early in January 1981, as President Carter, having lost his bid for reelection to the buoyant Ronald Reagan, approached the end of his term. In an act most certainly of personal vengeance and contempt, the Ayatollah Khomeini delayed the actual release of the hostages until January 20, the very day of Ronald Reagan's inauguration. To President Reagan's enduring credit, he bestowed on Carter the honor of traveling to a U.S. air base in West Germany as his special envoy to welcome the returning hostages. They had endured 444 days of captivity, at gunpoint, and always under threat.

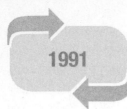

1991

The Cold War Ends

On December 25, 1991, Mikhail Gorbachev resigned as president of the Union of Soviet Socialist Republics. In point of fact, by this time, Gorbachev was a president with neither a party (the Communist Party had effectively dissolved) nor a nation (many of the "republics" that had formed the Soviet Union had declared independence, and those that remained re-formed themselves into the Commonwealth of Independent States). On that momentous day in Russian history, a long chapter of American history also closed. Since the end of World War II, much of our history had been defined by the "Cold War" against communism, which, most of the time, meant a Cold War against the Soviet Union. Now, suddenly, that opposition ideology and force against which the United States had for so long defined itself was gone.

The collapse of the Soviet Union was sudden, but the Soviet system bore within itself the seeds of its own destruction. It may well be impossible for any state to forcibly hold and sustain its people in a demand economy when the nature of human society embraces free-market capitalism. Certainly, Gorbachev did not set out to hasten the end of Soviet communism. Quite the contrary, he sought to preserve it by reforming it. When he succeeded Konstantin Chernenko as general secretary of the Communist Party of the Soviet Union after Chernenko's death in 1985 (in the USSR, leadership of the party entailed de facto leadership of the government), Gorbachev was, at fifty-four, the youngest party head ever. In contrast to his much older predecessors, he was willing to confront the reality that the Soviet economy was stagnant and there-

fore doomed. He called for a crash program of technological in-
novation and increased productivity from a workforce that, guaranteed an income, had become apathetic. He moved aggressively
to streamline the doddering complexity of the Soviet bureaucracy.
Yet even as he carried out his reforms, Gorbachev realized that
they were insufficient, and so, during 1987–1988, he instituted
two vast initiatives: *glasnost* ("openness") and *perestroika* ("re-
structuring"). Under traditional communism, culture and government had been paranoically closed and secretive. All news was
stringently filtered through party channels, paramountly *Pravda*
("Truth"), the party newspaper. Now, in a single stroke, the press
was given vastly expanded access to information and was encouraged to report the news fully and with candor. Equally significant
was the opening of at least certain elections to multiple candidates,
not just the individuals handpicked by the party. New laws began
to open the Soviet economy to private enterprise and free-market
mechanisms. This last reform was the principal thrust of *perestroika.*

While the Soviet Union was experiencing the tremors that her-
alded its demise, Germany, ever since the end of World War II divided into a communist East and a democratic West, moved
toward reunification. East Germany had come into being as a puppet of Moscow, and Erich Honecker, the communist functionary
who assumed leadership of East Germany in 1971, was content to
keep things that way—at first. But when the western democracies—including, ultimately, West Germany—extended to East
Germany long-withheld recognition as a sovereign nation, Honecker started to navigate a more liberal course, hesitantly, clum-
sily, and grudgingly opening up East Germany to the West.
Spiritually and politically, the Berlin Wall—that brick, mortar, and
barbed-wire symbol of the division between Free World and Communist World—was coming down.

The actual wall had stood since 1961. It was built because,
since 1949, when East Germany was created, some 2.5 million
East Germans had fled to the West. After erection of the wall,
about 5,000 East Germans managed somehow to overcome the

barrier and reach West Berlin, but at least 5,000 more were captured and 191 killed. By the 1970s, increased contact between
East and West heightened the discontent of East Germans, who
saw how meanly they lived, compared to those on the other side of
the wall. Honecker sought to reverse his own liberal reforms, but
as the volume of protest increased, he executed a new about-face
in the 1980s, this time even allowing East Germans to visit the
West. In October 1989, the East German politburo replaced Honecker with Egon Krenz. Although he was a hard-line communist,
Krenz yielded to the impossibility of controlling the flow of
refugees, and so opened East Germany's borders. On either side of
the Berlin Wall, East and West Germans began physically tearing
it down, brick by brick.

The symbolic dismantling of communism was counterpointed
to its collapse throughout eastern Europe, and the fall of the Berlin
Wall was the death blow for the Soviet Union. Mikhail Gorbachev
repudiated the so-called "Brezhnev Doctrine," promulgated by
Leonid Brezhnev (president of the Soviet Union from 1977 to
1982), asserting the right of the USSR to crush any uprisings
within Soviet satellite nations. As soon as Gorbachev put an end to
this policy, many of the Soviet republics declared themselves sovereign or independent.

Gorbachev scrambled to renegotiate relations with the fifteen Soviet republics, nine of which agreed to a new union treaty, but hard-line Soviet Communists organized a coup d'etat on August 19, 1991, and attempted to take back the government from Gorbachev. In Moscow, Boris Yeltsin, president of the Russian republic, led the resistance against the coup, which collapsed within days of its beginning. On December 25, 1991, what had been the Soviet Union and what was now a smaller Commonwealth of Independent States was in the hands of Boris Yeltsin. America's Cold War enemy had not surrendered. It had crumbled, evaporated, vanished, and the United States stood as the one great superpower of the post–Cold War world.

Impeachment of Bill Clinton

On September 11, 1998, the Republican-controlled U.S. Congress published on the Internet the full text of a report written under the direction of Kenneth Starr, an "independent counsel" appointed to investigate allegations of possibly impeachable offenses committed by President Bill Clinton. Millions of Americans were free to read laboriously detailed accounts of the president's sexual liaison with a twenty-one-year-old White House intern, Monica Lewinsky.

The "Starr Report" was the culmination of a four-year, $40-million-plus investigation into a number of questionable aspects of Clinton's conduct. It had begun as an inquiry into the involvement of the president and first lady in a shady real estate undertaking known as Whitewater (a name that coincidentally echoed the culminating scandal of the Nixon presidency, Watergate) and other possible financial improprieties. When Starr failed to find evidence of wrongdoing in these areas, he focused instead on the President's sexual behavior, creating a luridly documented account of Clinton's affair with Lewinsky. The details notwithstanding, Starr and the other investigators insisted that sex was not the issue in question. The issue, they claimed, was that the president had violated his oath of office by lying about the affair in a sworn deposition he had given in a sexual harassment civil lawsuit brought against him by a former Arkansas state employee, Paula Jones. It was alleged that the president had also lied about the affair to a grand jury.

Based on the Starr Report, Congress voted, along strict party lines, to impeach President Clinton, and, for the first time since

Andrew Johnson was impeached in 1868, the U.S. Senate was the scene of an impeachment trial.

Although Republicans held a simple majority of Senate seats, removal of a president from office requires more: a two-thirds Senate vote. Because no one believed that such a vote would be forthcoming, the months of congressional proceedings that followed made for engrossing television, but also struck many Americans as a time-wasting exercise in partisan vindictiveness. True, the American people generally deplored President Clinton's unbecoming behavior and were often vocal in their criticism of his character, yet they also overwhelmingly approved of his performance as a chief executive presiding over a booming economy. Most people believed that, even if true, the charges against the president did not "rise to the level" of removal from office, and even in the midst of the impeachment proceedings, public-opinion polls gave Clinton his highest approval ratings ever.

Heedless of popular sentiment, the Republican-controlled Congress pressed on with what members solemnly called their "constitutional duty." Nevertheless, on February 12, 1999, to no one's surprise, the Senate acquitted the president, and a potentially momentous national event receded into the media circus that had all along surrounded it, only to fade from the airwaves and the printed page—and, apparently, the consciousness of the American public.

The Supreme Court "Elects" a President

The lackluster presidential campaign of the year 2000 pitted Democrat Al Gore against Republican George W. Bush, the son of President Bill Clinton's predecessor, George H. W. Bush. Few were enthusiastic in their support of either candidate, who differed so little from one another that third-party spoiler Ralph Nader referred to them as Tweedle-Dee and Tweedle-Dum, and the election ended as too close to call. The first complete returns gave Gore 50,996,116 votes against Bush's 50,456,169. Gore led by a margin of more than half a million votes, but it is the electoral college that puts a president into office, and it was soon apparent that the election hinged on who would capture the twenty-five electoral votes of Florida.

In that state, which happened to be governed by candidate Bush's younger brother, Jeb, the vote was stupefyingly close. The tally on the day after the election gave Bush a lead of 1,784 votes over Gore, but Florida law required an automatic recount of votes when the difference between totals was less than half a percent. The result of the automatic recount, reported on November 9, two days after the election, cut the Bush lead to 327 votes. Three hundred twenty-seven votes would determine who would next occupy the White House and who would hold the reins of the most powerful government on the planet.

In an automatic recount, the ballots were simply run through the vote-counting machines a second time. (It was later revealed that, in some counties, the actual rerun of votes never took place; officials just rechecked tally-sheet totals.) Deeming the automatic recount insufficient, Democrats demanded a recount by hand in four counties: Palm Beach, Miami-Dade, Broward, and Volusia—all counties in which the Gore camp expected that a manual recount would net the vice president more votes. Why make such an assumption? After all, in the twenty-first century, in the most technologically sophisticated nation in the world, how could one fail to trust that the machines would do an accurate job of such a simple task as counting votes?

In Palm Beach County, a long list of candidates for local office had prompted election officials to design a ballot with enough space to accommodate all the names. The result was a punch-hole ballot consisting of two facing pages, a so-called butterfly ballot. The trouble with this design was that while the punch hole for Bush appeared directly to the right of his name, the punch hole below belonged to right-wing extremist Patrick J. Buchanan. In third place was the punch hole for Gore. Immediately following the election, officials were flooded with calls, mostly from elderly Jewish voters, who, confused by the butterfly ballot, claimed to have realized (*after* voting) that they had mistakenly punched the hole for Buchanan—widely believed to be an anti-Semite—when they had meant to vote for Gore. Democrats wanted this investigated.

In Palm Beach and the other three counties, Democrats were also concerned that many of the punch-card ballots were faulty, that votes were not counted simply because voters had not pushed the stylus all the way through the card. If a punch-out wasn't clean, the resulting hole could be blocked by a tiny rectangular fragment of cardboard—called a "chad"—and the vote would not be counted. Florida law required election officials to evaluate disputed ballots in a way that attempts to "determine the intention" of the voter. Democrats wanted each ballot inspected for "hanging chad." Where this was found, a vote should be counted. Some Democrats called for even more: an inspection for what was called (incredibly enough) "pregnant chad," chad that had not been punched out on *any* of its four sides, but bulged—evidence that some stylus pressure had been applied. Now it seemed as if the fate of the nation and the free world rested on a few infinitesimally small pieces of scrap cardboard.

On November 11, candidate Bush filed a federal lawsuit to stop the manual recounts. The court rejected the suit, even as Katherine Harris, Florida's secretary of state, declared that she intended to certify the election—with Bush as winner—on the legal deadline for certification, November 14, and that, in her official opinion, manual recounts should not be permitted. Gore supporters in Florida and across the nation were not a little concerned that Harris, the state's top election official, was not only a Republican, but had served as a Bush delegate to the Republican National Convention and was one of eight cochairs of the Bush campaign in Florida.

Over the next several days, manual counts started and stopped in the disputed counties, and a battle raged in the Florida courts, with one legal decision countering another. At last, Secretary of State Harris denied a request from Palm Beach County for more time to complete its recount, and, on Sunday, November 26, certified George W. Bush as the winner in Florida by 537 votes.

The certification of the Florida vote did not end the battle, however. On December 1, the U.S. Supreme Court began hearing arguments in Bush's appeal of a Florida Supreme Court decision to extend the deadline for certification, and on December 9, voting

Associate Justice Stephen Breyer was one of four U.S. Supreme Court justices who dissented from the majority decision overturning the order of the Florida Supreme Court to resume the manual recount of disputed ballots. This is from the conclusion of Breyer's dissenting opinion:

". . . Although we may never know with complete certainty the identity of the winner of this year's Presidential election, the identity of the loser is perfectly clear. It is the Nation's confidence in the judge as an impartial guardian of the rule of law. . . ."

five to four, the justices of the U.S. Supreme Court ordered the manual recount to stop. On December 12, the high court overturned the Florida Supreme Court, again by a five-to-four decision, thereby rejecting all further manual recounts. Al Gore conceded the election to George W. Bush on December 13.

Even for supporters of the winning candidate, the election of 2000 was largely a dispiriting and unnerving business. It spoke of voter apathy, it made many ask why candidates for the highest office in the land should be so uniformly unimpressive, and it suggested just how fragile the mechanics of democracy are. On the other hand, the nation swore in a president, the forty-third since 1789, and it did so without violence and without serious political protest.

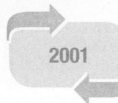

2001

Terrorist Attacks on New York and Washington, D.C.

At 8:45 (EDT) on the morning of September 11, 2001, a Boeing 757 passenger jetliner (later identified as American Airlines Flight 11 out of Boston) exploded into the north tower of the 110-story World Trade Center in lower Manhattan. Live television pictures of the disaster were beamed across the nation and the world almost immediately, and millions stared in disbelief at the great gash in the gleaming steel skin of the building, evil black smoke roiling out of it. The news camera video was rolling when, at 9:03, a second 757, United Airlines Flight 175, also out of Boston, hit the as-yet-undamaged south tower.

Emergency workers, firefighters, and police officers rushed to the site. At 9:30, President George W. Bush, attending an education-related function in Sarasota, Florida, announced that the nation had suffered "an apparent terrorist attack."

But that attack was far from over.

At 9:40, for the first time in American history, the Federal Aviation Administration (FAA) shut down all United States airports. Three minutes later, American Airlines Flight 77 burrowed into the Pentagon, America's military headquarters. Two minutes after this, the White House was evacuated, and, back in New York, at 10:05, the south tower of the World Trade Center collapsed: 110 stories of steel, concrete, glass, and humanity suddenly folded in on itself amid a death-dealing cloud of billowing smoke and debris. Just five minutes later, in Arlington, Virginia, a section of the wounded Pentagon also fell in, and, at almost exactly that moment, United Airlines Flight 93 tore into the soil of rural Somerset

County, Pennsylvania, not far from Pittsburgh. At 10:28, the north tower of the World Trade Center collapsed, ejecting a monumental plume, as if it had been swallowed into a volcano.

How many lives were lost in the space of less than two hours? No one knew. Asked to speculate, New York mayor Rudolph Giuliani replied quietly, "More than any of us can bear." (Ultimately, the death toll would approach 3,000—devastating, but, miraculously, far lower than had been feared.)

President Bush was flown from Florida, not to the White House, but to a "secure location" at Barksdale Air Force Base, Louisiana, and, later, to Offutt Air Force Base, outside of Omaha, Nebraska, a facility built to withstand thermonuclear attack. He finally returned to the White House shortly before 7 P.M. By that time, another part of the World Trade Center, the forty-seven-story Building 7, had collapsed, and the media was reporting that the airplane downed in Pennsylvania had been headed for the White House or the United States Capitol.

Although no organization claimed responsibility for the attacks, it was soon discovered that all four aircraft had been hijacked by terrorists executing carefully planned suicide missions. Later, the nation learned that cellphone calls made by crew members and passengers on the doomed aircraft—calls made to airline supervisors, to 911 operators, and to family members—described how the terrorists had operated. Handguns are difficult to smuggle on board an airplane, so the hijackers used small knives and box cutters to take over the aircraft, break into the cockpit, kill or disable the pilots, and commandeer the controls. The first three planes hit their targets in rapid succession: the south tower of the World Trade Center, the north tower, the Pentagon. But by the time the fourth plane was being taken over, passengers who made cellphone calls were told of the attack on the World Trade Center. A group of passengers on that fourth plane decided to attempt to seize control. The result was a terrible crash—but a crash in Shanksville, Pennsylvania, and not at the White House or the Capitol.

"The First War of the Twenty-First Century"

As early as 4 P.M. on September 11, the day terrorism struck at the United States, CNN correspondent David Ensor reported that U.S. government officials had "good indications" that Osama bin Laden was involved in the attacks. Forty years old, heir to a great fortune, Yemenite by birth, Saudi by nationality, and now living in Afghanistan, bin Laden routinely financed and sponsored terrorist acts while enjoying the protection of Afghanistan's radical Islamic Taliban government. Osama bin Laden was the suspected mastermind behind the bombings of two U.S. embassies in 1998 and the attack on the U.S. guided missile destroyer *Cole,* in port at Yemen, on October 12, 2000. At least since the early 1990s, bin Laden had led al-Qaeda (Arabic for "The Base"), a center for training, coordinating, and financing Muslim terrorists in a jihad (holy war) directed against Israel, the West, and, above all, the United States. President Bush, addressing the nation at 8:30 in the evening, vowed to "make no distinction between the terrorists who committed these acts and those who harbor them." It was, in effect, a declaration of war, and the very next day the president remarked that "We have just seen the first war of the twenty-first century."

Following the September 11 attacks, American military forces were deployed to strategic positions from which they could readily attack Afghanistan. The Bush government launched an intense diplomatic effort to secure the support—and in some cases, the direct aid—of many nations in fighting what was frankly described as a *war* against terrorism. Even Islamic nations voiced their opposition to terrorism; several, including Afghanistan's neighbor, Pakistan, promised support for American action.

Without a formal declaration of war, the first air attack against the Taliban government was launched at 16:38 Greenwich Mean Time, October 7—nighttime in Afghanistan. Over the next several weeks, U.S. and some British aircraft bombed Taliban military targets. Small groups of U.S. and British ground forces worked with indigenous opposition to the Taliban and, by the end of the year, had almost completely taken control of the country. While many al-Qaeda and Taliban troops and leaders were killed or captured, Osama bin Laden remained at large.

Most Americans knew little about Afghanistan and were far more anxious over the fact that terrorism had penetrated the American homeland. FBI and other investigators quickly discovered that the suicide hijackers of the four September 11 flights, all of Middle Eastern origin, had trained in small American flight schools and had lived not in secret safe houses but in ordinary American motels and apartment complexes while hardening their bodies in neighborhood gyms. How many more terrorists were among us? American and international law enforcement agencies made many arrests and detained more than a thousand suspects on immigration violation.

In the meantime, on October 4, even before the war got under way in distant Afghanistan, U.S. health officials reported that a Florida man, a photo editor for a supermarket tabloid, had contracted anthrax—the only case in the United States since the 1970s. At first, authorities discounted any link between the infection and terrorism, but after the Florida man succumbed to the disease on October 5, a second instance of exposure was discovered on October 8, and a third on October 10. More followed, including the cutaneous anthrax infection of a personal assistant to the popular NBC news anchor Tom Brokaw. The infections were traced to letters laced with dry anthrax spores—clearly a "weaponized" form of the anthrax bacillus—and in the course of October, at least forty persons were found to have been exposed to anthrax. A minority of these became ill, either with the highly treatable cutaneous form of the disease or the far more lethal inhalation anthrax. One anthrax-laced letter reached the office of Senate minority leader Tom Daschle, and on October 17, thirty-one members of Daschle's staff tested positive for anthrax exposure. The Capitol and several Senate and House office buildings were temporarily shut down, but, by this time, the tainted letter (or perhaps other tainted mail) had contaminated a Washington, D.C., postal facility, fatally infecting two postal employees. Two additional fatal cases followed, and as of April 2003, the perpetrator or perpetrators remained at large.

It was not determined what relation, if any, the anthrax attacks bore to the terrorism of September 11, 2001.

As for the war against terrorism, it seemed to go well, both in Afghanistan and elsewhere, although, as of April 2003, Osama bin Laden remains at large. By late 2002, it became apparent that President Bush was targeting Iraq as the next theater of the war. Although no direct link was demonstrated between the repressive regime of Saddam Hussein and the events of 9/11, the Bush Administration argued that Saddam's possession of weapons of mass destruction required action. Key UN Security Council members opposed U.S. military intervention and favored a lengthy program of UN-led weapons inspections. Despite widespread opposition at home and abroad, U.S. and British forces invaded Iraq, beginning on March 20, 2003, with the avowed objective of removing Saddam Hussein and his two sons from leadership in Iraq.

SCIENCE

A.S.A.P*

*As Soon As Possible,
As Simple As Possible

What This Is and What This Isn't

S cience *A.S.A.P.* has been written as an informal, very readable, and highly efficient one-stop source for all the science the general reader needs in order to stake a legitimate claim to cultural literacy. The book is not a compact review of scientific principles, nor is it a brief encyclopedia. Instead, it looks at science historically, highlighting key discoveries, inventions, and theoretical formulations everyone needs to know about, and it uses them as sturdy springboards to related discoveries, inventions, and theories and, even more important, to the ideas, concepts, and themes that underlie and inform the scientific approach to reality. Counting the main entries as well as the sidebars within some of those entries, there are only 202 items here, but they are leveraged into a full-scale appreciation of the movement of science from 500,000 B.C. through 2003—the year this book was completed.

ANCIENT
SCIENCE

Homo Erectus Tames Fire

The first hard archaeological evidence of the purposeful use of fire is found in a cave near Beijing, China. Here, along with remains of *Homo erectus*—a hominid, precursor of today's human beings (*Homo sapiens*), who lived between one million and three million B.C.—are traces of campfires.

The controlled use of fire—starting, perpetuating, applying, and stopping it—is not only essential to the activities of human society; it is also a basic skill that sets human beings apart from other animals. No wonder the ancient Greeks thought of fire as the divine gift to humanity, conveyed by Prometheus. Fire provides us with light that defies the night, with heat that defies the climate, with a weapon against stronger animals, and with a means to cook their meat—to render otherwise unpalatable, even inedible, foods useful. Fire also opened the way to myriad processes of transforming raw materials into useful objects. Its "discovery" by *Homo erectus* was the foundation of all technology.

Agriculture and Irrigation Develop in Northern Iraq

Before about 8000 B.C., human beings were largely wanderers, their nomadic mode of existence dictated not by some romantic wanderlust, but by the way they got their food: afoot and on the hoof. People were chiefly hunters who followed the migrating herds, though they also gathered whatever wild edibles grew nearby. Even those groups living among nonmigrating animals did not put down roots. Animals that stayed in one place were not, alas, to be had in limitless supply, so when the edible beasts dwindled in one location, it was time to move on to another.

The paramount feature of nomadic life is impermanence. Nomads do not build; their energies are directed toward moving, hunting, and moving again. There is no impetus or incentive to invest in, to improve, or to enhance any particular place.

Based on archaeological evidence, it is apparent that a new mode of living appeared around 8000 B.C. People began purposely planting seeds, watching them grow, watering them, then harvesting the results. No one has any idea how—or even why—this invention, agriculture, came about, but it did. And it gave groups of people a reason to stay in one place, especially when animal herding was added to agriculture. No longer did the source of food have to be ceaselessly pursued. Like the plants they cultivated, people began to put down roots.

The idea that food could be actively produced rather than passively followed was a great advance in what we think of as civilization: the creation of continuous, cohesive settlements and cultures.

Settlement called for building—not just shelters, but structures of all kinds, including structures of the intellect: ideas and systems. For now there was time to sit and think and formulate and invent. As great a step as agriculture was, there was still much that lay beyond the human capacity to control. One could plant a seed, but if a steady supply of water were not present, the seed would not become food. If human beings were no longer shackled to migrating herds, they were still the helpless vassals of rain and the victims of drought.

Archaeological evidence that people began to cultivate and harvest water as they had earlier begun to cultivate and harvest crops appears about 5000 B.C. Rain falls on land as well as on bodies of water. Rivers run with water long after a rain shower ceases. By about 5000 B.C., people began to dig ditches from the riverbanks into the land nearby. In this way, more land became productive more dependably and for longer periods. Of course, this required work—and not just a one-time commitment to dig ditches. The water flowing through them wore the ditches away, brought silt, caused them to collapse. Irrigation ditches required continual maintenance. Cooperation, collaboration, coordination were called for, and this required leadership, the rudiments of social structure, law, and government. If agriculture gave people a reason to stay put and the means to do so, irrigation provided a motive for the creation of what we call the city-state, the forerunner of nations.

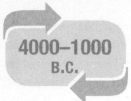

4000–1000 B.C.

Copper, Bronze, and Iron Come into Use

Archaeologists believe that hominids, the precursors of current human beings, learned how to use tools and weapons long before they learned to use fire—although the use of fire certainly enabled the creation of more and better tools and weapons. Stone, bone, and wood were the readily available materials from which the tools were fashioned, and since stone is by far the most durable, it is the stone tools that archaeologists have found in greatest abundance, and the period in which human beings used stone tools is generally called the Stone Age.

Over the centuries, early makers and users of stone tools must have devoted a great deal of time to searching out stones, and some that they found were unusual, heavy, shiny, and malleable—that is, when struck, they did not split or shatter, but dented and spread. These were metals, albeit the relatively rare metals that, chemically inert, do not combine with other substances readily. Most metal ore is exclusively found combined with nonmetallic stuff in rocks and so just looks like more rock. But relatively inert metals such as silver, gold, and copper are sometimes found in a free state, as pure metal nuggets.

By 5000 B.C., people were trading nuggets and even beating them into ornaments—they were too small to do much else with—but within a thousand years, people began separating metal from nonmetallic ore. Copper was the first. When copper ore is heated over a hot wood fire, the carbon liberated from the burning wood combines with the oxygen in the ore and forms carbon dioxide, which escapes to leave behind not a conglomerate of metal and nonmetal, but pure copper.

How was something so momentous discovered? No one knows. We can only assume that various people at various times during this period either built wood fires atop copper ore and noticed the result or perhaps deliberately experimented to see what would happen if certain rocks were thrown into a very hot fire.

Separation of copper from copper ore was an important advance in the science of metallurgy, and it allowed for the increased production of copper ornaments, which, in turn, fostered the wider development of trade among peoples. However, copper was not very practical for making tools. Soft, copper is easily bent and blunted. But those who spent a lot of time extracting copper from ore must have noticed that *some* copper comes out harder than other copper. Why? Because the hard copper is not pure copper, but a combination of copper and tin, which, when smelted from the mixed ore, produces an alloy of the two metals, bronze.

In contrast to copper, bronze is hard. Whereas a copper tool quickly became dull, a bronze tool held its edge. Soon, metalworkers did not rely on the chance finding of mixed copper and tin ores to produce bronze, but purposely smelted the two metals together, creating the bronze alloy at will and giving rise to the so-called Bronze Age, characterized by the production and use of vast quantities of bronze tools, armor, and edged weapons.

Bronze held sway as literally the cutting-edge material of civilization for some two thousand years, from about 3000 to 1000 B.C. During this period—and, doubtless, even earlier—people knew of another metal, even harder and heavier than bronze. They knew it from occasional rocks that fell from the sky, iron meteorites, the only rocks in which iron occurs free from nonmetallic substances. Meteors are extremely rare, and the iron ones must have been prized as precious, because the metal made a supremely strong tool—or weapon.

Before 1000 B.C., metalworkers had obtained copper, gold, silver, bronze, lead, and tin from ore, simply by using very hot wood fires. But a wood fire was not sufficient to free iron trapped in ore.

How to make fire hotter?

If wood is burned in the presence of relatively little oxygen, it produces charcoal—carbon—which, in turn, burns without flame, but at temperatures much greater than those of burning wood. By about 1500 B.C., the Hittite people of Asia Minor produced charcoal and, using it, they were able to smelt iron from ore. But it was never as good as that rare meteoric stuff (which, it turns out, is actually an alloy of iron and nickel); it simply wasn't as hard as a good piece of bronze. It took several hundred more years to discover that if the iron ore was smelted so that some of the resulting iron combined with the carbon in the charcoal, the resulting metal was very hard indeed. In fact, the carbonized iron was steel. By 1000 B.C., this metal was being turned out in great quantity, and the Bronze Age yielded to the Iron Age.

Egyptians Invent the Sundial and the "Modern" Calendar

The measurement of the most abstract of quantities, time, was a great advance in civilization. With it came the capacity to coordinate the actions of many individuals and, therefore, the ability to direct, manage, and govern complex enterprises and societies.

To be sure, human beings must have "told time" since early pre-history, simply by noting the passage of days, the changes of season, and almost certainly, early on, the phases of the moon. Most likely, they also divided the day into some sort of segments based on the position of the sun. But it was not until the appearance of the sun-dial, apparently in Egypt and probably about 4000 B.C., that any degree of accuracy in the division of the day was achieved. It is known that the Egyptians made extensive use of sundials—little wonder in a sunny climate and location—and that they divided the day into twelve equal parts, named hours.

The systematic measurement of time in the longer term seems to have originated about 2800 B.C. among the peoples of the "fertile crescent," the region watered by the Tigris and Euphrates. However, it was the Egyptians, shortly after this period, who developed a calendar that seems more familiar to us—although it was based on a more local phenomenon than the moon. By careful observation, Egyptian priests discovered that the Nile flooded every 365 days, which coincided with the time it took the sun to make what appeared to be its circuit of the heavens relative to the stars. Using these two coincidental cycles, the Egyptians developed a solar calendar. Returning to the lunar cycles, they divided the year into twelve months, making each month exactly 30 days long—without trying to synchronize the months with the actual phases of the moon. The result was a calendar year of 360 days, to which the Egyptians appended 5 more days at the end, so that the year would reflect the workings of river and sun. The Egyptian calendar was much simpler than anything that had come before, which made it that much more flexible and useful for measuring time across the long term and for planning the future.

The First Calendar, About 2800 B.C.

By about 2800 B.C., the people of the lands adjacent to the Tigris and Euphrates created a calendar—the first of which we have archaeological evidence—that attempts to reconcile the variations in the cycles of the moon with a consistent method of marking the passage of seasonal time. It takes twenty-nine or thirty days for the moon to go through all of its phases, and the cycle of the seasons consumes twelve or thirteen of these cycles. The Tigris-Euphrates calendar was projected over a cycle of nineteen years, during which some years had twelve and others thirteen lunar months. By this means, the lunar calendar meshed with the seasons.

1800 B.C.

Sumerians and Babylonians Create Mathematics and Astronomy

Who knows when human beings first began to count and to manipulate quantities? It is impossible to say. But the earliest known civilization that went beyond counting and quantities to develop a genuine system of numbers was that of the Sumerians, the people centered in what is today southern Iraq.

By 1800 B.C., they had developed a number system based not on the familiar ten, but on sixty. It is a most intriguing number on which to base a number system. Sixty is easy to manipulate, in that it is readily divisible by many numbers, even and odd: two, three, four, five, six, ten, twelve, fifteen, and thirty. This is ideal for a people heavily engaged in trade and commerce. But the choice of sixty likely went beyond mere convenience, and it is almost certainly no coincidence that, as the Sumerian number system is the earliest of which we have a record, so the immediate successors of the Sumerians, the Babylonians, are remembered as the world's first astronomers. Consider: There are six-times-60 degrees in a circle—360—which very nearly duplicates the apparent movement of the sun around the sky: about 1 degree per day, or 365 degrees per year, which is very close to the 360 degrees of a circle.

From virtually the earliest *recorded* times, then, mathematics and astronomy were joined. Numbers were very useful for counting cattle, people, and goods, but, thousands of years ago, those who watched the skies discerned a deeper significance in numbers. They felt a higher connection, between numbers and the motions of what

The Invention of Writing, About 3500 B.C.

The Sumerians produced writing long before they created mathematics. By 3500 B.C., a pressing need to track grain production and trade prompted the Sumerians to create unique symbols to stand for certain numbers and certain items, such as *grain, cow, human being,* and so on. The earliest symbols were, in effect, crude drawings of the objects represented. These evolved into standardized wedge-shaped indentations made with a stylus in a soft clay tablet: *cuneiform,* from the Greek for "wedge-shaped," writing.

Since the eighteenth century, when it was first described, cuneiform has been assumed to be the oldest surviving writing. However, in April 2003, archaeologists announced the results of preliminary analysis of symbols carved into eight, 600-year-old tortoise shells found in twenty-four Neolithic graves at Jiahu in Henan province, western China. It is quite possible that these signs, thousands of years older than cuneiform, will prove to be the earliest examples of writing, although it will require a good deal of study to determine if the symbols really belong to a genuine writing system.

they saw in the heavens. In the simultaneous formulation of mathematics and astronomical observation by the peoples of the great valley of the Tigris and the Euphrates we have the first evidence of what we today call science: the postulation of theory, the discernment of system and meaning in the world, a connection between mind and universe, a passion to look beyond the visible and the apparent for an explanation of all that is visible and apparent.

580 B.C.

Thales Conceptualizes the Elements

Great science has always asked the big questions, and few questions are bigger than "What is the universe made of?" Certainly, thoughtful people asked this question before 580 B.C., but the answers they came up with were based on myth, tradition, or faith rather than reasoning built on observation. When the Greek philosopher Thales asked the question in 580 B.C., he did not base his answer on religion, legend, or folk wisdom, but on observation, which he used to formulate a theory.

In itself, this was a great advance in science, whose very core is rational inquiry. As for the theory Thales formulated, well, it was, on the face of it, wrong! He concluded that all matter was water, either in the familiar form of liquid water or water in a transformed or altered state. Today, of course, no scientist believes that everything is made of water, but look deeper into Thales's theory and it is apparent that he conceptualized a cornerstone of modern physics and chemistry: the idea of elements as the building blocks of all matter. Wrong in the details, Thales was quite right in the concept.

Alcmaeon Performs the First Recorded Human Dissection

Science is about rational inquiry, yet it is also driven by a powerful human passion, for which the word *curiosity* seems pale, weak, and inadequate. Driven by the passion of their curiosity, many scientists have defied religious dogma and social convention. One such was Alcmaeon, who, about 500 B.C., became the first physician (of whom we have record) to dissect a human corpse—in bold defiance of Greek religious scruples and traditions. Alcmaeon was able to differentiate between veins and arteries, and he observed that the organs of sensation were linked to the brain by nerves. Beyond this, he did not leave any detailed anatomical studies, but his action broke new ground by elevating firsthand observation to the status of a scientific necessity above all other considerations.

440 B.C.

Democritus Proposes the Atom as the Smallest Particle of Matter

I n 440 B.C., the Greek philosopher Democritus took the idea of the element, as advanced by Thales (see "580 B.C.: Thales Conceptualizes the Elements"), much further by theorizing that all matter consists of tiny particles, too tiny to see and so small that nothing smaller was possible. With the keen logic of the Greek philosophical tradition, Democritus reasoned that if a particle were the smallest particle possible, it was by definition indivisible. This got to the true nature of an *element* as the basic, irreducible substance of matter. Democritus called such particles *atoms,* from a Greek word signifying indivisibility.

Unlike Thales's water theory, the atomic theory of Democritus was not based on observation, but speculation. This, too, is permitted in science, but such reasoning is never complete without experimental—observational—proof. In the case of atoms, that would not come for some two thousand years. During the long period of Western history known as the Dark Ages, roughly A.D. 476 to 1000, and far into the Middle Ages, the brilliance of Thales, Democritus, and most of the other philosophers of classical Greece would be forgotten, or even surpressed.

Euclid Creates the Elements of Geometry

Zoser, first king of Egypt's Third Dynasty, came to power in 2650 B.C., whereupon construction was begun on a massive "step pyramid," about 200 feet high and on a base of approximately 400 feet by 350 feet. It was the first of the pyramids and, perhaps, the first large stone structure ever built. Today, it remains as the earliest large-scale human structure in existence. From it, we can only infer that the Egyptians, at least as early as 2650 B.C., had developed considerable knowledge of geometry, at least on a practical, journeyman level. It was not until millennia later, however, about 300 B.C., that the Greek mathematician Euclid lifted geometry from the realm of the builder and artisan to that of the philosopher. In a book he titled *Elements,* Euclid compiled and synthesized all that was known of geometry at the time.

Analyzing a vast body of geometrical observation, Euclid developed a handful of axioms, a foundation of principles whose self-evidence required no proof. Building on these, Euclid constructed a series of theorems, the proofs of which depended on the axioms and on theorems previously proved.

Euclid's achievement in *Elements* has, of course, contributed mightily to the human-built world, but his contribution to thought and the intellectual process is even more profound. For Euclid removed from the physical world such tangibles as points, lines, curves, planes, and solids, and imported them into the realm of the mind. He did what countless scientists have done and continue to do daily: modeled reality in the imagination, where it can be examined, manipulated, and extended in myriad ways impossible or impractical in the physical world.

The Abacus, About 500 B.C.

Euclid's genius was in elevating the physical world to the realm of abstract idea. However, physical calculation—arithmetic—remained an important aspect of mathematics long after Euclid. The ancient computer known as the abacus may well have existed before 500 B.C., when it is known that Egyptians were using it, but the earliest archaeological evidence dates from this time. The abacus is an elegantly simple means of manipulating numbers by exploiting the base of a particular number system. Beads are strung on a series of wires suspended in a frame. In a base 10 system (the decimal system we are familiar with), ten beads are strung on each wire. The beads of the first wire represent ones, those of the second, tens, those of the third, hundreds, and so on. With practice, the basic arithmetical operations can be performed quickly.

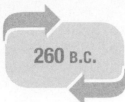

Archimedes Articulates the Principle of the Lever

As with the wheel and axle, the inclined plane, and other simple machines, the inventor of the lever is unknown. Doubtless, there was no single inventor, in any case, just practical people who, at various times, used a stick to pry up a rock or other heavy object, then, intuitively, figured out that it made even more sense to put a rock or other object (we call this a fulcrum) under the pry stick, and press down rather than pull up.

Intuitive, practical engagement with the world around us is a wonderful and highly useful thing, but it is hit or miss, and it holds little hope for any significant technological progress. How far would technical civilization progress if each individual had to discover the lever and fulcrum for himself and on his own, or if he depended on lore or even imitation for his knowledge of this simple machine, not to mention the others?

Scientists neither ignore nor disdain the practical and intuitive, but, for them, these things are never enough. Their urge is to reach behind and beyond the surface of practice and intuition, to develop the principles from which phenomena, actions, and causes and effects flow. This is the creation of theory, and one of the most brilliant theorists of the classical world was Archimedes.

An acute observer of the physical world, Archimedes was even more incisive in his ability to reduce what he observed to precise mathematical description. About 260 B.C., he worked out the mathematics of the lever, providing a theoretical means by which the most mechanically efficient length of lever and placement of fulcrum could be determined based on the weight of the object to be lifted and the height to which one wished to elevate it. Because he had established a complete mathematical theory of levers, Archimedes was able to declare with more than boastful hyperbole, "Give me a lever and a place to stand, and I'll move the world."

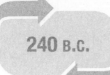

240 B.C.

Eratosthenes Calculates the Size of the Earth

Virtually all science begins with intense and original observation. Typically, the things others overlook or take for granted are precisely what draw the attention of the scientist. Take Eratosthenes (ca. 276–194 B.C.), who observed that, at the town of Syene (present-day Aswan, Egypt), southeast of Alexandria, the rays of the sun were precisely vertical at noon during the summer solstice. Separately, he observed that, at Alexandria, at exactly the same date and time, the sunlight fell at an angle of 7.5 degrees from the vertical. The difference was small, but Eratosthenes craved an explanation for it, small or not.

Eratosthenes assumed—correctly, as it turns out—that the sun was very far from the earth. This being the case, for all practical purposes, its rays are parallel when they strike the earth. He further believed, as Aristotle had taught, that the earth was a globe. Now, a circle—the flat representation of a globe—contains 360 degrees, and 7.5 degrees (the extent to which sunlight falling on Alexandria at the summer solstice varied from the vertical) is approximately one-fiftieth of 360. Therefore, Eratosthenes concluded, the circumference of the earth must be fifty times the distance between Alexandria and Syene. As measured in Eratosthenes's time, the distance between these two places was 5,000 *stadia,* so he concluded that the circumference of the earth was 250,000 *stadia.* Modern scholars assume that the *stadion* is equivalent to 521.4 feet; therefore, Eratosthenes's calculation of the earth's circumference comes out to 23,990.4 miles and the diameter to 7,578.6

miles. These figures are startlingly close to what we know today as the earth's circumference—24,887.64 miles—and its diameter, 7,926 miles.

Using the apparently meager information available to him, and without instrumentation of any kind, Eratosthenes made a measurement far beyond any physical capacity to do so. It was a triumph of inference.

In addition to measuring the circumference of the earth, Eratosthenes also accurately measured the tilt of the earth's axis, and he compiled an accurate and enormously impressive star catalog. The calendar he formulated was the first to include leap years. For all these reasons, many historians of science consider Eratosthenes the first astronomer in anything approaching the modern sense of the word. That is, he used his senses to make penetrating, remarkable observations precisely in order to move beyond what his mere senses could tell him.

Mapping the Stars, About 350 B.C.

About a century before Eratosthenes calculated the size of the earth, another Greek, Eudoxus, looked to the stars. About 350 B.C., this Greek mathematician who had already drawn the best map of the known world up to his time, created the first known star map, inventing, in the process, a system of lines of longitude and latitude to impose order on the apparently random distribution of the stars.

MEDIEVAL SCIENCE

Diophantus Writes the First Algebra Text

Geometry dominated Greek mathematical thought through most of the great classical age of Greece, and the development of geometry represented a profound progress from merely managing quantities and shapes to creating theories that allowed the logical and imaginative manipulation of numbers and space. The next step was to integrate numbers and symbols, and the first text that accomplished this was written about A.D. 250 by the Greek mathematician Diophantus. In effect, this is the first known algebra text—although the word *algebra* would not come into existence until much later, when the Persian mathematician Muhammad ibn al-Khwarizmi wrote in 825 a text titled *Hisab al-jabr w'al-musqabalah* (Science of the Reunion and the Opposition). It was this volume that introduced algebra into Europe, and the word *al-jabr*, roughly signifying the transposition of terms from one side of an equation to the other, became Latinized as *algebra*. (See "825: Muhammad ibn al-Khwarizmi Conceptualizes Zero.")

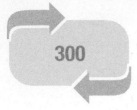

300

Zosimus Writes the Book on Alchemy

Just as no one knows when, precisely, human beings began to use tools to manipulate and modify their world, it is impossible to say when people began purposefully combining various substances to create new ones. But it was about 300 that an Egyptian named Zosimus wrote a text summing up, systematically, all that was known about chemical change. Because the work of Zosimus combined much mysticism and lore with something approaching practical chemistry, the text is considered the first work of alchemy rather than chemistry. Whereas chemistry is the science of the structure, composition, properties, and reactions of matter, alchemy is a mystical philosophy involving the manipulation of substances and aimed not so much at systematically understanding the nature of matter as at transforming "base metals" (lead and iron, for instance) into gold. Nevertheless, modern chemistry is clearly rooted in ancient alchemy, and Zosimus's study must be seen as a forerunner of a science that would create far more important and numerous miracles than the mere creation of gold from lead, a process modern scientists can now, in fact, carry out using particle accelerators or nuclear reactors—although at a cost far greater than mining and refining gold ore.

825

Muhammad ibn al-Khwarizmi Conceptualizes Zero

For many centuries after the appearance of mathematics, there was no concept, no symbol, for zero-ness. This lack must have greatly retarded the ability to make complex computations, or, at least, to express and further manipulate them. While an abacus can easily represent, say, the number 204 by moving two abacus beads on the wire representing hundreds, and four on the wire representing ones, how do you indicate, without the abacus, the null status of the tens?

Historians of mathematics believe that the concept of—and symbol for—zero first appeared in India about A.D. 500, specifically to indicate that the beads on one or more of the abacus wires hadn't been moved. Arab traders probably took the concept from the Hindus around 700, and, about 825, the Persian mathematician Muhammad ibn al-Khwarizmi used it in his groundbreaking algebraic text, *Hisab al-jabr w'al-musqabalah* (see "A.D. 250: Diophantus Writes the First Algebra Text"). Thus zero was conceptualized, and al-Khwarizmi gave the world a crucial tool for working with numbers at a higher level. Unfortunately, most of the world was slow to accept and appreciate this gift. Especially in backward Europe of the Dark Ages, most people continued to labor with crude arithmetical systems that had no zero.

1025

Alhazen Establishes the Science of Optics

The scientific study of optics, which Sir Isaac Newton would elevate to its first great height in 1704, began with an Arab physicist known (much later) to Europeans as Alhazen. About 1025, he wrote that vision was the result of rays of light entering the eyes. Prior to this, the prevailing view was that the eyes emitted rays of light, which created vision.

Beyond this landmark insight (so to speak), Alhazen also experimented extensively with lenses and demonstrated that their ability to magnify images was a function of their shape, not a property of the matter of which they were composed.

Alexander Neckam Introduces the Magnetic Compass to the Western World

The etymology of the word *magnet* may be traced to Magnesia, the city in Asia Minor near which (it has long been believed) a shepherd boy discovered in the sixth century B.C. that a certain ore attracted iron. While the phenomenon of magnetism was therefore long familiar, apparently no one thought to apply it to direction finding until the eleventh century A.D., even though the Chinese, as early as the second century A.D., observed that a sliver of magnetic metal, if allowed to rotate freely, always came to rest in a north-south orientation.

In 1180, an Englishman, Alexander Neckam, transmitted to Europe the ancient Chinese observation on the directional quality of magnets. Almost immediately, this led to the creation of the compass—a freely rotating magnetic needle mounted on a card inscribed with the four cardinal directions—north, south, east, and west—as well as those in between. This appropriation and new application of ancient lore empowered European navigators to explore the world and, ultimately, to dominate much of it.

1300

An Alchemist Known Only as the False Geber Discovers Sulfuric Acid

t is all too easy to mock medieval alchemists for confusing science with mysticism and frittering away time and effort in a hopeless search for the "philosopher's stone," a magical rock that would transform base metal into gold. But it is also true that many of the alchemists were, in fact, tireless experimenters and scholars who made valuable discoveries and who laid the foundation for modern chemistry.

We know little about most of the alchemists, and the name of one—sort of—survives only because he was associated with the discovery of the first industrially important chemical beyond those that occur naturally (such as water and air). The "False Geber" wrote a treatise around the year 1300 in which he described, among other things, sulfuric acid. It could be used to dissolve many substances, to etch metal, and to bring about a dazzling array of chemical reactions to produce many different substances.

While the False Geber, like the other alchemists, failed to transform lead into gold, he discovered a powerful acid essential to the transformation of many other things into useful substances. In this, we may see the origin of industrial chemistry.

1335

The City of Milan, Italy, Erects Perhaps the First Mechanical Clock

Time is at once the most ruthless and ephemeral dimension of the reality we know. Ancients measured it by the sun and the moon, and, about 270 B.C., the Greek inventor Ctesibius invented a water clock—the *clepsydra,* or "water stealer"—which "ran" by means of the regular dripping of water from an upper container to a lower one. This had obvious advantages over the sundial—it was usable in any weather, day or night, and it was portable—but it was still pretty clumsy and not terribly accurate.

The *clepsydra* used dripping water—that is, the force of gravity itself—to measure time, and in the fourteenth century people began to devise new ways to harness gravity—a force science had yet to name, although its effects were known intuitively—for the purpose of uniformly dividing up the day and night. Weights attached to an array of gears drove a dial on a clock face, which thereby "told" the time. Because the motive force was gravity, it was helpful to provide plenty of space for the descent of the weights. This naturally suggested a tower, which was a convenient thing, because it meant that the clock face could be fixed high up above a public square, and, in this way, the time it told could be shared by many people at once.

As clock makers became more skilled, they devised ways of linking gravity to gears, which would not only drive a clock dial, but would also audibly toll the hours, by ringing a bell. This greatly extended the range of the public clock. You didn't have to be close enough to see it, just close enough to hear it. It is believed that a tolling tower clock erected in Milan in 1335 was the first public mechanical clock.

RENAISSANCE SCIENCE

Johannes Gutenberg Invents the Modern Printing Press

Ask just about anyone to list the top two or three inventions in history, and it's almost certain that the printing press will figure among them. In itself, the "invention" of writing was a tremendous step forward (see sidebar: "The Invention of Writing, About 3500 B.C."), but writing was a laborious process and, except in the case of brief public inscriptions, the product of writing was not always easily shared among large numbers of people.

It is believed that the Chinese, by about 350, had hit upon a technology to distribute the written word more widely. They began carving characters into wooden blocks, inking them, then pressing the carved and inked blocks onto paper. The result was an impression that could be reproduced as many times as one wished. Within a few hundred years, the Chinese were printing entire books on a regular basis—while European scribes still labored to produce a few multiple copies of a work by quill and hand.

Printing came to Europe during the fourteenth century. As the Chinese had done, the first European printers carved their texts into blocks of wood—one block for each page of text. The work of carving was tedious, time-consuming, demanded great skill, and was very unforgiving of error. Once the block was carved, however, one could print as many pages as needed.

It was in 1454 that the German printer Johannes Gutenberg perfected an idea he had been working on at least since 1435. Instead of creating a uniquely carved block for each page of each book, Gutenberg decided to break the process down. Books are made of words, and words are made of letters. Gutenberg reduced the process to this basic element—the letter—and carved sets of these, which could be assembled at will into whatever words were required. Once the book was printed, the carved letters could be reused to make different words for different books. The famed Gutenberg Bible of 1454 is the first book printed using "movable type," a technology that made possible the increasingly rapid multiple production and wide distribution of an ever-growing number of books. Knowledge, which had been the exclusive property of the very few who could afford to acquire a small number of precious handwritten books, was now available to the many, and as more and more people gained access to knowledge, knowledge itself was transformed with greater and greater rapidity. Movable type moved civilization itself.

1543

Andreas Vesalius Develops the New Anatomy

Galen, a Greek physician who lived from 129 to about 199, combined his experience as a surgeon attached to a gladiatorial school with systematic dissection of animals to assemble the first attempt to account comprehensively for the human anatomy. Galen's work was extraordinary, but, of course, limited and riddled with guesswork and error. Nevertheless, in Europe, physicians relied on it through the Middle Ages. At last, in 1543, the Flemish physician Andreas Vesalius boldly dissected human cadavers and did so with unprecedented skill and thoroughness. He dared to challenge Galen, as well as all other received anatomical wisdom, and published the results of his work in *De Corporis Humani Fabrica* (On the Structure of the Human Body), which was illuminatingly illustrated by the artist Jan Stephan van Calcar, a student of no less a figure than the great painter Titian. Vesalius's *De Corporis* revolutionized medicine and the understanding of the human body.

1543

Copernicus Proposes a Heliocentric Model of the Universe

The notion that human knowledge "progresses" from point A to point Z via an orderly course through all the letters of the alphabet is a myth. Understanding goes forward and back innumerable times. As early as 280 B.C. the Greek Aristarchus imagined that the sun was the center of the universe, and the planets, earth included, revolved around it. About 150 B.C., however, Hipparchus voiced his belief that the earth lay at the center of things and, just a few years later, Ptolemy produced the mathematics to "prove" the validity of the geocentric—the earth-centered—universe.

Human beings are by nature egocentric, and so it is not a surprise that a collective expression of egocentrism, the geocentric universe, should hold more appeal than a system centered on another heavenly body. For about sixteen centuries the Ptolemaic geocentric system was accepted as an accurate model of the way things were.

And who was in a position to disprove years of theory and tradition? After all, there was no way to get above it all, above the earth and beyond the sun, to see just what revolved around what. But there was one apparent problem with the Ptolemaic scheme. Careful observation revealed that the sun and moon moved steadily across the sky, but the planets, from time to time, seemed to reverse direction and, furthermore, grew brighter and dimmer as they traversed the sky.

Ptolemy didn't ignore the "retrograde motion" of the planets, but cobbled together exceedingly complicated mathematical explanations to account for these variations in motion. In 1507, the Polish astronomer Nicolaus Copernicus became bothered by the clumsy, inelegant mathematical contortions Ptolemy required. He couldn't prove them wrong, but he had an instinctive grasp of what modern scientists accept as a general test of a theory's validity. Provided that two different theories fully account in some way for some set of phenomena, the simpler theory is most likely to be the correct one. Copernicus just could not rest content with Ptolemy, and it occurred to him that if one returned to the view that all the planets, earth included, revolved around the sun, retrograde motion became much easier to explain as an appearance caused by the earth's own motion around the sun. Moreover, the heliocentric—sun-centered—model of the solar system also made it possible to account for why Venus and Mercury at all times remained near the sun and also why the planets appeared to grow brighter and dimmer.

Copernicus did not merely revive an ancient idea. Aristarchus had offered heliocentricism speculatively, as a way of imagining the universe. Copernicus worked it all out mathematically, and he took such care in this process that he didn't publish his work until 1543. He wanted to be very sure he was right, especially since the suggestion that the earth did not lie at the center of creation courted a charge of heresy, and, in the 1500s, the Catholic church did not hesitate to dispose of heretics—at the stake. Copernicus had the added good sense to dedicate his *De Revolutionibus Orbium Coelestium* (On the Revolution of the Heavenly Bodies) to Pope Paul III.

Despite his careful math, Copernicus hadn't gotten it completely right. He remained attached to the belief that the planets orbited in perfect circles. As Johannes Kepler would demonstrate mathematically in 1609, their orbits are ever-so-slightly elliptical. Nor did the nod to the pope prevent his book from being added to the infamous "Index"—the church's roster of books condemned as heretical. In a way, Copernicus was probably fortunate that he died immediately after *De Revolutionibus* was published in 1543. He was even more fortunate that the widespread adoption of printing (see "1454: Johannes Gutenberg Invents the Modern Printing Press") quickly circulated too many copies for the church to seize and destroy.

Geronimo Cardano Conceptualizes Negative Numbers

Like the concept of zero (see "825: Muhammad ibn al-Khwarizmi Conceptualizes Zero"), the idea of negative numbers, numbers less than zero, seems to us self-evident—yet it wasn't until 1545 that negative numbers were conceptualized in *Artis Magnae Sive de Regulis Algebraicis Liber Unus* (The Great Art), a mathematical treatise by the Italian Geronimo (or Girolamo) Cardano. Before this, people understood the concept of debt—that it was possible (all too possible) to have, in effect, less than zero funds—but, until Cardano, no one had thought of treating negative numbers as real numbers. The concept was indispensable to the development of advanced mathematics.

Ambroise Paré Lays the Foundation of Modern Surgery

Beginning with the classical Greeks, science moved from the outer world to the inner world of the mind. Theory was valued over experimentation and practical knowledge. The European Middle Ages took this approach even further, and medieval scholars debated such questions as the number of teeth in a horse's mouth without deigning actually to count them.

In this cultural climate, physicians did not treat patients with surgery, which partook more of the butcher's trade than the doctor's, but left such procedures to the barber, a tradesman who doubled as a surgeon. One such was Ambroise Paré of France, who revolutionized surgical technique by lifting it, at long last, far above the level of butchery. While he did not introduce antisepsis—no one had any notion of bacteria in 1545—he did insist on cleanliness, because he found that, if the patient, the wound, and the surgeon's hands were all kept clean, the chances of postoperative infection were reduced. He had, of course, no anesthetics at his disposal, so he concentrated on formulating procedures that would be as quick, efficient, and painless as possible. Whereas most surgeons poured boiling oil into wounds as a means of cleaning them, Paré prepared soothing oils instead. While the prevailing surgical practice was to control bleeding by cauterizing severed arteries with a red-hot instrument, Paré developed the technique of tying off arteries. Not only were his procedures much less painful, they did far less damage to tissue, and the result was a significantly greater cure rate.

Fortunately for medicine, Paré described his procedures in a book. Unfortunately for sixteenth- and even seventeenth-century patients, however, Paré, a lowly barber-surgeon after all, was literate in French, but not the more learned Latin. Few physicians or scholars would descend to the vulgar tongue of the people. If Paré couldn't write it in Latin, it probably wasn't worth reading—and so the development of surgery was retarded for the next 150 years.

Rhäticus (Georg Joachim Iserin von Lauchen) Develops Trigonometry, and Erasmus Reinhold Uses It to Prepare Accurate Planetary Tables

Rhäticus—the learned pseudonym of German mathematician Georg Joachim Iserin von Lauchen—was a student of the great Copernicus, who developed the first mathematical model of a sun-centered solar system (see "1543: Copernicus Proposes a Heliocentric Model of the Universe"). To help his master calculate the orbits of the planets, Rhäticus created a set of trigonometric tables, working out the ratios of the length of the sides of triangles to each other for different angles. This provided an extraordinary tool for creating a fuller, mathematically complete model of the solar system, and, in 1551, another German mathematician, Erasmus Reinhold, used the trigonometric tables of Rhäticus to create tables by which the motions of the planets could be more precisely determined. With this, astronomy was carried beyond what one could see by looking up at the sky and began to emerge as a picture of an awesome system in dynamic motion.

Galileo, Observing Falling Bodies and Moving Bodies, Lays the Foundation of Experimental Science

C ommon sense is often the greatest enemy of science. A most seductive faculty, it leads us away from questioning our perceptions and lulls us into accepting as true whatever *seems* true. Thus when the great Greek philosopher Aristotle said that the heavier an object was, the faster it would fall, no one thought to question it—not only because the authority of Aristotle was rarely questioned, but also because Aristotle seemed here merely to state the obvious. The philosopher agreed with common sense.

But the Italian physicist and astronomer Galileo Galilei was not one to respect authority blindly, whether it was the authority of Aristotle or that of his own common sense.

Both, one, or neither of the following stories may be true. One story says that the Dutch mathematician Simon Stevin simultaneously dropped a heavy rock and a light one from a height. They hit the ground at exactly the same instant. The other story says that Galileo climbed the Leaning Tower of Pisa and dropped two cannonballs, one much heavier than the other, with the same result. Whichever story is true—if either is—it was Galileo and not Stevin who, in 1589, commenced a series of exacting tests to study the motion of falling objects.

It was easy enough to drop objects from a height and judge whether or not they hit the ground at the same time. However, no instruments were available in Galileo's day to measure any acceleration such objects underwent. It all happened too quickly. Therefore,

Galileo constructed an experiment that closely modeled the phenomenon he wished—but was unable—to study directly. He reasoned that the force that caused objects to fall (years later, Isaac Newton would name this force gravity) was the same that caused them to roll down an inclined plane. Both motions were downward, toward the center of the earth, but allowing the force to work at an angle rather than straight down provided sufficient time for an observer to measure, carefully and accurately, the behavior of these "falling" objects.

Galileo confirmed that (discounting wind resistance) objects fall at the same rate, regardless of weight. Aristotle and common sense were thus overturned.

He further demonstrated that objects fall at a constant, not variable, rate of acceleration, from which he reasoned that the force acting on them was constant. The conclusion Galileo drew from this was profound—and another blow to Aristotle. The Greek philosopher, again building on common sense, declared that an object would remain in motion only as long as a force was applied to it. Remove the force, and the object would come to a halt. Because all objects required a push, medieval thinkers concluded that the planets were propelled by an external force, almost certainly supplied by

The Thermometer, 1592

Just as Galileo was the first scientist to think systematically about gravity, a very basic force, so he was the first, in 1592, to create an instrument to measure the very basic sensations of hot and cold. Galileo secured a glass tube, open at one end and with a bulb blown at the other. He warmed the bulb, then placed the open end of the tube in a container of water. As the warm air within the bulb cooled, it contracted, thereby decreasing the pressure within the bulb and tube. This decrease in pressure drew the water up into the tube. If the bulb was again heated, the expanding air created an increase in pressure, which drove the column of water down. The column varied with the temperature and could be measured precisely. This thermometer was a basic scientific instrument, the purpose of which was to objectify a common and essential environmental condition.

angels. Galileo's observation of constant acceleration led him to conclude that, if friction could be discounted, an object, once set into motion, would keep moving, without the need for angelic intervention.

Galileo's observations on falling bodies added immeasurably to the science of physics and laid the foundation for the science of planetary motion. Even more important, by challenging received wisdom and common sense with a carefully constructed, infinitely repeatable experiment, Galileo created experimental science itself, the basis of all serious intellectual inquiry into the nature of the physical universe.

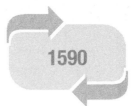

1590

Zacharias Janssen Invents the Microscope

By the close of the sixteenth century, Dutch opticians were the most accomplished in the world and regularly turned out eyeglasses to correct the most common fault of human vision, nearsightedness. These convex—outwardly bowed—lenses, of course, magnified objects, and, in 1590, the Dutch lensmaker Zacharias Janssen reasoned quite simply that if one lens magnified objects x times, then the combination of two lenses would magnify them at some multiple of x times. In order to juxtapose the two lenses, he placed them at either end of a tube. In this way, he invented the microscope, which, in the next century, another Dutchman, Antonie van Leeuwenhoek, would perfect and use to study a whole new world (see "1676: Antonie van Leeuwenhoek Perfects the Microscope and Opens to Study the Universe of Microorganisms").

1608

Hans Lippershey Stumbles Upon the Telescope

Just as a Dutch optician combined two lenses to invent the microscope (see "1590: Zacharias Janssen Invents the Microscope"), another Dutch lens maker, Hans Lippershey, invented the telescope.

He didn't mean to. In 1608, he was just an apprentice spectacle maker, and, like most apprentices, spent as much time goofing off as he did working for his master. One day, he idly juxtaposed two lenses, looked through one and then through the other. He pointed them out the window, toward a distant church steeple. With a start, he saw that the steeple had been "brought" much closer to him. What's more, it had been turned upside down!

He called his master over to look. The man wisely told his apprentice to mount the lenses in a tube, and thus the telescope was born.

Word of the accidental invention spread quickly, and other lens makers assembled similar instruments. In Italy, Galileo got a hold of one right away—in 1609—pointed it at the moon, and was stunned to discover craters, mountains, and dark areas he thought were oceans (*maria,* he called them, using the Latin word for seas). Directed at just this single heavenly body, the telescope shattered a much-cherished vision of the moon as a glowing orb of light, a perfect fixture in God's heaven. Galileo saw that it was a world, scarred and imperfect, not unlike the earth itself.

1609

Johannes Kepler Describes the Planetary Orbits

As far as anyone knows, the Greek philosopher Plato was the first to describe planetary orbits as circles, about 387 B.C. Ever since that time, everyone who thought about the subject, from Aristarchus in 280 B.C. to Copernicus in 1543 (see "1543: Copernicus Proposes a Heliocentric Model of the Universe"), assumed that the planets traveled in circles. Copernicus put the sun at the center of the solar system, which was quite correct, of course, and he worked diligently to formulate the mathematics of the circular orbits around that body. The trouble was that the math never quite worked out. In the late 1500s, the Danish astronomer Tycho Brahe made more careful observations, concentrating on Mars. Tycho was a great observer, but he was not much of a mathematician. At his death, he left a mountain of meticulous observations, from which he had drawn relatively few conclusions. His assistant, a German named Johannes Kepler, inept as an observer, but brilliant as a theoretician, studied his master's observations and, with infinite patience and insight, worked his way through them. His object was to calculate, once and for all, accurate orbits for the planets.

The trouble was, year after year, wrangling with one heap of data after another, he couldn't do it. Something always went wrong.

A scientist sees as much value in error and negative results as he does in apparent success. Kepler didn't give up. Instead, in a stroke of genius, he decided to see what would happen if he assumed the orbits were ellipses rather than circles. In 1609, he published the results of this radical new vision in the aptly title *Astronomia Nova*—The New Astronomy.

Kepler formulated the elliptical planetary orbits as the First Law of Planetary Motion. From this, he drew a second law, describing how the velocity of planetary orbits varied with their distance from the sun.

There was more work to be done by later heads and hands. Kepler had exaggerated the eccentricity of the orbits—he made them too elliptical—but he had cracked open a two-thousand-year-old mystery and had made a giant stride toward a full understanding of the solar system and of the mathematics of orbits, which, some four and a half centuries later, would help make possible the launch and orbit of artificial earth satellites.

John Napier Develops the Concept of the Logarithm

Arithmetic is necessary to the work of the mathematician and scientist, but the work of calculation is often tedious and time-consuming. By streamlining arithmetical mechanics, mathematicians may broaden the scope of their creative vision. Early in the seventeenth century, the Scottish mathematician John Napier realized that the great labor-saving expedient known as the exponent could be expanded to save even more work. In exponential form, 3×3 is written 3^2. In multiplying exponential numbers, we may just add the exponents instead of multiplying the numbers. Thus $2^2 \times 2^4$ may be expressed as 2×2 (4) added to $2 \times 2 \times 2 \times 2$ (16) equals 64. Or it may be expressed $2^2 \times 2^4 = 2^6$. The sum of the exponents is 6. In this way, multiplication can be simplified to addition and, likewise, division can be simplified to subtraction.

Working with exponents in this way is easy, provided that the exponents are whole numbers. For example, 2^4 is 16, and 2^5 is 32. But how do we derive, exponentially, the numbers in between 16 and 32? If there were an easy way to obtain the exponents between the whole numbers, all multiplication could be handled as addition, and all division as subtraction. This would greatly reduce and simplify the arithmetic and let mathematicians devote themselves to math.

Napier created formulas that enabled him to get at the numbers between the whole numbers. With these, he developed tables of what he called *logarithms* (Greek for "proportionate numbers"), which mathematicians and scientists could use to simplify and therefore speed their work, enabling them to get more done, more accurately, with greater speed, and in realms of increasing complexity. In the years, decades, and centuries before computers, Napier's logarithms energized all branches of inquiry requiring complex and extensive calculation.

Francis Bacon Proposes the Scientific Method

I n 1620, the daring British philosopher Francis Bacon published *Novum Organum,* or *The New Organon,* an answer to the much venerated *Organon* of Aristotle, the book that had dictated the rules of philosophy—and, therefore, the rules of science as well— since it was written, about 350 B.C. Where Aristotle had extolled the sovereign authority of deductive reasoning for all inquiry, Bacon declared that while deduction worked for mathematics, it was inadequate for scientific inquiry. This, he proposed, required induction—generalization based on a mass of precise observation derived from actual experience and deliberate experiment. In short, Bacon proposed what has come to be called the scientific method: knowledge arrived at through experiment analyzed inductively. It was a bold proposal, which has had a profound and well-nigh universal impact not only on science, but on thought itself.

Willebrord Snel Creates the Science of Refraction

People have been using and manipulating lenses of various sorts since at least the days of classical Greece, but it wasn't until the early seventeenth century that anyone thought of studying the action of lenses systematically—which is to say, mathematically. In 1621, the Dutch mathematician Willebrord Snel founded the science of refraction, which is the foundation of practical optics, by demonstrating that the sine of the angle to the vertical of light leaving a lens is in a constant relationship with the sine of the angle to the vertical of the light that hits the surface of the lens. Armed with this mathematical constant, lens makers could now design a wide array of lenses and lens assemblies for many purposes.

Jan Baptista van Helmont Coins the Term *Gas* to Describe Matter in "Chaos"

As the classical Greeks saw it, physical reality was made up of four earthly elements—earth, water, fire, and air—and one heavenly element, aether (the word means, roughly, "blazing"). This view remained largely unquestioned for many centuries, well into the seventeenth century. In the 1620s, however, the Flemish physician Jan Baptista van Helmont worked experimentally with a number of vapors. His observations made it apparent to him that not all vapors behaved in the same way as air did and, in fact, one vapor behaved differently from another. By 1624, Helmont decided that the various vapors formed a unique class of substance. For all their differences, they shared certain salient characteristics, the most striking of which was that they had no specific volume, but did fill any container. Thus Helmont concluded that vapors were matter in utter *chaos*. Transliterating that Greek word in tune with his Flemish ear, Helmont created the term *gas*.

In time, the concept of gas drew scientists away from the classical Greek picture of the five elements. Instead, they depicted matter in states—solid, liquid, and gaseous—and this made room for the modern vision of many elements, all of which may exist, depending on external conditions, in solid, liquid, or gaseous state.

1628

William Harvey Describes the Circulation of Blood

In the centuries after Galen, a number of physicians attempted to describe the circulation of blood, but they could not fully account for the fact that the heart is a double pump. A popular early view was that one portion of the heart fed the lungs, while the other part supplied blood to the rest of the body. The details, of course, were never worked out—mainly because this view, though pervasive, was just plain wrong.

As a student of the Italian physician Girolamo Fabrici, Harvey had learned of valves in the veins that kept blood flowing in one direction only. Armed with this knowledge, Harvey experimented with animals. He tied off a vein and noted that blood accumulated in the vein on the side away from the heart even as it simultaneously piled up in an artery on the side toward the heart. From this, Harvey concluded that blood flowed away from the heart in the arteries and toward the heart via the veins. He continued his experiments and observations until he had accumulated enough data to publish in 1628 a slim, concise volume titled *Exercitatio Anatomica de Motu Cordis et Sanguinis in Animalibus* (On the Movement of the Heart and the Blood in Animals). In it, he traced the circulation of blood from the right ventricle of the heart to the lungs, and, ultimately, back to the left ventricle. From here, it is pumped out to the body generally, whence it returns to the right ventricle—all in continual circulation.

The stodgy medical establishment of the seventeenth century

was slow to accept Harvey's elegant picture of circulation, but the physician did have the satisfaction of seeing it generally accepted before he died in 1657. That was certainly gratifying. But even Harvey didn't grasp the magnitude of what he had done, which was to create the modern science of physiology.

Galileo Is Charged with Heresy

G alileo was a great scientist and a man of principle. However, he was also a practical realist. His reason and his own observations had led him to accept the view of Copernicus, that the earth and the other planets orbited the sun in a heliocentric—sun-centered—solar system (see "1543: Copernicus Proposes a Heliocentric Model of the Universe"). However, Galileo also understood that to espouse this point of view in Italy, which was dominated by the Catholic church, was dangerous indeed. The position of the church was unalterably geocentric—earth-centered—and to assert anything contrary to this was to be guilty of heresy, a crime punishable by burning at the stake.

At last, in 1632, Urban VIII ascended the papal throne. Because Urban was a friend of Galileo's, the scientist felt emboldened to publish a book he hoped would promote and explain definitively and once and for all the logical superiority of the Copernican view versus the geocentric view. Galileo's *Dialogue on the Two Chief World Systems,* published in 1632, was not a sober-sided scientific treatise, but a spirited and witty dialogue among an advocate of the Ptolemaic, earth-centered system, a champion of Copernicus's heliocentric view, and a seeker of enlightenment.

Of course, the Copernican view won out—and that might not have been so bad, except that Galileo's book was so entertaining that it reached not just scientists and the learned minority, but that portion of the masses who were at least literate. Despite their friendship, Urban became alarmed, and, in 1633, hauled Galileo before the Inquisition to answer for his heresy. Perhaps because Urban was indeed his friend, Galileo was not punished. At age seventy,

Galileo Galilei was not interested in a trip to the rack, much less the stake. On June 22, 1633, he renounced the heliocentric picture, "admitting" to the Inquisitors that not the sun, but the earth, was at the center of the universe. Thus Galileo was released to a loose form of house arrest. Nevertheless, it is said that, as Galileo turned away from the Inquisitors, he muttered under his breath, "and yet it moves."

In a way, June 22, 1633, was a victory for coercive superstition and a dark day for the freedom of scientific inquiry. Yet it was a pyrrhic victory. Those who thought seriously about such things understood that Galileo had actually renounced nothing, and, thanks to the printing press, there were too many copies of his *Dialogue* in circulation to collect and destroy. Not only was the heliocentric model of the solar system taking ever firmer hold on the learned world, the spirit of scientific inquiry was stealing the march on received wisdom and superstition masquerading in the guise of religion.

ENLIGHTENMENT
SCIENCE

1642

Blaise Pascal Invents a Practical Adding Machine

The abacus (see sidebar: "The Abacus, About 500 B.C.") was almost certainly the earliest computer—if we take the term *computer* to include machines that do nothing more than calculate. The first significant advance in mechanical computing beyond the abacus did not come until more than 2,100 years after the Egyptians began using the device. In 1642, the French mathematician Blaise Pascal crafted a genuine calculating machine. It was an arrangement of wheels, each marked off from one to ten. When the right-most wheel, which represented ones, made a complete revolution, it engaged the wheel immediately to its left, which represented tens, and advanced it a single notch. That wheel engaged another, to its left, moving it a single notch when ten tens had been reached. This third wheel represented hundreds. And thus the wheels progressed through hundreds, thousands, and so on.

Pascal hoped to grow rich from his calculating machine, which he tinkered with from 1642 until 1649, when he produced a version he deemed worthy of a patent. The machine offered speedy calculations without the possibility of error—provided, of course, the information entered was correct. But the world was not yet eager for a calculating machine, and Pascal's pioneering computer never saw commercial success.

Robert Boyle Lays the Foundation
of Modern Chemistry

Jan Baptista van Helmont's description of gases (see "1624: Jan Baptista van Helmont Coins the Term *Gas* to Describe Matter in 'Chaos'") had begun to undermine the long-cherished belief that the earth consisted of four elements, fire, water, earth, and air, and the heavens of a fifth, aether, but this view nevertheless persisted well into the seventeenth century, greatly retarding the progress of chemistry, which continued to be dominated by alchemists—who were more sorcerer than scientist. The feisty Irish chemist and physicist Robert Boyle aggressively attacked both the dominance of the five-element view and the hegemony of the alchemist with his 1661 book *The Skeptical Chymist*. In it, he made three seminal points: First, he established chemistry as a field in its own right, distinct from the area of inquiry that had hitherto dominated it, medicine. Second, he held that chemistry could not be built on received wisdom, tradition, or even deduction. It had to be, he argued, an experimental science. Third, he proposed as the first appropriate goal of experimentation the discovery of the true elements. The fire, water, air, earth, aether model, he pointed out, did not adequately account for reality. An element, Boyle stated, was a substance that could not be simplified or broken down. Therefore, anything that could not be reduced to constituents was an element, and any candidate for elementary status had to be shown to be incapable of reduction to simpler constituents. Thus Boyle not only gave the concept of elements its modern definition, he provided a goal and purpose for the new science of chemistry—no longer to search for a way to convert lead into gold, but to discover just what substances made up the foundation of the physical world. And the only way to do this was by tireless experimentation.

Isaac Newton Describes the Visible Spectrum

Twenty-four-year-old Isaac Newton turned his prodigious intellect to the subject of light and discovered that white light, assumed to be the embodiment of purity itself, was actually composed of a spectrum of colors. The discovery was made when Newton methodically experimented with prisms. He observed that white light passing through a prism was broken into red, orange, yellow, green, blue, and violet, always in that order, beginning with the portion of the light that is least bent by the prism, red.

Newton was surely not the first person to pass light through a prism, but he was the first to draw conclusions from it. First, while others had assumed that the breakup of light into colors was due to some property of glass, Newton turned the focus back on the light itself, where it belonged. When he allowed the light to pass through two prisms, it entered the first, broke up into the color spectrum, then entered the second and emerged as white light again. Color, therefore, was a property of light, not glass. From this, Newton made one of the great quantum leaps of scientific reasoning, concluding that the phenomenon of color results from the property of various matter to absorb some portions of the spectrum and to reflect others. In short, *all* color was ultimately a property of light. The perception of color was the result of the action of light on matter.

John Wallis Formulates the Law of Conservation of Momentum, First of the Laws of Conservation That Are Fundamental to Our Understanding of the Universe

Our world is never static. It is, rather, dynamic, its varied constituents always in motion. We grow up with an intuitive understanding of movement (the Latin word for movement is *momentum*), learning by experience that kicking a soccer ball will send it far, but kicking a nice, round boulder will result in very sore toes. A big part of science is the rationalization and quantification of intuition, and momentum, long understood intuitively, was not explored mathematically until the Englishman John Wallis formulated his law of conservation of momentum in 1668.

It goes like this: Momentum is the product of mass multiplied by velocity. Momentum is neither created nor destroyed. It is merely transferred. Thus, in a closed system, a system in which no momentum is introduced from the outside nor any momentum is allowed to "leak" to the outside, the total momentum remains constant.

Understanding momentum intellectually—not just intuitively—enables many useful calculations concerning motion, which in turn makes it possible to design a vast array of machines, to calculate the energy required to accomplish various tasks, and to predict what will happen if the momentum of a Volkswagen Beetle meets that of an eighteen-wheel Peterbilt. Even more profoundly, understanding the law of conservation of momentum, that momentum is neither created nor destroyed, but merely transferred, contributes immeasurably to an understanding of the universe itself.

1668

Francesco Redi Disproves Spontaneous Generation

Most of us are disgusted by the sight of decomposition—the carcass by the side of the road, crawling with thousands of maggots. Yet, for centuries, people thought there was something miraculous about such a scene. Whereas the creation of human life and the more complex forms of animal life clearly required the mating of male and female, a long gestation period, and a dramatic episode of birth, some forms of life apparently sprang forth spontaneously from decaying matter. Let meat decay, and maggots appeared; their generation, as far as anybody could tell, was spontaneous.

Scientists look on the universe with a combination of wonder and skepticism. They are willing to be amazed, but, first, they need to test what everyone else simply assumes. Thus, in 1668, the Italian physician Francesco Redi designed an experiment to test spontaneous generation.

He took eight glass flasks and put into each a variety of meats. Four of the flasks he sealed. Four he left exposed. Only the exposed meat, on which flies could land, revealed the presence of maggots. Like the exposed meat, the sealed meat turned putrid—but it "produced" no maggots.

It occurred to Redi that the absence of sufficient air in the sealed flasks might have interfered with the process of spontaneous generation, so he redesigned the experiment, repeating it, but without sealing any of the flasks. Instead, he covered four with gauze, sufficient to exclude flies, but clearly porous enough to let in plenty of air. Once again, only the meat in the fully exposed flasks became infested. Thus Redi had created the first documented biological experiment employing "controls"—measures to ensure that the effect under study is produced by the cause under study, and not by something incidentally or accidentally introduced by the experimenter.

Even more important, Redi had provided experimental evidence for one of the bedrock principles of modern biology: All life comes from life and only from life.

1669

Newton and Gottfried Wilhelm Leibniz Independently Invent Calculus

I t may be the most famous moment in science. In 1665, young Isaac Newton had taken refuge on his mother's farm from the deadly bubonic plague that held London in its grip. Legend has it that Newton was reading under a tree when an apple fell on his head. According to Newton himself, however, he was gazing out of a window at a brilliantly moonlit night. The moon was so bright that he clearly saw an apple fall from a tree. It occurred to him in that moment: Why does an apple fall to earth, while the moon does not?

He reasoned that the moon was not exempt from gravity, and that, in fact, it *did* fall. However, because the moon was also moving horizontally, it fell exactly enough, from moment to moment, to make up for the curvature of the earth. Moving forward, the moon fell perpetually, thereby orbiting the earth—neither falling into it, nor shooting out, on a tangent, away from it.

Newton understood that this theory, brilliant though it was, meant little until it could be described mathematically. But the mathematical tools available to Newton were insufficient to produce the calculations he needed. How could he calculate a problem in which *all* of the earth, at every point, exerted a gravitational force on every point of the moon? Since both the earth and the moon have considerable volume—and are not the hypothetical spaceless points of mathematics—the force of gravity is exerted from a range of different distances and angles. Nothing existed to work such a complex problem.

So Newton set about inventing the tools he needed. In 1669, he began developing calculus, a method of dealing with multiple relationships, with limits and the differentiation and integration of functions of one or more variables. Calculus is ideal for working with bodies in motion, whose relationship to one another is dynamic.

Unknown to Newton, in Germany, the mathematician Gottfried Wilhelm Leibniz was also developing calculus. Newton probably beat him to the punch, but Leibniz created a more flexible and useful symbolic language by which problems could be expressed and resolved. At the time—and for some years afterward—proud Brits sparred with proud Germans in a struggle over who should be given credit for opening the door to higher mathematics. By now, that controversy has long been laid to rest, and both Newton and Leibniz are credited with having developed, independently from each other, calculus.

1675

Olaus Rømer Calculates the Approximate Speed of Light

At least as early as Galileo, there was curiosity about the speed of light. The Italian tried to measure it by stationing himself, with a lantern, atop one hill and a friend, also equipped with a lantern, on another. Once he and his friend were in place, Galileo would slide open his lantern, exposing his flame. His counterpart on the distant hill was to expose his flame as soon as he saw Galileo's. Galileo would time the delay between the exposure and the response and, from this, calculate the speed of light. The trouble was that, no matter how far apart the two men stationed themselves, the result was always the same. Galileo drew two conclusions: First, any elapsed time he measured represented nothing more than the time it took his counterpart to react to the sight of his light. The measurement had to do with physiology, not physics. Second, light traveled too fast to measure practically; indeed, some argued that light moved with infinite speed.

Almost a hundred years after Galileo threw in the towel concerning the speed of light, the Danish astronomer Olaus Rømer revisited the problem. He had not intended to do so, but something he observed awakened his curiosity. He was working at the Paris Observatory, studying the motions of Jupiter's moons. The Italian astronomer Gian Domenico Cassini had, about ten years earlier, timed these motions carefully, especially noting just when each moon passed behind Jupiter and was therefore eclipsed. Scientists learn much from repeating the experiments and observations of others. Like Cassini, Rømer timed the eclipses. To his profound surprise, his figures differed from Cassini's. And there was even more: The eclipses came progressively earlier during the season at which the earth was closer to Jupiter than when its orbit was receding from Jupiter's.

In science, discovery sometimes comes in great leaps and momentous revelations, but even more often it comes from recognizing subtle differences in minute measurements. Rømer theorized that the variation in timing came about because the light he saw had to travel farther when the Earth and Jupiter were farther apart; therefore, light must have a finite, and not an infinite, speed. Using what he knew about the distance separating the earth from Jupiter, Rømer calculated the speed of light at 141,000 miles per second.

He was, in fact, wrong. The speed of light is approximately 186,000 miles per second. Yet he was not *very* wrong, getting within almost 76 percent of the correct answer—and doing so based on the observation of a single phenomenon.

Antonie vanLeeuwenhoek Perfects the Microscope and Opens to Study the Universe of Microorganisms

The Dutch lens maker Antonie van Leeuwenhoek did not invent the microscope (see "1590: Zacharias Janssen Invents the Microscope"), and he was not even the first to use it to investigate the structure of life, but he did build a microscope of unprecedented power—creating exquisitely ground lenses capable of 200 times magnification—and he used it to open many views of a hitherto unknown world.

In 1676, Leeuwenhoek put under his lens a drop of pond water. What he expected to see we don't know. But what he actually saw amazed him: The droplet was alive with myriad microoranisms—Leeuwenhoek called them animalicules—entirely invisible to the naked eye.

The "Cell" Described, 1665

In 1665, the English scientist Robert Hooke used the microscope to examine a dazzling array of specimens and produced a beautifully illustrated compendium of his observations in the 1665 book *Micrographia.* His single most fascinating observation was the result of examining a paper-thin slice of cork. Hooke noted that the cork consisted of tiny rectangular holes, which, because they reminded Hooke of little rooms, he called *cells.* To be strictly accurate, Hooke had not discovered the cells themselves, but their remains—their dead shell, as it were. In a living specimen—not dead cork—each rigid cell would be filled with fluid (cytoplasm) around a nucleus and other structures (organelles). Nevertheless, Hooke had coined the term, alerting other scientists to this all-important structural and physiological constituent of plant and animal life.

1687

Newton Publishes the *Principia,* in Which He Formulates Three Laws of Motion

n 1669, Isaac Newton developed calculus as a tool for explaining how the moon orbited the earth by, in effect, perpetually falling toward it (see "1669: Newton and Gottfried Wilhelm Leibniz Independently Invent Calculus"). This led in 1687 to the publication of *Philosophiae Naturalis Principia Mathematica* (Mathematical Principles of Natural Philosophy), usually called simply the *Principia.* In this volume, perhaps the single greatest book ever written on a scientific subject, Newton explained not just how the moon orbited the earth, but why the planets maintained their orbits and why these orbits were elliptical. To arrive at this explanation, he had to codify, mathematically, Galileo's observations on falling bodies (see "1589: Galileo, Observing Falling Bodies and Moving Bodies, Lays the Foundation of Experimental Science"), proposing three Laws of Motion.

The first law sets forth the principle of inertia: A body at rest remains at rest and a body in motion remains in motion at a constant velocity until an outside force or forces act upon it.

The second law defines force as the product of mass times acceleration.

The third law holds that for every action there is an equal and opposite reaction.

From these three laws, Newton derived the basic mathematics of modern physics, and others who followed him used them as the basis for describing virtually all mechanical effects, from simple machines to the motions of celestial bodies.

SCIENCE IN THE AGE OF REASON

1712

Thomas Newcomen Invents a Practical Steam Engine

The motive power of steam was first demonstrated about A.D. 50 by the Greek engineer Hero. His "steam engine" was a hollow sphere from which two bent tubes protruded, their openings pointing in opposing directions. The sphere was filled with water and heated. When the water boiled, the escaping steam propelled the sphere, causing it to rotate.

Hero's engine was a brilliant little device, but no one thought of putting it to any practical use, and it wasn't until some seventeen centuries later that the British engineer Thomas Newcomen invented a practical, if quite inefficient, steam engine, in which the steam was used to push a piston and, in its initial application, drive a pump to eject water from coal mines.

Lady Mary Wortley Montagu Introduces Inoculation into Europe

Smallpox, one of the great epidemic scourges of humankind, was doubly cruel. Many died from it; however, most people survived the attack, only to emerge from it badly disfigured by pockmarks, deep scars left by myriad pustules. The only mercy the disease showed was this: If one survived, one never contracted smallpox again. And then there were also certain fortunate people who contracted only a mild form of the disease. This left them only slightly disfigured, if at all, and yet conferred exactly the same immunity as in major cases.

People would sometimes seek out an individual suffering from mild smallpox, get close to him, and hope to contract the disease—in its mild form. In Turkey, by the eighteenth century, some people were going a step further. They pricked a pustule from an individual who had contracted a mild case of smallpox, then scratched the matter into the skin of a healthy person, thereby *inoculating* him or her with the disease. Lady Mary Wortley Montagu, a poet and the wife of Britain's ambassador to Turkey, noted that, most of the time, those inoculated suffered only a mild case. *Most* of the time. She also noted that, occasionally, the person inoculated would come down with a severe case, either fatal or disfiguring. Nevertheless, she was sufficiently impressed with inoculation to bring news of it back to England, where many people were willing to risk death or disfigurement by deliberate infection rather than wait for the disease to do its evil work in its own time.

Edmond Halley Describes the Movement of Stars

Nothing in creation seems more permanent than the stars. Although the planets, the sun, and the moon move (or seem to move) relative to the stars, the stars themselves remain fixed. This had been believed since ancient times, and thus the heavens were called the "firmament."

It is the business of scientists to question accepted perceptions of reality, and it is, in particular, the business of astronomers to make seemingly impossible observations. To practically everyone the stars always appeared motionless. To look at the night sky, night after night, was, apparently, to confirm this universally held notion. However, the great British astronomer Edmond Halley took a different view. He carefully determined the position of the very bright stars Sirius, Procyon, and Arcturus. He compared what he observed with the positions recorded by the ancient Greeks thousands of years earlier. There was a marked difference. Even more tellingly, there was a difference between his observations in 1718 and those made by the famously careful astronomer Tycho Brahe in the late sixteenth century.

From his observations and those of the past, Halley concluded that the stars moved, and that only their great distance from earth made them appear to stand still. This conclusion, built on careful observation and close comparison with the observations of others over time, was a revolution in how we perceive the universe and our place in it. The cosmic stability promised by the ancients, by the church, and even by the testimony of our own senses was a fiction. A new vision emerged.

1729

Stephen Gray Experiments with Electrical Conduction

Early eighteenth-century "natural philosophers" (as scientists generally called themselves) were fascinated by static electricity and performed an array of experiments to explore it. One of the most important was that of the British scientist Stephen Gray, who, in 1729, found that if he generated a static charge in a long glass tube, corks stoppering either end of the tube were also charged, even though they had not been directly contacted. Gray concluded from this that electricity traveled, and, to find out just how far, he used long lengths of twine to conduct charges. He induced a charge to travel as much as 800 feet.

Gray believed that electricity was a type of fluid substance and that its fluid nature enabled it to travel. Moreover, the fluid theory explained (as far as Gray was concerned) why electricity traveled more easily in some substances than it did in others. Later experimenters built on this observation, deeming some substances "conductors" and others "nonconductors."

1735

Carolus Linnaeus Creates a Taxonomy

The Swedish naturalist Carl von Linné—who always signed his scientific work with the Latinized form of his name, Carolus Linnaeus—was not the first person to attempt the systematic classification of plant and animal life, but he did so in a way that was more thorough and useful than what any of his predecessors had produced.

In 1735, Linnaeus's *Systema Naturae* presented a classification of a dazzling catalogue of plants. His system grouped living things into a nesting set of classifications, beginning with the broadest, *kingdom*. Linnaeus distinguished only two of these, plant and animal. Next came *phylum*, then *class, order, family, genus,* and *species*. Plants or animals (in later editions of *Systema Naturae*, Linnaeus classified animals as well as plants) of related classes were put into the same phylum; those of related orders were put into the same class; of related families into the same order; and so on, down the line narrowing toward greater and greater specificity.

Taxonomy Before Linneaus, 1686 and 1691

In 1686, John Ray, a British naturalist, published his classification of some 18,600 plant species in a way that pointed toward ideas of evolution by underscoring the relationships among various species. Ray did the same for animal species in 1691, isolating the most telling characteristics that relate one type of animal to another. Although Ray's classification was neither as thorough nor as systematically cohesive as that of Linnaeus, it was the first attempt at a truly scientific classification.

From the last two categories, genus and species, came the Latin name of the plant or animal. So compelling was this system that biologists still use it, and, therefore, human beings are still known as *Homo sapiens.* The genus is *Homo,* the species *sapiens.* This is known as binomial nomenclature.

What's in a name?

By looking at plant and animal life as he did, Linnaeus introduced an orderly way of looking at life, a way that both invited and demanded drawing connections between organisms that were clearly related, yet also differentiated. This approach paved the way for an evolutionary view of life on earth, because it suggested that individual species branch out from common genera, which, in turn, evolve from even more common families, and so on, *up* the line of classifications. The implication is that some common ancestor or precursor once existed from which all the variety of life developed over many, many years.

Pieter van Musschenbroek Invents the Leyden Jar, a Device for Storing Electricity

The varied phenomena of static electricity had fascinated people since at least the time of the ancient Greeks, and, early in the eighteenth century, Francis Hauksbee, a British physicist, invented a simple machine (a glass sphere turned by a crank) to generate static electric charges at will. But the first significant advance in the manipulation of electricity was made by the Dutch physicist Pieter van Musschenbroek at the University of Leyden.

The device, which came to be called a Leyden jar, was a metal container hung from insulating silk cords and containing water. A brass wire pierced a cork that stoppered the container and terminated in the water. Static electricity could be generated outside the Leyden jar, and the charge conducted through the brass wire and into the water. The Leyden jar *stored* the charge—which could be released (discharged) as a great spark if any grounded object was brought near the brass wire. If that object happened to be a human finger, the discharge produced a painful jolt of electricity.

The Leyden jar was a curiosity that swept Europe, but it was also a tool that interested serious experimenters, including Benjamin Franklin (see "1752: Benjamin Franklin Tames Lightning").

Jean-Antoine Nollet Describes Osmosis, Thereby Laying the Foundation for a Theory of Molecular Behavior

The word *osmosis* is derived from a Greek root, meaning "to push." It is an apt description of a phenomenon first noted by the French natural philosopher Jean-Antoine Nollet in 1748. He filled a small container with an alcohol solution, covered it with a portion of pig bladder, then immersed this in a tub of water. He observed that, over time, the bladder bulged and, eventually, burst.

Nollet correctly concluded from his observations that more water entered the alcohol solution than left it, thereby building up pressure against the bladder. He further concluded that this meant that the water alone could penetrate the bladder membrane, but that once it was in solution with the alcohol, it could not penetrate the bladder—so it pushed against it, causing it to distend and, finally, to burst.

Why this should be the case, Nollet could not explain. He did not understand that what he was really observing was the behavior of molecules of different sizes. The relatively small molecules of pure water could pass through the bladder membrane, whereas the relatively large water-alcohol molecules could not. Nevertheless, the observation of osmosis laid the groundwork for a theory of molecular behavior, which would begin to emerge by the end of the eighteenth century.

Georges-Louis Leclerc de Buffon Estimates the Age of the Earth

The most respected naturalist of his age, Buffon was given to sweeping speculations that, while grossly inaccurate in their specifics, foreshadowed the profound discoveries of a later age. It was Buffon who was the first to propose a theory of evolution, although his theory might be more properly called a theory of devolution. For he believed that species became differentiated from one another not through a process of positive development, but through one analogous to rotting or decay, degeneration. Thus, to Buffon, donkeys were descended from horses; that is, they were a species of degenerate horse. Similarly, apes were a degenerated species of human beings.

In the same massive work in which he discussed evolution/devolution, his multivolume *Natural History,* Buffon also speculated on the age of the earth. His theory was that the earth and the other planets had been formed by the collision of the sun with a comet—which he thought of as an extremely massive object. If this indeed had been the case, Buffon reasoned, it should be possible to determine the age of the earth by calculating how long it would take an object the size of the earth to cool from a temperature approaching that of the sun to the planet's present temperature. By his calculations, the earth was 75,000 years old. And he took this figure a step further by calculating not just how long it would take the earth to cool to its present temperature, but how long it would take for it to cool sufficiently to support life. He pegged this at about 35,000 years. Furthermore, taking his calculations forward, Buffon estimated that the earth, continuing to cool, would reach a frigid temperature incompatible with life in about 90,000 years.

All of Buffon's figures, we now know, were wildly wrong. Yet he had taken an important step away from theology and into science. In Genesis, all creation spans just six days. Buffon's observations and reasoning concerning evolution and the age of the earth suggested that the sun and at least one other object (the "comet") existed before the earth. The earth required thousands of years to cool sufficiently to support life. Life itself appeared, then evolved (or degenerated).

Not only did Buffon's picture of creation span far longer than the biblical six days, it all must have predated the biblical creation. In 1650, the Anglican bishop James Ussher used the ages of the prophets and other hints in the Old Testament to calculate the date of creation. It came out to 4004 B.C. In 1654, another British theologian, John Lightfoot, pinpointed creation to October 26, 4004 B.C., at 9 A.M. Buffon's evidence indicated a date much, much earlier.

1752

René-Antoine Ferchault de Réaumur Describes the Process of Digestion in Animals

Some science is driven by pure curiosity—How does *this* work? What does *that* mean?—whereas some science is driven by the nagging need to settle an argument.

For many years, naturalists had debated the process of digestion. By the eighteenth century, there were essentially two opposed points of view. One held that digestion was mainly a mechanical process, in which the stomach, through muscular action, ground up food. The other view argued that digestion was mainly chemical in nature, perhaps a variety of fermentation.

René-Antoine Ferchault de Réaumur was a physicist, not a biologist or physiologist, but he hit upon an ingenious experiment to settle the debate. He knew that hawks tore at their prey, swallowing down large chunks of meat, digesting some of it, and regurgitating what could not be digested. As Réaumur saw it, this habit of regurgitation made the hawk an ideal experimental subject. He put meat in a small metal cylinder. The ends of the cylinder were covered with gauze. Réaumur forced the hawk to swallow the cylinder and, after a time, the bird regurgitated it. Examining the meat, Réaumur observed that it had been extensively dissolved. Because the meat had been encapsulated in the cylinder, Réaumur knew that this dissolution could not have been the result of any mechanical grinding. Therefore, it must be the product of a chemical process. But what kind of chemical?

Réaumur devised a second experiment to find out. He induced

the hawk to swallow an indigestible sponge, which it duly regurgitated after a time, soaked through with digestive juices. Réaumur squeezed out the contents of the sponge, placed a piece of meat in the fluid and watched as the fluid began to dissolve the food. Réaumur concluded that the stomach secretes an acid, which digests food. To demonstrate that this was not peculiar to hawks, he repeated the experiment with dogs.

1752

Benjamin Franklin Tames Lightning

Like another of the Founding Fathers, Thomas Jefferson, Benjamin Franklin was as interested in science as he was in government and diplomacy. Also like Jefferson, Franklin was a man of brilliance and brilliant insight.

Attracted to the phenomena of electricity, Franklin experimented with static charges and Leyden jars (see "1745: Pieter van Musschenbroek Invents the Leyden Jar, a Device for Storing Electricity"). It was Franklin who first proposed the concepts of negative and positive charges, suggesting that negative charges repelled each other, as did positive charges, but a positive charge was drawn to a negative. True, Franklin thought (as did others) that electricity was a fluid. What he called *positive electricity* was an excess of electric fluid. What he called *negative electricity* was a deficiency of fluid. Obviously, an excess of fluid is repelled by another excess of fluid. Likewise, a deficiency of fluid cannot be attracted to another deficiency, because neither could bring anything to the other. But an excess of fluid would naturally flow toward a deficiency.

Like everyone else at the time, Franklin was wrong about the fluid nature of electricity, but he had provided, in the idea of positive and negative charges, a valuable insight into how electricity behaves.

More dramatic was the intuitive association he made between static electricity and lightning. When a static charge that had been transferred to a Leyden jar was "drawn off" by bringing a conducting object close to the wire protruding from the jar, a spark and crackle were produced. Franklin reasoned that these were, in essence, miniature lightning and thunder discharges. To test his hypothesis, in 1751, he launched a kite into a thunderstorm. He had fitted a metal rod to the kite, because he knew metal was a conductor, and he ran down from the rod a long silk thread. Attached to that thread, which was soon soaked in the rain, was another dry silk thread, tied to a brass key. As the storm raged, Franklin observed that the fibers of the dry silk threat began to stand up, repelling each other, thereby indicating that a charge was traveling through the thread. Franklin brought his knuckle near the key, and a spark arced from the key to his knuckle. When he brought the key into contact with the wire from a Leyden jar, the jar became charged. Thus Franklin demonstrated that lightning is an electrical discharge.

If Franklin was a brilliant theoretician, he was even sharper when it came to the practical application of theory. His kite experiment had shown him that the electrical charge of lighting could be conducted artificially. Lightning was responsible for many fires in colonial America. Anything tall—especially church steeples—were often set ablaze by lightning strikes. In 1752, in the pages of his famed *Poor Richard's Almanack*, Franklin proposed that a long metal rod be fastened to the tallest part of a building, and a wire run down from the rod, away from the building, and into the ground. The lighting, always attracted to the tallest conductor, would strike the rod rather than the building, and its charge would be conducted, harmlessly, down the wire and dissipated in the ground. The lightning rod had been born, and a destructive natural force tamed—at least to a significant degree.

1766

Albrecht von Haller Establishes the Science of Neurology

Greek anatomists recognized the existence of nerves, but believed they served as a kind of circulatory system, conveying a fluid the nature and function of which were unknown to Western medicine. This nonexplanation had been accepted for centuries before the Swiss physiologist Albrecht von Haller began to experiment with nerves.

Actually, he began with muscle tissue freshly dissected from an animal. He demonstrated that muscle was *irritable*. That is, a slight stimulus to the exposed muscle would cause it to contract. But Haller took this further, demonstrating that if a nerve connected to the muscle was stimulated, the muscle would contract even more dramatically. Furthermore, the muscle would contract even if a very, very small stimulus was applied to the nerve—smaller than that required to induce contraction when it was applied directly to the muscle. From this, von Haller concluded that, in a living animal, stimulation of the nerves—not of the muscles—caused and controlled muscular movement.

Haller went another step further. Noting that all the nerves ultimately went to the brain or the spinal cord, both of which had been identified long ago as the centers of sensation and perception, Haller concluded that nerves were not only responsible for causing and regulating movement, but for generating sensation, which was processed by the brain. In almost a single stroke, therefore, Haller founded neurology, the science of nerves, the nervous system, and the brain.

Antoine-Laurent Lavoisier Describes Combustion

Up through most of the eighteenth century, chemists cared remarkably little about making precise measurements. They combined substances and noted the results. The French chemist Antoine-Laurent Lavoisier took what was a new approach by measuring quantities with great precision before and after a chemical process. In 1772, he applied this technique—call it quantitative chemistry—to the problem of combustion. The leading theory of combustion held that combustible objects were rich in a substance called *phlogiston* (from the Greek, "to set on fire"). Burning consumed phlogiston, leaving as a residue that portion of a substance deficient in phlogiston.

As proof of the phlogiston theory, the German chemist George Ernst Stahl pointed out that combustible materials lose mass (as evidenced by the fact that they weigh less) when burned. The lost mass was assumed to be due to the consumption of phlogiston. Stahl did not address an important contradiction in this theory, however. To his credit, he believed that the rusting of metal was a form of the same process that takes place during combustion. (Today, it is recognized that both combustion and the rusting of metal are oxidation processes.) Stahl believed that the rust was the substance left behind as the phlogiston in a metal was consumed. The contradiction here was that metals actually gain mass (as evidenced by an increase in weight) when they rust. Stahl and other chemists were apparently willing to overlook this paradox because the gain in mass was quite small, too small, they believed, to be significant.

It is the apparently insignificant paradoxes and inconsistencies that modern scientists pounce on, seeking to explain. Lavoisier burned various substances in enclosed containers. He found that the weight of the enclosed substance after burning was greater than its weight before burning. Lavoisier reasoned that if the substance remaining after burning was heavier than the substance before burning, it must have gained its weight from something. The only "something" in the enclosed container was air. Lavoisier further reasoned that if, in fact, the burned substance gained weight from the surrounding air, a partial vacuum must be produced in the enclosed container. This he proved simply by opening the container and hearing the air rush in. Furthermore, when he weighed everything after the container had been opened, he discovered that the weight of the air that had entered the container was equal to the weight gained by the substance that had been burned.

These experiments, painstakingly measured, disproved the phlogiston theory. Combustion was not the loss of phlogiston, but, rather, the *combination* of the burning (or rusting) substance with some element of the air. In the process of beginning to explain combustion, Lavoisier laid the groundwork for modern chemistry, which is founded in precise measurement and the significance of precise measurement.

Conservation of Mass, 1789

In 1789, Lavoisier published the fruits of a lifetime devoted to chemistry, a major textbook. His devotion to precise measurement had led him to confirm by observation one of the cardinal tenets of chemistry and one of the great discoveries of physical science, the law of conservation of mass. In any closed system, Lavoisier wrote, the total amount of mass remained the same, regardless of what physical or chemical processes were at work. In short, matter is neither created nor destroyed, merely transformed. In any closed system, provided that measurements are made precisely, what goes into one substance must come out of another.

1779

Jan Ingenhousz Discovers Photosynthesis

In 1771, the British chemist Joseph Priestley was curious about a possible connection between the fact that carbon dioxide supported neither combustion nor life. At least, that was the common conclusion, and, certainly, animals died if they were shut up in a container in which the oxygen had been replaced by carbon dioxide. To check if this principle held true for *all* life, Priestley tested a plant. He lit a candle and lowered a bell jar over it. When the candle guttered out, he knew that the oxygen had been consumed and replaced by carbon dioxide. Priestley quickly placed a glass of water containing a sprig of mint into this carbon dioxide environment. He expected that it would soon die. In fact, the specimen flourished.

That was a surprise. But there was even more. When Priestley placed a mouse into this environment, expecting that it would die, it survived very nicely. Clearly, the plant had somehow restored breathable elements to the environment. It had converted the carbon dioxide into oxygen.

Eight years later, a curious Dutch physician, Jan Ingenhousz, reading of Priestley's remarkable result, wanted to see it for himself. Scientists routinely repeat the experiments of others, in part to confirm the result, in part to see if they can add to the original observations, and in part to introduce new variations to the experiment. Ingenhousz repeated Priestley's procedure, but added a crucial element to the experiment. He found that the conversion of carbon dioxide to oxygen took place only in the presence of sunlight. A plant left in the dark behaved exactly as an animal did: It consumed oxygen and produced carbon dioxide. Although Ingenhousz didn't come up with a name for this process, he had discovered photosynthesis, one of the most basic processes of life and the key to the ecological relationship between plants and animals.

1783

The Montgolfier Brothers Devise a Hot-Air Balloon

Joseph-Michel Montgolfier and his brother Jacques-Étienne, French paper manufacturers, became interested in a common phenomenon: the fact that warm air rises. They reasoned that if they could trap warm air in a bag made of light paper—put, as they lyrically said, "clouds into bags"—the bag would rise. On a small scale, this worked very well. Air heated in a small bag buoyed the bag to the ceiling. But on a larger scale, the brothers had no luck. One of them realized that it was very difficult to get *dry* warm air into a large bag. Most likely, by the time a sufficient volume of damp hot air was inside the bag, the paper would become sodden and, therefore, too heavy to rise. How to solve this? One of the Montgolfiers noticed that smoke always billowed upward from the chimney of their factory. What if hot smoke were put into a large paper bag?

The bag floated.

With their basic problem solved, the Montgolfiers perfected bigger and bigger bags, some made of silk lined with paper. By the time they announced a public demonstration, they had produced a 24,000-cubic-foot globe of buttoned linen lined with paper. They called this a *ballon*.

Suspending the *ballon* over a large fire in the marketplace of their hometown, Annonay, they freed it. It soared 6,000 feet high and traveled more than a mile before landing.

Two years later, in June 1782, the French Academy of Sciences decided it could improve upon the Mongolfiers' achievement. Academicians had taken samples of the heated air, the so-called "Mont-golfier gas," within the balloon. They determined that this hot air weighed about half as much as cool air. The academicians were aware that, in 1766, the British amateur scientist Henry Cavendish had isolated a gas of extreme lightness he called hydrogen, and that, subsequently, a Scottish chemist, Joseph Black, had speculated that if a bladder could be filled with hydrogen and both the bladder and the gas weighed less than the air they displaced, the bladder would rise. In fact, the academicians knew that hydrogen was not half the weight of air, but that it was *forty times* lighter. They reasoned that a balloon filled with hydrogen would rise higher and fly farther than one filled with hot air.

The French Academy assigned one of their number, Jacques Charles, to come up with a method of producing a large volume of hydrogen. While Charles worked on this problem, two brothers—known to history only by their last name, Robert—were commissioned to build a balloon made of silk rendered airtight by impregnation with rubber. The balloon, christened the *Charlière,* was ready ten weeks later. It was inflated by holding it over the device Charles had invented: a series of lead boxes filled with iron filings over which the chemist poured diluted sulfuric acid. The action of the acid on the iron produced a massive volume of hydrogen.

Once inflated to a diameter of thirteen feet, the *Charlière* was ceremoniously escorted to the Champs de Mars in Paris. A spectacular crowd of some 300,000 witnessed the ascent of the balloon, which reached approximately 20,000 feet before it exploded and fell to earth near Gonesse, about fifteen miles from the Champs de Mars, creating great terror among the villagers. (A pair of local monks informed the people that it was the skin of a "monstrous animal," which they attacked with stones, pitchforks, and flails. Then the village curate sprinkled the burst balloon with holy water—just to be safe. The villagers tied the remains of the slain *Charlière* to a horse and dragged it in triumph.)

In response to the French Academy's project, the Montgolfiers decided to take the ultimate step and launch a man into the sky. In September 1783, with Louis XVI, Marie Antoinette, and the court of Versailles watching, they sent a sheep, a rooster, and a duck up in their hot-air balloon, to see if living, breathing creatures could survive in the atmosphere aboveground. All three animals made it. Next, an intrepid young physician named Pilâtre de Rozier persuaded the brothers to let him be the first human aeronaut. He and the Montgolfiers experimented with tethered flights; then, on November 21, 1783, in company with a dashing French infantry major, the Marquis d'Arlandes, Rozier undertook the first free flight in a balloon.

No less a dignitary than Benjamin Franklin, resident in France throughout the American Revolution as the special envoy of the United States, was among those who witnessed the twenty-five-minute, five-mile flight above the rooftops of Paris.

Ten days after this, Professor Charles and one of the Robert brothers flew for two hours and over twenty-seven miles, not in a hot-air balloon, but in one filled with hydrogen. Immediately after this flight, Charles decided to go aloft alone. Without the added weight of a second passenger, however, the balloon shot up to ten thousand feet so fast that the terrified Charles barely managed to scrawl a few observations: The air was punishingly cold, and his ears ached terribly—but the great altitude gave him the thrill of watching two sunsets in a single day.

"Nothing," he wrote later, "can approach the joy that possessed me." But he never flew again.

1785

William Herschel Formulates
the Concept of a Galaxy

Britain's foremost astronomer, William Herschel, was well aware that other astronomers had speculated that the earth and the solar system were parts of a much vaster structure, a galaxy, which some had even theorized was lenticular, or lens-shaped.

It was an interesting speculation, but how could it be supported by actual observation, given the vastness of the objects involved?

Herschel was one of the greatest observational astronomers in history. He decided that the only way objectively to determine the shape of the galaxy was to count stars. Gazing with a telescope into the night sky during an era before hundreds of thousands of artificial lights obscured the heavens presented an array of stars far beyond anyone's capacity to count. Herschel, therefore, invented statistical astronomy. He divided the sky into 638 regions distributed across the entire visible hemisphere. Then he concentrated on carefully counting stars within these regions. In this way, he developed a thorough picture of the statistical distribution of stars.

He found that the number of stars per region steadily rose as one neared the Milky Way. At the plane of the Milky Way, the number was at its maximum. In the direction of right angles to the plane, it was at its minimum. This distribution could be explained if one imagined the shape of the galaxy as that of a giant lens, the Milky Way demarcating the longest diameter of the lens all the way around. How many stars were in this lens-shaped galaxy? Herschel estimated one hundred million—a staggeringly large number, which proved to be a gross underestimation. Nevertheless, Herschel was the first to image the larger structures of the universe, and the first to use actual observation to give spatial dimension to the concept of a galaxy.

1789

Martin Heinrich Klaproth Discovers Uranium

The German chemist Martin Heinrich Klaproth had a great interest in discovering new elements. With the Austrian mineralogist Franz Joseph Müller von Reichenstein, he had discovered tellurium in 1782, and he was now fascinated by a mineral known as pitchblende. This black ore contained a yellow substance, which Klaproth identified as a new element. He decided to name it after the newly discovered planet Uranus and called it uranium.

Klaproth's discovery generated moderate excitement in the scientific community, but no one at the time had a clue as to the monumental impact the discovery of uranium would have on the course of history.

Thomas Robert Malthus Formulates a Scientifically and Socially Momentous Theory of Human Population

Through most of history the subject of human population has been treated much like the weather: You can *talk* about it, but you can *do* nothing about it. Common sense made it clear that the population of a given region tended to rise in times of peace and prosperity and fall during war, famine, or disease.

In 1798, the British economist Thomas Malthus made a leap beyond common sense by publishing *Essay on the Principle of Population,* in which he argued that population tended to increase geometrically, whereas the supply of food tended to increase arithmetically. That is, population increased in this fashion—2, 4, 8, 16, and so on—whereas the food supply increased this way—2, 3, 4, 5, and so on. The inescapable conclusion was that the demands of population would always outpace the supply of food, and, therefore, humanity would always be subject to famine and disease, as well as war (the cause of which, Malthus believed, was, at bottom, a struggle over scarce resources).

This outlook was grim, of course. Yet it also suggested that famine, disease, and war were not catastrophic aberrations, but normal and even necessary features of human existence. However, Malthus did not believe that these things were inevitable. He proposed population planning to curb population growth and bring it into line with the food supply. He recommended sexual abstinence and delayed marriage. What he did not foresee is that science and technology would provide some alternatives to his gloomy calculus.

On the supply side, farming, food production, and food distribution methods would be improved, as would the science of medicine. On the population side, birth control without sexual abstinence would become a reality—although one that, for religious, cultural, or economic reasons, is hardly practiced universally, with the result that, in many places on the planet, overpopulation remains a catastrophic problem.

Oral Contraception, 1954

The birth-control pill, an orally ingested hormone that, timed with the menstrual cycle, brings about temporary sterility in women, was developed by Gregory Goodwin Pincus, an American biologist. Years of clinical tests would follow before "the Pill"—as it was popularly called—became generally available. Its cultural effect was momentous, and many historians see oral contraception as the trigger of the "sexual revolution" that revised the mores of the 1960s. Would Malthus have welcomed this alternative to abstinence?

Humphry Davy Discovers Nitrous Oxide, Laying the Foundation for Anesthetic Surgery

In 1800, the British chemist Humphry Davy discovered nitrous oxide. In Davy's day, chemistry was in large part a science of the senses, so the scientist took the potentially hazardous step of sniffing at his new discovery. It made him feel light-headed and giddy, so Davy and others took to calling it "laughing gas." Soon, among elite London society, laughing gas parties became the rage.

But Davy also made another important observation about nitrous oxide intoxication. Under its influence, one felt little or no pain. Immediately, a practical application suggested itself to him. Nitrous oxide could be used as a dental and surgical anesthetic. Dentists began using nitrous oxide within years of Davy's discovery, but surgeons were more reluctant to adopt it. Nevertheless, nitrous oxide was the first chemical anesthetic, and its discovery began to take the terror out of surgical procedures and to open the door to more complex and time-consuming operations, which, without an anesthetic, would not only be unbearable, but impossible.

1800

Herschel Discovers Infrared Radiation

I n 1666, Isaac Newton divided white light into its spectrum of colors (see "1666: Isaac Newton Describes the Visible Spectrum"), and in 1800 the British astronomer William Herschel decided to measure the heat produced by the different parts of this spectrum. His question was: Did different colors of light produce different degrees of heat? What he discovered is that not only did different colors produce different levels of heat, but that more heat was produced the closer he moved toward the red end of the spectrum. Just to check his results, Herschel moved his thermometer beyond the red portion of the spectrum—that is, beyond the red, where the light clearly stopped. To his surprise, he found that the temperature rose even higher just beyond the visible red end of the spectrum.

Herschel had discovered that the visible spectrum was not the total spectrum of light, that some light was invisible, and he called the region just below visible red *infrared* ("beneath red"). Herschel concluded that the sun transmitted heat rays as well as light rays. Only later, about half a century after Herschel's initial observations, did it become clear that infrared light behaved just like visible light, except that the human eye did not detect infrared light waves. The invisibility of infrared was a matter of perceptual limitation, and it did not signify that infrared was a "heat ray." It was light, electromagnetic radiation in a part of the spectrum we couldn't see.

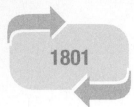

1801

Johann Wilhelm Ritter Discovers Ultraviolet Radiation

Just one year after William Herschel discovered infrared radiation (see "1800: Herschel Discovers Infrared Radiation"), the German physicist Johann Wilhelm Ritter began studying the other end of the visible spectrum. As early as 1614, the Italian chemist Angelo Sala observed that exposure to sunlight turned silver nitrate, normally a white substance, dark. Ritter decided to see how different parts of the spectrum would affect silver nitrate. Accordingly, he soaked paper strips in silver nitrate solution and exposed them. He found that the red end of the spectrum had the least pronounced darkening effect, whereas the violet end had the most. Almost certainly inspired by Herschel's experience with infrared radiation, radiation beyond the visible spectrum, Ritter tried exposing a piece of silver nitrate–soaked paper just beyond the visible violet band. He found that the specimen darkened at an even faster rate than the one exposed to the visible violet light. If the portion of the spectrum below visible red was called infrared, that above violet, Ritter decided, should be dubbed *ultraviolet*—beyond violet.

PRELUDE TO MODERN SCIENCE

1803

John Dalton Advances Atomic Theory

Robert Boyle's work with the compression of gases (see "1661: Robert Boyle Lays the Foundation of Modern Chemistry") launched a long period of interest in discovering the atomic nature of matter. The idea of the atom as the elemental unit of all matter was first put forth speculatively by the Greek philosopher Democritus (see "580 B.C.: Thales Conceptualizes the Elements" and "440 B.C.: Democritus Proposes the Atom as the Smallest Particle of Matter"), but empirical evidence for atomic theory was slow in coming.

In 1803, the British chemist John Dalton synthesized all that had been speculated about the atomic nature of matter and, using Democritus's term, *atom,* put forth the atomic theory.

Dalton proposed that matter was made up of indivisible particles, atoms. However, whereas the ancient Greeks had speculated that the differences between different kinds of matter were the result of differences in the shape of the atoms, Dalton brilliantly proposed that the differences were not a function of atomic shape, but atomic weight. This was not guesswork, but the product of careful observation and measurement. Dalton observed, for example, that it takes eight grams of oxygen combined with one gram of hydrogen to produce nine grams of water. He assumed water consisted of one atom of hydrogen and one atom of oxygen. Therefore, an oxygen atom must be eight times as massive as a hydrogen atom. Thus oxygen may be said to have an atomic weight of eight, versus an atomic weight of one for hydrogen.

As it turned out, Dalton's assumption that water was made up of one hydrogen atom and one oxygen atom was wrong (it is made up of two hydrogen atoms and one oxygen), as were the assumptions he used to calculate other atomic weights. Nevertheless, the underlying idea was right on the mark, and a truly useful atomic theory, the key to modern chemistry and a basic understanding of matter, was born.

George Cayley Lays the Foundation for Aerodynamics

In 1783, the Montgolfier brothers created a hot-air balloon capable of lofting a person into the air (see "1783: The Montgolfier Brothers Ascend in a Hot-Air Balloon"). However, the true dream of flight was to give people the wings of a bird, enabling controlled and powered flight at will. During the Renaissance, the great artist and inventor Leonardo da Vinci drew up fanciful designs for human wings and flying machines, but it wasn't until 1809 that an English scientist, George Cayley, carefully designed genuine flying machines, complete with most of the parts essential to modern aircraft: fixed wings with moveable control surfaces, a tail system, and various mechanisms for propulsion.

The technology of Cayley's time did not enable him to realize his designs in a working aircraft, but, nevertheless, he had laid the foundation for the scientific study and development of flight: aerodynamics.

Jöns Jakob Berzelius Establishes the First Reliable Table of Atomic Weights

n 1803, the British chemist John Dalton formulated the break-through theory that atoms were the basis of all matter and that differences among matter were not due to variations in shape among the atoms, but were the product of atomic weight (see "1803: John Dalton Advances Atomic Theory"). Dalton took a stab at calculating the atomic weight of various elements, but the tables he produced were based on many erroneous assumptions. Other chemists, excited by the atomic theory, also attempted to calculate atomic weights, and one of these, the Swedish chemist Jöns Jakob Berzelius, spent many years in the meticulous analysis of more than 2,000 substances. The result was the first reasonably reliable table of atomic weights. Berzelius supplemented this data with calculations of molecular weights of many common compounds.

Hans Christian Ørsted Demonstrates Electromagnetism

Hans Christian Ørsted, a Danish professor of physics, demonstrated what many scientists had long expected: a strong relationship between the phenomena of electricity and the phenomena of magnetism. The intuition that the two sets of phenomena were related was based on the fact that both magnetism and electricity involved opposites: north and south poles in the case of magnetism, and positive and negative charges in the case of electricity. Moreover, the opposites behaved similarly in both electricity and magnetism: Opposites attracted one another, and like charges or orientations repelled one another. Additionally, in both cases, the force of the attraction or repulsion diminished in proportion to the square of the distance separating the source of the charges or the two magnetic poles.

Ørsted created a practical demonstration in which he brought a compass near a wire through which an electric current was passed. As the compass neared the wire, its needle pointed at a right angle to the wire. If the direction of the current was reversed, the compass needle swung 180 degrees around, pointing in the opposite direction, although still oriented at a right angle to the wire.

Interestingly, Ørsted did not feel moved to pursue the full implications of his demonstration. It was left to other scientists, most notably the Frenchman André-Marie Ampère, to make the further observations that clearly established the field of electromagnetism as one of the cornerstones of modern physics.

1821

Michael Faraday Demonstrates That Electrical Forces Can Produce Motion, Thereby Laying the Foundation for Field Theory

The British physicist Michael Faraday, one of the great experimenters of science, tirelessly pursued the implications of the exciting new area of electromagnetism. In 1821, he set up an experiment with two electrical circuits and two magnets. In one circuit, the electric wire was fixed near a movable magnet. In the other circuit, the wire was movable and the magnet fixed. When the circuits were energized, the movable magnet revolved around the fixed wire, and the movable wire revolved around the fixed magnet.

The most immediate conclusion Faraday drew from this was that electricity could produce motion—a discovery that would have tremendous practical application in electric motors and like devices. But Faraday went beyond the immediate and practical. He concluded that magnetism is a field, a field that extends from its point of origin, weakening with distance. Moreover, Faraday reasoned, it is possible to chart this field by drawing imaginary lines that connect all points of equal magnetic intensity. Thus the field could be delineated as "lines of force."

Faraday's early formulation of a field theory provided an important foundation of modern physics, which pictures the universe itself as a set of fields, each originating in particles of matter. Faraday's experiment and the conclusions he drew from it provided an early window into the structure of the universe.

1822

Charles Babbage and Lady Ada Lovelace Begin to Develop the First Modern Computer

B y the nineteenth century, calculating machines were hardly new. In ancient times, the abacus appeared (see sidebar: "The Abacus, About 500 B.C."), and the mathematicians Blaise Pascal and Gottfried Wilhelm Leibniz had, independently, created more complex mechanical calculators in 1642 and 1693, respectively. In a sense, all of these devices were computers—but only in a sense, and certainly not in the full modern sense. A computer is not a calculator—although it can be used as one—but a machine that can be programmed at will to perform many different tasks based on logic and calculation. Working with another brilliant mathematician, Lady Ada Lovelace, the British mathematician Charles Babbage began to design a machine that could perform varied and highly complex tasks by means of actual programming—the instructions supplied on punched cards. This idea had come to Babbage from his observation of how a Jacquard loom works. It creates complex weave patterns in cloth by following instructions punched into cards. Babbage and Lovelace even went beyond the notion of programming, proposing a machine that could store information and partial answers to problems and that could even print out the results of calculations.

Babbage and Lovelace began work on this machine in 1822. Babbage carried on the project until the end of his life in 1871, but the machine was never fully completed. His design was severely limited by the technology available in his day. The device he envisioned required monumentally complicated systems of wheels and gears, which could not be made efficient and accurate enough to do the work he wanted the machine to do. What was required was a multitude of electronic switches—but the technology of electronics lay many years in the future, and the Babbage-Lovelace computer remained one of history's greatest incomplete inventions.

Georg Simon Ohm Formulates Ohm's Law, Cornerstone of Electrical Science and Engineering

George Simon Ohm, a German physicist, tackled the problem of calculating the flow of electricity between the two points, positive and negative, of an electric circuit. He experimented with wires of varied gauges (thicknesses) and lengths connected to an electrical source of known strength. What he found was that the quantity of electrical current transmitted through a conductor was inversely proportional to the length of the wire and directly proportional to the cross-sectional area of the wire. This allowed him to define the resistance (opposition to the passing of current) of a given wire. In 1827, he stated his observations in a form that is known as Ohm's Law: "Current through a conductor is directly proportional to the potential difference and is inversely proportional to the resistance." This formulation provides the key for many other calculations, which enable the design of a myriad of practical electric and electronic devices. On Ohm's Law, the science and technology of electrical engineering is built.

Friedrich Wöhler Synthesizes Urea, Thereby Demolishing the Notion That Only Organisms Can Produce Organic Substances

Many scientists agreed that organic substances could be produced only by living organisms, that these substances were the product of some special force or divine essence of life. Theologians and other conservative thinkers were heartened by this view, called vitalism, which seemed to uphold the supernatural sacredness of life. In 1828, however, the German chemist Friedrich Wöhler made an accidental discovery that exploded the vitalist view.

He was heating ammonium cyanate, a garden-variety inorganic substance, and found that, heated, the substance formed crystals that looked to him like urea, the chief constituent of mammalian urine, including human urine. He subjected the crystals to analysis and confirmed that they were indeed urea. The wall between organic and inorganic chemistry dissolved and, with it, the long-cherished notion that life was a divine and supernatural phenomenon.

Faraday Invents the Electric Generator, and Joseph Henry Invents the Electric Motor

L ittle more than a decade after Ørsted demonstrated that electric current creates a magnetic effect (see "1820: Hans Christian Ørsted Demonstrates Electromagnetism"), the great British experimentalist Michael Faraday reasoned that the reverse must also be true: Magnetism could produce electric current.

In 1831, Faraday wound a wire coil around a portion of an iron ring and attached the wires to a battery. When current flowed, a magnetic field was created. He wrapped a second coil around another portion of the ring, connecting these wires to a galvanometer, a compass-like device that indicated the presence of an electric current. When he connected the first coil to the battery, the galvanometer needle jumped—but then returned to a neutral position until the current was removed. The needle then jumped in the opposite direction.

Faraday had discovered electromagnetic induction, the principle behind an electrical transformer. He explained the failure to induce a continuous flow of current by reasoning that, when the current was applied, magnetic lines of force crossed to the second coil, inducing a current. When the current was removed, the lines of force crossed back from the second to the first coil, inducing an electrical current in the opposite direction. However, when the current was applied continuously, equilibrium was reached: No lines of force crossed the second coil in either direction.

Faraday reasoned that there was a technical way to cut across the lines of force in continual fashion. He set up a copper wheel so that its rim passed between the poles of a permanent horseshoe magnet. Wires led from the copper wheel. As long as the wheel was turned, continuously cutting through the lines of magnetic force, an electric current flowed in the wheel. The current produced could be transmitted through the wires to do work. Faraday had invented the generator.

Later the same year, another English scientist, Joseph Henry, inverted Faraday's generator. He reasoned that if rotary motion could produce an electric current, an electric current should be able to produce rotary motion. He improved Faraday's generator, then supplied current to the machine, which, acting on the permanent magnet, forced the wheel to move. The electric motor, in effect the mirror image of the electrical generator, was born. Together, the generator and the motor opened the door to a vast new range of electrically driven technologies and industries.

Anselme Payen Isolates Diastase, the First Enzyme Active Outside of a Living Organism

The French chemist Anselme Payen was a sugar refiner, who managed a factory that extracted sugar from sugar beets. In 1833, he was able to separate from malt extract a substance that catalyzed (accelerated) the conversion of starch to glucose. He called this substance *diastase*, a name derived from the Greek verb meaning to separate, because diastase separated the components of starch into the units of glucose.

Diastase was the first organic catalyst—or enzyme—isolated from the living matter that had produced it. Moreover, it was the first enzyme made active outside of a living organism. It represented a giant leap in the development of organic chemistry and the commercial exploitation of organic chemistry.

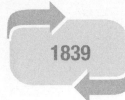

1839

Louis-Jacques-Mandé Daguerre Invents Photography

L ouis-Jacques-Mandé Daguerre, a French artist, was highly familiar with the camera obscura, a device at least as old as the Renaissance, which projected a focused image on a plane, and which artists had for centuries found highly useful in painting landscapes and other scenes in realistic perspective. Daguerre wanted to take the camera obscura image a step further. Instead of tracing the projected image, he wanted to find a way to fix that image permanently using a chemical process.

Daguerre understood that silver salts darkened upon exposure to light. By focusing an image on a surface coated with a suspension of silver salts, the chemical would be darkened selectively, depending on the intensity of the light falling on any given area. Normally, however, silver salts continued to darken as they were further exposed to light, thereby destroying the image. Daguerre's breakthrough came in 1839 when he discovered that he could bathe the photographic image in sodium thiosulfate solution, which would dissolve whatever silver had not been acted on by the light. Once dissolved and washed away, there was no unexposed silver to darken, and what was left behind was the light-transformed silver, which recorded the image of the light to which it had been exposed. The age of photography had begun.

Christian Johann Doppler Describes the Doppler Effect, a Cornerstone of Modern Astronomy

The distinctive sound of a locomotive whistle—rising in pitch as the train approaches, descending in pitch as it passes and recedes—fascinated people in the early days of the railroads. One person, the Austrian physicist Christian Johann Doppler, decided to dig beneath the fascination. He proposed that the change in pitch was caused by the fact that the sound waves partake of the motion of their source. As the locomotive approaches the listener, the sound waves reach the ear at progressively shorter intervals; therefore, the frequency is higher and so is the pitch. As the locomotive moves away, the sound waves reach a stationary listener at progressively longer intervals, the frequency is lower, and so, of consequence, is the pitch.

Doppler became so intrigued by the mathematics of waves from moving sources that he arranged for a locomotive to pull a flatcar on which trumpet players sounded various notes. Stationed at intervals along the track were musicians with perfect pitch, who were asked to record exactly what note they heard. In this way, Doppler was able to measure the degree of the "Doppler effect" by noting the variation between the note sounded and the note perceived.

The Doppler effect provided important insight into the nature of waves, light (electromagnetic) waves as well as sound waves. In the twentieth century, the American astronomer Harlow Shapley would use the Doppler effect to demonstrate that the universe was not only expanding, but expanding at an accelerating rate. In this insight was the birth of modern cosmology—the science of the birth, structure, and evolution of the universe.

1844

Samuel F. B. Morse Perfects the Telegraph

amuel F. B. Morse was not trained as a scientist, but as a painter. While returning from a stay in Europe—European credentials were essential to the success of an American painter in those days—Morse met and spoke with fellow passenger Thomas Jackson, a British scientist. The conversations gave Morse the idea that electrical current could be used as a medium for communication.

When he arrived home, Morse did not take up his brushes, but instead designed and built what he called the *telegraph,* a word from two Greek roots, *tele,* meaning distant, and *graph,* signifying writing.

In a scientific journal, Morse read about Hans Christian Ørsted's demonstration of electromagnetism and induction (see "1820: Hans Christian Ørsted Demonstrates Electromagnetism"). Morse wasn't the first to follow up on Ørsted. Several scientists experimented with "deflecting-needle telegraphs," essentially compass needles that moved in response to a current, and William F. Cooke and Charles Wheatstone installed a working deflecting-needle telegraph along an English rail line in 1837. But the device was not practical. Morse decided that electromagnetism rather than mere induction was a more robust technology, and he built his device around an electromagnet. When energized by a current from the line—when the remote operator pressed his "telegraph key"—an electromagnet attracted a soft iron armature, which was designed to make marks on a moving strip of paper. If the telegraph key was held down very briefly, a short mark, or dot, was inscribed. If held down longer, a longer mark, or dash, was produced. Using combinations of these two symbols, dot and dash, Morse created a logical system for encoding the entire alphabet, numbers, and punctuation: the Morse code.

Morse was not only a brilliant practical inventor, he was a highly competent self-promoter, who quickly persuaded Congress to finance a test wire between Washington, D.C., and Baltimore, a distance of about forty miles. On May 24, 1844, he transmitted the first telegraphic message over that wire: "What hath God wrought?" Within ten years, those forty miles of wire grew to 23,000. The age of electromechanical communication was born.

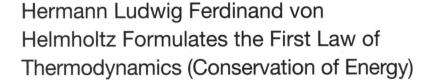

1847

Hermann Ludwig Ferdinand von Helmholtz Formulates the First Law of Thermodynamics (Conservation of Energy)

n 1668, John Wallis formulated the Law of Conservation of Momentum (see "1668: John Wallis Formulates the Law of Conservation of Momentum, First of the Laws of Conservation That Are Fundamental to Our Understanding of the Universe"), and in 1789, the French chemist Lavoisier demonstrated conservation of mass (see sidebar: "Conservation of Mass, 1789"). Some scientists began to speculate that energy might also be subject to conservation: that is, neither be created nor destroyed, but merely transformed. If this were indeed the case, the universe could be conceptualized as an ultimately finite place, in which transformations continually took place, but matter and energy remained constant.

In 1843, the British physicist James Prescott Joule experimentally demonstrated that work—the use of mechanical energy—produced heat. A fixed quantity of work yielded a fixed quantity of heat. (In fact, 41,800,000 ergs of work produce 1 calorie of heat.) This result suggested that energy was indeed conserved; that is, mechanical energy considered "lost" as friction was not lost at all, but merely converted to heat.

Four years after Joule's experiments, the German physicist Hermann Ludwig Ferdinand von Helmholtz synthesized Joule's data with his own and formulated a fully persuasive Law of Conservation of Energy: The energy in the universe is fixed and finite; it is neither created nor destroyed, but is converted from one form to another. Also called the First Law of Thermodynamics, conservation of energy stands as the most basic law of nature in that it describes a fundamental property of the universe.

1848

William Thomson, Baron Kelvin, Conceptualizes Absolute Zero

At the end of the seventeenth century, in 1699, Guillaume Amontons, a French physicist, observed that the volume of a fixed quantity of a gas increases with a rise in temperature and decreases with a fall in temperature. Looking back at this insight a century and a half later, the British physicist William Thomson, Baron Kelvin, realized that the important point was not the obvious one, the loss of volume with temperature reduction, but the loss of energy. He calculated the rate of energy loss to be such that "absolute zero"—a condition without energy—would be attained at −273°C (a figure modern scientists refined to −273.15°C or −459.67°F).

Kelvin suggested that scientists should work from a new temperature scale, one without negative numbers, an absolute scale beginning with absolute zero. Each degree of this new scale would correspond with one Celsius degree, so that water froze not at 0°C but at 273°K (or 273.15°K). (Kelvin himself proposed designating absolute temperatures with the letter "A," for absolute, but later scientists named the unit in Kelvin's honor, abbreviated "K.")

Why was it so important to rethink the temperature scale? The concept of absolute zero signified a state in which atoms are motionless, a state, that is, without energy. Only with atomic movement was energy—heat—generated. Thus absolute temperature was a true measure of energy and, therefore, a supremely useful tool for creating the science of thermodynamics.

Rudolf Julius Emanuel Clausius Formulates the Second Law of Thermodynamics (Entropy)

Conservation of energy, the First Law of Thermodynamics, was formulated in 1847 (see "1847: Hermann Ludwig Ferdinand von Helmholtz Formulates the First Law of Thermodynamics [Conservation of Energy]"). There was something profoundly comforting about this law, which affirmed the ultimate stability of the universe. Although no "new" energy could be created, none of the energy existing in the universe was ever lost.

Yet to anyone who ever did any work or operated any mechanical device, the notion of conservation of energy seemed to have little practical value. In a *universal* sense, energy was not lost, but in a *practical* or *local* sense, it was lost all the time. The French physicist Nicolas-Léonard-Sadi Carnot mathematically demonstrated the unavoidable inefficiency of steam engines, the fact that only a given amount of heat energy could be converted to mechanical energy. The rest, in practical terms, was "lost"—that is, unavailable for conversion. In 1850, Rudolf Julius Emanuel Clausius, a German physicist, generalized Carnot's finding to all energy conversions. Some energy was always "lost" to heat, and heat (as Carnot had demonstrated) could never be converted completely to any other form of energy. Thus, energy conversion was always inherently inefficient.

On the local level, the implication of this is that all machines are doomed to be more or less inefficient. Bad as this is, the implication is far more dire from the universal perspective. While energy is neither created nor destroyed, energy conversion is inefficient and, therefore, the energy of the universe is continually being degraded to heat, which, in turn, can never be fully converted to another form of energy. While the amount of energy in the universe remains constant, the amount of *useful* energy constantly decreases.

This, Clausius argued, could be demonstrated in a closed system. The ratio of the heat content of such a system would always increase during any process within the system. Clausius called this ratio—of heat content to absolute temperature—entropy. It is the heart of the Second Law of Thermodynamics. The amount of entropy in the universe always increases, destined to reach a maximum some day, at which point no useful energy will be left in the universe and, as a consequence, disorder will be literally universal. If the First Law of Thermodynamics signified that the universe was a system of ultimate order, the Second signified precisely the opposite, that it is a system of *ultimate* disorder.

1855

Alexander Parkes Dissolves Pyroxylin in Alcohol, Producing the First Synthetic Plastic

Chemists are inveterate tinkerers, and one of these, the Britisher Alexander Parkes, working with a partly nitrated cellulose called pyroxylin, discovered that if the substance was dissolved in a solution of alcohol, ether, and camphor, it emerged as a hard solid once the solution had evaporated. Moreover, this solid became soft and malleable when it was heated, then hardened again when cooled.

Parkes was a chemist, neither a businessman nor an inventor. He recorded the pyroxylin episode as a curiosity, but took it no further. In fact, he had created the first synthetic plastic, the material that, during the twentieth century, would come to constitute a great deal of the world's built environment.

William Henry Perkin Develops the First Synthetic Dye

Our manufactured world is varied and colorful. We take for granted that we can have paint and clothing in any color we can imagine. But this was not always the case. Through most of the history of civilization, color was a precious commodity. Fabrics were naturally off-white. They could be dyed with a few natural substances, but the resulting array of colors was limited and subject to fading. Many natural dye substances were also rare and costly.

William Henry Perkin, a British student of chemistry, was not thinking about dyes when he ambitiously engaged in a search for a process to synthesize quinine. In nature, quinine, an antimalaria drug, is derived from the bark of a tree. During the nineteenth century, quinine was vitally important to the British empire, which was continually expanding into tropical regions, where malaria was a grim fact of life. If quinine could be synthesized, greatly increased production of the drug would be possible. What Perkin did not realize, however, was that the molecular structure of quinine was far too complex for him to synthesize with the chemical technology of 1856. However, what he did manage to produce, quite by accident, was a purplish substance. Dissolving this in alcohol, he saw that it produced a gorgeous color that would, only later, be christened mauve.

Perkin was a better businessman than chemist, and he immediately saw the potential of the substance as a dyestuff. Once he confirmed that it could be used as a dye, he abandoned his chemistry studies, persuaded his family to invest all they had in setting up a factory, and William Henry Perkin became an enormously wealthy man as the creator and producer of the world's first synthetic dye. While this enriched Perkin, the discovery also opened the door to a dazzling array of synthetic dyes, which not only transformed the manufactured world into a colorful one, but set the stage for all manner of photographic reproduction technologies that would further transform and enrich modern life.

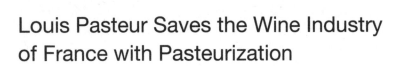

1856

Louis Pasteur Saves the Wine Industry of France with Pasteurization

The chemist Louis Pasteur, a scientist and French patriot, was deeply concerned by a crisis menacing his nation's economically crucial wine industry. During aging, wine was going sour at an alarming rate.

Pasteur investigated wine samples under the microscope and made the remarkable discovery that, in properly aged wine, yeast cells were visible as spherical globules, whereas in souring wine, the cells were oblong. Pasteur concluded that two types of yeast cells existed; the "bad" variety created lactic acid, which soured the wine. There was no way to regulate which type of yeast cell would form in the aging wine; therefore, Pasteur recommended that all yeast cells be killed after fermentation (the creation of alcohol) had taken place but before any lactic acid could be produced. To kill the yeast, he recommended heating the wine to 50°C, then allowing the product to age without yeast. Although conservative wine makers protested, they were willing to give the process a try, and when they discovered that it did not affect the quality of the wine, they adopted it universally. It was referred to as pasteurization.

Pasteurization soon found application in other food-related areas, particularly in the processing of milk, which often carried or supported the growth of disease-producing bacteria. As for Pasteur, the successful experience with the wine industry turned his attention increasingly to the power of microbes—mighty organisms too small even to be seen with the unaided eye.

1859

Charles Darwin Publishes
The Origin of Species

Charles Darwin was not the first naturalist to believe that modern life was the result of a process of evolution, but he was among the first to investigate just what forces propelled and governed evolution. His reading of Malthus's writing on human population (see "1798: Thomas Robert Malthus Formulates a Scientifically and Socially Momentous Theory of Human Population") struck a chord. The tendency to reproduce beyond the capacity of the available food supply was not, Darwin observed, peculiar to humankind, as Malthus thought, but was universal. It was as if nature created a competitive arena in which all living beings vied for survival and mastery. Thus, Darwin concluded, nature dictated conditions in which only the most capable offspring would survive to reproduce. Over time, therefore, traits favorable to survival would be bred into any given species, while those unfavorable to survival would disappear—because animals bearing those traits would die or be killed before reproducing.

Darwin formulated this idea, which he called "natural selection," as early as 1838, but he refrained from publishing it until he felt that he had sufficient observational data to support it. During the course of two decades, Darwin quietly and patiently amassed his data. Even so, it took the appearance of a theory of evolution proposed by another British biologist, Alfred Russel Wallace, to prod the cautious and diffident Darwin into finally publishing, in 1859, his *Origin of Species,* which developed in eloquent detail the theory of evolution by natural selection and thereby delivered to the world a compellingly dynamic picture of life on the planet.

Australopithecus Fossils, 1924

Darwin based his theory of evolution on the observation of living organisms, and he said very little about the evolution of humankind. The twentieth century would see an explosion in the study of fossil of evidence and major discoveries in human evolution. In 1924, Raymond Arthur Dart, an Australian-born South African anthropologist, came upon a fossilized skull in a South African stone quarry. He called it *Australopithecus,* meaning southern ape, but, in fact, it was a hominid, an ancestor of modern humankind, which had lived in Africa from the early Pliocene Epoch (beginning about 5.3 million years ago) to the start of the Pleistocene (some 1.6 million years ago). Today, most scientists classify Australopithecus as the earliest of the hominids and consider it the earliest form of humankind.

1862

Pasteur Advances
the Germ Theory of Disease

The French scientist Louis Pasteur, who had used microscopic analysis to rescue the French wine industry (see "1856: Louis Pasteur Saves the Wine Industry of France with Pasteurization"), was well persuaded of the existence and power of microorganisms. He was not alone. The most radical of mid-nineteenth-century biologists were already theorizing that microorganisms were responsible for causing many diseases, that they were, in effect, the "germs" from which much illness grew.

In 1862, Pasteur reviewed the state of research on the germ theory of disease and concluded that the theory was, indeed, valid. He published a seminal review and synthesis of all the evidence that had been gathered by others in support of the theory, and he lent this material the very considerable weight of his reputation.

Backed by Pasteur, the germ theory gained wide acceptance and motivated many scientists, including Pasteur himself, to set about identifying specific microorganisms as the cause of specific diseases. In this research, medicine entered its modern phase, approaching a time when physicians could, at long last, offer something more than well-meaning support to their patients. The germ theory identified an enemy in the war against disease.

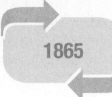

In a Dream, Friedrich August Kekule von Stradonitz Visualizes the Molecular Structure of Benzene, Thereby Providing the Basis for Organic Chemistry

S cience aims at the highest application of rational thought. Yet science is an intensely creative field of endeavor, and scientists learn to take their inspiration from wherever it comes, whether as a result of careful calculation or something very different.

In 1865, the German chemist Friedrich August Kekule von Stradonitz wrestled with what seemed an intractable problem. He could not understand—much less explain formulaically—how the important organic compound benzene behaved. How did the molecular structure of this molecule account for its properties? The benzene molecule has six carbon atoms and six hydrogen atoms. This defied chemical logic, as Kekule understood it, because there should be no way of combining six carbon and six hydrogen atoms without producing a highly unstable compound. Benzene, however, was eminently stable. How did this happen?

Exhausted by thought, Kekule was riding in a horse-drawn omnibus and began to doze. Suddenly, he found himself in the midst of a dream. He saw a snake engulf the tail of another snake in its mouth, and the first snake, in turn, take the tail of the second in *its* mouth. In this way, the snakes formed a ring, which began to spin.

Suddenly, Kekule awoke. He saw it all before him: The six carbon atoms of benzene formed a ring (actually, as Kekule conceptualized it, a hexagon); if each individual carbon atom were attached to a hydrogen atom, the result, in this molecular configuration, would be a stable compound. Kekule had visualized the first organic molecule, and on this structural foundation, many other organic molecules could be visualized. Organic chemistry was born.

Gregor Johann Mendel Creates the Science of Genetics

G regor Mendel was an obscure Augustinian monk and amateur botanist living in a remote Austrian monastery, far from the mainstream of nineteenth-century scientific thought. Curious about the mechanisms of inheritance, the subject that would become known as genetics, he experimented with pea plants in the garden of his monastery. Working alone and with the infinite care and patience befitting a monk as well as a scientist, Mendel made a series of extraordinary observations.

He noted that dwarf pea plants grew from seeds that had been produced by dwarf plants. These dwarf plants, in turn, yielded seeds that also produced dwarf pea plants. However, in the case of tall plants, some produced seeds that always grew into tall plants, while others produced tall plants 75 percent of the time and dwarf plants 25 percent of the time. When Mendel crossed a dwarf plant with a tall plant that always produced tall plants, the result was a tall plant. In effect, the dwarf trait seemed to have been suppressed. But not entirely. For when Mendel took the tall plants produced by a cross between tall and dwarf plants and allowed them to self-pollinate, they produced 75 percent tall plants and 25 percent dwarfs. Mendel thus identified the trait for tallness as "dominant," while that for dwarfness was "recessive"; it didn't disappear, but was temporarily suppressed.

Mendel expanded his experiments to examine a variety of traits, and he also established that the roles of the female and male in contributing to the inheritance of the offspring were equal. In

1865, after many years of observation, he published a paper in which he laid out a set of principles that formed the foundation of genetics and would be called the "Mendelian laws of inheritance." But that title would not be conferred until more than three decades after the publication, in 1865 and 1869, of Mendel's two research papers. Scientists were slow to recognize the work of an obscure monk. Once they did, however, the modern view of the natural world was dramatically transformed.

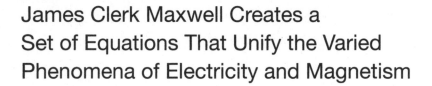

1865

James Clerk Maxwell Creates a Set of Equations That Unify the Varied Phenomena of Electricity and Magnetism

Ever since Isaac Newton had formulated a set of equations that tied together the phenomena of gravitation, physicists sought to accomplish the unification of apparently varied physical phenomena. The British physicist James Clerk Maxwell did this for electricity and magnetism, showing that both were manifestations of a single electromagnetic force.

Maxwell produced a set of equations showing that the oscillation of an electric current created an electromagnetic field that radiated from its source at a constant speed. He showed further that this constant was, in fact, the speed of light. From this, Maxwell concluded that light was a form of electromagnetic radiation. Indeed, Maxwell proposed that the nature of any type of electromagnetic radiation was a function solely of wavelength. For example, infrared radiation consisted of waves of longer wavelength than visible red light, which, in turn, was longer than ultraviolet radiation, and so on, across the spectrum. Thus Maxwell applied to what seemed entirely unrelated phenomena the same set of equations, thereby demonstrating the unity of magnetism, electricity, visible light, the infrared, and ultraviolet. After Maxwell, such unification increasingly became both the hallmark and the objective of modern physics.

1869

Dmitry Ivanovich Mendeleyev Creates the Periodic Table of the Elements

The concept of atomic weight had its origin in the work of the English chemist Robert Boyle (see "1661: Robert Boyle Lays the Foundation of Modern Chemistry"), and, at various times, chemists attempted to create an orderly table of elements based on atomic weight. The result was never entirely satisfactory.

At last, in 1869, the Russian chemist Dmitry Ivanovich Mendeleyev had the important insight of using both atomic weight and valence (the number of electrons in an atom's outer shell, electrons which it will lose, add, or share when it reacts with other atoms) as the basis of his table. This resulted in a table with rows ("periods") of varying length, a periodic table of the elements, which was published in 1869.

Not only did the periodic table provide a new picture of the order of the chemical universe, it provided a means by which the discovery of new elements could be predicted, because the arrangement of the known elements left gaps. Based on these gaps, Mendeleyev predicted the properties of elements that, in 1871 (the year he discussed the gaps), had yet to be found.

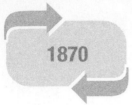

Heinrich Schliemann Locates the Site of Troy, in Effect Launching the Modern Science of Archaeology

Heinrich Schliemann was a poor German lad who made good, becoming a successful businessman. His lifelong motivation was not wealth for its own sake, but for the funding of a dream that had begun in childhood: an expedition to locate the lost city of Troy, fabled in Homer's *Iliad*.

Schliemann was a scientific amateur. At the time, this would have been true about anyone with Schliemann's interests. In 1870, archaeology did not exist as a professional scientific discipline. But he had devoured the *Iliad,* and, following its description of Troy, he identified precisely the right place in Turkey to begin his dig. He uncovered a trove: one ancient city built atop another. Not only did he prove the existence of Troy, he so thrilled the popular and scientific community that, single-handedly, he launched archaeology as a major field.

1876

Alexander Graham Bell Invents the Telephone

Alexander Graham Bell was a Scots immigrant to the United States, the child of a family of celebrated teachers of speech. As a young man, Bell decided to specialize in teaching the deaf to speak, and in 1872 he opened a school for the deaf in Boston. The following year, he was appointed professor of speech and vocal physiology at Boston University.

It was a noble calling, and Bell was good at it. But his imagination resisted confinement to any one profession. His study of the physiology and physics of speech soon expanded into a more general interest in sound and the recording and transmission of sound. Electricity, in the form of the telegraph, was already well established as a medium for communication (see "1844: Samuel F. B. Morse Perfects the Telegraph"), and Bell reasoned that if he "could make a current of electricity vary in intensity precisely as the air varies in density during the production of sound," he could "transmit speech telegraphically."

The concept was a breakthrough, but the problem remained: Just *how* could sound waves be converted into electrical impulses?

Bell set to work, and by 1876, after two years of experimentation, he had developed a microphone and a speaker. The first converted sound into a weak fluctuating electric current. The second converted that current into physical vibration—sound. Even before he had perfected the twin devices, Bell filed for a patent.

With the patent pending, he was now under increased pressure to turn a set of scientific principles into a device that actually transmitted and received sound. Painstakingly tinkering and adjusting, exhausted, Bell toppled a beaker of battery acid into his lap. The sulfuric acid burned clothes and flesh, and, without thinking about it, Bell called into the instrument on his workbench, summoning his assistant, Thomas Watson, who was stationed at the receiver in another room.

"Mr. Watson, come here. I want you."

They were the first words spoken over a telephone. Fittingly, they were a call for help, the most elemental form of human communication. They were prophetic words, a glimmer of just how indispensable the telephone would become to modern civilization.

1877

Thomas Alva Edison Invents the Phonograph and Records Sound

On the face of it, Thomas Edison showed little intellectual promise as a lad growing up in small-town Michigan. He was a poor student, soon dropping out of grade school to be tutored at home by his devoted mother, and he was partially deaf, the result of a childhood illness compounded by an injury. Initiative he did have, making his way as a "candy butcher," selling candy and newspapers to railroad passengers, earning money to finance his real passion, which was tinkering with chemicals. Fascinated by the telegraph, he became a journeyman railroad telegrapher, and this turned his tinkering to electricity. He made the decision to become an inventor.

After selling a telegraphic stock ticker to a group of Wall Street investors, Edison built a fine workshop and laboratory, first in Newark, New Jersey, and then, on a larger scale, in rural Menlo Park. He turned out inventions with such startling regularity that he was soon dubbed "the wizard of Menlo Park." But he plowed most of the money he made back into his work and, as a result, was chronically strapped for cash. Under the goad of necessity, one summer day in 1877, he rushed to complete the design for a machine that would transcribe telephone messages graphically. To do this, Edison used a stylus-tipped carbon transmitter, which made impressions on a strip of paper impregnated with paraffin. By accident, Edison discovered that, when the paper was pulled back beneath the stylus, the indentations that had been made by the original sounds reproduced those sounds—not well, but at least recognizably.

Edison had the happy faculty of combining accident with insight. He immediately sketched a crude diagram of a device that applied the stylus not to wax paper, but to a cylinder wrapped in tin foil. He handed the sketch to his chief engineer and said, simply, "Build this." He did not bother to explain what it was.

Building it was easy. There was very little to the machine, basically a cylinder attached to a crank. As soon as the machine was ready, Edison bent over a funnel-shaped object attached to a diaphragm, which, in turn, was linked to a stylus touching the cylinder. As he cranked the cylinder, Thomas Edison spoke into the funnel: "Mary had a little lamb. Its fleece was white as snow." Then he stopped talking and moved the stylus to the beginning of what he had recorded. He turned the crank, and the machine played back the nursery rhyme.

Edison had invented the phonograph. More importantly for the history of science and civilization, he had recorded *sound,* that most ephemeral of human products. If the telegraph and telephone annihilated space, Edison's phonograph arrested time by preserving, in grooves of foil and, later, wax, the past.

Edison Invents the Incandescent Electric Light

Thomas Edison, who would come to hold more than one thousand U.S. patents, is best known as the inventor of the electric light. In truth, electricity had been used for illumination since the beginning of the nineteenth century. Arc lamps, which produced a blindingly brilliant continuous spark between two carbon rods, were already used in some searchlights, theatrical lighting, lighthouse beacons, and even street lighting by mid century. What Edison grasped, however, was that arc lighting was of no use indoors, at home, in the office, or in the factory. He understood, as he put it, that the light needed to be "subdivided" to be made useful. And, if a way was found to subdivide it, electric lighting could replace gas lighting, which meant that a whole new industry would be created: the business of generating and selling electricity itself.

So, as Edison set about subdividing light, he understood that his aim was to do no less than transform civilization.

He developed the idea of *incandescence*, that is, causing a material—a filament—to glow by passing an electric current through it. The result would be sustained, safe, controllable, "subdivided" illumination. The practical obstacle to achieving this was the filament. Edison experimented with thousands of materials, including a whisker plucked from the beard of a workshop assistant, all to no avail. At last, on October 21, 1879, he "carbonized cotton" by pulling a piece of thread through lampblack—fine carbon. He put this thread into a glass bulb, pumped the air out to create a vacuum, and ran a current through it. For forty hours, it provided steady, usable, safe illumination.

Edison gave the first public demonstration of his incandescent electric lamp on December 31, 1879. He improved it, using new filament material and a new bulb design, so that it burned much longer. With financing from the nation's foremost venture capitalists, he founded the Edison Electric Light Company and, in 1881, opened the world's first commercial electric generating plant, the Pearl Street Station, in lower Manhattan. Before the century was out, all of the urban United States had been wired for electricity. Light had been subdivided.

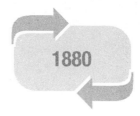

1880

Josef Breuer Describes the "Unconscious Mind"

Josef Breuer, a Viennese physician specializing in psychiatric disorders, was sent a patient he referred to only as Anna O, in deference to doctor-patient confidentiality. She suffered from what was called at the time "hysteria," a cluster of psychosomatic disorders—in her case, mainly sporadic paralysis—and other emotional problems. Breuer's approach to treatment employed hypnosis and, sometimes, just conversation. His idea was that both hypnosis and allowing the patient to talk about feelings and fantasies—to talk freely, without censorship of any kind—exposed a level of thought and feeling normally unavailable to conscious awareness. By verbalizing these "unconscious" thoughts, images, and ideas, they became available to consciousness and could then be discussed. The process of such discussion often improved the patient's condition and sometimes dramatically alleviated psychosomatic "hysterical" symptoms.

Breuer acquired a younger associate, Sigmund Freud, who systematized the notion of the unconscious and founded the single most influential theory of mind in modern times: psychoanalysis.

1885

Carl Friedrich Benz Invents the Automobile

By the beginning of the nineteenth century, steam had been harnessed to propel ships. By the end of the first third of the century, steam was being used to move locomotives along iron rails. But steam had not proved practical for driving vehicles across trackless land. Such vehicles were possible, but they remained awkward and commercially doomed.

In 1860, a Belgian, Jean-Joseph-Étienne Lenoir, invented an internal-combustion engine, which used a mixture of flammable vapor and air ignited within a closed cylinder to drive a piston. Lenoir even attached his engine to a carriage, which it successfully propelled. Nevertheless, the Lenoir engine was very inefficient, and it wasn't until 1876 that the German engineer Nikolaus August Otto developed a four-stroke internal-combustion engine. It worked like this: During the first stroke, as the piston moved outward, it drew into the cylinder a mixture of flammable vapor and air. During the second stroke, as the piston moved inward, the mixture in the cylinder was compressed. When the maximum degree of compression was reached, a spark was set off, which ignited an explosion. The force of this explosion drove the piston outward, sending it on its third stroke, which was the power stroke—the movement that did the engine's work. As the piston moved inward again—the fourth stroke—exhaust, waste gases, were pushed out, and the cycle began again.

The Otto four-stroke design greatly improved the efficiency of the internal-combustion engine, and once it was mated to an appropriate fuel—gasoline, which consisted of smaller molecules than the more familiar kerosene—it was even more appealing as a source of motive power. Recognizing this, in 1885, the German mechanical engineer Carl Friedrich Benz installed it in a small, steerable three-wheel carriage of his own design. Top speed was just under ten miles per hour, but it ran, ran reliably, and could be maneuvered easily. It was the first true automobile.

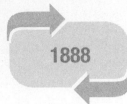

1888

Heinrich Wilhelm Gottfried von Waldeyer-Hartz Discovers the Chromosome

By the 1880s, scientists had described the events that accompanied mitosis—cellular reproduction. Among these events was the appearance of short threads of a substance called chromatin. A German anatomist, Heinrich Wilhelm Gottfried von Waldeyer-Hartz, focused on the appearance of these threads and proposed that the bodies be called chromosomes. This served to draw attention to them, although it would be many years before the genetic significance of chromosomes was discovered.

1889

Edison Invents Motion Pictures

The "movies" were not a single invention, but a complex technology of many inventions and innovations. In 1867, the zoetrope appeared in England and the United States. It had thirteen slots and thirteen pictures spinning around in a metal cylinder; by varying the number of pictures as seen through the slots, the movement of a figure could be simulated. Beginning at about this time, the British photographer Eadweard Muybridge developed the zoopraxiscope, which combined sequenced still photographs to create a "moving picture" representing the events of a specific span of seconds.

The single greatest advance in the creation of motion picture technology—the recording of light in motion—came in 1889, and it was produced by the American inventor who had already recorded sound. The American pioneer of photographic technology, George Eastman, had created a flexible film base to replace the existing technology of awkward glass-plate negatives. Edison realized that this flexible film, cut into long strips, could be used to record a great many separate photographs taken at extremely brief intervals. The resulting images could then be moved (pulled along by sprocket wheels engaging sprocket holes perforated into the sides of the film) in front of a light that flashed at an accurately timed rate. Because human visual perception is subject to the phenomenon of persistence of vision, the brain would tend to link, smooth out, and, in effect, fill in the intervals between the flashes of light, so that the succession of images would appear to be naturally continuous and moving.

Edison perfected his movie film in 1889, but it wasn't until

1891 that he patented a movie camera to expose the film sequentially. During 1893–1894, he developed the kinetoscope, a peephole motion picture viewer, "to do for the eye what the phonograph does for the ear."

While he perfected the kinetoscope, Edison built the world's first movie studio in 1893 and, the following year, produced the earliest surviving copyrighted film, *Fred Ott's Sneeze, January 7, 1894,* a motion picture record of one of Edison's engineers sneezing. Within two more years, Edison had made a genuine business out of his invention, creating and distributing movies for exhibition in "nickelodeons." The motion picture industry was launched.

1889

Camillo Golgi and Santiago Ramón y Cajal Prove the Neuron Theory

The German anatomist Heinrich Wilhelm Gottfried von Waldeyer-Hartz, the man who named the chromosome (see "1888: Heinrich Wilhelm Gottfried von Waldeyer-Hartz Discovers the Chromosome"), was also the first scientist to suggest that the nervous system consisted of individual cells, which were characterized by elongated extensions. The extension of one cell approached that of another very closely, without actually touching it. Thus each nerve cell, which Waldeyer-Hartz called a *neuron,* was separate. The German's notion that the nervous system is ultimately composed of many separate neurons was dubbed the neuron theory.

Camillo Golgi, an Italian histologist, built upon Waldeyer-Hartz's observations by using a special stain he had developed, which highlighted the neurons for microscopic study. Golgi focused on the gap between one neuron and the other. This he christened the *synapse.*

Finally, Santiago Ramón y Cajal, a Spanish histologist, refined Golgi's staining technique and used it to study the structure of the neuron in far greater detail. He showed how neurons made up the brain and the spinal cord, thereby providing the fullest elaboration of neuron theory. He and Golgi were jointly awarded the Nobel Prize for medicine and physiology in 1906.

1893

Freud and Breuer Publish *The Psychic Mechanism of Hysterical Phenomena,* Foundation of Modern Psychoanalysis

The Viennese physician Josef Breuer had put forth the concept of an "unconscious" in 1880 (see "1880: Josef Breuer Describes the 'Unconscious Mind'") and was soon joined by a younger colleague, Sigmund Freud, in studying the role of the unconscious mind in mental illness and, ultimately, in everyday life. In the process, the two physicians developed therapeutic techniques for accessing the unconscious, a region of thought ordinarily repressed and unavailable to consciousness. Breuer favored the use of hypnosis. Freud used it as well, but gradually turned to what he called "free association" instead. This was nothing more than encouraging the patient to speak randomly, to talk about whatever came into his or her mind, without any deliberate attempt to order the monologue or to censor or edit it in any way. Soon, Freud found that free association provided remarkable access to the unconscious. The more patients free associated, the less they censored. It was as if their own words caught them off guard—and yet they were aware of what they had said, although it took the analytical guidance of the therapist to assist in the interpretation of the free-associated discourse.

Based on what Freud and Breuer now called the "psychoanalysis" of the unconscious mind, the pair published in 1893 *The Psychic Mechanism of Hysterical Phenomena,* which was the earliest founding document of psychoanalysis, destined to be accepted as the most influential and profound psychological theory of the twentieth century and, perhaps, of all time.

THE ATOM AND THE AIRPLANE

1895

Wilhelm Conrad Röntgen
Discovers X Rays

The cathode-ray tube is a device in which electrons are accelerated by high voltage and formed into a beam that can be projected. In 1895, while studying how cathode rays caused various materials to fluoresce, the German physicist Wilhelm Conrad Röntgen noticed that certain substances glowed even after the cathode-ray tube had been turned off. He then observed that some of these materials fluoresced even if they were shielded from the active cathode-ray tube. Both of these observations persuaded Röntgen that radiation was projected from the cathode-ray tube and could excite as well as penetrate matter to some degree. Röntgen did not know what this radiation was, so he dubbed it *X rays*, "x" being the mathematical symbol for an unknown variable.

The discovery of X rays caused a sensation in the world of physics, because this form of electromagnetic radiation behaved unlike any other. While physicists were intrigued by the theoretical significance of X rays, the public was far more interested in the sensational practical application of the newly discovered ray. Once Röntgen saw that X rays penetrated various materials, he used the phenomenon to image the bones of his own hand. Profound as his discovery was for physics—and he was awarded the first Nobel Prize for physics in 1901—Röntgen had also given the science of medicine one of its most practical and powerful instruments.

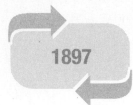

Joseph John Thomson Discovers the Electron, the First Subatomic Particle to Be Identified

The cathode-ray tube, which produced X rays (see "1895: Wilhelm Conrad Röntgen Discovers X Rays"), greatly interested physicists, who debated the nature of the rays produced by the tube. Were they truly waves? The fact that they could penetrate various matter argued for this. Or were they particles? In 1895, Jean-Baptiste Perrin, a French physicist, exposed a cylinder to a stream of cathode rays and demonstrated that, gradually, the cylinder became negatively charged. Based on this finding, Perrin concluded that cathode "rays" were actually streams of negatively charged particles.

But what was the nature of these particles?

In 1897, the British physicist Joseph John Thomson demonstrated that the cathode stream could be deflected by an electric field. By studying the degree of deflection, Thomson was able to gain an important insight into the particles. He could mathematically derive the ratio of the electric charge of the cathode-ray particle to its mass. To Thomson's amazement, the ratio was extremely high, which led him to conclude that the mass of the particle had to be vanishingly low, no more than a fraction of the smallest atom, hydrogen. Thomson christened this very low mass particle the *electron,* because he believed that the particle carried the fundamental unit of electric charge (which subsequent observation has indeed shown to be the case). The electron was the first subatomic particle—atomic constituent—identified.

Marie and Pierre Curie Investigate Uranium, Discover Polonium and Radium, and Coin the Term *Radioactivity*

The 1890s saw the rapid development of atomic physics based on the phenomena associated with radioactivity. After Röntgen discovered X rays (see "1895: Wilhelm Conrad Röntgen Discovers X Rays"), the French physicist Antoine-Henri Becquerel pursued the notion that fluorescent substances might emit X rays. What he discovered is that one such substance, potassium uranyl sulfate, emitted radiation capable of fogging photographic film. This prompted the Polish-born French chemist Marie Sktodowska Curie to carry out experiments to measure the radiation of a number of uranium-bearing compounds, including potassium uranyl sulfate. Her measurements proved that the radiation came not from the compounds, but exclusively from the uranium atom. This meant that radiation was an atomic and not a molecular phenomenon.

With her husband, the French chemist Pierre Curie, Marie Curie launched an exhaustive investigation of the radiations produced by uranium. When the pair discovered that thorium, like uranium, a heavy metal, also produced radiation, Marie Curie coined the word *radioactivity* to describe radiation-producing properties of certain elements. She and her husband then set about identifying more radioactive materials. They observed that some uranium ores were more highly radioactive than others, but that these variations were not proportionate to the amount of uranium present. Marie Curie concluded the ores must also contain very small (and, hitherto undiscovered) quantities of other radioactive elements, which had to be much more radioactive than uranium itself. Acting on this insight, she and her husband were able to isolate in July 1898 an element they called polonium (after Marie's native land) and, in December, radium, which was very intensely radioactive. The Curies' discoveries took physics to a new level of understanding and opened the door to the eventual exploitation of atomic energy (see "1901: The Curies Discover the Enormous Energy Potential of Radium, Setting the Stage for the Development of Atomic Energy and Atomic Weaponry").

1900

Karl Landsteiner Identifies the Basic Human Blood Types

At least as early as the 1700s, physicians reasoned that withdrawing blood from a desperately ill patient and replacing it with blood from a healthy person (or, sometimes, even an animal) might bring about a cure. In practice, the results were extremely varied and unreliable. While it was true that such transfusions sometimes dramatically improved the patient's condition, it was also true that, very often, the transfusion brought about almost immediate death. Not surprisingly, the practice of blood transfusion fell into disrepute, and, by the mid nineteenth century, was almost never attempted.

At the turn of the nineteenth century, the Austrian physician Karl Landsteiner undertook an extensive study of the nature of blood. He discovered that plasma (the liquid fraction of blood) from one donor would cause the blood of some recipients to clump up. This clumping would block blood vessels and bring about death. However, that same plasma would cause no clumping in other recipients.

Landsteiner set about classifying blood "types," so that physicians could match a compatible donor and recipient in order to save lives with transfusions instead of cause death with them. He discovered that human blood could be classified into four broad groups, which he called O, A, B, and AB. Transfusing blood from a donor of one type into a recipient of the same type was almost always completely safe; however, in a pinch, it was also reasonably safe to transfuse type O blood into any recipient. Type A blood could go only to a type A or a type AB recipient, and type B blood only to a type B or type AB recipient. AB donors could give blood safely only to AB receivers.

Landsteiner's discovery was a medical triumph, which made lifesaving blood transfusions safe and practical. The discovery also had a side benefit for the field of forensics. Now criminal investigators could analyze bloodstains found at the scene of a crime and determine the blood type, which might therefore enable easier identification of a victim or a perpetrator. Landsteiner received a Nobel Prize in 1930.

1900

Max Planck Formulates Quantum Theory

A s far as most scientists were concerned, Sir Isaac Newton had nailed just about all of the basic laws of physics by the end of the seventeenth century. For example: Newton viewed light as a product (radiation) produced by energy. Heat an object, and its atoms vibrate—become more energetic—thereby producing light. In terms of Newtonian physics, the more you heat a thing, the faster its atoms vibrate, and the light radiated would accordingly rise in frequency, from red, to orange, and on up through the spectrum into the far ultraviolet.

One problem: This did not happen.

The light radiated from heated objects did not move toward the ultraviolet. Because Newtonian physics seemed to break down when applied to this apparently simple phenomenon, physicists called it the "ultraviolet catastrophe." It cried out for an explanation.

The German physicist Max Planck confronted the ultraviolet catastrophe head-on—until it dawned on him: Energy was not radiated continuously, but in discrete chunks or packets. The size of each "packet" of energy was, in fact, fixed. It was inversely proportional to the wavelength of the radiation in question. Since the wavelength of violet light is half that of red light, the energy packet for violet light "contains" twice as much energy as that for red light.

Planck called each energy packet a *quantum* (the Latin word for "how much?"), and he worked out the relationship between energy and wavelength using a vanishingly small number, 6.6×10^{-27} erg-seconds. This number represented the "graininess" of energy; that is, the only permitted energies in the universe are whole number multiples of this number (which scientists soon dubbed "Planck's constant") multiplied by frequency.

Quantum theory changed our perception of the world—sort of. In everyday terms, for most of us, Planck's constant and quantum theory are of little practical use. That is, on a large scale, the macro scale, the scale we can see and feel, energy does appear to behave as if it were radiated continuously, just as Newtonian physics assumes it is. Only when we penetrate to the micro scale, the scale of the atom, does the quantum "graininess" of energy become apparent.

Even Planck himself did not take quantum theory very far. Its greater implications would be explored by Einstein a few years later in the century (see "1905: Albert Einstein Resolves the Argument Over Whether Light Consists of Waves or Particles").

The Curies Discover the Enormous Energy Potential of Radium, Setting the Stage for the Development of Atomic Energy and Atomic Weaponry

Having discovered radium (see "1898: Marie and Pierre Curie Investigate Uranium, Discover Polonium and Radium, and Coin the Term *Radioactivity*"), the Curies next explored its prodigious energy potential. Pierre Curie found that radium produced 140 calories per gram per hour and did so, it seemed, without diminution. (Actually, the radiation did diminish—but very gradually. The concept of radioactive half-life, which measured the decay of radioactivity over time, was developed later. In the case of radium, the energy output was found to diminish by 50 percent only after 1,600 years.) It was clear to the Curies that the energy produced by radioactive radium was far beyond what any conventional chemical reaction could generate. The Curies' work provided compelling insight into a new universe of energy.

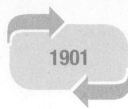

Guglielmo Marconi Demonstrates Radio

I n 1888, the German physicist Heinrich Hertz described long-wave electromagnetic radiation, the totally invisible and, to the human senses, imperceptible energy waves that would later be called radio waves. Following up on this discovery, other experimenters explored mechanisms by which radio waves might be used to transmit information—to take the place of the wires that tethered the telegraph to the ground.

One of the experimenters was an Italian named Guglielmo Marconi, who focused on creating a practical transmitter and a receiver (which he called a "coherer"). After working on the problem during the 1890s, Marconi was persuaded that radio waves did offer an opportunity for the creation of a revolutionary system of communication. In Italy, however, he found no one willing to finance his research; therefore, in 1896, he went to London, where he secured assistance from Sir William Preece, chief engineer of the royal post office.

By 1899, Marconi created a transmitter capable of generating a reasonably powerful signal, and in September he equipped two American ships with transmitters to broadcast to receivers in New York newspaper offices the progress of the America's Cup yacht race. This demonstration created sufficient stir to bring meaningful financial investment.

Marconi next decided to send a message across the Atlantic. A number of prominent mathematicians predicted that the effort was doomed. Radio waves, like any other form of electromagnetic radiation—visible light, for instance—travel along the line of sight. The earth, of course, is curved; therefore, some claimed, any radio message would get no farther than the horizon before it traveled out on an unrecoverable tangent into space. Marconi countered this position by arguing that radio waves would conform to the curvature of the earth because of the earth's magnetic field and certain reflective properties of the atmosphere.

On December 12, 1901, he attached an antenna cable to a balloon, which he lofted high into the air. At the other end of the antenna was a radio transmitter fitted with a telegraph key. Marconi tapped out a Morse code signal from his location at the southeastern tip of England. It was instantly picked up by the receiver he had stationed across the Atlantic, in Newfoundland. The age of radio—and electronic communications—had dawned.

The Wright Brothers Make the First Successful Sustained Flight in a Heavier-Than-Air Machine

In 1896, two Dayton, Ohio, bicycle mechanics, Orville and Wilbur Wright, read an account of the death of Otto Lilienthal, a German aviation pioneer killed in the crash of one of his experimental gliders. The fact of Lilienthal's death did not interest the Wrights, but the gliders he designed did, and the pair began devouring every aeronautical book and article they could find. Their object was to perfect glider design and, ultimately, mate it to an internal-combustion engine to achieve powered flight. By 1899, they had completed their first man-carrying biplane kite, and, acting on wind research obtained from the U.S. Weather Service, they decided to test their machine on the beach at Kitty Hawk, North Carolina. When the glider and a subsequent design failed to perform to their satisfaction, however, the Wrights concluded that all published tables of air pressures on curved surfaces were wrong, so they designed and built, in 1901, the world's first wind tunnel to test some 200 different wing designs. Based on the wind tunnel experiments, they drew up the world's first reliable tables of air pressures on curved surfaces. This in itself was a giant stride in aerodynamics, albeit an unglamorous one.

In 1902, the Wrights built a better glider, which they flew and tweaked more than a thousand times. With the aerodynamics determined, they fitted a 170-pound, twelve-horsepower motor of their own design to the 750-pound fabric-and-wood aircraft. On December 17, 1903, the brothers flipped a coin, Orville won the toss—heads—and he assumed his position at the controls, lying on his belly across the bottom wing of the craft.

At Kill Devil Hills, Kitty Hawk, North Carolina, the engine coughed into life, the aircraft raced down a rail track the aviators had laid across the beach, and, for twelve seconds, over a distance of about 120 feet, it flew.

That day, the Wrights made three more flights, Wilbur managing to remain aloft for almost a minute, over a distance of 852 feet. Quietly, the brothers telegraphed their father, who was back in Dayton: "Success. Four flights Thursday morning . . . Inform press. Home Christmas."

1905

Albert Einstein Resolves the Argument Over Whether Light Consists of Waves or Particles

I n 1900, Max Planck laid the foundation for quantum theory by demonstrating that energy is not radiated continuously, but in discrete "packets," or quanta, each inversely proportional to the wavelength of the radiation under consideration (see "1900: Max Planck Formulates Quantum Theory"). Two years after Planck's quantum theory, the German physicist Philipp Lenard discovered the photoelectric effect by demonstrating that light falling on certain metals generated electrical activity. This was the result of the emission of electrons from the surface of the metal. Only light of a certain wavelength or shorter could excite emissions from a particular metal. Depending on the metal, light of different wavelengths was necessary to excite electron emission. Moreover, increasing the intensity of light on a metal resulted in the emission of a greater number of electrons, but the energy of the individual electrons remained fixed. If, however, the wavelength of the light were decreased, the fewer electrons emitted had higher energy. If the wavelength were increased, the greater number of electrons had lower energy. The reason for this relationship between wavelength and the energy of the electrons emitted was a mystery.

Then, in 1905, Einstein solved the mystery of the photoelectric effect by applying quantum theory to it. First, he had to challenge both prevailing theories about the nature of light by assuming that light was neither a continuous wave (one theory) *nor* a stream of particles (the other theory), but, rather, consisted of quanta, discrete packets of energy. If this were the case and, as Planck had explained, the energy of each quantum was inversely proportional to the wavelength of the light, then the atoms on the surface of the metal could absorb only intact quanta. Quanta of long wavelength would not furnish sufficient energy to eject an electron from the metal. This was true regardless of the intensity of the light. But, reduce the wavelength, and each quantum would grow larger, reaching a point at which each was sufficiently energetic to eject an electron from the surface of the metal, thereby producing the photoelectric effect. Shorten the wavelength beyond this point, and each electron would be ejected with greater energy and, therefore, greater velocity. Some metals hold electrons more tightly than others; therefore, the "critical wavelength"—the wavelength just short enough to eject electrons—varied from metal to metal.

Explaining the photoelectric effect was a significant accomplishment, but, even more important was the fact that it had been explained by the application of quantum theory. This proved that, despite Planck's own doubts, quantum theory was a real explanation of nature, not just a mathematical device. Most important of all, the explanation resolved the wave versus particle debate over the nature of light. In some respects, quantum theory showed, light behaved as a particle; in other respects, it behaved as a wave. That is, Einstein demonstrated, light had properties of both a particle and a wave. Later physicists would encapsulate both of these properties of light in the concept of the *photon*.

Einstein Formulates the Theory of Special Relativity

Born in Ulm, Germany, and raised in Munich, Albert Einstein was so slow to speak that his parents feared he was retarded. In school, he was bored, misbehaved, and was expelled. Bridling under strict German habits of thought and discipline, he left his native country in 1901, settled in Switzerland, became a citizen there, and found work not as a physicist and mathematician, which he was trained to be, but as an examiner in the Swiss patent office. That post did give him time to explore a problem that had resulted from the Michelson-Morley experiment, something that had perplexed physicists ever since the experiment had been performed.

In 1881, the German-born American physicist Albert Michelson built an interferometer, a device that split a light beam in two, then brought the two beams back together. His purpose was to measure the earth's "absolute motion"—the motion of the earth against what was assumed to be the substance of space, a "luminiferous ether," believed to be absolutely without motion. The interferometer would split a beam of light at right angles, sending one half in the direction of the earth's motion. That half of the beam should complete its round trip a little later than the other beam. By measuring the width of the difference between the two beams, Michelson reasoned that he could measure the motion of the earth with respect to the absolute, the "ether."

But it didn't work. There was no difference between the beams.

Michelson kept working, and, in 1887, with the American chemist Edward Williams Morley, he refined the experiment sufficiently to conclude that, in fact, the speed of light was apparently the same, regardless of the motion of the light source relative to the observer.

How could this be? The experiment seemed to indicate that either the earth was motionless with respect to the "luminiferous ether," or the earth dragged this substance with it. However, neither of these cases seemed possible.

In 1905, Einstein put his hand to the problem. He started with the assumption Michelson and Morley had arrived at experimentally (though Einstein later claimed to have been unaware of their result): that the only constant in the universe was the speed of light through a vacuum. In this fact, Einstein reasoned, was the answer to the problem. The Michelson-Morley experiment did not work as expected precisely because there is no absolute in the universe other than the speed of light. There is no such thing as absolute motionlessness, and, therefore, no absolute motion. In short, Michelson and Morley's error lay in attempting to measure something that didn't exist.

Then Einstein stepped beyond merely explaining a failed experiment. Taking the fact of the absolute speed of light, he deduced that length contracted and mass increased with velocity, while the rate of time flow decreased. To say that this was revolutionary is to put it weakly. For Einstein held that everything people thought of as absolutes—space, mass, and even time—were not absolute at all, but, rather, relative to the observer's frame of reference within the very dimensions of space, mass, and time. Since relativity was at the heart of his conclusion, Einstein called his formulation a *theory of relativity*—or, more precisely, a special theory of relativity, because it applied only to the "special" instance of objects moving at constant velocity. (Later, Einstein also developed a "general" theory; see "1916: Einstein Advances the General Theory of Relativity, Thereby Establishing the Science of Cosmology.")

The implications of Einstein's special relativity theory forever changed our picture of the universe, instantly removing it from the comfortable realm of our senses and our common sense. We cannot help but think of space, mass, and time as very separate and distinct things. Einstein suddenly linked them all together, making each a variable relative to and dependent on the others.

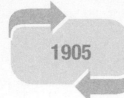

Einstein Proposes That Mass and Energy Are Equivalent: E = mc²

The most famous—and momentous—mathematical expression to come out of the theory of relativity (see "1905: Einstein Formulates the Theory of Special Relativity") expressed the relationship of equivalence between matter and energy: $E = mc^2$.

The equation demonstrated that matter and energy are not the radically separate entities common sense tells us they are, but are, in fact, readily convertible one to the other. In essence, one may see matter as concentrated energy. A quantity of energy, E, is equal to an amount of mass, m, multiplied by the square of the speed of light, c^2.

This equation was nothing less than a brand-new lens through which to view the universe. But its implications reached far beyond theory.

The speed of light is an extremely large number—about 984,000,000 feet per second. Square that number—that is, multiply it by itself—and you get an enormously larger number. Multiply this huge product by a given quantity of matter, and you arrive at a measure of the amount of energy that would be produced *if* a process could be found to convert matter to energy very, very efficiently. The necessary efficiency would exist on a subatomic level—that is, only if the energy (later called the "strong force") holding together the nucleus of the atom could be liberated by the "splitting" of the atom. In 1907, no such process existed. Before mid century, however, a process would be found—with devastating results that ended the century's second world war.

Paul Ehrlich Develops the First Chemotherapy, Using Trypan Red to Cure Sleeping Sickness

The idea of curing disease with chemicals is very old. When alchemists took time off from the search for a means of changing base metal into gold, they often experimented with curative substances—sometimes with disastrous results. At the beginning of the twentieth century, the German microscopist and bacteriologist Paul Ehrlich reflected on the significance of the earlier work of Walther Flemming, who, in 1882, observed that certain synthetic dyes combined with (and colored) some parts of cells but not others. Ehrlich reasoned that if a chemical could be found to combine with (and kill) disease-causing cells while leaving healthy cells alone, physicians would have what Ehrlich called a "magic bullet" to fight disease.

After much research, Ehrlich, in 1907, identified a dye he called Trypan red, because it combined with the trypanosome, the unicellular organism that, transmitted by the bite of the tsetse fly, caused sleeping sickness. Trypan red had no effect on other cells. It therefore became the magic bullet for sleeping sickness, and it was the first effective chemotherapy agent ever discovered. Ehrlich's achievement was recognized the following year with the Nobel Prize for physiology and medicine.

Ivan Pavlov Describes the Conditioned Response, Establishing the Basis of Behavioral Psychological Theory

The Russian physiologist Ivan Pavlov observed that dogs salivated at the mere sight or smell of food, not just during the actual process of ingestion. He decided to see if he could artificially create a new pattern, by which salivation would be induced by some stimulus totally unrelated to food or digestion. In a series of landmark experiments, Pavlov showed dogs food simultaneously with the sound of a bell. He attached a surgical drain to the dogs' salivary glands, so that he could precisely measure the amount of saliva produced. He discovered that the dog would soon associate the sound of the bell with the sight of the food and would salivate. After a certain number of repetitions of the ringing bell with the sight of the food, the dog could be made to salivate merely at the sound of the bell, in the absence of food. Pavlov called this a "conditioned response," and it was the basis of a new branch of psychology, behaviorism, which introduced new theories of learning and behavioral development in many animals, including human beings.

Building on the Work of Einstein, Hermann Minkowski Formulates a Theory of Space-Time, a Fourth Dimension of Reality

One of the most brilliant thinkers to grapple with the implications of Einstein's Theory of Relativity (see "1905: Einstein Formulates the Theory of Special Relativity") was the Russian-born German mathematician Hermann Minkowski. In a book called *Time and Space,* published in 1907, Minkowski concluded that Einstein's theory made it necessary to expand the view of the universe beyond the traditional three dimensions and add to these the dimension of "space-time." For Minkowski proposed that Einstein's universe did not permit the separate existence of space and time, but required a special fusion of these two dimensions.

In the so-called Minkowski universe, the traditional geometric dimensions apply within any closed system of reference ("inertial reference frame"); however, when the view is expanded to the universe, apparent space and time intervals between events become relative to the velocity of the observer. For this reason, on the universal level, the space-time dimension becomes critically important.

The space-time concept helped Einstein develop his theory of relativity further, to apply it to accelerated motion so that it could account for gravitational interactions. Ultimately, the space-time concept guided modern theories concerning the shape, extent, origin, and fate of the universe.

1908

Fritz Haber Develops a Process for Fixing Atmospheric Nitrogen to Synthesize Ammonia and Nitrates—a Momentous Scientific Discovery That Also Gives His Native Germany the Power to Manufacture the Explosives Needed to Wage Sustained War

N itrates are essential to two important products: nitrogen fertilizer and high explosives. Early in the twentieth century, Germany, like other European nations, was preparing for what it anticipated would be a war among the major powers of the continent. German military planners realized that the principal source of nitrates was northern Chile. Those planners also understood that the mighty British navy controlled the seas and, therefore, could cut off access to Chilean nitrates at will. A call was put out to patriotic German scientists to find a synthetic alternative to natural nitrates.

Among those who answered the call was the great German chemist Fritz Haber. He realized that nitrates are nothing more than atmospheric nitrogen that has been "fixed"—converted by leguminous plants and deposited into the soil. He therefore searched for an alternative means of fixing atmospheric nitrogen and found that if nitrogen mixed with hydrogen was placed under high pressure in the presence of iron, which served as a catalyst, the resulting product would be ammonia. The process of extracting nitrates from ammonia was well known and therefore was an easy step once the ammonia had been obtained.

The "Haber process" was a great leap forward in the chemistry of synthetics. It did indeed liberate Germany from reliance on Chilean and other sources of natural nitrates. And it thereby enabled Germany to fight World War I without fear of running out of an essential raw ingredient for the manufacture of explosives.

Ernest Rutherford Proposes the Nuclear Atom

The British physicist Ernest Rutherford spent several years conducting experiments in which he bombarded various objects with alpha particles. His purpose was to learn about the structure of the atom.

Rutherford fired his alpha particles at a wide variety of materials, including an ultrathin sheet of gold, which, at one-fifty-thousandth of an inch, was a barrier only two thousand atoms thick. By studying the images the alpha particles created on a photographic plate, Rutherford was able to determine, roughly, what proportion of alpha particles were able to penetrate the sheet. He found that particles did pass through, yet some proportion of them were significantly deflected. From this, Rutherford concluded that the atom was mostly empty space, but did contain a "nucleus" of relatively dense mass.

After gathering more data, Rutherford proposed the "nuclear atom": a structure with almost all of its mass concentrated in a nucleus, which bore a positive electrical charge, surrounded by enough negatively charged electrons—of far less mass—to neutralize the positive charge of the nucleus and thereby render the atom neutral. The structure of the atom, at least at its most basic, was now understood.

Heike Kamerlingh Onnes Discovers Superconductivity (Electrical Conductivity with Virtually No Resistance) Near Absolute Zero

eike Kamerlingh Onnes, a Dutch physicist, liquified helium in 1908, achieving temperatures within just four degrees of absolute zero. This opened up a whole new reality to explore, and Kameringh Onnes set about studying the behavior of matter at these temperatures. One property that greatly interested him was electrical conductivity, which, he knew, tended to increase at lower temperatures; that is, matter became less resistant. Kamerlingh Onnes predicted that resistance would drop to zero at absolute zero; however, when he tested mercury, he discovered, to his astonishment, that electrical resistance dropped to zero at 4.2°K— more than four degrees above absolute zero. He soon found that some other metals behaved similarly at very cold temperatures, their resistance also dropping to zero.

Kamerlingh Onnes called this phenomenon superconductivity. It would take several decades, however, after the field of electronics and computers was well advanced, for practical applications to be found for superconductivity: the creation of supercomputers of prodigious speed and computational power, their circuits unfettered by resistance.

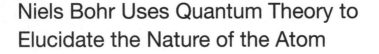

1913

Niels Bohr Uses Quantum Theory to Elucidate the Nature of the Atom

Ernest Rutherford had painted the broad strokes of atomic structure in 1911 (see "1911: Ernest Rutherford Proposes the Nuclear Atom"), but a significant problem remained unresolved. Take the simplest atom, that of hydrogen. As Rutherford pictured it, it consisted of a positively charged nucleus around which a single negatively charged electron orbited. What was wrong with this picture? The orbiting of the electron around the nucleus should result in the production of electromagnetic radiation, which, in turn, would result in energy loss for the electron, so that it would ultimately be attracted to the more massive nucleus and collapse into it.

No such thing happened.

To explain this apparent anomaly, the Danish physicist Niels Bohr applied quantum theory (see "1900: Max Planck Formulates Quantum Theory") to further explain the structure of the atom. Instead of radiating energy continuously, Bohr theorized, the orbiting electron could radiate it only in quanta, discrete packets of energy that were (on an atomic scale) quite large. Thus the electron, when it radiated, would lose a quantum of energy, which would cause it not to spiral down into the nucleus, but, rather, to descend to a lower orbit—an orbit (or shell) nearer the nucleus. Each time it radiated a quantum, the electron would descend to the next lower orbital shell until it reached the lowest one, below which it could not descend, because it could emit no more energy.

If an atom absorbed, rather than radiated, energy, the electron would rise to a higher orbit, stepwise, with each quantum absorbed. If it absorbed sufficient energy, it would break free of its nuclear orbit. The resulting atom would then be an ion, an atomic fragment bearing a positive charge equal to the number of electrons that had departed.

The rise and fall of orbiting electrons did radiate energy, but only in quantum packets; therefore, the radiation produced would be emitted only at certain fixed wavelengths. Moreover, the reverse was also true: The electrons would absorb energy only at those same wavelengths. By determining these wavelengths, Bohr was able to create a picture of the simple hydrogen atom, showing just what electron orbits would yield the wavelengths represented by the spectrum hydrogen produced.

Other physicists would add much more to the "Bohr atom," but it demonstrated the basic relationship between quantum theory and atomic structure, providing a new understanding of matter and energy.

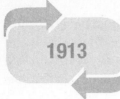

1913

Frederick Soddy Conceptualizes the Isotope

The periodic table of the elements was a great advance in chemistry (see "1869: Dmitry Ivanovich Mendeleyev Creates the Periodic Table of the Elements"), but research into radioactivity, which spanned the late nineteenth and early twentieth centuries, posed a perplexing challenge to the table. Almost fifty new "elements" had been apparently discovered, but the periodic table had no more than a dozen predictive "blanks" to fill. Was the table wrong? Or was it simply invalid for radioactive elements?

The British chemist Frederick Soddy addressed this puzzle. He formulated the radioactive displacement law, which successfully shoehorned multiple elements into the same available space on the periodic table.

According to the radioactive displacement law, when an atom radiates an alpha particle, that particle has a positive charge of two and a mass of four. This causes the atom that has lost the alpha particle to become a different atom, its nuclear charge reduced by two, and its mass reduced by four. When an atom loses a beta particle, negative charge one, the atom, in effect, gains a positive charge—that is, it gains a larger nuclear charge. The loss of the almost massless electron has virtually no impact on the mass of the new atom. As for any gamma rays the atom may emit, this radiation reduces the energy content of the atom, but, because gamma rays lack both charge and mass, the radiation does not affect the essential nature of the atom.

Soddy concluded that these radioactive changes produced substances that were equal in nuclear charge but different in mass; therefore, they were not separate elements, but could occupy the same place in the periodic table. Soddy called these radioactive variants *isotopes*, derived from a Greek word meaning "same place."

Henry H. Dale Isolates Acetylcholine, Key Chemical in the Transmission of Neural Impulses

Investigating ergotism—a disease caused by eating grain tainted by the ergot fungus and sometimes characterized by gangrene of the extremities, sometimes by severe psychiatric and neurological disorders—the British biologist Henry Hallett Dale isolated acetylcholine from the fungus. He found that this substance could affect certain organs just the way the nerves that governed those organs affected them. Although Dale did not fully appreciate it at the time, he had discovered the key chemical responsible for the transmission of neural impulses across the synapse (physiological gap) separating one neuron from another.

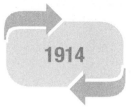

1914

Henry Moseley Develops the Concept of the Atomic Number

The British physicist Henry Moseley improved on the periodic table of the elements (see "1869: Dmitry Ivanovich Mendeleyev Creates the Periodic Table of the Elements") in 1914 by developing the concept of atomic number. In the Mendeleyev periodic table, the elements are arranged in order of increasing atomic weight, which created a problem, because it made it necessary to alter the order of some elements to keep them in their appropriate families. Moseley used the phenomenon of characteristic X rays—the fact that when elements were bombarded by X rays, they emitted X rays of characteristic (and precisely measurable) wavelengths—to demonstrate that characteristic X rays decreased in wavelength in proportion to the weight of the element emitting the X rays. The heavier the element, the shorter the wavelength emitted. The cause of this, Moseley concluded, was the increasing positive charge of a heavier nucleus. Moseley called this positive charge the "atomic number" of the element, and by ordering the elements by their atomic number instead of by their atomic weight, he was able to correct the deficiencies in the original periodic table. This made the table an infallible predictor of how many new elements awaited discovery and exactly where in the table they would occur.

In 1915, the year after Moseley explained the atomic number concept, he was killed in World War I.

Einstein Advances the General Theory of Relativity, Thereby Establishing the Science of Cosmology

In 1905, Albert Einstein formulated his special theory of relativity, which was "special" in that it applied only to systems moving at a constant velocity relative to each other (see "1905: Albert Einstein Formulates the Theory of Special Relativity"). After years of work, he published, in 1916, his *general* theory of relativity, which extended relativity to systems moving relative to each other at any velocity, however variable.

In order to generalize the special theory, Einstein had to assume that mass derived from measurements of acceleration—inertial mass—was identical to mass derived from measurements of gravitational intensity—gravitational mass. Furthermore, he had to assume that space was curved in the presence of mass, so that gravitation was not a force, but the result of objects in motion following the shortest path in curved space. Thus gravity was not a function of massive objects attracting one another, as Newton had explained, but was a field, in effect the deformation of space itself in the presence of mass. These conclusions necessitated nothing less than equations that implied the nature of the structure of the universe. Therefore, Einstein's general theory of relativity also marked the birth of modern cosmology, the science that seeks to explain the origin, structure, and fate of the universe.

Using Einstein's Relativity Equations, Astronomer Karl Schwarzschild Describes the Black Hole Phenomenon

The German astronomer Karl Schwarzschild eagerly seized upon Einstein's equations supporting the general theory of relativity (see "1916: Einstein Advances the General Theory of Relativity, Thereby Establishing the Science of Cosmology") to arrive at solutions outlining the nature and structure of the universe. He paid particular attention to what happens to the gravitational field in the vicinity of a very massive star that has collapsed so that its mass is concentrated in a point. Ultimately, he calculated what would happen if a star collapsed to the extent that its volume was zero, and its gravitational pull at its surface was without limit. Anything that approached closer than a certain distance from this point—what astronomers now call the "Schwarzschild radius"—would be unable to achieve sufficient velocity to escape the gravitational pull of the collapsed star. That "anything" includes electromagnetic radiation, light. Because light could not escape, there would be no way to know anything about the star; that is, no information could escape from it. Although Schwarzschild himself did not use the term (it was coined years later), the massive collapsed star acted like a "black hole," a bottomless pit from which nothing escaped.

1917

Using Einstein's Relativity Equations, Astronomer Willem de Sitter Calculates That the Universe Is Expanding

Albert Einstein was a genius, but he was not infallible. His equations for the general theory of relativity (see "1916: Einstein Advances the General Theory of Relativity, Thereby Establishing the Science of Cosmology") assumed that the universe was essentially changeless, static. The trouble was that the theory did not imply this, and, in order to make the equations work—that is, to allow them to apply to a static universe—Einstein had to introduce an arbitrary constant.

Willem de Sitter, a Dutch astronomer, decided to find out what would happen if he approached the equations without the "gravitational constant." The result was not a static universe, but one that expanded. Einstein himself pointed to this result as evidence of the need for his constant, since the idea of an expanding universe seemed absurd. Later, when the American astronomer Edwin Hubble observed that the galaxies were receding, thereby confirming that the universe was, in fact, expanding (see "1929: Edwin Hubble Observes the Expanding Universe"), Einstein called his gravitational constant the greatest mistake of his scientific career.

1919

Rutherford Creates the
First Nuclear Reaction

The British physicist Ernest Rutherford performed a series of experiments in which he bombarded various gases with alpha particles. With certain gases, such as hydrogen, the bombardment produced scintillations—flashes of light—on a specially coated screen, indicating that it had been struck by an energetic subatomic particle. Rutherford concluded that the brightest scintillations were produced when an alpha particle struck a hydrogen nucleus, propelling a proton into the screen.

When Rutherford bombarded a more complex atom, that of nitrogen, he also saw the scintillations, but the number of these decreased over time. Rutherford concluded that the alpha particles occasionally knocked one of the seven protons out of the nitrogen nucleus, but, after a time, an increasing number of the nitrogen nuclei absorbed the alpha particles—hence the reduction of scintillations. If this was the case, the following should also be true: a nitrogen nucleus, with a charge of +7 (seven protons), loses a proton but absorbs an alpha particle, which has a charge of +2. The net result should be a nucleus with a +8 charge (eight protons), which is an oxygen atom. Thus Rutherford had combined a helium nucleus (a two-proton alpha particle) with a nitrogen nucleus to form a hydrogen nucleus (a single proton) and an oxygen nucleus (eight protons). Rutherford had produced an extraordinary chemical reaction, actually transferring particles inside the atomic nucleus, whereas ordinary chemical reactions involved merely the transfer or sharing (bonding) of electrons. His experiments produced the first artificially induced nuclear reactions.

Frederick Grant Banting Isolates Insulin

By very early in the twentieth century, there was a rudimentary understanding of the function of hormones in the human body. Physicians at this time also began to suspect that diabetes was caused by some deficiency in the pancreas, and some guessed that this organ produced a hormone that controlled carbohydrate metabolism, without which diabetes ensued. It was suggested that structures within the pancreas known as the islets of Langerhans were responsible for producing the hormone, which might be called *insulin*, from the Latin word for island. However, all of this was speculation, because no one had been able to identify the hormone. The problem was that the pancreas itself digested and destroyed any insulin produced before it could be isolated and extracted.

Frederick Grant Banting, a Canadian physician, had read of an experiment in which the pancreatic duct of an experimental animal was tied off, thereby causing a degeneration of the pancreatic tissue. He reasoned that if the pancreas were caused to degenerate, the islets of Langerhans would still produce insulin, but the pancreas would not be able to digest and destroy it; therefore, it could be extracted directly from the degenerated organ.

With a physiologist, Charles Herbert Best, Banting operated on a number of dogs, tying off their pancreases. Once the organ had degenerated, the doctors were, indeed, able to extract insulin, which they used to stop the symptoms of diabetes. Hormone therapy had been discovered.

Max Born, Werner Heisenberg, and Erwin Schrödinger Develop Quantum Mechanics

Making sense of the Bohr atom (see "1913: Niels Bohr Uses Quantum Theory to Elucidate the Nature of the Atom"), the Austrian physicist Erwin Schrödinger concluded, required thinking of the electron, a particle, as behaving like a wave. Schrödinger called this wave mechanics, and it represented an elaboration of the work of the German physicist Werner Heisenberg, who had earlier developed matrix mechanics.

The German physicist Max Born developed matrix and wave mechanics a step further by treating the electron as both a particle and a wave. That is, he developed equations to predict the behavior of an electron as a particle existing at certain points in a "wave packet" or quantum. Collectively, Schrödinger, Heisenberg, and Born developed quantum mechanics, the physics of atomic and subatomic systems and how they interact with radiation, based on observable quantities. Quantum mechanics brought physics down to a scale of almost unimaginable smallness, in which events can no longer be described in terms of classical Newtonian physics, which is exclusively suited to macro scales.

OUTER SPACE, INNER SPACE, AND CYBERSPACE

Robert Goddard Fires
the First Liquid-Fuel Rocket

Rocketry was not new in 1926. Armies had been firing small rockets at one another since the era of medieval China. Nor was it a new idea to use a rocket to achieve sufficient velocity to escape the earth's gravitational pull; Sir Isaac Newton had speculated on this in the seventeenth century. But rockets that used gunpowder as fuel—and all early rockets did—could never achieve sufficient thrust to go very far, let alone to achieve escape velocity (the velocity needed to "escape" the earth's gravity), and, equally important, they required air to support combustion, so they could not function once they were beyond the earth's atmosphere.

The American physicist Robert H. Goddard, who, as a boy, dreamed of building a rocket that would loft him to Mars, pondered the problems of thrust and combustion beyond the atmosphere. He decided that a liquid-fueled rocket, running, say, on gasoline, could develop far more thrust than a solid-fuel rocket. What is more, if the rocket could carry its own oxidizer (Goddard decided on liquid oxygen), its fuel could sustain combustion without the presence of an atmosphere.

Goddard built his first liquid-fuel rocket early in 1926 and test flew it on March 16, from a "launch pad" on property owned by his aunt. Just four feet long and about half a foot in diameter, it didn't look like much. Nor did it get very far: perhaps 200 feet in altitude. But it was the first liquid-fueled rocket, and it represented a major stride forward in the science and technology of rocketry. In subsequent experiments, Goddard identified and solved—at least in a basic way—every major problem of liquid-fueled rocketry, including the development of fuel pumps, self-cooling rocket motors, and other devices required for an engine suited to power missile weapons or vehicles to carry human beings into space.

Heisenberg Formulates the Uncertainty Principle

While much of scientific and technological history is the story of how human beings increased their knowledge and power, the tale also has a counterplot in the discovery of certain limitations. Copernicus, for example, took the earth away from the center of the universe. Breuer and Freud demonstrated that human beings have only limited conscious control over their own thoughts and actions.

Then came the German physicist Werner Heisenberg. By way of exploring the implications of quantum mechanics, Heisenberg proposed that there was a finite limit to what can be measured and known, no matter the skill of the observer or the exquisite nature of the instrument used.

Heisenberg postulated that the momentum of a subatomic particle could be determined to an infinite degree of precision. Likewise its position. However, both momentum and position could not be precisely determined at the same time. The more precisely you attempted to determine momentum, the less certain you could be about position, and vice versa. Moreover, the degree of uncertainty in momentum multiplied by the uncertainty in knowledge of position was equal to Planck's constant (see "1900: Max Planck Formulates Quantum Theory"). This equivalence was no coincidence. It meant, according to Heisenberg, that Planck's constant expressed the "graininess" of the universe—the point beyond which one could gain no more information. Think of a photograph. You can magnify its detail to a certain extent, until you no longer see a clear image, but, rather, the grain of the film's emulsion. From this point on, further magnification will reveal no new information—just bigger clumps of grain.

Looked at from one perspective, the uncertainty principle represents the absolute limit of possible knowledge. Looked at a bit differently, it is simply an operating principle of the universe, which explains certain phenomena that otherwise defy human reason and common sense.

1928

Alexander Fleming Discovers Penicillin

Alexander Fleming was a Scottish-born British physician who became keenly interested in bacteriology while working as a military surgeon during World War I and seeing soldiers survive initial wounding only to succumb later to infection. Fleming was determined to identify substances that could kill bacteria without destroying healthy cells. In 1921, he isolated the enzyme lysozyme, a constituent of human tears and mucus, which, he found, attacked many types of bacteria. But he could derive nothing of practical value from it.

He kept working. In 1928, he was culturing experimental staph bacteria in a petri dish when he noticed that one of the cultures had been contaminated by a mold, *Penicillium notatum.* He was about to discard the petri dish in disgust, but, being a scientist, he looked more closely at it, and he saw that surrounding the mold growth was a circle free from bacteria. Something in the mold had killed the staph.

Fleming set about making sense of this laboratory accident. He soon was successful in isolating the substance in the mold that was responsible for killing the bacteria. He called the material penicillin, and further tests demonstrated that it was effective not just against staph, but a wide range of bacteria. Most important of all, it was nontoxic. And so medicine had its first antibiotic, a substance that transformed physicians from observers of disease and providers of often feeble comfort, to scientists armed with a powerful weapon that could actually fight—and defeat—disease.

The First Sulfa Drug, 1935

Fleming discovered the first antibiotic, a substance that stimulates the production of antibodies, which fight disease. A few years later, in 1935, the German biochemist Gerhard Domagk synthesized the most important early antibacterial, a substance that does not stimulate antibodies, but that is directly effective against infection. He discovered that a dye, Prontosil, was, like Trypan red (see "1907: Paul Ehrlich Develops the First Chemotherapy, Using Trypan Red to Cure Sleeping Sickness"), effective to some degree against bacteria. The problem was that Prontosil was a complex chemical, expensive, and difficult to obtain in quantity. Domagk looked for a way to dismantle the big Prontosil molecule and discover the fraction that was antibacterial. He found that sulfanilamide, a constituent of Prontosil, was highly effective against bacteria. This discovery led to the synthesis of a large family of sulfa drugs, which proved effective against a broad range of infections.

1929

John Douglas Cockcroft and Ernest Thomas Sinton Walton Invent the Particle Accelerator (Atom Smasher)

Ernest Rutherford (see "1919: Rutherford Creates the First Nuclear Reaction") and other early nuclear physicists used alpha particles as investigative "bullets" to bombard atoms and to create nuclear reactions. Alpha radiation, however, was not very penetrating, and, therefore, it was quite limited as an investigative tool. Scientists looked for a means of accelerating ordinary nuclear particles, such as protons, and using these to bombard atoms under investigation.

In 1929, the British physicist John Douglas Cockcroft and his Irish colleague, Ernest Thomas Sinton Walton, built a "voltage multiplier," which created very high electrical voltages powerful enough to accelerate protons such that they became more energetic than naturally occurring alpha particles. This was the first device physicists called a particle accelerator and the general public dubbed an "atom smasher."

Cockcroft and Walton shared the 1951 Nobel Prize for having created an instrument valuable in the exploration of the atomic and subatomic realms.

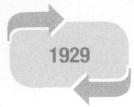

1929

Edwin Hubble Observes the Expanding Universe

The great American astronomer Edwin Hubble, in whose honor the Hubble Space Telescope is named, reviewed the work of Vesto Melvin Slipher and Milton LaSalle Humason, both of whom concluded that the galaxies they observed were receding from us. Hubble reasoned from their observations and his own that the galaxies receded at a rate proportional to their distance from us, a proposition subsequently called Hubble's Law. And he reasoned further that the galaxies were not receding from us, per se, but from any observer anywhere. If one inflated a balloon partway, then drew dots on it, then continued to blow it up, each dot would recede from the others. Take the perspective of any one dot, and the rest of the dots would appear to recede from this point of view.

If the galaxies were the equivalent of dots on a balloon, what was the balloon? The universe itself. Therefore, the explanation of receding galaxies was that the universe itself was expanding. This conclusion reshaped the science of cosmology and validated the equations Einstein originally introduced to support his general theory of relativity (see "1916: Einstein Advances the General Theory of Relativity, Thereby Establishing the Science of Cosmology").

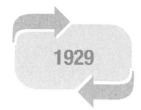

1929

Jean Piaget Formulates a Cogent Theory of Child Development

Jean Piaget, a Swiss national, had been trained as a zoologist, but he made his most important contribution to science as a psychologist, and he took as his subject of study the development of his own children. By carefully observing their development—and, later, the development of others—Piaget formulated the first comprehensive, cogent, and empirically based theory of child development. Essentially, he saw psychological development as an orderly and universal four-stage journey away from egocentricism and toward a recognition of a self defined in relation to the rest of the world.

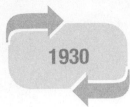

Paul Adrien Maurice Dirac Proposes the Existence of Antimatter

Paul Adrien Maurice Dirac, a British physicist, pursued the mathematical implications of the theory that electrons behave both as particles and as waves (see "1926: Max Born, Werner Heisenberg, and Erwin Schrödinger Develop Quantum Mechanics"). From his work, he concluded, at first, that electrons and protons (at the time, the only two known subatomic particles) existed in two energy states, positive and negative. He even postulated that electrons and protons were really the same particle in different energy states, positive or negative. However, the mass of the proton was so much greater than that of the electron that this seemed clearly false. Therefore, in 1930, Dirac postulated that both particles, the electron and the proton, were in the positive state, but that each could also exist in a negative state. That is, Dirac predicted the existence of a particle entirely like the positively charged proton, but with a negative charge. The same was true of the negatively charged electron; an antiparticle counterpart existed, identical in every way to the electron, except for a positive charge.

If protons and electrons made up matter, then antiprotons and antielectrons made up antimatter. For this remarkable concept, Dirac (with Erwin Schrödinger) was awarded the Nobel Prize in 1933.

1932

Karl Guthe Jansky Detects Radio Waves from Space, Inaugurating Radio Astronomy

As radio became an increasingly important medium not only for entertainment, but for communications, static—radio interference—became an increasingly serious problem. Bell Laboratories, the research arm of the Bell Telephone Company, put an electrical engineer, Karl Guthe Jansky, in charge of investigating the sources of static. Jansky built a large antenna at Bell Labs' New Jersey facility and used it to sample static. He soon detected a signal from outer space. At first, he assumed that its source was the sun, but after much observation, he concluded, in 1932, that the origin of the radio signal was in the direction of the constellation Sagittarius, the very direction that the astronomer Harlow Shapley had identified as the center of our galaxy, the Milky Way, in 1918.

From this humble beginning—a search for unwanted static—the science of radio astronomy was born. It would not seriously develop until the 1950s, but the idea had been planted: that the radio portion of the electromagnetic spectrum could now be added to the visible light spectrum as a medium through which the heavens might be studied.

Ernst August Friedrich Ruska Builds the First Electron Microscope

The microscope was a titanic advance for science (see "1590: Zacharias Janssen Invents the Microscope" and "1676: Antonie van Leeuwenhoek Perfects the Microscope and Opens to Study the Universe of Microorganisms"), but, no matter how well designed and how exquisitely made, optical microscopes have an important limitation: The degree of acuity—sharpness—with which the smallest objects can be viewed is inversely proportional to the wavelength of the viewing medium. The shorter the wavelength, the greater the acuity and the smaller the object that can be viewed. The longer the wavelength, the less the acuity, which makes it impossible to view extremely tiny objects, such as objects smaller than the smallest living cells.

The German electrical engineer Friedrich Ruska understood that electron waves were of much shorter wavelength than visible light. If a microscope could be designed to use electron waves rather than visible light waves, it could resolve much, much smaller objects with much greater sharpness than a conventional microscope. Ruska set to work to create an electron microscope, producing a working model—quite primitive by today's standards—in 1932. Over the years, the instrument was greatly refined and improved to the degree that viruses can be studied, as can molecules—objects much too small to be resolved by the relatively long wavelengths of visible light.

1935

Konrad Lorenz Establishes the Science of Ethology, the Study of Animal Behavior

Ethology, the science of animal behavior in natural environments, was unknown prior to the work of the German zoologist Konrad Lorenz, who made the breakthrough discovery of "imprinting"—a receptiveness to certain types of learning, which occurred only at specific, critical points in the life of an animal. For instance, chicks learned to follow a moving object very shortly after hatching. Normally, that object was the chicks' mother, but, Lorenz discovered, the chicks would follow any object if it was introduced during the critical imprinting period. Once the critical period was passed, however, imprinting would not occur again, and once imprinting had been accomplished, it continued to shape the animal's behavior, to some measurable degree, lifelong.

Alan Turing Creates Computer Science with the Turing Machine

The origins of the modern computer are many and varied. Important milestones are covered in "The Abacus, About 500 B.C." (sidebar), "1822: Charles Babbage and Lady Ada Lovelace Begin to Develop the First Modern Computer," "1946: John William Mauchly and John P. Eckert, Jr., Design ENIAC, the First Fully Electronic Computer," and "1981: IBM Introduces the Personal Computer." All of these steps in the evolution of an instrument now so central to our lives have one thing in common. They are all inventions, physical devices: machines.

But the "machine" on which computer science is most directly based was not a physical device at all, but a construct of the imagination.

During World War II, the British mathematician Alan Turing was part of a team dedicated to breaking the German master military code, the so-called Enigma cipher. To break this code, Turing used—in part—a concept he had created shortly before the war, in 1936. It was called the "Turing machine," but it was nothing mechanical or electrical. Instead, it was a "thought experiment," an idealized model. Turing imagined a machine consisting of an infinite paper tape on which a kind of "tape head" could read and write information. The tape head included a modifiable control mechanism, which could store directions from a finite set of instructions—that is, a "program." As Turing conceived it, the tape was divided into squares, each of which was either blank or bore one of a finite number of symbols. The tape head could move to, read, write, and erase any single square and could change from one "internal state" to another between one moment and the next, depending on both the internal state of the machine and the condition of the scanned square at a given moment. Once the machine had stopped the process of scanning, writing, and erasing, the result would be a solution to the mathematical query that had been presented to it.

The technology to realize a practical version of the Turing machine did not exist in 1936, but Turing had provided instructions for what to do when it became available. He did no less than outline the theoretical basis of computer science.

1941

Using an Engine Design Patented in 1930 by Frank Whittle, the First Jet Plane Is Flown

In 1930, the British aeronautical engineer Frank Whittle patented a design for a jet engine. It resembled a rocket, in that it burned fuel in such a way as to eject exhaust at extremely high speed, thereby providing thrust. In contrast to the rocket engine, however, the jet is air breathing—its supply of oxidizer, necessary for combustion, is not some onboard chemical, but the atmosphere itself.

A conservative aeronautical community was slow to buy into the Whittle engine and continued instead to rely on piston-powered propeller designs. However, in May 1941, during World War II, British aeronautical engineers experimented with the Whittle engine as a power plant for an aircraft, thereby coming to design and fly the first jet plane. Although it began later, development of jets proceeded more rapidly in Germany, but, even there, jets were developed too late and were produced in insufficient numbers to have significant impact on the outcome of World War II.

1942

Enrico Fermi Conducts the First Sustained Nuclear Chain Reaction

Albert Einstein's $E = mc^2$ equation described the equivalence of energy and matter, showing that the potential energy of matter, locked, as it were, within the "strong force" holding together the atomic nucleus, was tremendous: the product of mass multiplied by an enormous number, the square of the speed of light. However, a single atom is a very small thing, with a tiny mass. Split a single atom, liberate the strong force, and even multiplied by the square of the speed of light, the energy liberated will not be great from the macro perspective. However, in 1939, the Hungarian-born physicist Leo Szilard advanced the possibility that the fission (splitting) of a single atomic nucleus could induce a "chain reaction" in other atoms, the cumulative effect of which would yield amounts of energy unparalleled by any conventional chemical process.

In theory, a chain reaction would work like this: The particles split off from one atomic nucleus would have sufficient energy to split off particles in the nuclei of more atoms, which, in turn, would do the same to yet more.

That was the theory, and it might have remained on the theoretical level for a long time, had it not been for the advent of World War II and the fear, especially among scientists who had fled to America to escape Nazi persecution, that Germany would attempt to develop a fission weapon. At Szilard's urging, Albert Einstein—now living in the United States—wrote a secret letter to President Franklin Roosevelt, warning him of the danger and urging him to begin a project to develop a fission weapon: an atomic bomb.

That was the beginning of the "Manhattan Project," the greatest scientific, engineering, and manufacturing effort ever mounted by any nation. Its purpose was to beat the Germans to the creation of an atomic weapon. The first step toward this goal was to produce in actuality and under controlled conditions the kind of chain reaction Szilard had only theorized. This assignment was given to Enrico Fermi, a young physicist who had fled fascist Italy in 1938 on the heels of the anti-Semitic decree Benito Mussolini had promulgated in obedience to Hitler. Fermi's wife was a Jew.

Fermi oversaw the design and construction of an "atomic pile" reactor in a squash court under the stands of the University of Chicago's Stagg Field. Uranium and uranium oxide were piled up in combination with graphite blocks. Neutrons colliding with the carbon atoms in the graphite would not affect the carbon nuclei, but would bounce off them, giving up energy and moving slowly as a result, thereby increasing the chance that they would react with the uranium 235. By making the atomic pile large, the chances that neutrons would strike the uranium 235 were increased. However, it was essential that the pile be just large enough to achieve "critical mass," sufficient mass to start and sustain the chain reaction, without producing an uncontrolled reaction: an atomic explosion.

Indeed, Fermi and the other scientists recognized the need to control and shut down the reaction, so they inserted cadmium rods into the pile, to moderate the neutron action. When the pile approached critical mass, the rods would be slowly withdrawn, and the number of neutrons produced would increase. When the rods were sufficiently withdrawn so that more neutrons were produced than were being consumed by the cadmium, the pile would "go critical," and the nuclear chain reaction would begin. Fermi understood that if this were allowed to proceed unchecked, an uncontrolled chain reaction would take place—an atomic explosion. How destructive would that be? No one knew. Much of Chicago could be destroyed, or, some theorized, a chain reaction might be set off in the very atoms of the atmosphere, perhaps bringing the world to an end.

The pressures of war compelled the gamble, the gamble that the chain reaction could be produced—and that it could be controlled. So, just before 3:45 in the afternoon of December 2, 1942, Fermi ordered the withdrawal of the cadmium control rods. Geiger counters indicated a large release of energy—a chain reaction under way. At 3:45, the reaction became self-sustaining. When this occurred, Fermi directed that the rods be reinserted. The chain reaction stopped, and Chicago didn't vaporize, but the scientists were now ready to make a bomb.

Oswald Avery Discovers the Genetic Significance of DNA

The Canadian-American bacteriologist Oswald Avery was studying pneumococci, the bacteria responsible for pneumonia. He grew two strains in the laboratory, an "R" strain, which had a rough surface, and an "S" strain, with a smooth surface. The smooth surface was created by a carbohydrate molecule, which, Avery concluded, the "R" strain was genetically incapable of producing. He prepared an extract from the "S" bacteria, which contained genetic material but no actual cells. Using this substance, he was able to convert the "R" strain into the "S" strain, thereby demonstrating that the extract contained some genetic substance that triggered production of the carbohydrate coat.

In an effort to derive the exact nature of this genetic substance, Avery successively purified the "S" extract until he obtained a substance that still effected the conversion of the "R" to the "S" strain. That substance was DNA, deoxyribonucleic acid. The conclusion was inescapable: DNA was the substance that bore the genetic code of any cell. With this identification, the science of genetics made its greatest leap since the work of Gregor Mendel in the mid-nineteenth century (see "1865: Gregor Johann Mendel Creates the Science of Genetics"). Less than a decade later, two other scientists would discover the structure of this all-important molecule (see "1953: Francis Crick and James Watson Postulate the Double-Helix Structure of DNA").

Carl Friedrich von Weizsacker Proposes a New Nebular Hypothesis, Generally Accepted Today as the Most Plausible Explanation for the Origin of the Solar System

In the mid-eighteenth century, the German philosopher Immanuel Kant theorized that the solar system had begun as a nebula. This cloud of gas and dust, which slowly rotated, contracted until it became flattened into a spinning disk that, in various ways, coalesced into the sun and the planets. The French mathematician Pierre-Simon Laplace elaborated on this "nebular hypothesis" later in the century. Appealing as the hypothesis was, it ran up against a serious problem. Most of the angular momentum of the solar system—about 98 percent—was concentrated in the planets, which, however, constituted only one-tenth of 1 percent of the total mass of the solar system. The physics just didn't make sense.

The German astronomer Carl Friedrich von Weizsacker made a fresh approach to the nebular hypothesis by suggesting that the outer layers of the contracting nebula were subject to turbulence, which caused the planets to form in the orbits that were now observed. Weizsacker's modification of the nebular hypothesis is the most widely accepted explanation of the genesis of the solar system.

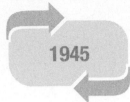

1945

A Massive American Research Team Led by J. Robert Oppenheimer Develops a Nuclear Fission (Atomic) Bomb

With the theory of the nuclear chain reaction proven in fact by Enrico Fermi (see "1942: Enrico Fermi Conducts the First Sustained Nuclear Chain Reaction"), the charismatic American physicist J. Robert Oppenheimer, in 1943, directed the establishment of a laboratory in what was then a remote mesa at Los Alamos, New Mexico. Here, some of the most prominent of the world's scientists gathered to complete the transformation of theoretical physics into a working bomb.

The raw materials were two radioactive isotopes, uranium 235 and plutonium 239, which were supremely difficult to obtain and which were required in sufficient quantity to create critical mass. Under U.S. Army general Leslie R. Groves, giant secret plants at Oak Ridge, Tennessee, and at Hanford, Washington, were constructed to separate uranium 235 from its natural companion isotope, uranium 238 (this was done at Oak Ridge), and to produce plutonium 239 (at Hanford). At Los Alamos, the scientists had to devise a way to reduce these fissionable products to pure metal, which could be shaped in order to bring the chain reaction to an explosive level. The material also had to be brought together instantly to achieve a supercritical mass, which would create an explosion. Moreover, the scientists had to figure out how to make all of this compact enough to be carried to a target by an airplane.

By the summer of 1945, sufficient amounts of plutonium 239 were available from the Hanford Works, and the physicists at Los

Alamos had designed a bomb, a device using conventional high explosives to compress the shaped plutonium tightly and instantaneously together, so that it would go supercritical and create a massively energetic chain reaction: an atomic detonation.

The first test of the bomb, code named "Trinity," took place in the Alamogordo desert near Los Alamos at 0529:45 on July 16, 1945. All who witnessed it described it in much the same terms: the explosion of a sun on earth.

The next month, on August 6, 1945, at 8:15 A.M. local time, a single B-29 Superfortress bomber, christened *Enola Gay* by pilot Paul Tibbets in honor of his mother, dropped a uranium-235 bomb on Hiroshima, Japan. The device bore the innocuous nickname of "Little Man," and it destroyed two-thirds of the city, killing tens of thousands instantly and more who succumbed to radiation sickness later. (By the end of 1945, 140,000 were dead.) Another bomb, a plutonium-239 device called "Fat Man," was dropped on Nagasaki on August 9. Of 270,000 people present at the time of the detonation, about 70,000 would be dead by the end of the year. Japan, for the first time in its entire history, surrendered to a foreign power, and the "Atomic Age" exploded into the reality of the modern world.

1945

Salvador Edward Luria and Alfred Day Hershey Discover Viral Mutation

ndependently of one another, the American microbiologists Salvador Edward Luria and Alfred Day Hershey demonstrated that viruses are subject to mutation, just as plants and animals are. This insight explained the difficulty of acquiring immunity to certain viral diseases. One might develop antibodies for one strain of a given virus, but the antibodies might not be effective against a mutated strain. A key (and highly vexing) disease process had been discovered.

1946

John William Mauchly and John P. Eckert, Jr., Design ENIAC, the First Fully Electronic Computer

The idea of a machine to perform calculations goes back at least as far as the abacus, which the Egyptians were using by 500 B.C. (see sidebar: "The Abacus, About 500 B.C."). It was not until 1822 that Charles Babbage and Lady Ada Lovelace began to develop the first computer in the modern sense: an "analytical engine" (as they called it), which was distinguished from a mere calculating device by the fact that it could be *programmed* to perform *any* logical operation capable of being expressed symbolically (see "1822: Charles Babbage and Lady Ada Lovelace Begin to Develop the First Modern Computer"). The pair never completed the machine.

It was the 1880 U.S. census that provided the next major impetus for the development of the computer. Following that event, worried officials estimated that the upcoming 1890 census would not be counted until 1902—two years *after* the 1900 census. Worse, the lag would become greater with each succeeding census. John Shaw Billings, a U.S. Army surgeon in charge of vital statistics at the Census Bureau, had the idea of using punch-hole cards to record and then process census information, and he gave the project to Herman Hollerith, who developed the cards and an electric machine to read them. Using the Hollerith machine, the 1890 census was completed in less than three years. Hollerith subsequently joined CTR (the

Computing Tabulating Recording Company), which later became International Business Machines—IBM.

By 1935, programmed electromechanical calculating devices were common in business. The next year, an English mathematician named Alan Turing formulated the essentials of modern computer science by developing the "Turing machine" (see "1936: Alan Turing Creates Computer Science with the Turing Machine").

With the outbreak of World War II, Turing joined the British team of mathematicians and others working to break the German "Enigma" code. In the meantime, across the Atlantic, IBM joined with a development team at Harvard University in 1939 to begin work on the Mark I, an advanced electromechanical device completed in 1944 and generally acknowledged to be the first truly modern programmable computer.

Yet it was only a prelude to what two University of Pennsylvania engineering professors, John William Mauchly and John P. Eckert, Jr., unveiled in 1946. "ENIAC" (Electronic Numerical Integrator and Computer) replaced the slow and cumbersome mechanical relays of Mark I and earlier devices with electronic "switches"—that is, vacuum tubes, eighteen *thousand* vacuum tubes—enabling it to perform very complex mathematical tasks with what was then unheard of speed and accuracy. The electronic behemoth, 3,000 cubic feet in volume, took up an entire room and weighed in at thirty tons. It kept a small army of technicians hopping to replace vacuum tubes, which burned out with great frequency. Although ENIAC was fully programmable, that task required extensive rewiring of massive switchboards and was, therefore, a major undertaking.

Realizing that ENIAC was unwieldy, Mauchly and Eckert acted on the suggestions of the mathematician John von Neumann and the American scientist John V. Atanasoff to develop UNIVAC (Universal Automatic Computer) in 1951. This differed from ENIAC in two very important respects. Programming was recorded on magnetic tape rather than accomplished by rewiring a switchboard, and UNIVAC was meant to be mass produced. There were still, of course, many difficulties to be overcome. Like ENIAC, UNIVAC was massive and depended on inherently unreliable vacuum tubes. But the work of Mauchly and Eckert had nevertheless changed our lives and created an industry. Over the next forty years, as electronic technology rapidly developed and the vacuum tube gave way to the transistor and the transistor to the integrated circuit ("chip"), computers would become progressively smaller, less expensive, more powerful, and, finally, ubiquitous, finding their way from government and military agencies, academia, business, and industry, into the home.

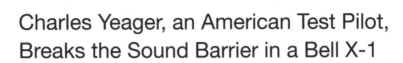

Charles Yeager, an American Test Pilot, Breaks the Sound Barrier in a Bell X-1

The speed of sound is generally placed at 1,088 feet per second at sea level at 32°F—about 740 miles per hour. The development of jet aircraft (see "1941: Using an Engine Design Patented in 1930 by Frank Whittle, the First Jet Plane Is Flown") greatly increased the maximum velocity of airplanes, and flying at the speed of sound came to seem an attainable goal.

Engineers spoke of this as the "sound barrier," because it did pose an aerodynamic challenge. At speeds under 740 miles per hour, air molecules slip smoothly over the surfaces of the plane, but, as the aircraft approaches the speed of sound, those molecules cannot move out of the way before they are overtaken. In effect, the air molecules pile up in front of the aircraft, forcing it to fly into a "wall" of compressed air. Some aeronautical engineers feared that hitting this wall would cause an aircraft to disintegrate. The engineers of the Bell Aircraft Company created an ultrastreamlined design, the X-1, which they hoped would minimize the effects of compressed-air turbulence.

On October 14, 1947, U.S. Air Force test pilot Charles E. Yeager flew the Bell X-1 faster than the speed of sound. Observers on the ground heard a loud "sonic boom," the effect of air piling up, suddenly slipping to one side of the aircraft, then rapidly reexpanding with a boom, like the crack of a giant whip.

Dennis Gabor Lays the Theoretical Groundwork for the Development of Holography

Photography is a two-dimensional medium because it records, chemically, the effect of a reflected-light image on a two-dimensional plane—photographic film. The Hungarian-born British physicist Dennis Gabor theorized, in 1947, that photography could be made three-dimensional. He proposed that a beam of light be split, so that part of it illuminated the object to be photographed, reflecting the surface of that object, no matter how irregular, and the other part of the light would be reflected from a mirror, without creating any irregularities. The two beams would come together again at the photographic film, which would record the interference pattern created by their convergence. By passing light through the developed film, the interference pattern would appear, creating not a two-dimensional image, but a *holograph* (the "holo" prefix meaning whole or entire) in three dimensions.

When Gabor proposed holography in 1947, the technology did not yet exist to transform theory into reality. Within less than three decades, advances in optics and, especially, the invention of the laser (see "1960: Theodore Harold Maiman Builds the First Laser") would make holography physically feasible.

1947

Willard Frank Libby Pioneers Carbon-14 Dating

The radioactive isotope carbon 14 was discovered in 1940 by Martin David Kamen. As with all radioactive isotopes, the radioactivity of carbon 14 degrades with time; however, as Kamen noted, this isotope has a very long half-life (the time it takes for the substance to decay to 50 percent of its radioactivity): 5,700 years.

Seven years after the discovery of carbon 14, the American chemist Willard Frank Libby took note of this long half-life and also of the fact that, due to cosmic ray bombardment of the earth, some of the nitrogen 14 in the atmosphere is converted into carbon 14. Thus new carbon 14 is always being formed as the old carbon 14 breaks down, creating a balance between old and new carbon 14. It occurred to Libby that plants absorb carbon dioxide during photosynthesis, so that carbon atoms, including trace amounts of carbon 14, would be present in plant tissue. Once the plant died, it would absorb no more carbon or carbon 14; therefore, the carbon 14 within the plant tissue would break down without being replaced. That is, only old carbon 14 would be present in the tissue. Using instruments to detect beta radiation, Libby concluded, it would be possible to measure the concentration of carbon 14 and, based on its half-life, determine how long ago the plant had died. Plants, of course, are used in many artifacts, including wooden objects, parchment, cloth, and so on. Therefore, carbon-14 dating techniques could be applied to human-made products, such as objects found in tombs or at archaeological sites. Science now had a tool to date the most ancient of archaeological finds, even in the absence of historical documentation.

George Gamow Formulates the "Big Bang" Theory of the Origin of the Universe

Born Georgi Antonovich Gamow in Odessa, Russia, George Gamow emigrated to the United States in 1934, anglicized his name, and became professor of physics at George Washington University in Washington, D.C. His special interest was cosmology, the origin, nature, and fate of the universe. Gamow was especially interested in three theories, those of the Dutch astronomer Willem de Sitter, the Russian mathematician Alexander Alexandrovich Friedmann, and the Belgian astrophysicist Georges Henri Lemaître.

In 1917, de Sitter, pursuing the implications of Albert Einstein's general theory of relativity (see "1916: Einstein Advances the General Theory of Relativity, Thereby Establishing the Science of Cosmology"), concluded that the universe is not static, but is expanding (see "1917: Using Einstein's Relativity Equations, Astronomer Willem de Sitter Calculates That the Universe Is Expanding"). In 1922, Friedmann—one of Gamow's teachers—created equations that took the mass of the universe into account and seemed to confirm de Sitter's concept of an expanding universe. Then, in 1927, Lemaître pondered the implications of an expanding universe, concluding that if the universe expands as time goes forward, it would contract if time were imagined to run in reverse. Lemaître reasoned that the implication of an *expanding* universe is that it began from what must have been a small, highly compressed body, which Lemaître called the "cosmic egg." How did it begin to expand? Lemaître believed that it must have exploded, sending out of itself the matter that is now the universe. The expansion of the universe is the ongoing thrust of the original explosion.

Gamow synthesized all three theories into a fully developed cosmology. He showed how the chemical elements were formed in the aftermath of the explosion, and he theorized that the blast had been unimaginably energetic, but that the universe had necessarily cooled as it expanded, so that it was now, on average, only a few degrees above absolute zero (217.15°K). Gamow believed that such a temperature would create a background of microwave radiation emanating at a certain wavelength. At the time, the technology did not exist to measure such radiation, but radio astronomers did detect it in 1964—compelling empirical evidence of Gamow's theory.

In 1948, many were impressed by Gamow's hypothesis. Not so, however, the eminent British astronomer Sir Fred Hoyle, who derided it as a "big bang." Unintentionally, that good-naturedly mocking phrase stuck, and it even served to popularize what most astronomers now believe is the most plausible theory of the origin of the universe.

1948

William Shockley, Walter Brattain, and John Bardeen Invent the Transistor

I n 1906, the American physicist Lee De Forest exploited a phenomenon known as the "Edison Effect" to create the Audion vacuum tube, a device that amplified a weak current, such as that produced by radio-frequency signals. In countless variations, the vacuum tube became the basis of all electronic circuits, from radio and television to the first electronic computers (see "1946: John William Mauchly and John P. Eckert, Jr., Design ENIAC, the First Fully Electronic Computer").

The vacuum tube is, in effect, an electronic valve, a necessary control for doing much of anything useful with electronics. Admirable though it was, the tube was plagued by many shortcomings. It was delicate, it burned out readily, it often operated unreliably or erratically, and it required relatively high voltages to operate.

The "Edison Effect," 1883

In 1883, while working on improvements to his incandescent electric light, Edison decided to see if putting a metal wire into the bulb, near, but not contacting, the filament, might improve the vacuum in the sealed bulb and thereby extend the useful life of the filament.

As it turned out, the wire did no such thing, but it did produce another phenomenon: a flow of current from the filament to the wire, across the gap separating them. Edison himself could think of no useful application for what was immediately dubbed the "Edison Effect," but, as applied in 1906 by Lee De Forest, it would prove to be a cornerstone of electronic technology.

Electrical engineers began looking for something to replace the vacuum tube, and, in 1948, Walter Houser Brattain, John Bardeen, and William Bradford Shockley, all scientists working for Bell Laboratories, collaborated on the semiconductor, a device that can control the electrical current that flows between two terminals by means of a low voltage applied to a third terminal. In short, it was an alternative electronic valve.

The three inventors called the most basic semiconductor device the transistor, which was a crystal grown from germanium, an element with excellent semiconductor properties. Later, silicon, much more abundant and cheaper than germanium, was found to possess equally suitable semiconductor properties. With this, the transistor emerged as a less expensive, more reliable, more efficient, lighter, and more compact alternative to the vacuum tube.

The transistor enabled the creation of ever more complex and affordable electronic devices, starting in the 1950s with portable "transistor radios," but soon finding uses in a dazzling array of sophisticated applications. By the 1960s, the individual transistor was being miniaturized to microscopic dimensions and incorporated into thin wafers of silicon called integrated circuits (ICs), chips, or microchips. The trend toward miniaturization and then microminiaturization created a virtually unlimited horizon for electronic technology (see "1960: Integrated Circuits—Chips—Are Introduced").

1948

Auguste Piccard Invents
the Bathyscaphe

In 1934, the American scientist Charles William Beebe created the bathysphere, a spherical diving bell with a heavy quartz window designed for very deep descents into the ocean. Using this craft, Beebe reached a record depth of 3,028 feet. Extraordinary as this achievement was, Beebe's bathysphere, tethered to a surface vessel, could not explore freely and independently. The daring French high-altitude balloonist Auguste Piccard decided to turn his attention from the upper atmosphere to the depths of the ocean and designed what he called a *bathyscaphe* ("ship of the deep"), which was an untethered very-deep-water one-man submarine. The first descent reached 4,500 feet, and, subsequently, the vessel was used to explore ocean depths few human beings had imagined and none had ever seen. The oceans, by far the largest features of earth, accounting for seven-tenths of the planet's surface, were at last opened to detailed scientific exploration.

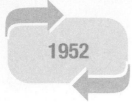

Harold Urey and Stanley Miller Model the Origin of Life

The American chemists Stanley Miller and Harold Urey conducted a remarkable experiment in an attempt to model the chemical and atmospheric conditions that produced life on earth, presumably more than four billion years ago. Within the confines of a five-liter flask, they created what they surmised to have been earth's primordial atmosphere, consisting of methane, hydrogen, ammonia, and water. They then wired the flask for an electric discharge, a spark they intended to simulate a source of ultraviolet photons. On the primordial earth, this source might have been lightning or some other form of energy, such as the shock wave of a meteor impact.

The result of the Miller-Urey experiment was not life, but it did create the organic constituents of life: amino acids, sugars, nucleotide bases, and other organic compounds. At the very least, the Miller-Urey experiment showed that, in the presence of certain chemicals and with the application of energy, the chemical building blocks of life would be created. In subsequent years, other scientists repeated and refined the Miller-Urey experiment, producing an even wider variety of organic molecules. The implications were unmistakable: The origin of life is consistent with the known laws of chemistry and physics and, apparently, required no supernatural intervention.

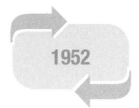

1952

Robert Wallace Wilkins Identifies the Tranquilizing Properties of Reserpine

During the first half of the twentieth century and earlier, institutions for the mentally ill were terrifying places. Some patients lived in dread of horrors only they knew. Others were uncontrollably violent, a danger to others and to themselves. For the first group, little could be done. For the second, there was no choice but a life of confinement, often under very harsh conditions.

As a last resort, barbiturate drugs could be administered. These, however, brought patients to a drowsy, subalert state. Barbiturates controlled behavior, but only by inducing a kind of suspended animation.

An alternative to incarceration and heavy drugging was identified in 1952 by the American physician Robert Wallace Wilkins, who reported his research on reserpine, a drug obtained from the root of a native American plant. Reserpine could produce sedation without diminishing alertness or bringing about sleep. Reserpine became the first in a galaxy of tranquilizers, a new class of drugs that transformed the treatment of the mentally ill and eased the lot of the chronically anxious.

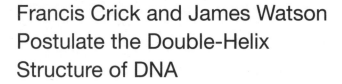

1953

Francis Crick and James Watson Postulate the Double-Helix Structure of DNA

In 1944, Oswald Avery identified DNA as the bearer of genetic information in living organisms (see "1944: Oswald Avery Discovers the Genetic Significance of DNA"), and in 1952, the British biophysicist Rosalind Elsie Franklin used an X-ray diffraction technique to explore the structure of the DNA molecule, discovering that it was a helix. Using one of Franklin's X-ray diffraction photographs, the American biochemist James Watson and the British physicist Francis Crick took the analysis of the structure of the DNA much further by explaining that it was two chains of nucleotides arranged as a *double* helix, resembling a spirally twisted ladder. The twisting sides of this ladder, Watson and Crick determined, consisted of alternate phosphate-sugar groups, while the rungs of the ladder were protein bases joined by weak hydrogen bonds. This double-helix structure enables DNA to replicate itself, which it does prior to cellular reproduction. When a cell divides to form two new cells, the double-stranded helix unwinds, the two sides of the ladder, in effect, unzipping, and each unzipped strand picks up complementary nucleotides, which, incorporated into those unzipped strands, create two new DNA molecules that are identical to each other and to the original molecule. Because the DNA molecule carries chemically coded genetic information for the transmission of inherited traits, when the double helix "unzips," that coded information is passed on.

As Watson and Crick explained, DNA has a dual function. The

process of replication of DNA during reproduction ensures that a baby born to a human mother and a human father will be a human being and not a mouse, a baboon, or a kumquat. Moreover, the DNA ensures that the offspring will inherit certain more specific genetic traits from the mother and father. However, even as DNA transmits characteristics common to the species and to the parents, it also ensures that each individual is unique.

In the case of human beings, each cell has twenty-three pairs of chromosomes containing the full DNA code, which is nothing less than the blueprint for everything needed to build the individual. One member of each chromosomal pair is inherited from the mother, and one from the father. The unique DNA pattern that results from this is copied in each and every cell of the body.

Maurice Ewing and Bruce Heezen Develop Plate Tectonics, the Study of the Evolution of the Earth's Crust

Maurice Ewing and Bruce Heezen, American *physicists,* made a *geological* discovery: a canyon or rift that runs along the Mid-Oceanic Ridge, a great, world-surrounding undersea mountain range. The scientists concluded that the rift actually broke the earth's crust into gigantic but distinctly defined plates, butted together as if by a carpenter. From this latter quality, Ewing and Heezen called the plates *tectonic plates,* from the Greek word for carpenter.

The discovery of the tectonic plates took geology to a new macro level, encompassing the entire earth as a single geologic system. Of the six major plates (there are also additional minor ones), the one that includes most of the Pacific Ocean was found to account for more than three-quarters of the energy released as earthquakes on the planet. The movement of the plates, relative to one another, explains much about seismic activity and has led to unprecedented understanding of earthquake phenomena.

1954

Jonas Salk Develops
a Successful Polio Vaccine

Poliomyelitis—infantile paralysis, or polio—had long been a dread disease, but beginning in 1942, it assumed truly terrifying epidemic proportions in the United States (and elsewhere) each summer. Cruelest of all, "infantile paralysis" usually struck infants and young children. For some, it came and went, having created no symptoms worse than a transitory case of the flu. For some, it was fatal. And for others—about 20 percent of those infected—polio resulted in paralysis. This varied greatly in severity. In some cases, the paralysis was temporary. In others, permanent, ranging from partial paralysis, to paraplegia, to paralysis so devastating that the nerves controlling respiration were damaged, so that the victim could breathe only with the aid of an "iron lung," a massive respirator that resembled nothing more than the iron maiden of medieval torture. In the worst epidemic year, 1950, there were 33,344 cases of polio in the United States, and summer became a season of anxiety, with public swimming pools closed and parents agonizing whenever they let their children play with others.

A young American physician, Jonas Salk, completed his training at New York University's medical school and, rather than go into practice, took up research on immunology under Dr. Thomas Francis at the University of Michigan. This institution produced the world's first killed-virus vaccine against influenza—a major breakthrough, because while scientists believed that vaccines prepared from dead bacteria were effective in immunizing against bacterial infections, they were persuaded that immunization against viruses required live-virus vaccines. And that was a dangerous proposition. Inoculating a patient with live viruses might very well result in infection with the very disease one was trying to prevent.

Moving to the University of Pittsburgh, Salk worked on a killed-virus vaccine for polio, and by 1954 had produced enough to begin patient testing. The following year, the U.S. Food and Drug Administration pronounced the "Salk vaccine" both safe and effective, and a nationwide vaccination campaign got under way. Within a very short time, polio was conquered.

George C. Devol, Jr., and Joseph Engelberger Patent a Robot

The notion of an automaton—a "mechanical man"—is quite old; during the eighteenth century, for instance, various charlatans claimed to have invented chess-playing automatons (which, invariably, proved to be humans disguised as mechanical men). Then in 1920, the Czech playwright Karel Čapek presented *R.U.R.*, which stood for Rossum's Universal Robots and was a political drama that centered on mechanical men manufactured as workers or serfs—the word "robot" is derived from a Czech word that can apply to either. The play is now largely forgotten outside of the Czech Republic, but the word *robot* stuck, and it served to revive the age-old interest in artificial beings, especially those that could perform useful—perhaps even superhuman—work.

The first actual patent on a robotic device was secured by the American inventor George C. Devol, Jr., financed by the visionary entrepreneur Joseph Engelberger. Over a period of two decades, the pair created robots to perform a variety of manufacturing tasks. These early devices were limited by the relatively rudimentary level of computer science at the time, but they were the start of an increasingly important robotics industry.

Surgeons in Boston Perform the First Successful Organ Transplant, a Kidney

Surgeons had long recognized that, in the event of the failure of an organ, death might be prevented by transplanting a healthy organ from another person. In the case of organs that are doubled in the body—the kidney—or that at least partially regenerate—the liver—the donation can come from a living volunteer. In the case of other organs, they can be "harvested" from persons very recently killed, typically by such sudden trauma as an automobile accident.

But it soon became apparent that, in most cases, the recipient's body rejects the donated organ, reacting to it as a foreign infection or as an allergen. In 1954, Boston surgeons determined that the only sure way around rejection was to make a transplant only from one identical twin to another—since identical twins are genetic duplicates. The first successful organ transplant, that of a kidney, was performed, and the recipient lived for eight years.

Since that time, transplant researchers have continued to develop tests for compatibility between recipients and donors who are not identical twins, and to find drugs and other treatments to suppress the immune reaction in the recipient, thereby suppressing organ rejection. Success has varied, but organ transplantation is now a common procedure.

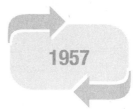

1957

The Soviet Union Launches *Sputnik,* the First Artificial Satellite

Robert Goddard, an American, developed the principles of liquid-fuel rocketry beginning in 1926 (see "1926: Robert Goddard Fires the First Liquid-Fuel Rocket"), but it was the Germans, during World War II, who made the most significant strides by developing the rocket as a weapon of terror. At the end of that war, both the United States and the Soviet Union began rocket-development programs by studying captured German V-1 and V-2 rockets and by employing the services of the German scientists who had developed them. For both countries, these scientists made up the core of national space programs, and although the most prominent of the German rocket scientists, Wernher von Braun, came to the United States, it was the Soviet Union that successfully orbited the first artificial satellite.

It was launched on October 4, 1957, from a site deep within the interior of the country. *Sputnik*—Russian for "traveler" or "satellite"—was no more impressive than its mundane name: a thirty-eight-pound metal sphere that contained only a radio transmitter and sported antennas. Yet it was nothing less than a new moon.

The sole purpose of *Sputnik* was to orbit the earth and broadcast radio beeps to enable tracking. However, to the Soviets, the satellite seemed a vindication of communism over democracy, and to the United States, it was a wake-up call. As many Americans saw it, *Sputnik* portended military disaster—the Soviet occupation of outer space, the ultimate high ground, from which weapons might be wielded against the United States. For others, it was simply a stinging attack on American pride.

In either case, the successful orbiting of *Sputnik* was the starting gun in a "space race" between the USSR and the United States.

First Communications Satellite, 1965

The first satellite with a practical, commercial use was developed by scientists in the United States. *Early Bird,* launched on April 6, 1965, was the world's first communications satellite. Two hundred forty voice communication circuits and one channel for television were available. This was the start of an orbiting network of satellites, which, well before the century was out, would transform the nature of communications on every level.

1959

The Soviet Union Launches the First Moon Probe

I n the space race triggered by the triumph of *Sputnik* (see "1957: The Soviet Union Launches *Sputnik*, the First Artificial Satellite"), the United States got off to a slow, stumbling start. The first several American launches after *Sputnik* were abject failures, and it wasn't until January 1958 that *Explorer I* was successfully orbited. However, on January 2, 1959, the Soviets stunned the world yet again by launching *Lunik I*. It was the first rocket to achieve and surpass escape velocity—about seven miles per second—the speed necessary to break free of the gravitational field of the earth.

That was a triumph in itself—although *Lunik I* failed in its stated mission, to land on the moon. It missed and ended up orbiting the sun, thereby becoming the first artificial planet. Later in the year, on September 12, *Lunik II* was launched, and it succeeded in hitting the moon—thereby becoming the first human-made object to reach another world. Less than a month after this, on October 4, *Lunik III* swung round the far side of the moon, sending back the first-ever images of something never before seen: the hemisphere of the moon perpetually hidden from earth.

Integrated Circuits—Chips—Are Introduced

Electronic circuits require the equivalent of valves to control current flow in myriad useful ways. The first valves were vacuum tubes, which were almost completely replaced by transistors (see "1948: William Shockley, Walter Brattain, and John Bardeen Invent the Transistor"). Among other things, the development of the transistor was the first major step toward the miniaturization of electronics—an evolutionary trend that continued apace during the 1950s. In 1960, each individual transistor could be made so small that it was no longer necessary to treat them as individual components. It now became both practical and desirable to manufacture transistors as components integrated into complete electronic circuits and subassemblies: *integrated circuits*.

ICs are small, thin wafers of silicon (or other semiconductor material), which are microscopically etched with transistor circuits. Because the wafers, originally about a quarter-inch square, resembled nondescript chips, they were informally and universally called chips.

Just about any electronic circuit can be designed onto a chip, and the chips can then be assembled into a wide variety of devices. Over a remarkably short period of time, the degree of specialization and complexity of available chips grew exponentially, so that now the chip at the heart of a desktop computer—the "microprocessor"—is, in effect, the computer itself. All of the other devices boxed along with the chip—hard drive, sound card, video card, and so on—are entirely subordinate to this small semiconductor wafer. The integrated circuit brought electronics into virtually every space and aspect of modern civilized life.

1960

Theodore Harold Maiman
Builds the First Laser

I n 1953, the American physicist Charles Hard Townes created the Maser (microwave amplification by stimulated emission of radiation), a device that bombarded with photons the molecules of ammonia vapor to create a high-intensity microwave beam. The maser principle was based on Albert Einstein's observation that if a photon of a certain size strikes a molecule, that molecule will absorb the photon and be elevated to a higher energy level. If, however, the molecule that was struck was already at a higher energy level, it will return to the lower energy level and, in the process, emit a photon of the same wavelength and moving in the same direction as the striking photon. Thus, two photons are set into motion, which then strike two more high-energy-level molecules, thereby producing four photons. Multiplied many times over, this process creates a flood of photons, all of identical wavelength and all moving in exactly the same direction (they constitute "coherent radiation"). In practical terms, the photon beam that results is extremely intense.

The maser principle was first applied to *visible* light by the American physicist Theodore Harold Maiman in 1960. He used a ruby rod through which an intense flash lamp emitted light that was thereby concentrated in a coherent beam into a tiny point that created temperatures hotter than the sun's surface. At first dubbed an optical maser, the device soon got a name of its own: *laser*, for light amplification by stimulated emission of radiation.

Initially, the intense laser beam was seen as a cutting tool or even a weapon, but it is now even more extensively used as a device for transmitting, recording, and reading digital data, music, and video.

1961

The Soviet Union Sends
Yury Gagarin into Space

Shortly after the successful orbital mission of *Sputnik* (see "1957: The Soviet Union Launches *Sputnik,* the First Artificial Satellite"), the Soviets lofted a dog into orbit, then, in 1960, launched two missions with dogs—and brought both of them back alive. Clearly, like the United States, the Soviets were preparing for manned space flight, and, on April 12, 1961, they launched "cosmonaut" Yury Gagarin into space, sending him on a single orbit around the earth. The United States sent its first "astronaut," Alan B. Shepard, into space a month later—but only on a fifteen-minute suborbital flight. It would be nine months before John Glenn embarked on an American orbital mission, by which time the Soviets had orbited a second cosmonaut—Gherman Stepanovich Titov—*seventeen* times around the earth in a daylong mission on August 6, 1961.

Murray Gell-Mann Describes Quarks

Particle physics, the science of subatomic particles, was exploding by the mid-twentieth century. To the well-understood atomic particles—protons, electrons, and neutrons—were added a host of "intermediate" subatomic particles, including the muon (or lepton, described in 1937), the pi-meson (or pion, described in 1947), and the so-called strange particles, the kaons and hyperons.

The discovery of so many particles was exciting but also overwhelming and puzzling, especially since they seemed to act in contradictory ways. The American physicist Murray Gell-Mann, who had already researched "strange particles," developed a means of grouping subatomic particles into families, which he called the Eightfold Way. The most exciting aspect of his classification system was that, as with the periodic table of the elements (see "1869: Dmitry Ivanovich Mendeleyev Creates the Periodic Table of the Elements"), it contained gaps, which Gell-Mann believed indicated the existence of particles yet to be discovered.

Gell-Mann's particle families were based on what he called *quarks* (the word was borrowed from James Joyce's arcane novel *Finnigans Wake*). These were a small set of particles, Gell-Mann theorized, each complemented by an antiquark, which, grouped together in varying combinations, accounted for all of the particles known as hadrons (including proton, neutron, lambda, sigma, xi, pion, kaon, J particle, and omega). That is, the hadrons were said to be composed of quarks.

The most revolutionary aspect of Gell-Mann's quark was that it carried fractional charges—for instance, plus or minus one-third or two-thirds. This goes against all that is known about the nature of electrical charges, yet it was undeniable that the quark accounted for so much in particle physics that even the notion of fractional charges won acceptance. As for Gell-Mann, the importance of his work in opening up the subatomic world was recognized by a Nobel Prize in 1969.

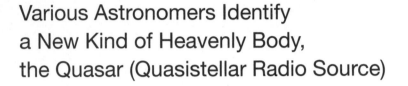

1963

Various Astronomers Identify a New Kind of Heavenly Body, the Quasar (Quasistellar Radio Source)

One of the cosmic mysteries radioastronomy revealed was a set of very strong sources of radio signals emanating from objects that appeared to be very dim stars. How could such faint objects be responsible for such powerful signals? Indeed, because the disparity between the dimness of the objects and the strength of the radio signals was so striking, it was by no means certain that these objects were, in fact, stars, so they were dubbed quasistellar radio sources, or *quasars*.

And there was more strangeness to come. Spectrographic studies of the quasars revealed lines that could not be identified, that corresponded to no known elements. In 1963, the Dutch-born American astronomer Maarten Schmidt observed that the lines did make sense if they were viewed as the lines that would normally be in the ultraviolet portion of the spectrum, but had been displaced by a great redshift. The redshift phenomenon was first described in 1848 by the French physicist Armand-Hippolyte-Louis Fizeau, who pointed out that the Doppler effect (see "1842: Christian Johann Doppler Describes the Doppler Effect, a Cornerstone of Modern Astronomy"), which applied to sound waves, also applied to light waves. That is, just as the wavelength of a sound wave became longer as the source of the sound receded from the listener, so the wavelength of light waves would become greater if the source of the light receded from the observer. This effect would be apparent in a shift in the dark lines of the spectra. If the light source was approaching, the lines would shift toward the ultraviolet (shorter wavelength). If it was receding, the lines would shift toward the infrared (longer wavelength). This latter phenomenon astronomers subsequently called a redshift.

The detection of an enormous redshift in the quasar spectra signified that these sources were extremely distant, well over a billion light-years away. Dim though they were, the fact that they were detectable at all at such a distance meant that quasars had to be extremely energetic. Thus it was concluded that quasars are not stars, but galaxies with highly active centers. Moreover, some are at least 12 billion light-years away.

Now, that fact alone is astounding. But if we take into account the Big Bang theory (see "1948: George Gamow Formulates the 'Big Bang' Theory of the Origin of the Universe") as well as Willem de Sitter's idea of an expanding universe (see "1917: Using Einstein's Relativity Equations, Astronomer Willem de Sitter Calculates That the Universe Is Expanding"), then it becomes apparent that quasars are not merely very distant objects, but very old ones, objects that have expanded with the universe over billions of years and that appear to us now as messengers from a time very near to that of the Big Bang itself.

Elso Sterrenberg Barghoorn Discovers Microfossils, Windows on the Precambrian World

Fossils had been studied for years, but none older than about 600 million years—from the era of the dawn of the Cambrian era—had ever been found. The reason was simple. Organisms of the Precambrian era lacked shells and hard tissue; therefore, they rarely fossilized, but simply died without leaving a trace.

In 1965, the American paleontologist Elso Sterrenberg Barghoorn sought to push the fossil record as far back as possible by studying microscopic bits of carbonized material from very old rocks. His intuition was that these would reveal fossilized evidence of the bacteria that had been among the very first forms of life on earth. He made use of the electron microscope (see "1932: Ernst August Friedrich Ruska Builds the First Electron Microscope"), which revealed microfossils within the material, presumably dating back some 3.5 billion years. The microfossil record suggests that the earth was no more than a billion years old before the first forms of life began to appear on it.

MODERN SCIENCE

Robert Briggs, Thomas J. King, and John B. Gurdon Develop Cloning Techniques

Cloning is not unknown in nature. The very word *clone* is Greek for twig and reflects the fact that a twig may be grafted onto the branch of another tree and then grow. A variety of simple animal organisms—flatworms are a familiar example, as are starfish—can regenerate from a tiny portion of tissue.

Among the more complex animals, cloning does not occur naturally; however, in 1967, the British biologist John B. Gurdon employed the technique of nuclear transplantation (developed by the American biologists Robert Briggs and Thomas J. King) to produce the first clone of a vertebrate animal. Gurdon took a cell from the intestine of a South African clawed frog and implanted it in the ovum (egg cell) of another frog, having first removed the nucleus from the ovum. From the ovum, with the transplanted nucleus, a new South African clawed frog developed and was hatched.

At this point, cloning the more advanced vertebrates was years off. It was one thing to perform nuclear transplantation on an exposed amphibian egg, and quite another to carry out a cloning procedure on, say, a mammal, in which the ovum remains within the body (see "1996: Keith Campbell, Ian Wilmut, and Others of the Roslin Institute, U.K., Clone a Sheep from the Nucleus of a Specially Cultured Cell").

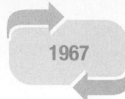

Astronomers Antony Hewish and Jocelyn Bell Are the First to Discover Pulsars

I n the 1960s, the British astronomer Antony Hewish directed construction of a new radio observatory, an array of more than two thousand receivers deployed over three acres and intended to detect minute changes in microwave intensities. In 1967, one of Hewish's graduate students, Jocelyn Bell, detected a remarkable radio source from deep space. Located between the stars Vega and Altair, it emitted a signal burst for a fraction of a second, then fell silent for precisely 1.33730109 seconds. It did this with a precision far in excess of any human timepiece. Shortly after Bell's discovery, other astronomers identified such "pulsating stars," which were eventually dubbed *pulsars*.

In the 1970s, Hewish offered an explanation of the pulsar phenomenon. Because the signal bursts were so precise, he concluded that the source of radiation was both rotating and very compact. He reasoned that only a relatively small object would produce such crisp, clean bursts of energy; a star-sized object would emit a more diffuse signal. Hewish believed that the compact, spinning sources were neutron stars, the superdense compact cores of massive stars that had undergone a supernova explosion. Such neutron stars spin rapidly and, because they are so massive and so dense, they create a magnetic field many times stronger than that of the parent star, a magnetic field many trillions of times stronger than that of the earth. The combination of rapid rotation and a powerful magnetic field creates very strong radiation that is emitted at the star's magnetic poles. The radiation "shines" out of these poles much as light shines from a rotating lighthouse beacon. The beacon is visible only when it rotates toward an observer. The radiation burst of the pulsar is "visible" only when it rotates toward a radio telescope.

The discovery of pulsars, energetic neutron stars that are, except for black holes, the most densely massive objects in the universe, is wondrous in itself. Subsequently, however, some pulsars were discovered that exhibit minute variations in their pulsations. This astronomers attribute to the pulsar's wobbling on its axis. What causes wobbling? Gravity—or, more precisely, the gravitational influence of planets. Thus, some pulsars indicate the presence of extrasolar planets—worlds outside of our solar system (see "1995–1996: The Discovery of Extrasolar Planets Is Announced").

Neil Armstrong and Edwin "Buzz" Aldrin, American Astronauts, Land on the Moon

Since the Soviet launch of *Sputnik* in 1957 (see "1957: The Soviet Union Launches *Sputnik,* the First Artificial Satellite") and the Soviet orbiting of the first human being in space (see "1961: The Soviet Union Sends Yury Gagarin into Space"), the United States had been playing catch-up in the "space race." To many, indeed, the speech President John F. Kennedy made on May 25, 1961, rang hollow with what seemed an impossible objective: "I believe this nation should commit itself to achieving the goal, before the decade is out, of landing a man on the moon and returning him safely to earth. No single space project in this period will be more impressive to mankind, or more important for the long-range exploration of space, and none will be so difficult or expensive to accomplish." Nevertheless, the moon became the target of America's manned space program.

The program was called *Apollo,* and it was the biggest, most complex, and most daring scientific and technological venture in the history of humankind. A mighty *Saturn V* multistage booster would carry the three-man *Apollo* craft beyond earth orbit on a two-and-a-half-day voyage. *Apollo* would enter lunar orbit, then the lunar excursion module (LEM), called *Eagle,* with two men aboard, would separate from the orbiting command module to land on the moon. The astronauts would explore the lunar surface for a time, return to *Eagle,* lift off, and dock with the orbiting command module, which would then slingshot around the moon, blast out of lunar orbit, and return to earth.

Could anything of this magnitude actually be pulled off? The program did not begin well. *Apollo 1*, undergoing a launchpad test, was swept by a catastrophic fire on January 27, 1967, killing astronauts Virgil I. "Gus" Grissom, Edward H. White, and Roger B. Chaffee. At the very least, it seemed that the program would be greatly delayed; perhaps it would even be scrapped. But the National Aeronautics and Space Administration (NASA), Congress, and the American people had the will to carry on, and, after a series of preliminary missions, including earth- and moon-orbital flights, *Apollo 11* was launched on July 16, 1969, crewed by Neil A. Armstrong, Edwin E. "Buzz" Aldrin, Jr., and Michael Collins. It was Armstrong and Aldrin who piloted the *Eagle,* while Collins remained in orbit, flying the command module.

The landing came on July 20, at 4:17 Eastern Daylight Time (8:17 P.M. Greenwich Mean Time). With billions watching live television pictures beamed to radio telescope antennas on earth, Armstrong descended the *Eagle*'s ladder.

"That's one small step for [a] man," he declared as he jumped off the module's ladder, "one giant leap for mankind."

The two astronauts spent twenty-one hours thirty-six minutes on the moon, collecting lunar soil and "moon rocks" as well as setting up a number of experiments. The landing was the culmination of a human dream certainly older than history, and in a politically turbulent period racked by war, the lunar landing spoke of the human spirit and, however briefly, united humanity in one of its greatest achievements.

ARPANET, Precursor to the Internet, Is Activated

In 1999, Vice President Al Gore remarked in a CNN interview that "During my service in the United States Congress, I took the initiative in creating the Internet." To many, this sounded as if Gore were taking credit for having invented the Internet, and he was given a lot of media grief over the remark. But this begs the obvious question: Who *did* invent the Internet?

As usual with any complex technological system, no single person "invented" it. Indeed, the Internet is not so much an entity, a thing that was invented, as it is a state of being or a fact: the fact of the interconnectedness of millions of computers and computer networks. And once this vast network became well established by the beginning of the 1990s, it took on a life of its own as a space—or "cyberspace"—in which data, ideas, images, and thoughts are transmitted, exchanged, and shared, and in which an increasingly vast amount of commerce—buying, selling, and advertising—takes place. Combined with the personal computer (see "1981: IBM Introduces the Personal Computer"), the Internet connects many (potentially, all) businesses, institutions, government agencies, and households to each other and to the world.

Yet the Internet does have a physical and temporal origin. In 1969, the U.S. Department of Defense established ARPANET, the Advanced Research Projects Agency Network, a computer-mediated communications network intended to link U.S. military forces together and to connect them with a network of institutional and governmental computers. Very soon after ARPANET commenced operations, researchers, not only in defense, but in other academic fields, used it. As they used it, they also contributed to it, and the network expanded steadily.

At first, ARPANET and the subnetworks it engendered could be accessed only by large mainframe computers in universities, government establishments, and research-oriented industries. But as personal computers began to proliferate and as these were equipped with modems enabling them to receive and transmit data via the telephone lines, ARPANET blossomed into the Internet, ultimately exploding beyond the confines of any government, corporation, or institution. The American citizen—the American family—embarked on the "information superhighway."

Hamilton Smith and Daniel Nathans Develop Recombinant DNA, First Step Toward Genetic Engineering

The genetic significance of DNA was well established by Crick and Watson in 1953 (see "1953: Francis Crick and James Watson Postulate the Double-Helix Structure of DNA"), and, in 1970, two American microbiologists, Hamilton Smith and Daniel Nathans, found an enzyme capable of cutting the DNA molecule at certain specific places. The DNA fragments that resulted still contained viable genetic information, which implied that fragments could be artificially recombined with other fragments to create new genes that did not exist in nature.

Smith and Nathans's discovery opened the door to the development of recombinant DNA, DNA that permits genetic engineering, the modification and transfer—or even wholesale design—of genes to create organisms with desired characteristics. The possibilities of genetic engineering with recombinant DNA are intensely exciting—the genetic prevention of cancer, for example—and also frightening—the engineering of someone's idea of a "super race."

Fiber Optics Are Introduced

Since the last third of the nineteenth century, people had been familiar with conducting electric current through silver or copper wire. By 1970, glass fibers had been created to do much the same with light. The fibers were manufactured such that they not only transmitted light, but their internal coating reflected light, which allowed the light to follow any path, no matter how curved. Combined with lasers (see "1960: Theodore Harold Maiman Builds the First Laser"), fiber optics meant that light could be used to carry enormous amounts of data, thereby greatly improving communications and other data-intensive technologies.

CAT Scan Techniques Are Introduced

Wilhelm Röntgen's discovery of X rays in 1895 (see "1895: Wilhelm Conrad Röntgen Discovers X Rays") gave medical science a powerful diagnostic tool. Yet, because the X ray is essentially a photograph, it is a two-dimensional image of a three-dimensional space: the human body. To image the body in three dimensions, scientists developed computerized axial tomographic scanning, the CAT scan, which combines, by means of a computer, numerous X-ray images that, taken together, yield a three-dimensional cross-section of the body or area of the body under study. The CAT scan gives diagnosticians and surgeons a far more complete view and, in many instances, is a safe, noninvasive alternative to risky exploratory surgery.

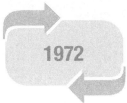

1972

The Laser Disc Is Introduced

Sound was first recorded mechanically, on foil or wax cylinders (see "1877: Thomas Alva Edison Invents the Phonograph and Records Sound") and, later, on vinyl discs. The technology prevailed for more than a century—the only alternative being magnetic wire recording (introduced as early as 1898) or, later, magnetic tape (patented in Germany in 1928). Vinyl discs were bulky, fragile, and subject to inevitable wear. Tape was also vulnerable. Moreover, both technologies were severely limited in the amount of information they could record and reproduce.

In 1972, the laser (see "1960: Theodore Harold Maiman Builds the First Laser") was first used to produce sound recordings. An amplifier modulated a laser beam, which, in response, microscopically pitted a plastic-coated metal disc. In a playback device, another laser beam picked up the pits and translated them into a modulated beam, which was converted back into sound. The laser disc was soon made quite compact—in the form of a compact disc, or CD—and it was capable of recording a huge amount of information. This meant recording more music and theoretically with greater fidelity than a conventional long-playing phonograph record. Moreover, CDs did not wear out with repeated playing and were also far more stable than magnetic tape.

Within another dozen years, an improved version of the CD was developed, the digital versatile disc, or DVD, which was capable of carrying even more information, so that it could serve as a practical medium for recording high-fidelity video as well as audio. By the late 1990s, both the CD and DVD formats would find widespread application as media to record computer-readable data, a use hardly foreseen in the 1970s.

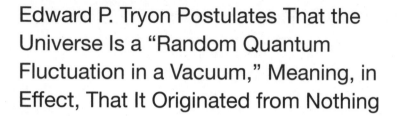

Edward P. Tryon Postulates That the Universe Is a "Random Quantum Fluctuation in a Vacuum," Meaning, in Effect, That It Originated from Nothing

Since the proposal of the Big Bang theory (see "1948: George Gamow Formulates the 'Big Bang' Theory of the Origin of the Universe"), cosmologists developed an extensive theoretical understanding of the probable evolution of the universe, including the first few fractions of a second after the initial "big bang." Yet accepting that the universe came into being as the result of an explosion of a supremely dense concentration of mass did not answer the most basic ontological question. Where did that mass, however infinitesimal, however dense, come from?

The American physicist Edward P. Tryon offered an explanation. A vacuum, a true vacuum—nothingness—can, according to quantum mechanics and the uncertainty principle, give rise to subatomic particles that disappear before they are detected. That is, within nothingness, particles will randomly appear and disappear. Randomly, from time to time, a particle may appear that is capable of developing the mass of the universe and that expands before it disappears. In this sense, then, the universe is a random quantum fluctuation in a vacuum, and thus did indeed originate from nothing.

1974

F. Sherwood Rowland and Mario Molina Demonstrate That CFCs Have the Potential for Destroying the Earth's Ozone Layer

As human settlement of the planet has became increasingly industrial, pollution has become an increasingly serious problem, posing a significant threat to the quality and even the continuation of life on earth.

Some sources of pollution are obvious, for example, exhaust gases from combustion processes, especially those associated with industry and automobiles. Other sources are more subtle, but, potentially, even more catastrophic. In 1974, two American researchers, F. Sherwood Rowland and Mario Molina, demonstrated that chlorofluorocarbons (CFCs), the compounds contained in freon, tend to break down some components of the atmosphere, especially the ozone layer. Chlorofluorocarbons were introduced in the 1930s. Mistakenly thought to be inert, CFCs seemed the ideal industrial chemical—highly useful, relatively cheap, and apparently harmless—so that, by the 1970s, they had become ubiquitous as refrigerants and aerosol propellants. Cumulatively, large amounts of CFCs escaped into the atmosphere.

The ozone layer serves as a natural atmospheric shield that reduces the amount of ultraviolet radiation reaching the earth. An increase in ultraviolet radiation is associated with various cancers (especially skin cancers) and other diseases in human beings. Moreover, too much ultraviolet radiation may kill valuable soil bacteria and ocean plankton—a key element in the food chain—thereby greatly disrupting the planetary ecosystem.

Atmospheric observations subsequent to Rowland and Molina's research confirmed the thinning of ozone layer, especially above Antarctica, and the United States banned the use of CFC refrigerants and aerosol propellants in 1978.

First "Test-Tube Baby" Is Born

People have always been fascinated by the idea of life produced, in some sense, artificially. The phrase "test-tube baby" is a media invention, smacking more of Frankenstein than of medical science, but it does have some validity as a description of what happened in England, on July 25, 1978.

On that day, a baby was born—not in a test tube, but from an ovum (egg) that had been fertilized outside of the womb, in laboratory glassware, using sperm donated by the father. The fertilized egg, after undergoing initial development, was then surgically reimplanted in the mother, where it continued to develop normally. The baby was also born normally.

The medical name for the "test-tube baby" process is *in vitro fertilization,* "vitro" being the Latin for glass. In vitro fertilization is used when, for various medical reasons, fertilization within the body (called *in vivo fertilization*) cannot take place.

Walter Alvarez Finds a Reason for the Extinction of the Dinosaurs

Historians generally agree: The further back an event, the more difficult it is to find out anything concrete about it. One thing is for certain: The dinosaurs became extinct a very long time ago.

Scientists had long wondered why. Why had so varied and, apparently, so well adapted a species suddenly ceased to exist some 65 million years ago, the point at which the Mesozoic Era transitions into the Cenozoic?

The American scientist Walter Alvarez was studying sedimentation rates in certain rocks in Italy when he detected an abnormally large concentration of the rare metal iridium within a narrow layer of the rock he was investigating. This layer corresponded to the late Mesozoic and early Cenozoic era—the period that saw the extinction of the dinosaurs.

Alvarez concluded that the concentration of iridium and the death of the dinosaurs was no coincidence. But where would so much iridium come from? Alvarez speculated that a very large meteor—or even a comet—colliding with the earth could have been the source. Such an impact would have caused great natural catastrophes, including tidal waves, earthquakes, volcanic upheavals, and the like. Perhaps even more destructive would have been the great cloud of dust raised by the impact. It would have filtered out much of the sunlight for a very long time.

By no means was Alvarez's explanation of the extinction of the dinosaurs universally accepted in 1979 or even today; however, evidence of a catastrophic meteor impact (indeed, multiple significant impacts) continues to accumulate, and the Alvarez hypothesis has steadily gained credibility.

The United States Launches the First Space Shuttle

The reality of both the Soviet and American space programs often rivaled science fiction's imaginings of space flight—except in one key respect. Science fiction writers almost invariably depicted space ships as vessels analogous to airplanes, which could be flown, landed, then flown again and again. Until 1981, all Soviet and American space flights had been made in one-way craft, space "capsules" lofted into orbit (or beyond) by nonreusable booster rockets, then returned to earth in a controlled descent. Soviet capsules parachuted onto the ground, whereas U.S. spacecraft parachuted to an oceanic "splashdown." In both cases, the capsules were not intended to be reused.

It is easier and faster to design "single-use" boosters and capsules than it is to engineer reusable spacecraft. This facilitated the kind of rapid development that a "space *race*" demanded. However, once the race had been won, American planners turned to the more demanding task of building of reusable vehicles, and the space shuttle was born. Although it was sent into orbit by a disposable booster rocket, the shuttle itself was capable of reentering the atmosphere and then, with its stubby delta wings, gliding to a nonpowered landing on specially prepared fields.

The idea behind the space shuttle was to make space travel less expensive and more routine. Not only would the Shuttle be used to explore space, it would perform practical (and even profitable) tasks, such as placing satellites into orbit and flying personnel to and from orbiting space stations. The first space shuttle flight took place on April 12, 1981, and there have been many more since then. However, critics of manned space flight point out that the shuttle has never proven profitable, that the scientific information gathered from shuttle flights has been minimal, and that manned programs drain precious funding from more scientifically productive unmanned exploration. As two fatal accidents proved—the *Challenger* disaster on January 28, 1986, and the *Columbia* catastrophe on February 1, 2003—manned spaceflight is an inherently hazardous undertaking.

1981

IBM Introduces the Personal Computer

Since 1946, when the first fully electronic computer was introduced (see "1946: John William Mauchly and John P. Eckert, Jr., Design ENIAC, the First Fully Electronic Computer"), computers assumed an increasingly important role in all aspects of life, from the most basic bookkeeping to the most advanced scientific research. Yet, to most people in the 1970s, computers were big, mysterious machines locked up in special rooms and so expensive that only mammoth corporations and the government could afford them. Then, in 1975, an article in the debut issue of *Popular Electronics* announced: "The era of the computer in every home—a favorite topic among science fiction writers—has arrived!"

The article was about the Altair 8800, a computer kit. Programmable not through software, but by means of an array of switches, the Altair 8800 produced its output not on a monitor screen, but by illuminating light-emitting diodes (LEDs) on its front panel. Today's desktop PC may contain 128 megabytes (128 million bytes) or, often, more of random-access memory (RAM); Altair maxed out at eight kilobytes (8,000 bytes). It was less a practical tool than an amusement for the geek hobbyist, and the *Popular Electronics* claim of a computer in every home was a bit premature.

But not by much. The Altair proved surprisingly popular, and by 1977, new companies such as Apple and Commodore were producing far more sophisticated computers running a relatively simple programming language (originally developed for large "mainframe" computers) called BASIC, which could be readily adapted to practical calculating and word-processing tasks. The major manufacturers of big "mainframe" computers, such as IBM, took little note of the new machines—at first. But, in 1981, IBM brought out a desktop computer of its own and dubbed it the *personal computer,* or *PC.* And that started a revolution.

The PC brought computing to the people. It decentralized many office tasks. It empowered lower-level employees, greatly democratizing the workplace. And, with the rise of the Internet (see "1969: ARPANET, Precursor to the Internet, Is Activated"), the PC became a veritable window to the world, an advance in the creation and dissemination of knowledge paralleled only by the invention of printing (see "1454: Johannes Gutenberg Invents the Modern Printing Press").

Robert K. Jarvik Develops an Artificial Heart

The American physician Robert K. Jarvik did not invent the concept of an artificial pump to replace the heart—these had been tried, with little success, as early as 1969—but he did develop the first truly promising one. A "Jarvik heart" was implanted into the chest of Barney Clark on December 1, 1982. He lived 112 days with it.

The Jarvik heart was a technological wonder, which promised to free persons with irreparable heart ailments from having to wait for a suitable organ donor and heart transplant surgery, but it also made dramatically clear the limits of technological attempts to duplicate the wonders of the human body. The Jarvik heart extended life somewhat, but that life was significantly degraded in quality. Moreover, the powerful pump required an external power source, which meant that the recipient was more or less tethered for the duration of whatever life he or she had left. A handful of other patients received the Jarvik heart, but the device was soon abandoned.

Since then, some artificial-heart research has continued. The so-called AbioCor Replacement Heart, developed by Abiomed, Inc., at the beginning of the twenty-first century, is more self-contained than the Jarvik heart. On September 13, 2001, Kentuckian Tom Christerson received the AbiCor heart in a surgery performed by Drs. Laman A. Gray, Jr., and Robert D. Dowling. Christerson died, at age seventy-one on February 7, 2003, the longest-surviving artificial heart recipient.

Karl Alex Müller and Johannes Georg Bednorz Identify Ceramic Materials Capable of Superconductivity Well Above Absolute Zero

I n 1911, Kamerlingh Onnes discovered the phenomenon of the superconductivity of certain metals as temperatures approached absolute zero (see "1911: Heike Kamerlingh Onnes Discovers Superconductivity [Electrical Conductivity with Virtually No Resistance] near Absolute Zero"). The idea of superconductivity, which would enable extraordinarily efficient electronic circuits (a boon to the development of supercomputers, among many other things), was highly attractive; however, achieving and maintaining temperatures close to absolute zero is expensive, difficult, and, in everyday applications, highly impractical. Through much of the twentieth century, scientists and engineers searched for a way to achieve superconductivity at higher temperatures, such as those achievable by immersion in cheap, easily managed liquid nitrogen. All tests on metals and metal alloys failed.

Then something entirely unexpected happened. A Swiss physicist and his German colleague, Karl Alex Müller and Johannes Georg Bednorz, began experimenting with ceramics, which are not metals, but do contain mixtures of metallic oxides. To their astonishment, they found that they could attain superconductivity at 30°K—well above the near-absolute zero temperatures achievable only with costly and difficult liquid helium cooling.

The discovery ignited a flurry of experimentation, and, soon, ceramics were found that enabled superconductivity at even higher temperatures, including the range achievable by immersion in liquid nitrogen, a cheap and safe substance. Only two problems remained: one practical, the other intellectual. Ceramic substances are not easy to standardize chemically, nor are they very easy to fabricate into such traditional conductive media as wire or film. On the intellectual front, no one has yet been able to explain just *why* ceramics permit "warm superconductivity."

Climatologists Identify a Global Greenhouse Effect

C arbon dioxide in the earth's atmosphere allows the passage of relatively short-wavelength radiation, but filters out longer wavelengths. That is, the CO_2 acts like the glass of a greenhouse. It admits sunlight, but traps the longer waves of heat that are radiated by the ground and other objects within the greenhouse.

Climatologists focused worldwide attention on the "greenhouse effect" of CO_2 when they identified it as the cause of the warmest weather ever recorded in 1987 and 1988. They pointed out that industrial and automotive pollution was greatly adding to the concentration of CO_2 in the atmosphere, and they called for a general reduction in CO_2 emissions—lest the temperature continue to rise, creating disastrous drought conditions and, perhaps, even melting the polar ice caps, causing devastating floods.

NASA and the European Space Agency Deploy the Hubble Space Telescope

Throughout much of the twentieth century, astronomers were engaged in a kind of telescope race, designing and building successively larger optical telescopes, culminating in the two Keck telescopes, which became operational in 1992 and 1996 atop Mauna Kea in Hawaii. Each instrument is equipped with the equivalent of a 10-meter (393-inch-diameter) reflector, making them the largest telescopes on earth.

The operative phrase here is "on earth." For no matter how large a telescope is, it will always be limited by the interposition of the earth's atmosphere, which acts like a giant screen or filter between the telescope lens and the cosmos. The ultimate means of eliminating atmospheric interference with astronomy is to get above the atmosphere, and that is just what the National Aeronautics and Space Administration (NASA), in collaboration with the European Space Agency (ESA), did with the Hubble Space Telescope (HST).

In 1990, the HST was lofted into orbit by the space shuttle *Discovery*, which deployed it from its cargo bay, setting it on an earth orbit. The HST is equipped with a 2.4-meter reflecting telescope, capable of ten times the angular resolution of the gigantic Keck telescope and approximately thirty times more sensitivity to light. At least, that was the plan. Because of a manufacturing flaw, however, the curvature of the 2.4-meter mirror was machined inaccurately by literally less than a hair, having been made too flat by one-fiftieth of the width of a human hair, an infinitesimal error nevertheless sufficient to throw the instrument out of focus. In 1993, astronauts aboard the space shuttle *Endeavour* intercepted the HST in orbit and installed a system of small corrective mirrors, which completely fixed the problem. Immediately, HST began transmitting unprecedented images of the universe, including the very first images of stars as actual bodies rather than just points of light and images of galaxies so distant that they are veritable ambassadors from the era of the origin of the universe.

The Discovery of Extrasolar Planets Is Announced

In 1983, it was observed that the star Beta Pictoris is surrounded by a disk of gas and dust. This led to speculation that planets may form—or have already formed—around the star, creating something like our own solar system. The observation led to a search for other stars that may have planets orbiting around them. The difficulty of such a search is that stars are very bright and very distant, whereas planets have no light of their own and, compared to stars, are extremely small. Looking for planets orbiting distant stars has been compared to trying to detect the light of a firefly in front of a searchlight. Rather than attempt visual identification, astronomers have used the Doppler shift phenomenon (see "1842: Christian Johann Doppler Describes the Doppler Effect, a Cornerstone of Modern Astronomy") to detect gravitational effects caused by orbiting planets. Planets orbiting a star may be expected to cause a distinctive shift in the spectrum detected from the star. In 1995, Michel Mayor and Didier Queloz of Geneva Observatory announced that they had observed such a shift in the spectrum of the star 51 Pegasi, forty-two light-years from earth. Then, in January 1996, two American astronomers, Geoffrey Marcy and Paul Butler, announced the discovery of planets orbiting the stars 70 Virginis and 47 Ursae Majoris. Like their European colleagues, they used the Doppler shift technique, but they achieved more definitive results. The star 70 Virginis is about seventy-eight light-years from earth, 47 Ursae Majoris about forty-four light-years away. Moreover, using formulas that balance the sunlight absorbed and the heat radiated, Marcy and Butler calculated the temperature of the 70 Virginis planet at about 85°C or 185°F—compatible with the existence of liquid water and complex organic molecules. The star 70 Virginis is almost identical to our sun. It is also believed that the planet orbiting 47 Ursae Majoris may have a region in its atmosphere that allows liquid water. In both cases, the implication is that these planets may be capable of supporting life.

Since 1995, several dozen extrasolar planets have been discovered, and the list grows continually. Most scientists believe that many of these planets are capable of supporting life.

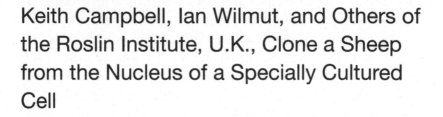

Keith Campbell, Ian Wilmut, and Others of the Roslin Institute, U.K., Clone a Sheep from the Nucleus of a Specially Cultured Cell

In 1970, recombinant DNA was developed (see "1970: Hamilton Smith and Daniel Nathans Develop Recombinant DNA, First Step Toward Genetic Engineering"), enabling DNA molecules from two or more sources to be artificially combined and then inserted into host organisms. As laboratory techniques were honed, such gene cloning could produce new genetic combinations to produce organisms with traits deemed desirable: genetically engineered bacteria to fight disease, new crops resistant to insects and parasites, or even genetically modified human beings. In 1980 and 1986, the U.S. Department of Agriculture approved the sale of the first living genetically altered organism—a virus, used as a pseudorabies vaccine—and, since then, several hundred patents have been issued for genetically altered bacteria and plants.

For the most part, this revolution in genetic engineering proceeded quietly. Then, in 1997 came the stunning news of the birth, in England, of a quite ordinary-looking lamb, named Dolly.

Ordinary-looking though she was, Dolly, unlike any other mammal in history, had no parents in the conventional sense, but was an exact duplicate of her "mother." Dolly was a clone.

Researchers had removed the nuclei from various sheep cells and implanted them into unfertilized sheep eggs, from which the natural nuclei had been removed using highly refined microsurgery techniques. This transfer gave the recipient eggs a complete set of genes, just as if the eggs had been fertilized by sperm. The eggs were cultured and then implanted into sheep. Only one of the implantations was carried to term, and the result was Dolly.

Most significant, the transferred cell nuclei did not come from embryonic cells, but from mammary cells. In other words, the cloning process did not use reproductive cells—just ordinary body cells. Traditional biology argued that no cell from any complex animal could be used to regenerate an entire organism. The successful cloning of Dolly shattered this long-held belief. However, even more shattering was the realization that a sheep, in genetic terms, is quite similar to a human being. If Dolly could be cloned, so could a human being. As had occurred on more than one occasion in the past, a great scientific advance instantly created new moral, legal, and ethical frontiers, and when Dolly developed lung disease and was euthanized on February 14, 2003, many questioned whether clones necessarily suffered health defects.

NASA Deploys *Mars Pathfinder*

Mars has long held a special place in the imagination of scientists as well as others. The most earthlike of the planets in the solar system, Mars has invited speculation that it might, like earth, harbor life. In 1906, the American astronomer Percival Lowell wrote about what he called the "canals" of Mars, thereby exciting speculation that the planet might not only support life, but intelligent life, life capable of civilization.

Well before the National Aeronautics and Space Administration (NASA) launched three important unmanned Mars probes, most scientists had stopped believing in the existence of Martian civilization, and they understood that the so-called canals were nothing more than natural formations. However, Mars continued to cry out for close exploration—and there was still the very real possibility of *some* form of life on the planet.

Mars Observer was launched on September 25, 1992, but, unfortunately, was lost on August 22, 1993. Next came *Mars Surveyor,* launched on November 7, 1996, which, after entering Mars orbit, began the long, automated process of creating a detailed low-altitude map of the Martian surface.

Mars Surveyor was a stupendous achievement, but the public was even more excited by the mission of *Mars Pathfinder.* Launched on December 4, 1996, the spacecraft landed on Mars the following summer. It employed a combination parachute and rocket-braking system, as well as an air bag system, to achieve a soft, upright landing on the Martian surface. Once it was safely landed, the spacecraft deployed a "microrover" vehicle, which traversed the area near the landing site and began transmitting some of the most extraordinary pictures human beings have ever seen. In thousands of images, ranging from broad panoramas to tight close-ups and all available to the public on a special Internet site, *Mars Pathfinder*'s microrover recorded the Martian landscape in exquisite detail.

In 1969, human beings explored a small piece of the surface of the moon (see "1969: Neil Armstrong and Edwin "Buzz" Aldrin, American Astronauts, Land on the Moon"). In 1996, using the remote-controlled microrover, *Pathfinder* did the same for a tiny patch of a planet. As for the question of life on Mars, it remains tantalizingly unresolved.

1998

The Super-Kamiokande Experiment Finds Evidence for Neutrino Mass, Providing a Clue to the Nature of 90 Percent of the Universe

Using well-established physical laws, astronomers can calculate the mass of our galaxy, the Milky Way. When they do so, they find that the visible matter in the galaxy—principally stars—accounts for only about 10 percent of its mass, perhaps even less. That is, at least 90 percent of the galaxy is invisible in the most profound sense: It does not produce nor does it reflect electromagnetic radiation at any wavelength. Extrapolating the results for the Milky Way to the universe as a whole, we must conclude that at least 90 percent of the universe likewise consists of what astronomers call "dark matter," material for which no scientist could account.

Then, in 1998, the results of the Super-Kamiokande Experiment were announced. The Super-Kamiokande Experiment uses an enormous 50,000-ton tank of highly purified water, located about 1,000 meters underground in the Kamioka Mining and Smelting Company's Mozumi Mine, Japan. This massive volume of water acts like a trap to allow study of extremely elusive neutrinos, which are created when cosmic rays, fast-moving particles from space, bombard the earth's upper atmosphere and produce cascades of secondary particles, which shower down upon the earth. Most of the neutrinos thus produced pass through the entire earth itself unscathed, undetected, and, because they were thought to be without mass, undetectable. Using the Super-Kamiokande tank, however, it is possible to image faint flashes of light given off by the neutrino interactions in the water. These flashes are detected by more than 13,000 photomultiplier tubes, which greatly amplify faint light. Using this equipment, physicists concluded that muon neutrinos oscillate, changing their type back and forth, as they travel through space or matter. Such an oscillation can occur only if the neutrino possesses mass and is not, as previously thought, massless. The Super-Kamiokande Experiment indicates that muon neutrinos oscillate into tau neutrinos, a subatomic particle that, in 1998, had yet to be detected (but see "2000: The Tau Neutrino Is Detected, Third and Last Neutrino to be Confirmed on the Standard Model of Elementary Particles").

So, what's important about discovering a neutrino with mass? As the Super-Kamiokande experimenters commented when they announced their result: "We note that massive neutrinos must now be incorporated into the theoretical models of the structure of matter and that astrophysicists concerned with finding the 'missing' or 'dark matter' in the universe must now consider the neutrino as a serious candidate." In this all-but-undetectable subatomic particle may be found 90 percent of the mass of the universe.

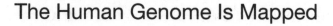

2000

The Human Genome Is Mapped

On April 6, 2000, Celera Genomics, a privately funded, for-profit corporation, announced that it had finished sequencing—"mapping"—the entire human genome, thereby beating the federally funded Human Genome Project, which was working toward the same goal. As the CEO of a rival firm, Neomorphic, remarked, "It's awesome. It's an incredible scientific feat. They really pushed the envelope of the technology and they've done what nobody thought could be done . . . well ahead of schedule—it's remarkable."

What had been achieved?

A "genome" contains all of the genetic material in the chromosomes of a particular organism. To sequence the human genome meant creating a map of some three billion units of DNA. With this information, it becomes possible to find a particular gene's location in the genome, to identify and find other genes in the same region, to correlate many diseases to specific genes, and to develop possible "gene therapies" to cure, prevent, or eliminate various diseases.

The genome maps resulting from both the Celera and the federally funded projects are now available to all researchers. Thus the fruits one of the greatest scientific achievements in history have been made available, worldwide, entirely free of charge.

The Tau Neutrino Is Detected, Third and Last Neutrino to Be Confirmed on the Standard Model of Elementary Particles

An international consortium of fifty-four physicists working at Fermi National Accelerator Laboratory (Batavia, Illinois) announced on July 21, 2000, the first direct evidence for a subatomic particle called the tau neutrino. Past experiments had provided hints of the particle's existence, but it had never been directly observed. The tau neutrino is the third and last neutrino to be confirmed on the "standard model" of elementary particles, the most widely accepted theoretical description of the basic constituents of matter and the fundamental forces of nature. Previously discovered were the electron neutrino and the muon neutrino (see "1998: The Super-Kamiokande Experiment Finds Evidence for Neutrino Mass, Providing a Clue to the Nature of 90 Percent of the Universe"). Thus the discovery of the tau added a new dimension to an understanding of the universe at its most basic and elemental level.

The work of discovery began in 1997, when scientists used the laboratory's gigantic Tevatron accelerator to produce an intense neutrino beam, which was passed through a three-foot-thick target of iron plates sandwiched with layers of emulsion, which recorded the particle interactions. In this massive target, one out of one million million tau neutrinos interacted with an iron nucleus and transformed into a tau lepton, a particle that leaves a small (one millimeter long) track in the emulsion. That is, the tau lepton leaves tracks in the emulsion much as visible light creates an image on photographic film, but the tau does so in three dimensions. Scientists spent years sorting through approximately six million potential interactions recorded in the emulsion, until they identified a mere four events that provided convincing evidence for the tau neutrino.

Scientists Grow Tadpole Eyes from Stem Cells

In April 2002, two Japanese researchers, Makoto Asashima and Ayako Sedohara of the University of Tokyo, announced that they had successfully grown—from scratch—tadpole eyeballs and had transplanted them into tadpoles. As Asashima remarked to the press, "None of the eyes were rejected and none dropped out. All of the frogs can see."

For some years prior to this, scientists had been researching stem cells as (among other things) a source of organs for transplantation. Stem cells can be cultured in the laboratory and divide for indefinite periods, giving rise to specialized cells, such as those of specific organs.

Where do these stem cells come from?

When a sperm fertilizes an egg, a single cell is created, which has the potential to form an entire organism. The fertilized egg is said to be "totipotent," its potential for development total. Within hours after fertilization, the totipotent cell divides into identical totipotent cells. About four days after fertilization and several more cell divisions, the totipotent cells start to specialize, becoming a hollow sphere of cells known as a blastocyst. From the inner cell mass of the blastocyst the tissues of the body will form. These inner cell-mass cells are called "pluripotent" because they can give rise to many types of cells, though not all types of cells necessary for fetal development. They are also called stem cells.

Some researchers have developed techniques for isolating stem cells from blastocysts—in animals as well as human beings. Others have isolated stem cells from fetal tissue obtained from terminated pregnancies. Other techniques that do not require cultivating blastocysts or using aborted embryos are also under development.

By culturing stem cells, it is possible to perform research to better understand the events that occur during human development, including the development of disease-causing problems. Stem cells are also potentially valuable for testing and developing new drugs. But most exciting of all is the possibility of generating cells and tissue for so-called cell therapies. Pluripotent stem cells may become a source of replacement cells and tissue to treat many diseases and conditions, including (for instance) Parkinson's disease, Alzheimer's disease, spinal cord injury, stroke, burns, heart disease, diabetes, osteoarthritis, and rheumatoid arthritis.

As with many scientific advances, stem cell research has met with religious and moral objections, because human embryonic tissue is involved and because some individuals believe that science has "crossed the line" into attempting to create life. At present, the stated position of the U.S. government is ambivalent. In a policy statement of August 9, 2001, President George W. Bush announced that research using existing embryonic tissue now in laboratories would be eligible for federal funding, but research involving the harvesting of new tissue would not. In Congress, competing legislative initiatives promote stem cell research or seek to limit it severely.